Performance and Transformation

Performance and Transformation

New Approaches to Late Medieval Spirituality

Edited by Mary A. Suydam and
Joanna E. Ziegler

St. Martin's Press
New York

PERFORMANCE AND TRANSFORMATION
Copyright © 1999 Mary A. Suydam and Joanna E. Ziegler. All rights reserved. Printed in the United States of America. No part of this book may be used or reproduced in any manner whatsoever without written permission except in the case of brief quotations embodied in critical articles or reviews. For information, address St. Martin's Press, 175 Fifth Avenue, New York, N.Y. 10010.

ISBN 0-312-21281-X

Library of Congress Cataloging-in-Publication Data

Performance and Transformation : new approaches to late medieval spirituality / edited by Mary A. Suydam and Joanna E. Ziegler.
    p. cm.
  Includes bibliographical references and index.
  ISBN 0-312-21281-X
    1. Mysticism—History of doctrines—Middle Ages, 600–1500.
  2. Spirituality—History of doctrines—Middle Ages, 600–1500.
  3. Feminist theology. 4. Theater—Religious aspects—Christianity.
  I. Suydam, Mary A., 1951– . II. Ziegler, Joanna E.
  BV5083.P47   1999
   248.2'2'0902—dc21   98-40688
                                                            CIP

First Published: May, 1999
10 9 8 7 6 5 4 3 2 1

Contents

About the Contributors

Laurie A. Finke received her Ph.D. in English Literature from the University of Pennsylvania and her B.A. from Lake Forest College. She is currently director of Women's and Gender Studies at Kenyon College. Her publications include *Feminist Theory, Women's Writing* (Cornell University Press, 1992), *Medieval Texts and Contemporary Readers,* which she edited with Martin B. Shichtman (Cornell University Press, 1987), and, most recently, *Women's Writing in English: Medieval England* (Longman, 1999).

Mary E. Giles received her Ph.D. in Romance Literature from the University of California, Berkeley. She taught in the California State University system for 36 years, teaching Spanish Literature, Humanities, and Religious Studies. She is Professor Emeritus of Humanities and Religious Studies from California State University, Sacramento. She has published several books on women's spirituality and Spanish mysticism. Her most recent books are *Prison of Women: Testimonies of Resistance in Franco Spain, 1939–1975* (SUNY Press, 1998) and *Women in the Inquisition: Spain and the New World* (Johns Hopkins Press, 1999).

Rosemary Drage Hale received her Ph.D. from the Committee on the Study of Religion, Harvard University, in 1992. As Associate Professor of Religion at Concordia University in Montreal, Quebec, she teaches courses in comparative mysticism and women and religion. Currently she is the Associate Dean of the School of Graduate Studies.

William F. Hodapp received his Ph.D. in English, with a concentration in medieval languages and literature, from the University of Iowa in 1994. Presently, he is an assistant professor of English at the College of St. Scholastica, Duluth, Minnesota, where he teaches literature and writing and coordinates the college's Medieval and Renaissance Studies Minor. With research interests in the high to late Middle Ages, he has published articles on Geoffrey Chaucer, the *Gawain*-Poet, John Lydgate, Charles d'Oréans, and John Peckam, as well as Richard Rolle and other English mystics. He is particularly interested in relationships between devotional literature and drama, in medieval theories of translation, and in dream-vision poetry. He lives in Duluth, Minnesota, with his wife and four children.

Nanda Hopenwasser received her Ph.D. in English Literature from the University of Alabama in 1992. She is currently an adjunct instructor at the University of Alabama, English Department. She has published numerous articles about Margery Kempe, as well as Chaucer's Wife of Bath, William Butler Yeats's Crazy Jane, and is now collaborating with Signe Wegener (English Department, University of Georgia) on an article on the Alabama Red Cross nurse and organizer Annie Wheeler. She is also (with Signe Wegener) writing a two-woman "show" for the upcoming SEMA conference on St. Birgitta and Margery Kempe—"Mother Always Knows Best."

Catherine Müller received her Ph.D. in French literature from the Department of Foreign Languages and Literatures, Purdue University (West Lafayette, Indiana), in 1996. She also has an M.A. in languages and literatures with majors in French and Italian, and a minor in German, from the University of Geneva, Switzerland, 1984 (Licence ès lettres de l'Université de Genève). She has published numerous articles as well as *Marguerite Porete et Marguerite d'Oingt de l'autre côté du miroir*. Currents in Comparative Romance Languages and Literatures, eds. Tamara Alvarez-Detrell and Michael G. Paulson, New York: Peter Lang, 1998. She currently teaches medieval French literature at the University of Lausanne, Switzerland.

Susan Rodgers has done research on oratory and the politics of print literacy issues since her first work in the Angkola Batak area of North Sumatra, Indonesia, in 1974. After a 1978 Ph.D. in Cultural Anthropology from the University of Chicago she taught for 11 years in the anthropology program at Ohio University. Now Professor of Anthropology and Chair of the Department of Sociology and Anthropology at the College of the Holy Cross, Worcester, MA, she is the co-editor, with anthropologist Rita Smith Kipp, of *Indonesian Religions in Transition* (University of Arizona Press, 1987). Among her other studies of Indonesia are *Power and Gold: Jewelry from Indonesia, Malaysia, and the Philippines* (2nd ed., Prestel Verlag, 1985), *Telling Lives, Telling History: Autobiography and the Historical Imagination in Modern Indonesia* (University of California Press, 1995), and *Sitti Djaoerah: A Novel of Colonial Indonesia*, (University of Wisconsin Center for Southeast Asian Studies, Monograph 15, 1997), a translation of a 1927 Angkola novel by Soetan Hasoendoetan.

Claire L. Sahlin is the Director of Women's Studies at the University of North Texas in Denton, Texas. She teaches courses concerning women and religion, feminist thought, the history of Christianity, and world religions. The recipient of a Ph.D. from Harvard University in the Study of Religion, she is presently completing a book on Birgitta of Sweden and her voice of prophecy.

Mary Suydam received her Ph.D. in History from the University of California at Santa Barbara in 1993. She has published numerous articles about Hadewijch of Antwerp. She has taught History, Religion, and Women's and Gender Studies at Kenyon College in Gambier, Ohio. She is currently teaching Medieval History at Ohio Wesleyan University.

Robert Sweetman teaches History of Philosophy at the Institute for Christian Studies in Toronto. He received his Ph.D in Medieval Studies from the University of Toronto in 1989. His interests center on the dissemination of theory beyond the academy and the impact of ordinary ways of experiencing reality upon theoretical formulations, focusing particularly upon Dominican preachers and their pastoral care.

Joanna E. Ziegler is Associate Professor and Chair of the Visual Arts Department at College of the Holy Cross in Worcester, Massachusetts. She is the author of *Sculpture of Compassion: The Pietà and the Beguines in the southern Low Countries, c. 1300–1600*, Studies over kunstgeschiedenis/ Études d'histoire de l'art 6 (Brussels: Institut Historique Belge de Rome/Belgisch Historisch Instituut te Rome, 1992), and numerous articles on devotional art.

Acknowledgments

I would like to thank the many people who helped make this volume a reality. In particular I would like to thank the International Congress on Medieval Studies at Kalamazoo, Michigan, for providing the interdisciplinary forum in which colleagues could exchange information and be inspired by each other. I would like to thank Michael Flamini, Elizabeth Paukstis, Jennifer Simington, and Ruth Mannes at St. Martin's Press for their faith in the project and their invaluable editorial assistance. I am grateful to Vernon Schubel, Religion department, Kenyon College, for his comments and advice on the introductory chapter. I would like to express my appreciation to the Information and Computing Services at Kenyon College for their help in translating the computer formats of our contributors. Finally, I would like to thank my husband, Michael Levine, without whose patience, inspiration, insights, and last but hardly least, editorial abilities, this volume would never have come to fruition.

—Mary Suydam

Although acknowledgments must for the most part be taken essay by essay, thanks are to be given more broadly, nonetheless. For continued support of this project from its inception as conference papers, College of the Holy Cross is owed special thanks. The Committee on Research and Publication and the Office of the Dean of the College have generously subsidized the research, travel to conferences, and most importantly, time to think. Many institutions and professional societies hosted this research at earlier stages in the form of conference papers and public lectures; I wish I could thank here all those involved personally in that critical stage of the work. Colleagues have been generous with bibliography and ideas, as well as reading and listening to my musings along the way. I have also had the distinct privilege of being exposed to the intensely interesting faculty who comprise a reading group at the College; I remain grateful to their sparkling wit and intelligence. Since only a few names can be singled out here, I wish to thank Kermit Champa for showing me many years ago that dance was worth pursuing as a way of retrieving history and Mary Paula Hunter for choreographing and dancing Elisabeth's "dance," which led me to rethink Elisabeth in totally unforeseen ways. I am grateful to Hilde Hein, Susan Rodgers, and Walter Simons for sound critical reading. For their patience, encouragement, editing, and abiding intellectual faith in my ideas, I cannot thank sufficiently Kathryn Brush, Christopher Dustin, and Robert A. Warren. Finally, for Joe Vecchione, my "word meister," I reserve those special unspoken words which go to the one who makes all of this worthwhile.

—Joanna E. Ziegler

Introduction

Joanna E. Ziegler

In this collection of essays, 11 scholars look at some of the most startling writings on religious behavior ever produced by Christian believers. The present work is set apart from previous studies by a common theme: a perception of the mystics as performers, actors, and dancers—in short, as artists who *performed* their mysticism. This new performance-oriented perspective offers a more accessible and humanizing view of the participants themselves, as well as of the medieval writings that recorded the often incomprehensible activities of the pious mystics.

The historical texts preserve the extreme form of spirituality known as mysticism through autobiographies and *vitae*, devotional and meditational treatises, sermons, letters, and records of visions and other ecstatic experiences. Perhaps one of the best known examples of this type of intense spirituality is the sixteenth-century Saint Teresa of Avila, who, following her ecstatic experiences, wrote that at the moment of union with the Divine, she felt her heart pierced [transverberatio] by the arrow of God's love.[1] Teresa conveys many of the images we associate with mystical spirituality: rapture, transport, ecstasy, eroticism, pain and pleasure intertwined, submission, and extreme physical sensations. These images recur throughout the writings by and about women like Teresa, though the mystics discussed in this anthology preceded Teresa by nearly two centuries.

These writings have been available to scholars for quite some time. In this anthology, however, we adopt a new approach by looking at the subjects of those writings—the people, activities, events—not only as examples of piety or spirituality, but also as performance and theater. These mystical and devotional texts are spectacular examples of the scriptures' admonition to "suffer like Christ out of love for Christ." Yet most people— even those who take their spiritual lives seriously—are unfamiliar with mysticism, especially its medieval manifestations. This is unfortunate, because medieval mysticism is one of the richest chapters in the history of Christianity. The later Middle Ages, the period we explore here, was a time when believers expressed their piety fearlessly and in astonishingly creative and dramatic ways—and most of the practitioners were women.

Although these mystical texts are for the most part unfamiliar to Christians today, scholars have long been interested in them. At least since the nineteenth century, the texts have been the preserve of specialists— mainly historians of religion and theologians. During the past two decades, however, this distinctly academic context has broadened. The study of medieval mysticism has become a trendy topic in academe. Now it is a major theme in undergraduate courses in medieval history and religion; doctoral dissertations abound; there are sessions, conferences, books, and articles proliferating within the academic sphere at a remarkable pace.

The authors in this anthology are representative of this resurgent interest. The past decade or so has been a dynamic, exciting time to explore mysticism, when scholars no longer saw it as some spiritual irregularity but rather as a meaningful, even exemplary expression of one of the central Christian themes—piety as manifested through suffering. Our work on mysticism differs from the approach and language of those who pioneered in the field 10 or 20 years ago.

A certain tension underlies the writings in this anthology. We still fashion our ideas according to an epistemology of "the body" and "physicality" that we have inherited. Nor have we abandoned a type of social history that follows the claims of physicality, especially in the history of the beguines. However, we are now working more with theories of performance than physicality, for we seek an understanding of mystical texts from the perspective of drama, theater, and spectacle. We see spirituality as a wide-ranging cultural product or artifact, as much as a category of faith and belief. In short, we are reorienting the discourse on the body, which we've inherited, toward a more performance-sensitive perspective.

For those who are not academics, our views will seem self-evident. Most contemporary Catholics, for example, probably perceive the Mass as *inherently theatrical*—a spectacle to behold on the stage of the altar, with clergy dressed in regal gowns, a singular time where belief reigns supreme during the consecration of bread and wine into the Body and Blood of Christ. In other words, the Mass is regarded as a dramatic spectacle, with an audience in attendance. Though the celebration of the Mass has changed radically since Vatican II was held in the 1960s, we believe that the Mass-as-theater is a common presumption today. For scholars, however, this is a different matter. Thus for us to proclaim the radical innovation of our interpretation—our theory of a theatricalized, performed religion in devotional and mystical actions—requires some explanation.

First, our theory revises the way in which scholars understand and project these phenomena. It conceptualizes mysticism in ways that differ from those to which we are accustomed. This is not to be taken lightly. It may seem strange, but scholars have been overly caught up in what is uncommon, even bizarre or freakish, about mystical experience. In 1902, the renowned pragmatist philosopher William James sought to persuade his audience not to brand mystics as "sick souls,"[2] suggesting a more positive interpretation of the pain and suffering that attach to mysticism. For James, that nature is best grasped by comparing it to the emotional condition of the artist and the lover. Although the present writers do not discuss James directly, we reinstate his passionate belief that mystical states are neither sick nor bizarre, but are more akin to what happens to a person who has been transported—made ecstatic—by listening to music, for example, or falling "madly" in love. He asks us, as we do our readers, to remember that lovesickness or aesthetic bliss will be foreign (even unbelievable and ludicrous) to those who have not had such experiences and yet inescapably definitive—if "ineffable," in James's terms—to those who have.

Indirectly, we take up James's call to remove mystical behavior from the categories of interpretation that foster and emphasize the aberrant and bizarre. Rather, we encourage our readers to consider what is *artistic* about mystical behavior, instead of what has been interpreted as psychologically and behaviorally grotesque. What, really, was being narrated in texts that describe women who swell as though with pregnancy in anticipation of receiving the consecrated Host, or who bleed from the five wounds of Christ on Fridays? It is tempting to presume that the accounts are largely imaginary or else that these women were indeed exceptional believers.

For nearly 20 years, scholars have pursued the latter course, with important results. They have established mysticism as a serious subfield of the major humanistic disciplines of history, art history, religion, and literature. Although certainly worthy of a detailed discussion, this body of literature is far too vast and complicated to cover adequately in this introduction. A few key points, however, may help to orient the reader to our new explorations.

Historian Caroline Walker Bynum looms large in all our reading, writing, and understanding of women's mystical behavior. In the late 1970s, she rescued the study of medieval holy women from an obscure corner of Christianity, giving it visibility and respectability in the academy. Bleeding and ecstatic virgins were hardly of interest to the "men of science" who comprised the field of medieval history until approximately two decades ago, with their emphasis on the related themes of war, politics, and finance. The study of women mystics was therefore reserved for philosophers and theologians, and a few literary truffle hounds, interested in the verse and style of mystical writings. Bynum changed this, and what an exciting change it was for academics! Scholars and students were fascinated by the women she wrote about: an entire new field of publication emerged, novels were written, and films were made. Bleeding, fasting, ecstatic girls— rapt in their own spiritual journey of pain and suffering—were suddenly of great interest.

Bynum concentrated on women's visionary writings and the *vitae*, or lives of holy women. This genre of writing was popular from the late twelfth century through approximately 1500 in the Low Countries and the Rhineland, regions that were home to many female mystics. Bynum emphasized two themes in these writings: Eucharistic piety (the fervent desire to see and receive the Body of Christ in the consecrated Host) and extreme asceticism.

Coupled with her distinctive writing style and visceral vocabulary, Bynum's themes linger. Readers could scarcely ignore the women's sensational eating habits and erotic, loving, sensory responses to Christ portrayed by Bynum: vomiting, starving, hacking off pieces of their own flesh, bloating, bleeding, lactating, and weeping copiously.[3] Bynum's achievement was to demonstrate that images such as these are prevalent in the medieval texts that record women's spirituality. Because of them, she claimed that the essence of female spirituality in the Middle Ages had been bodily and physical. To encapsulate this phenomenon, Bynum coined the term "physicality"—a word and concept that proved to be highly influential. Asceticism, eroticism (the Heavenly Bridegroom), illnesses (bleeding, paralysis), and lastly food (fasting, starvation, vomiting) have become, because of Bynum, the common themes of scholarly writings on the subject.

Bynum developed her perspective on physicality on the basis of a complex understanding of female piety in the medieval period.[4] Her claim is that women had a singular role in the Incarnation. They were solely responsible for the flesh of Christ—his human-ness—and thus women viewed their participation in his humanity as unique. For women, then, the central act of piety in the later Middle Ages, *imitatio Christi* (literally meaning the imitation of Christ), was understood quite literally: "No religious woman failed to experience Christ as wounded, bleeding and dying. Women's efforts to imitate this Christ involved *becoming* the crucified, not just patterning themselves after or expanding their compassion toward, but *fusing with*, the body on the cross."[5] Bynum argues, therefore, that women's participation was characterized by an excessive physicality, in which imitating or becoming Christ was manifested in physical and bodily ways.

It should not be hard to understand why Bynum's claims are persuasive. The women mystics, formerly the preserve of inaccessible and arcane studies, were suddenly seen as women with whom we could identify. Although often repulsive, their behavior is familiar to us, nonetheless. Feminism had made us acutely aware that women, far more than men, are subject to eating disorders and that, regardless of social class, they are susceptible to acts of self-mutilation. Writing to a post-Vietnam generation raised on a diet of images of violence and pathological disorders such as anorexia and post-traumatic stress—or so we've been led to believe[6]— Bynum produced images of holy women with which our generation easily identified. It is hardly surprising, then, that we took to her work enthusiastically, even zealously.

Yet, oddly, we write prolifically—often in graphic prose, but without emotion—about women who stood apart from ordinary people by virtue of their extraordinary pious practices. Perhaps because we live in a culture that with unthinking ease accepts and promotes the body as a convenient site for self-abuse, self-abhorrence, and violence, it is possible for us to distance ourselves, as only scholars can, from the fact that the medieval mystics were portrayed as transforming themselves in apparently unbelievable physical ways.

Although we do not write about these phenomena as pure empiricists (aren't many of us feminists, after all?), the fact remains that we still have not looked squarely at our interest in the public suffering of the medieval mystics. The "objectifying" impulse, which feminists today are so quick to condemn, operates even now. But these mystics about whom we write were deeply suffering and making that suffering a public affair.

I know of no scholar who has publicly questioned her or his own fascination with the material. We use highly charged, palpable language to investigate something we never question in print. Indeed, the scholarly writings on mysticism of the last 20 years constitute a significant cultural document, albeit one that testifies to minds operating in isolation from the senses and emotions. Why are we so intellectually interested in, indeed disposed to, these persons of such "unbelievable" physical existence—and yet, in our emotional and spiritual response, remain relatively detached?

By not attending to who we are, to what brings us to these worlds we study with such intensity and fervor, we have persisted in keeping mysticism as something arcane, remote, and alien. This has perpetuated a conception of spirituality that prevents us from realizing the human message that public, mystical suffering expresses.

In brief, earlier scholarship discussed the women as remote but socially explainable and, furthermore, as being clothed in symbolic images of the period. Because of their historical distance, then, we have remained intensely curious and analytical regarding the mystics but not connected with them in any emotional or immediate way. They were, frankly, interesting oddities. We lost their humanity through the prism of curiosity, just as we forget that circus "freaks" are human beings, too—more like us than we would care to admit.

In addition, earlier scholarship approached the mystical life as though it were more or less an unchanging entity between 1200 and 1500. But is this right; is this historically possible? In those centuries, culture and societal values would have changed dramatically. Yet that entire period is out there, a body of knowledge to be examined and analyzed *as religion*— which for scholars has been defined as an entity to be engaged only intellectually, not emotionally or spiritually. Scholars have been careful to differentiate themselves from theologians, believers, priests, monks and nuns; they "understand" but are loathe to embrace. Thus, when studying religion within the academy, scholars have been likely to suppress and repudiate the personal point of view, lest their enterprise be considered "unscholarly."

Our authors here attempt to reintroduce the personal element into their study of spiritual behavior. They do so as a critical activity though, not as a spiritual one. They acknowledge the historical nature of the material they work with—but they do this in order to explore the possibility that there may be more than just an intellectual investment in the material that fascinates them. We seek to lead our readers into perceiving the mystics as performers, actors, dancers: in other words, as artists. Mystics *performed* their mysticism. As this perspective repositions the participants, onlookers, and writers (including ourselves), we find ourselves standing on new ground, where the activities of religion and piety are no more remote nor foreign or alien than are theatrical devices, actors, and dancers.

When Cornwall gouges out Gloucester's eyes in Shakespeare's great tragedy, *King Lear*, we willingly suspend disbelief in the pretense, lest the profoundly human and tragic message of the physical pain—the suffering in all its glorious particularity, which rises from the depths of emotional pain and love—escape us. His case demonstrates vividly that the most unbelievable things happen to characters in the theater, as in life. Yet we know that this is not literally so; the actor did not in fact gouge out his eyes each night on stage. Yet, the audiences are horrified by the perception of it. They moan, recoil, and weep with the suffering king torn from what he loves most in the world—his youngest daughter. He wails the name Cordelia, embraces his dead daughter, and carries her gently in his arms. Love, pain, and suffering intertwine. The tragedy, indeed the very message of tragic human frailty, is utterly lost without that leap of faith that the audience takes into theatrical time and space, where the most fantastic things occur. It is not that we "believe" the actors and events; it is that we permit them to live within our psyche as *artistic* reality.

No one questions the propriety of that leap of faith into the extreme physical suffering of Gloucester and Lear that we take every time we watch the play. We all acknowledge that if we are to gain but a small glimmer of its meaning, we must allow ourselves to be transported, to be literally moved there by the actors' and writer's artistry.

The present writers believe that something of this sort was happening with the mysticism we deal with here. There is an underlying, pervasive message in the mystics' activities. Let us not forget that love of Christ Jesus propelled the mystic to act. That love was intimately bound to public pain and suffering, which expressed the mystics' love, for these acts provided the model of Christ on earth that they emulated. This process of identification through suffering was not a medieval invention. The Scriptures are rife with images of terrifying, even incredible suffering. From Job to Paul, the texts proclaim that one way of loving Christ is by becoming Christ; one way to know that one is loved by God is to accept that the true believer must suffer most. In Job (30: 27–31) we read: "My inner parts have boiled without any rest, the days of affliction have prevented me. I went mourning without indignation; I rose up, and cried in the crowd. I was the brother of dragons, and companion of ostriches. My skin is become black upon me, and my bones are dried up with heat. My harp is turned to mourning, and my organ into the voice of those that weep." Surely, these are mystical images.

The method adopted in this anthology is less concerned with documentation of physical phenomena than with the significance of the appearance of such phenomena upon the audience in the context of a convincing ritual performance by the mystic. Whether or not the mystics believed, or were perceived to believe, that transformance actually took place is not the essential point. Rather, it is that the audience at that moment is affected by the performance and—as a theatrical audience may forever be somewhat changed by the momentary effect of a persuasive performance—so, too, were those witnessing the ritual performance of a mystic changed by their perception of the message of the performance.

The viewer is affected to one degree or another—even subconsciously—in a way that will become a factor in shaping his or her interior philosophical landscape. We are, after all, the sum of every event that occurs in our perception—from those having little significant effect to others that are life transforming.

If we miss the relationship between love and suffering in mysticism, we have missed its meaning altogether. By entering mystical behavior as theater, as artistry—with an audience hoping to make a leap of faith—we begin to understand the most incredible acts of public pain and self-affliction. As in theater, that audience is moved to believe, to feel the pain and suffering, and to witness the effects of love. The freakish, outlandish, bizarre acts of personal piety that accompany mysticism, if interpreted as performance, may then be seen as dramatic vessels from which pour forth the entire and glorious range of ecstatic revelation.

Notes

1. Michael Walsh, ed., *Butler's Lives of the Saints: Concise Edition* (Kent: Burns and Oates, 1981), 336.
2. William James, *The Varieties of Religious Experience: A Study in Human Nature* (1902; reprint, Canada: Mentor Books, 1958).
3. Caroline Bynum, "Women Mystics and Eucharistic Devotion in the Thirteenth Century," *Women's Studies* 11(1984): 179–214; and *Holy Feast and Holy Fast: The Religious Significance of Food to Medieval Women* (Berkeley: University of California Press, 1987).
4. For a postmodern reading of Bynum, see David Aers and Lynn Staley, *The Power of the Holy: Religion, Politics, and Gender in Late Medieval English Culture* (University Park, PA: Pennsylvania State University Press, 1996).
5. Caroline Walker Bynum, "Women Mystics and Eucharistic Devotion in the Thirteenth Century," 193. Emphasis in original.

6. For a chilling example of the process of creating disorder, see Jerry Lembcke's discussion of the association between mental illness and Vietnam veterans in *The Spitting Image: Myth, Memory, and the Legacy of Vietnam* (New York and London: New York University Press, 1998).

CHAPTER ONE

Background: An Introduction to Performance Studies

Mary Suydam

The essays in this volume represent a diverse array of medieval scholars who share a commitment to exploring how the burgeoning field of performance studies can expand and deepen the study of medieval devotional practices and textuality. These essays demonstrate the wide variety of approaches to performance studies in the fields of English literature, the visual arts, history, religious studies, and anthropology. Because many of the late-medieval texts we study were written in the vernacular, we have chosen contributors who have expertise in each of the following medieval religious cultures: English, Flemish, German, French, Spanish, Swedish, as well as Latin. Thus the collection examines a wider spectrum of European cultures than each author could provide alone. This collection is truly more than the sum of its parts. We hope to encourage further cross-cultural examinations of medieval devotionality, especially with regard to Mediterranean and eastern European cultures.

Much of the impetus for the renewed attention to performance in all disciplines has come from the field of literary criticism, which has been increasingly unraveling and problematizing the once-tidy categories of text, author, editor, translator, and performer. The de-emphasis on the single author and his/her authorized text, as well as the conception of texts as performances, provides a background for this collection.[1] This area of literary criticism has itself drawn heavily upon the disciplines of theater studies, anthropology, and religious studies. Theater studies have always been concerned with defining and differentiating particular aspects of theatrical performances. Since the 1970s "performance studies" has also become extremely important in defining and highlighting aspects of religious ritual. Ritual, originally defined in Christianity as the order for conducting liturgy, now usually refers to a type of action being performed generally in public (we speak of civic rituals, for example, in addition to religious rituals) that also carries symbolic meaning and is characterized by formality, fixity, and repetition.[2] To study ritual from a performance standpoint means to examine what ritual *does*, rather than focusing primarily upon the meaning behind or embedded within the ritual. Performance studies scholars attempt to highlight action, space, emotion, and sensory dimensions rather than the intellectual content of the ritual text.[3] The result has been a complete reassessment of the concept of ritual itself.

For those readers who are new to performance studies, this chapter will sketch some basic components of general performance studies and ritual studies, and identify the issues surrounding the boundaries (if any) separating theatrical, ritual, and less-formal devotional performances.[4] First and foremost, in order to apply performance studies to ritual and/or devotional practices, it is important to define what we consider to be the major issues surrounding the term "performance." Each discipline has a different lens with which to view different aspects of performance. Not surprisingly, each contributor to this volume works with a different conception of performance. Indeed, we hope that bringing together many performance perspectives will spark a meaningful dialogue among scholars of different disciplines. We also suggest that there may not be a universal definition of performance, but rather different performance perspectives that are useful for understanding particular types of performances. Hence, rather than supply one definition of performance, we will examine some of the performance perspectives that have been most influential for the contributors to this volume.

Anthropology and Ritual Studies: Victor Turner

The field of performance studies and its relationship to religious ritual was revolutionized by the pioneering works of Victor Turner, assisted by his wife, Edith. Before Turner, the sociological field of religious studies was dominated by the ideas of Émile Durkheim (1858–1917). Durkheim regarded rituals as the collective expression of the social order, a set of rules by which people sacralize their social structure, enabling them to experience that structure as part of a larger reality (often imagined as a transcendent being).[5] This view assumes a unity underlying the social order with which individuals identify. Thus rituals are conservative and serve to stabilize the social order.

Victor Turner (1920–1983), on the other hand, observed that societies continually wrestle with tension, ambiguities, and conflicts. Such conflicts generate change in dynamic ways, a process Turner called "social dramas." Turner identified five stages of social drama: breech/crisis/redress/reintegration *or* schism. By focusing upon social change as drama, he defined the dramatic impulse as the ground of social life. Among the Ndembu people Turner studied, he discovered that "a multiplicity of conflict situations is correlated with a high frequency of ritual performance."[6] Thus Turner began to associate rituals with social dramas. In fact, rituals may serve as a redressive phase in social dramas: "I consider the term 'ritual' to be more fittingly applied to forms of ritual behavior associated with social transitions, while the term 'ceremony' has a closer bearing on religious behavior associated with social states. . . . Ritual is transformative, ceremony confirmatory."[7]

Turner was particularly interested in the type of ritual called "rites of passage," in which an individual's status is changed. During such rituals individuals frequently spend periods of time in which they have left their previous social state but have not yet completed the transition to a different social state. Following the research of Arnold van Gennep (1873–1957), Turner used the term "liminality" to describe states that are "not this/not that" or "betwixt and between."[8] In these liminal states brought about by some kinds of rituals, there is the potential for creativity. Although the goal of such rituals is reintegration into communal norms, the reflexivity and sense of being "outside the bounds" occasioned by liminal states may in fact subvert those norms. Thus Turner transformed the definition of ritual from that of conservative guarantor of the status quo (now confined to the concept of "ceremony") to one with the possibility of dynamic social change. Eventually Turner located liminality in more diffuse and less formal situations (which he called "liminoid"), especially in industrialized cultures, in which people of different social statuses could take part: civic parades and games, pilgrimages, the arts, and even subversive literature.[9]

Turner has provided scholars with a model in which formalized rituals and other more diffuse performances such as pilgrimages or visionary states are one important way in which social conflict is addressed, redressed, ignored, and/or transformative. Catherine Bell notes that "[Turner's] emphasis on how ritual does what it does by means of a process of dramatization led him and other scholars to explore ritual as performance."[10] On the other hand, Turner was never very clear about the exact components of drama. Ronald Grimes has noted that for Turner, "a ritual drama . . . depends less upon formal qualities of the performance itself than upon the connection of a ritual enactment with a social drama."[11] Consequently, although Turner provided a model of ritual that was dynamic and performative, others have had to specify what qualities belong to the dramatic and performative genres. Because theater has always been concerned with the mechanics of theatrical performance, the insights of theater studies have been especially helpful for scholars of religious performances.

In this collection, Mary Giles's essay directly applies Turner's concept of liminality to Spanish visionary women. Giles views women in visionary states as liminal people in the more diffuse liminoid sense described by Turner: as people who occupy a status "betwixt and between." Her essay examines the creative possibility for people in such states to reaffirm or to subvert the status quo, and the ways in which audiences, then and now, perceive such people as normative or "outside the bounds."

Performance Studies, Theater, and Ritual

Theatrical theorists are primarily concerned with how theater does what it does: what exactly constitutes performance (speech, gestures, space, audience?) and how theatrical performances differ from other kinds of performances—individual, cultural, and ritual. In modern westernized secular theater, the differences may seem obvious, but even there theatrical performance proves surprisingly difficult to isolate from other types of performances (for example, giving a speech to an audience of business people).

Although the hypothesis that modern drama emerged from medieval liturgy has been vigorously challenged, no one denies that there are obvious affinities between the drama of theater and the drama of ritual.[12] Like their colleagues in the performing arts, theorists of ritual have attempted to specify what constitutes religious or ritual performance, and what criteria, if any, separate ritual from theatrical performances. Thus, theorists of both religion and theater have devoted considerable energy to differentiating theatrical from religious performances, although such considerations tend to blur, not sharpen, the perhaps artificial boundary between them. The models of Richard Schechner, Manfred Pfister, and Ronald Grimes have been especially helpful for the study of religious and theatrical performances. It is important to note that Schechner, Grimes, and Turner all developed their ideas in dialogue with each other.[13]

Richard Schechner: From Ritual to Theater and Back

Schechner's influential book *Essays in Performance Theory* (1977) defines performance as a "quality of action," emphasizing that the performer *does* something. Moreover, the performer does something in the presence of and for an audience.[14] Schechner claims that types of performances can be viewed from two perspectives. The first posits a continuum ranging from performances in everyday life (for example, gestures of greeting, the "performance" of an academic professional at a conference) to those of religious rituals and ceremonies (for example, the rite of baptism). Schechner further notes that all performances involve some degree of ritualization, that is, the use of conventions that an audience can recognize. The second perspective is that of a web of differing types of performances, all of which interact with each other within a culture.[15] For example, within the formal ritual of the Mass are recognized social gestures of greeting and eating. Conversely, modern Veterans Day parades often reflect their origins in civic religious processions—the parade of civic leaders, the placing of wreaths on monuments, the participation of important local clubs and civic groups. Thus, for Schechner, the qualities of action and audience are the two most critical components of performance. Within the category of "action," various types of action are treated for the purposes of this definition as equivalently performative—speech, gesture, use of space, dance, and music.

Schechner is also concerned with the relationships between performance, ritual, script, play, theater, and drama. Western theatrical performances, such as Shakespeare's *Hamlet*, involve some sense of separation from "real life" and their primary purpose is entertainment. They involve play or pretence; they take place in delineated spaces; they often occur "outside time," and the audiences understand themselves to be witnesses rather than participants. Schechner separates such performances—even those with re-

ligious themes—from rituals by stipulating that rituals such as the Mass
are "efficacious," meaning that they cause something to happen or they
bring something into being. Rituals are also public and participatory.[16]
    So, for Schechner, the Mass is a ritual rather than a performance.
Its participants are not a passive audience, but active performers themselves. Further, its purpose is not to entertain, but to bring about a
transformation in that participating audience. For Schechner, the efficacy-
entertainment binary is more important than the ritual-theater opposition.
Some theatrical performances may indeed be efficacious, while some rituals
may be more valued for their entertainment traditions than for efficacy
(for example, the recitation of the story of Esther and Haman, complete
with costumes, masks, and noisemakers, at Purim).[17]
    Schechner does acknowledge, however, the transformative potential
of theatrical performance. Unlike ritual, this transformative potential is for
the witnessing audience, not the performers: "Aesthetic drama works its
transformations on the audience. In aesthetic drama the audience is separated both actually and conceptually from the performers."[18] For Schechner, this transformation is effected through the here-and-now performance
rather than through the scripted drama being performed. Thus, however
one defines and categorizes performance, it has transformative qualities.
For Schechner, then, Western theatrical performance is characterized by
action in the here-and-now; it requires an audience; and in its spontaneity
it has transformative potential.

Manfred Pfister: Dramatic and Literary Texts

Manfred Pfister's *The Theory and Analysis of Drama* (1977) is concerned with
specifying how drama differs from literature. Like Schechner, Pfister also
emphasizes the necessity of an audience for theatrical performance. A literary text is generally written by one author and read by one individual
at a time; in contrast, theatrical performances are characterized by a "collectivity of production and reception."[19] By "collectivity of production"
Pfister means that no one person is solely responsible for a theatrical production. By "collectivity of reception" Pfister means that a group of people
(an audience), rather than a single reader, engage with the work.
    Drawing on J. L. Austin's and J. Searles's concept of "speech acts"
(10), Pfister further argues that dramatic dialogue is "spoken action," that
is, each utterance is meaningful not solely in terms of content, but as a
type of action itself. Performative dialogue is therefore different from both
narrative dialogue and philosophical dialogue. Moreover, the presence of

nonlinguistic signs, spatial orientation, and attention to physical movement are characteristic of dramatic texts and form part of the "multimediality" of such texts. In other words, "the multimedial dramatic text contains more information" than purely verbal narratives (9–10).

According to Pfister, these features of drama are also present in other public performance activities, notably games, sports, ritual, and unstructured play. He is less concerned than Schechner with differentiating theatrical performances from ritual, noting in passing that "ritual may be interpreted as a phylogenetic precursor of drama" (12). Thus, for Pfister, the qualities that constitute performance—performative speech and dialogue, multimediality, and collectivity of production and reception—are found across all performance genres.

In this collection, Mary Suydam's essay on Flemish beguines examines their textuality using Pfister's concept of performative texts (decentered author, multimedial, and audience-oriented) rather than that of a literary (authorized and individual) perspective. Suydam also employs Jean Alter's model of the "staged text" to argue that devotional and ecstatic texts by and about beguines construct an ethic of performative and transformative reading.

Ronald Grimes: Performance Studies and Ritual Studies

Scholars in the field of ritual studies also examine ritual performances to determine how ritual activities differ from those of everyday life. For example, how does the Eucharistic meal differ from an everyday meal? A performance perspective is concerned not only with the symbolic meanings within the meal, but the actual activities of eating and drinking.[20] One of the most influential theorists and practitioners of ritual from the field of religious studies is Ronald Grimes. He is less interested in constructing academic boundaries between ritual, theater, and myth than with elaborating processes of "ritualization" in which performance is the key component.

Grimes calls ritual "theater's next of kin," noting that the western separation of ritual and drama is absent in many cultures, and in fact may be a recent and temporary phenomenon in the history of western culture. He is interested in the ways in which ritual and theater may intersect, especially in postmodern theater performances such as Jerzy Grotowski's Poor Theatre.[21] Grimes lists as common components of ritual and theatrical performances "the fundamental impulse toward stylization, mimesis, and transformation."[22] By performance Grimes means actions that eliminate the dichotomy between thought and action and that focus upon the body as the center for such fused thought-action dynamics.[23] Some features of this type of performance in both ritual and theatrical contexts include:

1. avoidance of mental rehearsal and planning
2. insistence upon a concrete, associated image at the moment of execution
3. adaptation of the whole body and psyche to every movement
4. action from bodily centers outward to extremities and voice
5. surpassing fatigue, chatter, self-indulgence, and masks for the sake of revelation. (172)

According to Grimes, these qualities embody a "ritual ethic" of creativity, and thus Grimes does not see ritual as necessarily conservatively repetitive or a method of social control. For Grimes, ritual studies and ritual theater intersect when they seek to enact dynamic flow and process. Yet because Grimes studies ritual, which is repetitive in nature, he recognizes that this "dynamic flow" may be called forth through stylization and practice. Indeed, such repetition may be necessary to allow the performer to reach the point where one's whole body "surpasses fatigue, chatter, and self-indulgence."

Grimes is also concerned with performance and audience. An important corollary of his "ritual ethic" is his belief that detached observation of performances is impossible; the observer is necessarily a participant. In this way Grimes restores to ritual studies the sense of audience that is so prominent in theater performance studies. Grimes believes that in order to study ritual one must adopt a method of "going with," which means acknowledging one's participation in the process, articulating as part of the data one's own gestures and actions, and, perhaps most important, developing all the senses, not just the visual and verbal: "The goal of field study is to maximize the process of interaction, not to arrive at conclusions" (19–20). This methodology is completely at variance with traditional scholarly reliance upon verbal communication, detached observance, and articulation of meaning: "Studying ritual will only be fruitful if we recognize that we can only articulate meaning after we have been grasped by its sense" (23).

For Grimes, studying ritual means examining and experiencing the spatial, emotional, and sensory components of both participants and observers. According to this perspective, the dichotomy between theater and ritual is artificial, because, just as in theater performances, observer/participants who do not share in the ritual activities may still transform and be transformed by rituals. An example is the annual religious fiesta at Santa Fe, New Mexico, in which the primary observers are now tourists and not native Hispanic Catholics, and whose observation/participation have changed the nature of the fiesta (10–13). There, Grimes observed that many of the participants and observers described their actions in terms of scholarly rather than traditional Catholic religious conceptions of their performance, mentioning Mircea Eliade and Carl Jung. The scholars, he wryly noted, have themselves become mythmakers.

One of the difficulties faced by scholars who characterize religious rituals as theatrical performances is that this perspective introduces the elements of repetition and artifice. In particular, the element of rehearsal conflicts with the desire for spontaneity in both ecstatic and theatrical performances. Yet, to bring about the "dynamic flow and process," both ritual and theater require preparation, repetition, and practice. This has obvious implications for scholars of mysticism, who have tended to regard religious ecstasies as spontaneous outpourings. For theater, too, the search for the "fully present moment" conflicts with the requirements of control and practice. Are spontaneous theatrical performances more or less "real" than consciously staged ones? Our essays' examinations of control and spontaneity grapple with this dilemma in divergent approaches to the phenomenon of ecstatic mysticism in the European Middle Ages. Mary Giles's essay on Spanish visionary women stresses the spontaneous nature of their mysticism in their inability to recall what had been said or done during moments of ecstasy. Susan Rodgers's and Joanna Ziegler's depiction of the trance dances of Elisabeth of Spalbeek, a Flemish beguine, emphasizes instead the elements of control, repetition, and stylization required by her repeated performances. Both essays rely upon concepts from Jerzy Grotowski's elemental theater.

The element of artifice is perhaps even more troubling for scholars of religion. After all, Schechner defined "play or pretense" as one of the major characteristics separating theater from religious ritual. In the Mass the priest is his role; in *Hamlet* the actor only pretends to be Hamlet. However, even in clearly theatrical performances audiences often highly value the actor who seems to have most "become" his part.[24] If religious performers are "only pretending," does that detract from their spiritual authenticity? In this volume, Rosemary Hale examines the use of infant cradles for some kinds of devotional performances. Are women who rock infant cradles pretending to care for the baby Jesus, or do they really believe he is there? Which kind of religious performance is more authentic? Hale argues that such questions ignore spiritual performances' potential for transformation. Through performance, the performer becomes his/her role, and the cradle does contain the infant Christ.

The question of authenticity is also addressed here in Nanda Hopenwasser's examination of Margery Kempe. If we view Margery as a self-conscious artist, do we admire her skill or denounce her as a religious fraud? Perhaps, as Jacques Derrida once remarked about the quest for authenticity, "A desire for centrality is a function of play itself; is it not indestructible? A ghostly center is calling us."[25] Perhaps, also, play or pretense is devalued when the transformative effect of pretense upon performer and audience is ignored.

To focus upon what performance does that may be transformative is to heed Grimes's call to develop all the senses, paying more attention to the nature of particular components involved in performance, rather than treating all actions (gestures, speech, song, movement) as equivalent. Three "qualities of action" that recur in most of our essays, and thus deserve some theoretical introduction, are speech, interpretive context, and space (including bodily movement).

Components of Performance

Linguistics and Performance Studies

J. L. Austin emphasized the performative quality of certain kinds of verbal statements. There are some statements in which an utterance, rather than describing meaning, is part of the "doing of an action."[26] For example, the words "I pronounce you husband and wife" effect a marriage; they do not describe it. Austin noted that social convention and context are necessary for such speech acts to be performative. For example, a stranger who says "I pronounce you husband and wife" to a couple sitting beside him at a football game does not effect a marriage. Similarly, the statement "I divorce you" only effects divorce in societies that accept this convention, and, in such societies, only in specifically understood contexts. Within the Christian liturgy of the Mass, the statement "This is my body" does not describe or explain the significance of the Eucharist; it performs the Eucharist. One important consequence of Austin's theory of "speech acts" is the breakdown of the boundary between ritual actions and ritual sayings.

Austin's theories seem to function most effectively in a context of sanctioned ritual events, such as the Christian liturgy. In this volume, Laurie Finke's essay on a fifteenth-century English translation of the works of Marguerite Porete examines the concept of speech acts in more socially ambiguous circumstances—the speech acts of an unsanctioned person outside the bounds of the ecclesiastical world. For Finke, Mikhail Bakhtin's concept of the "dialogic" voice provides a framework within which to understand such ambigous speech performances. For Bakhtin, dialogue involves the "intense interaction and struggle between one's own and another's word."[27] This opposition is not a binary struggle between self/other or orthodoxy/heresy, but a multiple layering of voices that are not reducible to clearly-marked authorial standpoints. Such "dialogues," in their attempts to mark authoritative spaces and to claim sites of authenticity, are performative and multidimensional. Finke's essay examines the "heteroglossia" of performative speech.[28]

Also in this volume, Catherine Müller's essay on the works of Marguerite d'Oingt compares performative writing to performative speech. Müller argues that d'Oingt's writings are themselves performative, that they enact their own meanings and allow the author and reader to transcend the oppositions of signifier and signified. Müller thus stresses the performative rather than the literary dimensions of mystical writing.

Framing and Interpretative Context

As used by Gregory Bateson, framing connotes the ways in which activities or statements provide interpretative frameworks for understanding other activities or statements. Bateson noted that, among Andaman Islanders, the framing of a ceremonial blow indicated whether one intended to make war or peace.[29] Framing, which tends to involve special kinds of speech, actions, or use of space, provides the interpretative context for ritual activities. For example, in the study of the religious ritual of the Mass, the concept of framing means studying the interpretative context in which the Mass takes place: the types of spaces in which it occurs and the people and objects who occupy those spaces; the use of particular symbols such as the altar, cross, and chalice; and the types of speech employed by the performers. Similar studies can be conducted for theatrical performances, raising questions such as: Are there frames that denote particular kinds of performances? What frames enable ritual, rather than theatrical or political, performances?

In connection with Austin's linguistic analysis, some scholars have concentrated upon the way in which some kinds of ritual are framed by particular kinds of ceremonial speech that contrast with less formal everyday speech.[30] Maurice Bloch, for example, has theorized that ceremonial speech is impoverished relative to normal speech, in that only certain forms are allowed and that Speech A must be followed by Speech B, rather than an infinity of possible responses. For example, during the Mass when the priest says "The Lord be with you," the audience response is dictated by the liturgy. According to Bloch, one consequence of formal speech is that it compels acquiescence: "It is because the formalization of language is a way whereby a speaker can coerce the response of another that it can be seen as a form of social control."[31] Bloch adds that this social control is reciprocal because Speaker A is also constricted in speech and action possibilities. In the example of the Mass, the priest's words are also dictated by the liturgy.

In this volume, Claire Sahlin examines the public performance of Birgitta of Sweden's sermons and exorcisms by male priests in terms of Bloch's ideas about formalized speech. She observes that Birgitta gained spiritual power through relinquishing her voice to others. She also explains how Birgitta's spirituality was framed in terms of speech and communication rather than private, closed experiences.

Bloch further argued that ritual speech, and especially song, do not explain anything and are not logical in nature. Hence, ritual studies that emphasize meaning, even according to Durkheimian explanations of one's place within social structure, fail to grasp the nature of ritual: "You cannot argue with a song" (36–37). Within the ritual context, one can only sing or refuse to sing the song.[32] Like Grimes, Bloch asserts the priority of action over meaning in the study of religious ritual. Rituals are not primarily theological concepts enacted. Bloch's emphasis upon performance elements within ritual argues against the older scholarly tendency to treat ritual activity as secondary to the symbolic meaning embedded within it.[33]

Unlike Grimes, Bloch believes that, in most societies, the element of social control present in ritual differentiates the performance qualities of ritual from those of theater. In fact, Bloch believes that ritual should be compared to political leadership and control. It is noteworthy that a focus upon performance does not necessarily lead to an equation of ritual and theatrical performances. Indeed, many of the essays in this volume record the dynamics of ecstatic performance in a dialogue, to use Bakhtin's term, with the performances of ecclesiastical orthodoxy. One of the paradoxes of performance is the collapse of simple binaries like orthodoxy/heresy, ritual/theater, or collective/personal.

Spatial Orientation and Sacred Space

Another component of performance that is related to framing involves heightened awareness of the placement of bodies, symbols, visual decoration, and architectural elements in ritual space. The notion of "sacred space," first elaborated by Durkheim, has been very prominent in ritual studies. For Durkheim, the "sacred" and the "profane" were opposing conceptual universes. Sacred space thus refers either to special locations, objects, or animals devoted to ritual, or to ordinary locations, objects, or animals demarcated as sacred through ritual actions.

Mircea Eliade (1907–1986), another influential theorist of religion and a contemporary of Victor Turner, argued against Durkheim's reduction of God to the social order. Like Rudolf Otto (1869–1937), Eliade saw the phenomenon of the "holy" as sui generis. For Eliade, rituals seek to reenact an original revelatory moment, an encounter with the sacred, that has been preserved in myth. Hence, rituals are a means to recapture the past.[34] Eliade's primary focus was upon the mythic symbols contained within rites: "A symbol and a rite . . . are on such different levels that the rite can never reveal what the symbol reveals."[35] Eliade theorized that ritual spaces such as temples attempt to re-create a "sacred center, where heaven and earth meet."[36]

In this collection, William Hodapp's essay on Richard Rolle's Passion meditations uses the theories of Mircea Eliade in a performance-oriented perspective. He notes that the re-enactment process described by Eliade, far from being static, seeks to actively "re-present" the long-ago hierophany in the fully present moment. Hodapp argues that such attempts to bring the past into the present, with all the instabilities and ambiguities that entails, have a dynamic "ritual-devotional impulse" that is not only symbolic, but performative.

Arnold van Gennep and Victor Turner, on the other hand, pioneered the concept that the sacred is relative to its nonsacred surroundings and may therefore change:

> Van Gennep saw the sacred not as some sort of absolute entity or quality but as a relative one that readily shifts in different situations and at different ritual stages. What he designated as the 'pivoting of the sacred' alerted scholars to the ways in which ritual can actually define what is sacred, not simply react to the sacred as something already and for always fixed.[37]

Van Gennep and later Turner connected space with the concept of liminality. For example, participants in the ritual of confession occupy different spaces and perform different roles before, during, and after the ritual. Before the ritual, they are in a state of sin and are not allowed to approach the altar nor participate in the Eucharistic "meal" of wafers. During the ritual, they occupy the role of penitent and are neither damned nor forgiven—a liminal space that has a definite corresponding physical space: the confessional booth. Afterward, they are restored to communion with the Church. "Liminality" thus has both metaphysical (marginal) and physical (spatial) connotations. Turner later theorized a more diffuse concept of liminality (called "liminoid" to distinguish it from the more formal "liminal") in which space may be less relevant.

Place, Space, and Bodies

Jonathan Z. Smith's *To Take Place: Toward Theory in Ritual* (1987) examined the concept of place itself and its relationship to space. Rather than human discovery and mapping of pre-existent places, Smith theorizes that humans create place from space: "It is the relationship to the human body, and our experience of it, that orients us in space, that confers meaning to place. Human beings are not placed; they bring place into being."[38] For Smith, sacrality is "a category of emplacement." Such a perspective entails an appreciation of the ways in which humans create sacred places through ritual, rather than ritual creating spaces for sacrality. A home wedding is a good example of an ordinary space that becomes the setting for a transformative ritual. Churches and temples are ordinary places that have become sacralized through ritual activities.

All of the essays in this volume seek to examine the relationship between place, sacred space, ritual, and performance. Nanda Hopenwasser's examination of Margery Kempe's pilgrimage narrative recognizes Kempe's conscious artistry as a writer through her descriptions of her movements through the pilgrimage spaces of Jerusalem, while William Hodapp argues that Rolle's Passion meditations seek to re-create those pilgrim spaces "at home." In a truly interdisciplinary essay, Joanna Ziegler and Susan Rodgers combine modern anthropological perspectives with those of the visual and performing arts to examine the way in which Elisabeth of Spalbeek occupied and defined particular spaces and made them sacred through the movement of her body.

Also in this collection is Rosemary Hale's analysis of the performative rituals and practices that surrounded women's use of Christ-child effigies and infant cradles, which were held, bathed, swaddled, caressed, and rocked. Hale emphasizes the performative—tactile and sensory—dimensions of these maternal activities, which have usually been described as "visionary" experiences. She argues that such tactile performances—(be)holding the divine—intersect with the transformative nature of mystical experience. Thus Hale expands our ideas about "visionary" mysticism to encompass the manipulation of bodies in space.

Postmodern Perspectives on Performance

These components of performance—speech, framing, and space—are also used by postmodern performance theorists. However, the meaning of performance in postmodern theories has different connotations than "activity expressing meaning." Instead, postmodern theorists tend to emphasize the contingent and strategic use of different kinds of performances to *generate* meaning or to question meaning altogether. In particular, religious performances can be viewed as a method of establishing, rather than expressing, identity. It is important to note that such ideas of performance have been developed in conjunction with the arts, anthropology, and religious studies.[39]

A number of postmodern theorists are interested in performance as part of their project to deconstruct the unitary concept of the individual. Rather than imagining a set of performances as equivalent expressions of an essential identity, scholars such as Judith Butler theorize that contingent identities are constructed through continual performances. Butler, for example, theorizes that sexual identity is constructed rather than essential:

> Rather, it is through the repeated play of this sexuality that the "I" is insistently reconstituted as a lesbian "I"; paradoxically, it is precisely the *repetition* of that play that establishes as well the *instability* of the very category that it constitutes. . . . And if the "I" is the effect of a certain repetition, one which produces the semblance of a continuity or coherence, then there is no "I" that precedes the gender that it is said to perform; the repetition and the failure to repeat, produce a string of performances that constitute and contest the coherence of that "I".[40]

This perspective depends upon the poststructuralist contention that meaning is not transparent or fixed by its referent (the sign), but contingently constructed and continually deferred: "In avowing the sign's strategic provisionality (rather than its strategic essentialism), that identity can become a site of contest and revision, indeed take on a future set of significations that those of us who use it now may not be able to foresee."[41] The consequence of this poststructuralist perspective for performance has been a fresh examination of the ways in which humans construct personal and social identities through performances. In particular, ritual and devotional practices can be analyzed as mechanisms for constructing, rather than expressing, identity. Ritual's performative practices can also be linked with other kinds of performances, most notably, theater. Sarah Beckwith notes that "In such an understanding of ritual practice no objective meanings can be assigned independently of material processes, and such meaning restores the practical moments of human agency that James' model of ritual has found it hard to locate. Space . . . comes to have meaning through practice itself."[42]

In this collection, Robert Sweetman's essay explores the ways in which Thomas of Cantimpré "becomes" the scripts with which he works. As exorcist and pastoral curé, Thomas's clerical persona—indeed, his identity—is positioned and shaped by the differing content of the texts he must enact in his religious roles.

Also in this collection, Mary Suydam's essay on Flemish ecstatic beguines examines the ways in which these women's religious identities were continually constituted through performances, rather than viewing performances as an expression of fixed identities. Such a conception of ecstatic performances focuses upon the strategies and interpretations of such religious performances by beguines and their audiences.

Practice Theory

Practice theory originally derives from the theories of Karl Marx and attempts to provide methodological tools for overcoming the dichotomy between subject and object (in this case, observer and rite observed). "Practice" as used by Marx indicates both "activity" and the theory of the process of that activity, just as "performance" often is used to mean either "the act of performing" or a theory about the process of that act.[43]

Catherine Bell, incorporating Pierre Bourdieu's concept of *habitus*, proposes that practice be considered an irreducible term for human activity.[44] She has also argued that performance theory, in spite of the many

new paradigms for emphasizing "qualities of action," continues to dichot-
omize thought and action, and often continues to operate in a theoretical
framework "in which activity is seen as dramatizing or enacting prior
conceptual entities in order to reaffirm or reexperience them."[45] After all,
giving priority to action over meaning reflects the belief that they are
dichotomized concepts. Her theory to elucidate the process of practice
argues that practice, or activity, has four features. It is (1) situational, (2)
strategic, (3) embedded in a misrecognition of what it is doing, and (4)
reproduces a vision of the order of the world. For Bell, ritual as an activity
also shares these four features. All of these features are intertwined with
practice's ability to construct a vision of an ordered world, or as Bell calls
it, "redemptive hegemony."[46]

Thus, Bell proposes deconstructing the strategies of ritual acts in
their particularity rather than generating abstract models of ritual. Bell
notes that some features that have been considered intrinsic to ritual,
namely formality, fixity, and repetition, may not be so much essential ritual qualities as frequent strategies for constructing ritual acts. Thus, the
term "strategies" points toward a more contingent and contextual framework for studying rituals, rather than a theory of ritual essentialism. The
performance perspectives elaborated in this volume may be useful in
particular situations rather than universally applicable. Our conviction
that we need to examine many kinds of devotional performances in particular cultures and time periods has inspired the production of this collection.

One question that arises is whether power and domination are the
most important constituents of human life. For example, Bell admits that
the very concept of "redemptive hegemony suggests that human practice
is characterized by relations of dominance and subjugation" (84). Indeed,
the omnipresence of power relations is a basic assumption of most modern
and postmodern theories. However, although the concept of power relations and dominance strategies is most useful for understanding how particular groups construct and resist activities, it may be that it is a model
particularly produced by western twentieth-century sensibility rather than
an essential part of medieval life. It is striking that all the medieval authors
in this collection were in some degree affirmed by those ostensibly in
power, in the sense that those "powers" transcribed, read, and preserved
their writings. An examination of the "interanimation" of medieval textual
and devotional communities may help scholars construct alternative strategic models devised by medieval people.

Feminist Studies and Performance

Feminist scholars in the area of performance and ritual studies have criticized the construction of many performative models for their masculinist bias. Most of the scholars we have surveyed tend to regard rituals as social constructions but have not questioned the possibility that such social constructions are gendered. Two examples, one from religious studies and one from theater studies, will demonstrate the potential of feminist studies for deconstructing perceived universalist paradigms. In fact, feminist critiques of performance argue that many "universalist" theories of performance are based upon masculine norms.

Caroline Walker Bynum has argued that van Gennep's and Turner's more formal concept of liminality is not relevant to women within medieval cultures. She suggests that liminality is a quality needed by those firmly situated within the social structure, and notes that within medieval cultures, women were always liminal to men.[47] According to Bynum:

> All Turner's ideas involve in some way the insight that, in explaining human experience, one is explaining process or drama rather than structure, and that liminality or suspension of social and normative structures is a crucial moment in the process . . . Turner's ideas describe the stories and symbols of men better than those of women. Women's stories . . . are in fact less processual than men; they don't have turning points.[48]

Thus, another fruitful dialogue that may follow from this volume is a fresh examination of the extent to which liminality and its cousin, the "liminoid," is a useful category for ecstatic performances, and the extent to which it is or is not gendered.

Sue-Ellen Case has also described the feminist critique of the theatrical model, inherited from Aristotle, of "the form of tragedy as a replication of the male sexual experience . . . foreplay, excitation and ejaculation (catharsis)."[49] Perhaps a more feminine model of theater might be composed of "multiple orgasms, with no dramatic focus . . . or necessity to build to a single climax." Rather than inscribing a gendered essentialism, Case is simply trying to deconstruct the ways in which traditional theater practices have been traditionally a male performative enterprise rather than a universalist one.

Feminist critiques have pointed out the necessity to examine whether or not any theoretical model of experience is based upon notions of male societal norms. Any examination of performance, whether theatrical, ritual, or social, needs to consider the gender and status of the performer(s) and audience.

The essays in this volume address the question of gender in different ways. Although it has long been claimed that women's spirituality is more "embodied" and more "affective" than that of men, it is striking that all of the religious women surveyed in this volume were admired and emulated by men, either as confessors, onlookers, transcribers, interpreters, or authenticators of their visions. Moreover, the presence of two male writers, Richard Rolle and Thomas of Cantimpré, both of whom were sympathetic to and surrounded by holy women, confounds the picture still further. An avenue for further research is the degree to which male appreciation, appropriation, and authentication of religious women makes gender comparisons difficult if not impossible to ascertain. It may mean that the "dialogic voice" described by Laurie Finke ultimately confounds binary categorizations of gender altogether.

From Ritual Studies to Devotional Texts and Practices

This volume expands the field of performance studies and ritual. The authors all share the belief that Christian ritual is more encompassing than the seven sacraments and their liturgies. Within this liturgical framework are a wide variety of Christian devotional texts and practices that are not intended to be performed by an elite priesthood. However, because devotional practices change throughout time and have not always been as meticulously recorded as more formal rituals, it is often quite difficult to summon up the ghosts of past performances. In fact, such devotionally-oriented texts have generally been studied as genres of religious literature rather than performance. Our intention is that a cross-cultural examination of devotional textualities and practices will foster a new appreciation of their performative dimensions. Moreover, we hope that attention to the questions asked by performance perspectives—about text and performance, sponaneity and repetition, gender expression and construction, authority and power, men's and/or women's spirituality—will spark a lively dialogue across disciplines and cultures about the importance of performance-oriented perspectives for understanding the complexities of medieval spiritualities within their cultures.

Notes

1. There is a large body of literature on this subject, especially in the area of Shakespearean studies. For a good introduction to the concepts of texts as performances, see D. C. Greetham, ed., *In the Margins of the Text* (Ann Arbor: University of Michigan Press, 1996).

2. Talal Asad, *Genealogies of Religion* (Baltimore: Johns Hopkins University Press, 1993), 55–57. There are also private rituals, such as the Jewish morning benedictions. For the medieval period, the terms public/private are somewhat misleading. The element of formality, fixity, and repetition is the most important part of the definition. For an overview and critique of the concept of formalization within ritual, see Catherine Bell, *Ritual Theory, Ritual Practice* (New York: Oxford University Press, 1992).

3. Catherine Bell's *Ritual: Perspectives and Dimensions* (Oxford: Oxford University Press, 1997), 72–83, provides a very useful overview of the history of performance studies scholarship.

4. It may be obvious but important nonetheless to point out that a short overview of complex ideas is necessarily somewhat of a disservice to the gifted writers surveyed here. The intention is to sketch some of the most important and influential ideas for performance studies in this volume, and let the bibliography at the end of this chapter direct the reader to the works themselves.

5. Émile Durkheim, *The Elementary Forms of the Religious Life*, trans. J. W. Swain (New York: Free Press, 1965).

6. Victor Turner, *The Ritual Process: Structure and Anti-Structure* (Ithaca, NY: Cornell University Press, 1977), 10.

7. Victor Turner, *The Forest of Symbols: Aspects of Ndembu Ritual* (Ithaca, NY: Cornell University Press, 1967), 95.

8. Turner, *Forest of Symbols*, 95–97.

9. Victor Turner, *From Ritual to Theater* (New York: Performing Arts Journal Publications, 1982), 24–37. For Turner, the difference between agricultural and industrial cultures lay in the close connection between work and play in the former and their separation in the latter.

10. Bell, *Ritual: Perspectives and Dimensions*, 42.

11. Ronald Grimes, *Beginnings in Ritual Studies*, rev. ed. (Columbia: University of South Carolina Press: 1995), 151.

12. Osbourne B. Hardison, *Christian Rite and Christian Drama in the Middle Ages* (Baltimore: Johns Hopkins Press, 1965).

13. It was Turner who suggested that Grimes study the Santa Fe fiesta. Grimes discusses some of his exchanges with Turner in *Beginnings in Ritual Studies*, 10–12. Schechner and Turner participated in the 1977 Burg Wartenstein Symposium, and Turner participated in workshops at Schechner's Department of Peformance Studies at NYU,

as Schechner explains in *By Means of Performance*, ed. Richard Schechner and Willa Appel (Cambridge: Cambridge University Press, 1990), xv.

14. Richard Schechner, *Essays in Performance Theory* (New York: Routledge: 1988), 30.

15. Schechner, *Essays*, xii-xv.

16. For a similar perspective on the public nature of liturgy, see Cheslyn Jones, Geoffrey Wainwright, and Edwin Yarnold, S.J., *The Study of Liturgy* (New York: Oxford University Press, 1978), 13: "Liturgy is celebrated *with* others and the relationships between the members of the worshipping community are of the highest importance. *Private* acts of *public* worship are a contradiction in terms."

17. One should note that if "efficacious" is meant to imply "personal transformation," then Purim celebrations do not qualify. If "efficacious" is broadened to mean "good for the community," then Purim, as a celebration of Jewish survival, is indeed efficacious in that sense.

18. Schechner, *Essays in Performance Theory*, 171. Turner also characterized actors as liminal people (*From Ritual to Theater*, 40).

19. Manfred Pfister, *The Theory and Analysis of Drama* (Cambridge: Cambridge University Press, 1988), 11.

20. Talal Asad has pointed out that one of the earliest definitions of ritual was simply "a book directing the order and manner to be observed in celebrating religious ceremonies." The entire concept of something called "ritual" has been a product of the new disciplines of anthropology and religious studies that emerged in the late nineteenth and early twentieth century. Asad demonstrates that the concept of ritual is a western phenomenon that is problematic for other cultures. For a good overview of the development of ritual studies, see Asad, *Genealogies of Religion*, 55–79, and Bell, *Ritual: Dimensions and Perspectives*.

21. Grimes, *Beginnings in Ritual Studies*, 164–188. For more on Growtowski's "ritual theater" see Mary Giles's and Susan Rodgers's and Joanna Ziegler's essays in this volume.

22. Grimes, *Beginnings in Ritual Studies*, 164. As discussed above, ritual is often characterized by qualities of formality, fixity, and repetition (Bell, *Ritual Theory, Ritual Practice*, 88–93). By choosing "transformation," Grimes argues for the creative power of ritualization.

23. It is important to emphasize that many theater performers would not agree with Grimes. Grimes is concentrating upon a particular type of theater that he feels has closest affinities with ritual processes.

24. In this regard Herbert Blau's wry observation of theater applies in reverse to religious ritual: "If theater were real, we wouldn't bother with it. When it's not real, we complain." To paraphrase, "If ritual were 'not real' we wouldn't bother with it. When it is real we complain." "Letting Be the Finale of Seem," in Michel Benamou and Charles Caramello,

eds., *Performances in Postmodern Culture* (Madison, WI: Coda Press, 1977), 61.

25. Quoted in Benamou and Caramello, eds., *Performances in Postmodern Culture*, 5.

26. J. L. Austin, *How to Do Things with Words* (Cambridge: Harvard University Press, 1955), 5.

27. Mikhail Bakhtin, "Discourse and the Novel," in *The Dialogic Imagination*, trans. Michael Holquist and Caryl Emerson (Austin: University of Texas Press, 1984), 354.

28. For the term "heteroglossia" see Laurie Finke, *Feminist Theory, Women's Writing* (Ithaca, NY: Cornell University Press, 1992), 13.

29. Gregory Bateson, *Steps to an Ecology of Mind* (New York: Ballantine Press, 1978), 179–189.

30. See the work of Erving Goffman, *Frame Analysis: An Essay on the Organization of Experience* (New York: Harper and Row, 1974), and Maurice Bloch, *Ritual, History, and Power: Selected Papers in Anthropology* (London: Athlone Press, 1989).

31. Maurice Bloch, *Ritual, History, and Power*, 29.

32. Of course, Durkheim would not disagree. He also believed that ritual was not rational for the participants, but he did attempt to explain the social meaning embedded within ritual that scholars could recognize. Bloch is less interested in such scholarly explanations.

33. In this regard see Bell, *Ritual Theory, Ritual Practice*, 30–46.

34. Mircea Eliade, *The Myth of Eternal Return; or, Cosmos in History*, trans. Willard Trask (Princeton, NJ: Princeton University Press, 1954).

35. Mircea Eliade, *Patterns in Comparative Religion*, trans. Rosemary Sheed (New York: New American Library, 1963), 9.

36. See the discussion of Eliade in Jonathan Z. Smith, *To Take Place: Toward Theory in Ritual* (Chicago: University of Chicago Press, 1987), 13–15 and n. 42, 131.

37. Catherine Bell, *Ritual: Perspectives and Dimensions*, 37. See Arnold van Gennep, *Rites of Passage*, trans. M. B. Vizedom and G. L. Caffee (Chicago: University of Chicago Press, 1960).

38. Smith, *To Take Place*, 28.

39. For example, Benamou and Caramello, eds., *Performance in Postmodern Culture*, published in 1977, contained essays by Turner, literary critics, and theater theorists.

40. Judith Butler, "Imitation and Gender Insubordination," in Linda Nicholson, ed., *The Second Wave: A Reader in Feminist Theory* (New York: Routledge, 1997), 304.

41. Butler, 305. Even before the advent of poststructuralism, structuralists like Claude Lévi-Strauss argued that human beings construct symbolic systems in order to organize social relations. As a structuralist, Lévi-Strauss believed that such systems, like language, were constructed by means of binary oppositions. Poststructuralist thinkers, however, have

de-centered meaning more radically, demonstrating that meaning is never defined by such oppositions, but continually deferred. See Claude Lévi-Strauss, *The Elementary Structures of Kinship*, trans. James Harle Bell, John Richard von Sturmer, and Rodney Needham (Boston: Beacon Press, 1969); *Totemism*, trans. Rodney Needham (Boston: Beacon Press, 1963); and Jacques Derrida's critique of Lévi-Strauss in *Of Grammatology*, trans. Gayatri Chakravorty Spivak (Baltimore: John Hopkins University Press, 1976), 101–140.

42. Sarah Beckwith, "Ritual, Theater, and Social Space In the York Corpus Christi Cycle," in Barbara Hanawalt and David Wallace, eds., *Bodies and Disciplines: Intersections of Literature and History in Fifteenth-Century England* (Minneapolis: University of Minnesota Press, 1996), 67–68.

43. Bell, *Ritual Theory, Ritual Practice*, 74–78.

44. Pierre Bourdieu, *Outline of a Theory of Practice*, trans. Richard Nice (Cambridge: Cambridge University Press, 1977).

45. Bell, *Ritual Theory, Ritual Practice*, 38. Bell also has critiqued the analogy between ritual activities and other performative acts. First, because performance theorists regard ritual as a series of symbolic actions meant to have an impact upon an audience, the scholar/observer is invited to incorporate his/her own meaning with that of the ritual. Second, performance becomes the criteria for what is or is not a ritual. Yet she believes that performance theorists have not effectively differentiated types of performing. As Clifford Geerz demonstrated, the analogies between "game," "text," and "drama" tend to illuminate some features and confuse others. Is everything analogous to everything else? If one does not differentiate, how can any statement be meaningful?

46. Bell, *Ritual Theory, Ritual Practice*, 81–83.

47. "Liminality itself . . . may be less a universal moment of meaning needed by human beings as they move through social dramas than an escape for those who bear the burdens and reap the benefits of a high place in the social structure." Caroline Walker Bynum, *Fragmentation and Redemption: Essays on Gender and the Human Body in Medieval Religion* (New York: Zone Books, 1991), 34.

48. Bynum, *Fragmentation and Redemption*, 31–34.

49. Sue-Ellen Case, *Feminism and Theater* (New York: Methuen Press, 1988), 129.

Bibliography

Asad, Talal. *Genealogies of Religion*. Baltimore: Johns Hopkins University Press, 1993.

Austin, J. L. *How to Do Things with Words*. Cambridge: Harvard University Press, 1955.

Bakhtin, Mikhail. "Discourse and the Novel," in *The Dialogic Imagination*, trans. Michael Holquist and Caryl Emerson. Austin: University of Texas Press, 1984.

Bateson, Gregory. *Steps to an Ecology of Mind.* New York: Ballantine Press, 1978.

Beckwith, Sarah. "Ritual, Theater, and Social Space in the York Corpus Christi Cycle." In *Bodies and Disciplines: Intersections of Literature and History in Fifteenth-Century England,* ed. Barbara Hanawalt and David Wallace. Minneapolis, MN: University of Minnesota Press, 1996.

Bell, Catherine. *Ritual: Perspectives and Dimensions.* Oxford: Oxford University Press, 1997.

———. *Ritual Theory, Ritual Practice.* New York: Oxford University Press, 1992.

Benamou, Michel, and Charles Caramello, eds. *Performances in Postmodern Culture.* Madison, WI: Coda Press, 1977.

Bloch, Maurice. *Ritual, History, and Power: Selected Papers in Anthropology.* London: Athlone Press, 1989.

Bourdieu, Pierre. *Outline of a Theory of Practice.* Trans. Richard Nice. Cambridge: Cambridge University Press, 1977.

Butler, Judith. "Imitation and Gender Insubordination." In *The Second Wave: A Reader in Feminist Theory,* ed. Linda Nicholson. New York: Routledge, 1997.

Bynum, Caroline Walker. *Fragmentation and Redemption: Essays on Gender and the Human Body in Medieval Religion.* New York: Zone Books, 1991.

Derrida, Jacques. *Of Grammatology.* Trans. Gayatri Chakravorty Spivak. Baltimore: Johns Hopkins University Press, 1976.

Durkheim, Émile. *The Elementary Forms of the Religious Life.* Trans. J. W. Swain. New York: Free Press, 1965.

Eliade, Mircea. *The Myth of Eternal Return; or, Cosmos in History.* Trans. Willard Trask. Princeton, NJ: Princeton University Press, 1954.

———.*Patterns in Comparative Religion.* Trans. Rosemary Sheed. New York: New American Library, 1963.

Finke, Laurie. *Feminist Theory, Women's Writing.* Ithaca, NY: Cornell University Press, 1992.

Goffman, Erving. *Frame Analysis: An Essay on the Organization of Experience.* New York: Harper and Row, 1974.

Greetham, D. C., ed. *In the Margins of the Text.* Ann Arbor: University of Michigan Press, 1997.

Grimes, Ronald. *Beginnings in Ritual Studies.* Columbia: University of South Carolina Press: 1995.

Hardison, Osbourne B. *Christian Rite and Christian Drama in the Middle Ages.* Baltimore: Johns Hopkins Press, 1965.

Jones, Cheslyn, Geoffrey Wainwright, and Edwin Yarnold, S.J. *The Study of Liturgy.* New York: Oxford University Press, 1978.

Lévi-Strauss, Claude. *The Elementary Structures of Kinship.* Trans. James Harle Bell, John Richard von Sturmer, and Rodney Needham. Boston: Beacon Press, 1969.

———. *Totemism.* Trans. Rodney Needham. Boston: Beacon Press, 1963.

Pfister, Manfred. *The Theory and Analysis of Drama.* Cambridge: Cambridge University Press, 1988.

Schechner, Richard, and Willa Appel, eds. *By Means of Performance.* Cambridge: Cambridge University Press, 1990.

Schechner, Richard. *Essays in Performance Theory.* New York: Routledge: 1988.

Smith, Jonathan Z. *To Take Place: Toward Theory in Ritual.* Chicago: University of Chicago Press, 1987.

Turner, Victor. *The Forest of Symbols: Aspects of Ndembu Ritual.* Ithaca, NY: Cornell University Press, 1967.

———. *From Ritual to Theater.* New York: Performing Arts Journal Publications, 1982.

———. *The Ritual Process: Structure and Anti-Structure.* Ithaca, NY: Cornell University Press, 1977.

van Gennep, Arnold. *Rites of Passage,* trans. M. B. Vizedom and G. L. Caffee. Chicago: University of Chicago Press, 1960.

CHAPTER TWO

How to Do Things with Mystical Language: Marguerite d'Oingt's Performative Writing

Catherine Müller

Oh beautiful sweet Lord Jesus Christ, who gave me the audacity to speak of such marvelous things. (*Med* 8)[1]

The linguistic and philosophical concept of performative speech as employed by J. L. Austin in his well-known 1955 Harvard lectures entitled *How to Do Things with Words*[2] and by John R. Searle in his analysis of speech acts[3] becomes a useful tool for tracing action-producing utterances and analyzing aspects of empowerment in language. Based on these studies I have opted to define the term "performative" as "acting out its own meaning" or "producing an action by/while pronouncing or writing something." In the context of Western religious thought, this notion is particularly relevant, for it underscores the very foundation of Jewish and Christian beliefs. As we all know, biblical texts and their exegesis understand creation as the sole act of God's speech, thus considering the performative aspect of words an ontological truth. Furthermore, Christ the Logos is seen as an incarnation of divine words and a bodily re-enactor of prophetic words inscribed in the Old Testament: he is therefore both the Text and its most perfect Performance. Consequently, the Bible as God's Word becomes a literal transmission of divine performative power because it enables its readers or listeners to be affected by the inspired texts, to act according to their teachings, and to receive the necessary words to gloss them.

The medieval mystic Marguerite d'Oingt (d.1310) follows the church fathers in the same tradition when she draws on the biblical model of the "dixit et facta sunt" [God said and it was done] to show the transforming power of scriptural meditation. As a female mystic, however, she does more: incorporating in her work God's performative words "Ego dixi, dii estis"[4] [I said, you are gods], she justifies her own empowerment to write. The purpose of this chapter is to discuss Marguerite's use of performatives as a philosophical and poetic strategy.

A few examples taken from her Meditations (*Pagina Meditationum*) and personal *Letters* will be useful to understand Marguerite's belief in the performative power of spiritual language. Subsequently, two narrated visions will be taken into consideration, that of the inverted tree (*Med* 143–146) and that of the closed book (*Sp* 1–12)—both of which contain inscribed words and letters and appear as a mirror for writing, a reflection on signs, and a powerful call to action. I will argue that in Marguerite's theological system specular and speculative are intertwined and suggest that her implicit theory on language could lead to a new definition of subjectivity.

The *Pagina Meditationum* is a prime example of the immediate effects biblical words have on the mystic's thoughts and actions. In the opening paragraph, the first two Psalm verses Marguerite hears sung invite her at once to introspection. After she realizes that her sad thoughts can offer no solace, she remembers God's words of love and reports them in direct speech. Unlike the Psalmist, the divine "Ego" is successful in bringing forth immediate relief followed by confession and action (*Med* 2, 3):

> In the year of our Lord 1286, on the Sunday of Septuagesima, I [ego][5] Margaret, the maidservant of Christ, was in church at mass when, as an introduction to the mass, the following verse *was being sung*: "The sighs of death will surround me." And *I began to think* about the misery to which we are consigned because of the sins of the first parents. And while thinking about this *I began [to feel]* such fear and such pain

that my heart seemed to fail me completely, and because of this I did not know whether I was worthy of salvation or not. *When I heard* afterwards the introductory verse that David sung so sweetly to the Lord, "I love you, Lord etc.," *my heart was completely relieved* because I recalled *the sweet promise the Lord makes* [facit] *His friends when He says* [dicit]: "I [Ego] love those who love me," and because *I knew* that He is so good and so mild that He would never permit those who love Him to perish.

2. *And after I considered* the great sweetness and compassion which is in Him, filled with great pain, *I threw myself down* full length in front of His precious body and *petitioned* and *prayed* to Him humbly that He *give* me what He knows I need.

3. Then He, full of sweetness and gentleness, by His grace *visited me without delay* and *gave me* His sweet consolation and such a will to do good that it seemed to me that *I was all changed and renewed*. After that *I got up* and *kneeled* in front of the Lord and *confessed* to Him everything I could remember in which I may have offended Him and *promised* Him to amend myself now and hereafter. (*Med* 1–3)[6]

Later, her *Meditations* stress the absolute power of Christ's speech: "With a single word you can destroy and make perish the whole world and with another single word you can remake it better and more beautiful" (*Med* 13).[7] Jesus is also portrayed by Marguerite as a physical source of empowerment for the world: just touching and smelling him brings healing and life (*Med* 20–21): "You are the greatest health and the true physician whose touch healed the sick and whose fragrance resuscitated the dead"(*Med* 20).[8]

In other passages the power of language is illustrated by its potential danger. In a rather polemic text, the prioress shows how a corrupt religious community has become affected by evil words and is no longer able to react lovingly to insults. God's performative words have ceased to empower them, and instead of being transformed by divine speech they are being put to the test by it:

Oh, best Jesus Christ, what are your creatures *doing?* For I see hardly anyone who *knows* how to *love* or *understand* you; the religious *behave and speak so irregularly* that they are almost like secular people; and many are more eager to go to eat than to go to the matins or mass. They are very capable of drinking good wines and eating good food since they have it, but *they are incapable of remembering the smallest word told to them; on the contrary, by signs and words they return bad for bad*. (Med 64)[9]

The play on words and sounds in "bene potentes ad potandum bona vina" [very capable of drinking good wines] accentuates the connection between spiritual strength and verbal empowerment by stating the weakness of a religious community that has lost its sensitivity to the Word, misuses the gift of speech, and is reduced, as drunkards may be, to "babbling." Furthermore, as the beginning of the quoted passage suggests, speaking well is directly tied to loving and understanding God. Because for Marguerite—and for Carthusians in general—words heard always call for other words; silent contemplation is particularly important as it allows one to be transformed within before going on to speak and affect others.

In a letter to a "dear brother" seeking advice regarding penance, Marguerite makes clear that for her the best way to purify the inner being is to act out ("fayre") her meditation according to God's teaching ("signs"): "je me mis a *fayre* comme il mesmes m'*ensigna*" (Let 128).[10] She spiritually approaches first the Christ-child and then Jesus on the cross and performs the following deeds:

I spiritually *took* the glorious child into my arms. Thus I *carried* and *kissed* Him tenderly in the arms of my heart. . . . I *went* towards Him, with great respect, and removed the nails; then I *took* Him upon my shoulders and *took* Him down from the cross and *put* Him in the arms of my heart; and it seemed to me that I *carried* Him as easily as if He had been one year old. . . . in my spirit I *put* Him down on my bed and I *kissed* His tender hands and these blessed feet which were so cruelly pierced for our sins. And then I *bent down* towards that glorious flank which was so cruelly wounded for me. (Let 129–131)[11]

Just as successful teaching leads to action, so are meditating and doing posited by the prioress as virtually equivalent. In that context, writing becomes the means by which the heart can at once ("aussi tot") be relieved from otherwise overwhelming divine revelations. In Let 136–138, the author explains to a "dear father"[12] how she writes and wants her work to be considered. Her visions are said to have an immediate performative power, first transferred to her body, then to her writings. In fact, the words written in her heart are so strongly impressed that they keep her from thinking about anything else or performing the normal functions of life, even giving her an outward appearance of death: "[S]he had all these things written in her heart in such a way that she could think of nothing else, and her heart was so full that she could not eat, drink or sleep until she was so weak that the doctors thought she was on the point of death" (*Let* 137).[13] Only writing can bring life back to her being:

> She thought that if she put these things into writing in the same way that our Lord had put them into her heart, her heart would be unburdened. She began to write everything that is in this book, in the order that it was in her heart; and as soon as she had put the words into the book, everything left her heart. And when she had written everything down, she was all cured. I firmly believe that if she had not put all this down in writing, she would have died or gone mad, because for seven days she had neither slept nor eaten and she had never before done anything to get her into such a state. And this is why I believe that all this was written down through the will of our Lord. (*Let* 138).[14]

A comparison with the above quoted passage on the healing power of Christ's body (*Med* 20) attests once more to the parallel the writer draws between the divine Logos and human words. Whether heard sung, contemplated through a vision, caught in a conversation, seen written in her heart, or expressed in her own writing, words have a transformative effect in the mystic's work.

To stress the performative quality of writing, Marguerite uses two separate visions in which words and letters produce meaning by/while acting out their own significance. Drawing attention to what may seem insignificant details, the narrator develops what I believe to be a profound reflection on language itself. In fact I would state with Michel de Certeau that one recurrent characteristic of mystical writing in general may well be an acute sensitivity to the apparently banal:

> The mystic discourse transforms the detail into myth; it catches hold of it, blows it out of proportion, multiplies it, divinizes it. It makes it into its own kind of historicity . . . the minute detail suspends meaning in the continuum of interpretation. A play of light arrests the reader's attention: ecstatic instant, a spark of insignificance, this fragment of the unknown introduces a silence into the hermeneutic medley. Thus, little by little, common everyday life begins to seethe with a disturbing familiarity—a frequentation of the Other.[15]

This is particularly well illustrated in Marguerite's vision of the tree (*Let* 143–146):

> 143. Not long ago some good people were together in a house and spoke of God. There was a worthy man who said that once he had asked a lady what the word *"vehemens"* meant and that the lady had answered that it meant *"strong."* There was a person present [Marguerite herself] who was *deeply touched by this word,* and it seemed to her that all this was *of great importance,* but she never dared to ask him to *explain the word "vehemens" to her.*
>
> 144. Nonetheless she subsequently asked a lot of people what that word meant, but she could find no one who could answer her to her satisfaction. *This word was so deeply driven into her heart* that she could not get rid of it, not while she was praying nor under any other circumstances, until she finally addressed a fervent prayer to the Lord that He in His great goodness may *teach* her *what this word meant* and *remove it from her heart.* (*Let* 143–144)[16]

God responds to this longing by means of a vision that has the twofold objective to comfort her and draw her spirit closer to him, that is, fill her heart with a teaching that is both affective and intellectual, since the word "ensegnyer," already encountered before, means to give signs, to show physically and to teach. It is noteworthy that Marguerite rarely uses the words "body" and "soul"—so often opposed in scholastic theology—and privileges the word "heart" ("cuer," "cuor"), which is repeated three times in *Let* 144. In conformity with its common meaning in the Middle Ages, the heart takes on for her the activity of thinking and feeling and designates an instrument of meditation, knowledge, and writing. As she will explain later in her *Speculum,* looking into her heart is synonymous with seeing herself and God in a perfectly transparent mirror.[17] First, the meditative activity prepares the heart to receive the vision:

> 145. Before she had finished her prayers, the one who is filled with sweetness and pity wanted to comfort her and to draw her spirit towards him; and He did this in such a way that it seemed to her that she was in a large deserted open space where there was only one high mountain, and at the foot of this mountain there stood a *marvelous tree.* This tree had *five branches* which were *all dry* and were *bending*

downwards. On the leaves of the first branch there was written "visu" (sight); on the second was written "auditu" (hearing); on the third was written "gustu" (taste); on the fourth was written "odoratu" (smell); on the fifth was written "tactu" (touch). On the top of the tree there lay a large circle, similar to the bottom of a barrel, which covered the tree completely so that neither the sun nor the dew could get to it.

146. And after she had looked attentively at the tree, she raised her eyes towards the mountain, and she saw a great stream descending with a force like that of the sea. This stream rushed so violently onto the bottom of this tree that all its roots were turned upside down and the top was struck in the earth; and the branches which had been bent downwards were now stretching towards heaven. And the leaves which had been dry were all green, and the roots which had been in the earth were all spread out and pointing towards the sky; and they were all green and full of leaves as branches usually are. (Let 145–146)[18]

If one assumes that the tree represents a human being, and more precisely the narrator-visionary herself, one might be struck not only by the reversal of the tree, but by the absence of hierarchy. As R. Howard Bloch usefully reminds us in his discussion on medieval misogyny, the tree is often used to render the hierarchical structure between spirit and senses, head and body, meaning and signs.[19] For Marguerite, this dichotomy between sensual and spiritual seems irrelevant. The senses emanating from her heart are the very thrust of her inner being, the only way to attain perfect knowledge of the divine, and, as I propose to show, the source of writing, inner transformation, and action. Senses are the vehicle through which God chooses to transmit his power.

In Marguerite's vision, the weight is placed on the five senses as each one of them is written in Latin to establish a correspondence with the mysterious word "vehemens." The auditory sensitivity the narrative's persona demonstrated for the word "vehemens" is echoed in the importance given to the written word. Since in Marguerite's Franco-Provençal the use of Latin is otherwise reserved for biblical citations, the Latin inscription of the senses is clothed with sacred, inspirational, and scriptural value. Moreover, the inscribing of the words "visu," "auditu," "gustu," "odoratu," and "tactu" has been privileged over any metaphorical phrase or descriptive explanation such as "the tree had five branches which represented the five human senses," thus insisting on the words as graphic signs and alluding to the author's vision in her *Speculum*, namely that of the letters appearing on the book Christ holds in his hand (see below). Senses and writing are indeed connected, even on the literal level.

The reversal of the tree illustrates the elevation of the self from a state of inner drought and absence of divine grace (symbolized by the sun and the dew) to a state of plenitude and fertility.[20] The water falling down from above and uprooting the tree—the violence of which is an illustration of the word "vehemens" itself—represents both the creative force of divine love and the visionary's vehement desire to be showered by it. This image underlines the importance of the textual body (the body as text and the text as body) as a place of encounter between her Self and God, between her Self and writing. Again, human beings are not characterized as body and soul but as entities composed of five sacred senses, both physical and spiritual, allowing for metamorphosis and fertility. In order to bear fruit, humans have to gaze upon their own dryness and elevate their eyes toward that which surpasses and surprises them. When the high and the low exchange place and logic is turned upside down (as is the envisioned tree), then something truly new, truly "meravillous" can happen. In her desire for wholeness and understanding, Marguerite's persona is made into a new creation capable of perpetuating in her and through her this creative power, equated here with a blossoming of the foliage, a rebirth of all the senses.

The *Speculum* carries a similar image of the heart as a scene of divine drowning and renewal, a place of desire and reflection where God grants perfect knowledge of him through a stimulation of all the senses: the visionary *sees* his delicious and glorious light (*Sp* 16), *smells* his great fragrance (*Sp* 17), *touches* him in a loving embrace (*Sp* 17), *feels* an immense joy (*Sp* 17), and *hears* a beautiful melody (*Sp* 18). In fact, the senses are necessary means to approach and portray the divine because, as her *Pagina Meditationum* puts it, Jesus is an embodiment of all senses: "You are the sweet electuary in which are all good flavors and of whose goodness live the holy souls in paradise. . . . You are the glorious rose in which are all good odors and colors" (*Med* 23, 25, etc.)[21]

In the examined passages, a connection has been established on the one hand between the senses and writing (the written words on the leaves), and on the other between the senses and performance (the uprooting and vitality of the tree). Senses can thus be considered in Marguerite's text as a sacred path to the divine and a powerful means for change.

Just as one word, "vehemens," was the starting point of thought and meditation in the heart, so too it is through linguistic signs that in Marguerite's *Mirror* the self is brought to a vision and knowledge of the divine. Within the text written by the narrator and entitled *Speculum* are enclosed several books in a structure of *mise en abîme*. The second level represents the heart of the visionary, which is seen as a book containing another book held by Christ with the purpose of showing and teaching (here again the term used is "ensennier"). On this book are engraved many letters, but unlike those written on the leaves of the tree, they do not form words but are given as mirrors of a discourse (*Sp* 2–5, 7–12):

2. By the grace of our Lord, this creature had written into her heart the holy life that Jesus Christ had led on earth, His good examples and His good teachings. She had put sweet Jesus Christ so firmly into her heart that it sometimes seemed to her that He was present and that He held a closed book in His hand in order to teach from it.

3. The outside of the book was completely covered with white, black and red letters; the clasps of the book had golden letters on them.

4. In the white letters was written the saintly life of the blessed Son of God who was all white through His great innocence and His holy works. In the black letters were written the blows and the slaps and the filthy things that the Jews had thrown at His saintly face and His noble body until He looked like a leper. In the red letters were written the wounds and the precious blood that was shed for us.

5. There were also two clasps that closed the book; they had gold letters on them. On one of them was written: "Deus erit omnia in omnibus" (God will be everything [in] everyone). On the other one was written: 'Mirabilis Deus in sanctis suis' (God is marvelous in His saints).

7. After she had looked into this book carefully, she began to read in the book of her conscience which she found full of falsity and lies. When she considered the humility of Jesus Christ, she found herself full of pride. When she thought of how He wanted to be scorned and persecuted, she found herself just the opposite. When she considered His poverty, she did not find it in her that she wanted to be so poor that she would be scorned. When she considered His patience, she found none in herself. When she thought of the way in which He was patient until death, she did not find herself as obedient as she should have been.

8. These were the white letters in which the life of the blessed Son of God had been written. Then, when she had well considered all her faults she made an effort to correct them, as much as she could, following the example of the life of Jesus Christ.

9. Then she studied the black letters, in which were written the evil things which had been done to Jesus Christ: in these letters she learned to bear tribulations with patience.

10. Then she studied the red letters, in which were written the wounds of Jesus Christ and the shedding of His precious blood. In these letters she not only learned to bear tribulations with patience, but also to enjoy them, so that all the pleasures of this world became detestable to her; and to such an extent that it seemed to her that there was nothing in this world as worthy and as sweet as suffering the pains and the torments of this worlds for the love of her creator.

11. Then she studied the gold letters. There she learned to desire the things of heaven.

12. In this book she found written the life that Jesus Christ led on earth, from His birth until the time when he went up to heaven.[22]

In *Sp* 4 and later in 7–11, the particle "en" repeated ten times as well as the repetition of the verb "regarder" and the reflexive "se" (in "se estudiavet," "se trovavet") insist on the fact that knowledge of Christ is achieved through contemplation in a mirror. Besides, the term "essemplayre" (*Sp* 8) designates a model, a mimetic image, an original manuscript to recopy, thus connecting with the idea of mirror that of a translation or multiple writing. The clasps on Christ's book are also engraved with letters, which in turn contain in them biblical verses dealing themselves with the theme of inclusion and enclosure: "Deus erit omnia *in* omnibus" and "Mirabilis Deus *in* sanctis suis." The book held by Jesus contains on the outside the book of his life and part of the Holy Scriptures. When the book is opened, it becomes an infinitely wide mirror within which Christ is also said to be a mirror[23] reflecting all pure human beings who are themselves transparent mirrors of the Trinity (*Sp* 24, 29, 35). Moreover, Marguerite states that in the marvelous world mirrored in the opened book springs forth an unceasing and always new song, thus emblematically creating within this textual *mise en abîme* a place of joy and poetic renewal: "This sweet song makes its way through all the orders of the angels and the saints, from the first to the last. And this song is hardly finished when they start another one, also all new. And this song will last forever" (*Sp* 18).[24]

Let us now consider the two visions again. This creative power is well illustrated in the episode of the inverted tree. At the onset of her account, Marguerite affirms that the word "vehemens" falls in her heart in a very strong way ("chait forment") and cannot leave from there until it is completely understood and produces desired effects (*Let* 143). This word, she says, may be explained and erased from her heart only by God himself; even prayers are not strong enough to divert the persona's attention from its linguistic power. At the reading of *Let* 143 (see above), one stumbles on a paradox about the so-called meaning of "vehemens." After the narrator has heard the translation of the word ("the lady had answered that it meant 'strong'"), why does she repeatedly ask for its significance to be unveiled? Why is it so vital for her to know more? I would suggest that what she attempts to grasp is the divine essence of language and its transforming power, or in literary terms its figurative and performative meaning. Obviously, through the vision of the tree, God grants her the perfect knowledge she sought, since after retelling the event, the author has no need to interpret it. I believe the image calls for no further decoding because its gloss is already self-contained; the word "vehemens" leaves on the visionary the effect produced by its own significance. The structural and semantic parallel between the two phrases "cete parole chait forment el cuer" and "cele yeve chisi si tres duremant au pie de cel arbre"—using the same verb, "chair" (to fall), and two adverbial synonyms, "forment" and "duremant" (strongly)—stresses the performative quality of the enigmatic word. Language, here, enacts its own meaning by *strongly* impressing itself on the heart of the visionary and by creating an emblem (the water, symbol of divine inspiration and love) that *empowers* her being (the tree) and makes her words to flourish. The narrator is thus given to feel language as performative in her body and to transcend the dualistic opposition between signifier and signified thanks to a word ("vehemens") that does what it says and is what it designates. Just as the dried-out tree was made to experience the impetuous watering coming down from above provoking an unexpected springing, the visionary is invited both to unfold an unattainable mystery (the meaning of a simple word) and to be transformed by this meaning. Through the vision, God grants her to see beyond what she thought were her limited views (her inner drought) and to conceive of her senses as perfectly capable not only of grasping the significance of words, but also of explaining divine understanding and language by means of her own writing, thus making the specular speculative.

In her *Speculum,* the opposition between signifier and signified is also dismantled since the letters inscribed on the book do not need to form words to take on meaning but have significance in and of themselves, and as such have the power to transform those who gaze upon their shapes and colors, meditate on Christ's life reflected in them, and interpret his speech. As mirrors of divine words, the letters on the clasps are also a guaranty of God's dwelling *in* the believers. It is therefore through writing that divine language is understood and oneness between God and Self achieved.

The performative power of the Logos culminates in *Sp* 37 when she quotes in direct speech the biblical "Ego dixi, dii estis," which not only affirms but textually creates sameness between human beings and their creator through a perfect mirroring of all transparent bodies. Moreover, this overwhelming divine statement literally empowers the saints (and by extension the narrator) to speak and tell ("dire") rather than maintaining them in a state of passive astonishment ("fall into a swoon"):

> I truly believe that he who would devote his heart to the contempla-
> tion on the great beauty of Our Lord and of the glory that He man-
> ifested in His saints, he could rightly say that these are true marvels,
> and I believe he would fall into a swoon; he could *say* that God kept
> the promise He made to His saints through the prophet David: "Ego
> dixi, dii estis" ("I sa[id], you are gods"). For it seems to everyone of
> them that he is a little god, because they will be His sons and heirs.
> (*Sp* 37)[25]

In short, words give birth to a vision, which in turn allows for words to be performative and for bodies to become transparent and divine.

As writing starts in the body and the body itself can only write after hearing or reading words, so does bodily transparency stem from and imply a transparency of language. In order for the narrator to rise above and thus eliminate the dualistic opposition between soul and body, male and female,[26] subject and object, divine and human, she presents mystical language and writing as a creative place beyond the paradox of silence and speech, where the frontier between signifier and signified is being erased. Through the metaphor of a beautiful melody, an eternal song emanating from the mystic's body, she symbolizes what Luce Irigaray designates as "a sensible transcendental,"[27] that is, a new transcendent subjectivity in the senses that has received from God the performative power to write and act. The empowered subject is now capable of envisioning a language no longer limited by the fallacy of signs, but inspired by divine music as a substitute for the beauty of God's unspeakable silence. To the patristic concept of the feminine as sign, to the rhetorical association of signs with the fallen, Marguerite opposes a new vision of the Self and God. She imagines a world in which signs, rather than being enigmas forcing humans to see through a glass darkly—thus maintaining them in a feeling of unworthiness and powerlessness—are transparent words allowing for immediate understanding and contemplation of God face to face.

The performative aspect of divine speech has therefore brought the mystic to a radical change of her being and to an understanding of writing as a source of ongoing transformation and performance. From her Self, she was lead to God and then back to her Self. But to a Self radically Other. As I hope to have shown, this transformative circular journey was mainly possible because at first her powerless reading into the book of her heart was producing no concrete vision of the power of divine language— best symbolized by the lack of understanding for the Latin (that is, sacred) word "vehemens." Once the senses—innermost part of a human being and source of his/her potential spiritual rebirth—had experienced the deeper meaning and performative quality of words, the Self (in the image of the tree) was literally "turned upside down," then (in the second vision) made to become "a little god," and finally empowered to disseminate divine words through human writing. Similarly to the way the Father was made flesh in the Son, God's performative Word has become meaning in/through Marguerite's body and will be perpetuated as an endless performance in/ through her writings.

From trying to decipher the meaning of one word, "vehemens," Marguerite's persona has thus come to see not only her Self as a spotless mirror of God, but also language as a transparent mirror of divine speech, a place of perfect knowledge and transformative power, the very source of her own creation. Marguerite d'Oingt's mystic search may therefore be equated with a poetic endeavor symbolized by this circular movement leading her from a performative word ("vehemens") to her own empowerment to write so that she may in turn empower those who hear, read, and meditate upon her words with a transparent heart. When the circle is closed, that which was considered at first utterly unspeakable[28] is becoming an echo of an audacious and new song written by a Self who is not only object of discourse and persona of narrated visions, but a subject who glosses them.[29] And if the purpose for writing is an unending pleasure of solitary remembrance and inner transformation—

I only wrote these things so that I could concentrate my thoughts on them while my heart was occupied with the things of this world, and so that I could turn my heart towards my Creator and away from the world.(*Let* 136)[30]—

I would claim that the ultimate performative act of the words engraved in the book of the heart is indeed for Marguerite d'Oingt that of making the writer into a reader of her own work, leading her back to the creative power of the original Word.

Notes

1. O pulcher dulcis Domine Jhesu Christe, quis dedit mihi audaciam dicendi tam mirabilem rem. All quotes in the original are from Antonin Duraffour, Pierre Gardette, and Paulette Durdilly, eds. *Les Œuvres de Marguerite d'Oingt* (Paris: Les Belles Lettres, 1965). Excerpts will be identified with the abbreviations *Med* for *Pagina Meditationum, Sp* for *Speculum* and *Let* for *Letters,* followed by paragraph numbers. All emphasis mine. The translations are from *The Writings of Margaret of Oingt, Medieval Prioress and Mystic (D. 1310),* trans. Renate Blumenfeld-Kosinski (Newburyport, MA: Focus Information Group, 1990). In the translations, all added emphases are mine as well.

2. J. L. Austin, *How to Do Things with Words,* ed. J. O. Urmson (London: Oxford University Press, 1962).

3. John R. Searle, *Speech Acts: An Essay in the Philosophy of Language* (Cambridge: Cambridge University Press, 1970.)

4. Psalm 81, 6.

5. In all passages quoted in translation, additions of original Latin terms are my own.

6. 1. Anno Domini millesimo ducentesimo, octogesimo, sexto, dominica in septuagesima, *ego* Margareta, ancilla Christi, eram in ecclesia in missa quando *incipiebat cantari* introitus misse, scilicet: "Circumdederunt me gemitus mortis," et *cepi cogitare* miseriam in qua sumus dediti propter peccatum primi parentis. Et in illa cogitatione *cepi* tantum pavorem et tantum dolorem quod *cor mihi deficere videbatur* ex toto, propter hoc quod nesciebam utrum essem digna salute an non. *Postea cum audivi versiculum* introitus quem David psallebat ita dulciter domino *dicens:* "Diligam te, Domine et cetera," *cor meum fuit totum alleviatum,* quia recolui dulcis repromissionis quam Dominus *facit* amicis suis *cum dicit:* "*Ego* diligentem me diligo," quia *bene sciebam* quod ipse est tam bonus et tam mittis quod nunquam permittit perire eos qui diligunt illum. 2. Et postquam *consideravi* magnam dulcedinem et misericordiam que est in ipso, *proieci* me totam extensam coram precioso corpore eius plenam magno dolore, et

petii et eum *rogavi* humiliter ut *daret* mihi quod sciebat mihi esse nec-
cessarium. 3. Tunc ipse, totus plenus dulcedine et pietate *visitavit me*
per suam gratiam sine mora, quia *dedit mihi* suam dulcem consolationem
et *donavit mihi* tam magnam voluntatem bene faciendi quod mihi videbatur quod *essem tota mutata et renovata.* Postea *surrexi* et *posui me* flexis
genibus coram Domino et *feci* ei confessionem de omnibus que potui
recogitare in quibus offenderam illum et promisi sibi emendationem ex
tunc et deinceps (*Med* 1–3).

7.   [U]no solo verbo potes destruere et perire totum mundum et uno solo
      alio verbo potes eum reficere meliorem et pulcriorem (*Med* 13).

8.   Tu eras summa sanitas et verus medicus cuius tactu infirmi sanabantur
      et cuius odore mortui resuscitabantur (*Med* 20).

9.   Hay, optime Ihesu Christe, quid *facient* tue creature? Quia ego non
      video fere unum qui *sciat amare* te, nec *cognoscere,* pene religiosi, quia
      portant se sic *inordinate in verbis suis* et continentiis sicut seculares; et
      multi sunt avidiores eundi ad mensam quam ad matutinas vel ad mis-
      sam. Ipsi sunt *bene potentes ad potandum bona vina* et ad manducandum
      bona cibaria cum habent ea, *sed ipsi impotentes ad ferendum unum parvulum
      verbum si dicatur eis; immo reponsdent per signa, per verba et reddunt malum pro
      malo* (*Med* 64). See also *Med* 70–72.

10.   I began to act just as He had taught me (*Let* 128).

11.   *Je pris* cel glorious enfant entres mes bras espiritualment . . . *je le portoie*
      et l'*enbracoe* tendrement entre les bras de mon cuer . . . *jo me traiot* ver
      lui a grant reverenci et le *declaveloye* et puis le *charioye* sus mes espaules
      et puys le *descendoye* de la croys et le *metoye* entre les bras de mon cuer
      et m'estoiet semblanz que jo le *portoye* a tant legierement come se fut
      de un ant . . . je le *metoie* en mont liet espiritualment et *baysoie* ses tein-
      dres mans et ces benoiz piez qui ensi durament furont percia per nos
      pechiez. Et poys *m'abeyssoye* sus ce glorious flan qui si cruelment fut
      navrez per moy (*Let* 129–131).

12.   This is probably the same Hugh, prior of Valbonne who insisted on
      making her *Speculum* known and handed it over to the General Chapter.

13.   [I]lli les ot totes escrites en son cuer en tel maneri que illi n'avoyt pueir
      de penser en autres chose, mais estoyt son cuer si plain qu'il non poyt
      ne mengier, ne beyre, ne dormir tanqu'ele fut en si grant defauta que
      li fisician la jugerunt a mort (*Let* 137).

14.   Ainsi com Nostri Sires li mit au cuer, elle se pensa que s'ela metoyt
      en escrit ces choses que sos cuers en seroyt plus alegiez. Se comenca
      a escrire tot co qui est ou livro, tot per ordre aussi come illi les avoyt
      ou cuer, et aussi tot come illi avoyt mis les mot ou livre et ce li sallioyt
      du cuer. Et quant illi ot tot escrit, illi fu tote garie. Je croy fermament
      se illi ne l'eust mis en escrit, que illi fut morta ou forsonet, quar illi
      n'avoyt de VII jors ne dormi ne mangie, ne jamais ne feit por quoy
      elle fut en tel poynt. Et por co je croy que ce fut escrit per la voluta
      de Nostre Segnour (*Let* 138).

15. Michel de Certeau, *The Mystic Fable,* trans. Michael B. Smith (Chicago: University of Chicago Press, 1992), 10.

16. Il n'a pas mout de teins que de bones genz estoyent assenble en une mayson et parloent de Diu. Si ot un prodome en la place qui recontait qu'il avoyt demande a une dame *que voloyt dire: vehemens,* et que la dama li dit *que co voloyt dire: fort.* En cele place ot una persona [Marguerite herself] cui *cete parole chait forment el cuer* e li fut semblanz que co fut *trop granz chosa,* mays illi ne li oset unques demandar que li *espondit cele parole: vehemens.* 144. Totes voys ele demanda apres a mout de genz *que voloyt dire cete parole,* mais elle ne trova qui li sout responndre a son *cuer.* Ciz mot li eret *si fichiez el cuor* que ele ne se puyt delivre ne en oreyson ne autra part tant que illi priat a Nostrum Segnour forment qu'il per sa tres grant bonte li volit *ensegnyer* que *voloyt dire cete parole* ou qu'il la li *ostat dou cuor* (*Let* 143–144).

17. For a more detailed reading of her *Speculum,* see my book, *Marguerite Porete et Marguerite d'Oingt de l'autre côté du miroir,* Currents in Comparative Romance Languages and Literatures 72. Ed. Tamara Alvarez-Detrell and Michael G. Paulson (New York: Peter Lang Publishing, 1999). This study argues that mirror metaphors in Marguerite d'Oingt's work function as a theological and poetic strategy to dismantle the traditional subject/object paradigm and propose a new model for defining the knowledge of God and Self.

18. Devant que celi out fayt ses preeres ne que se movit de la place, cil qui est plains de doucour et de pidie la vot confortar et trahire son espirit a se, en tel maneri que oy li fut semblanz que illi eret en un grant leu desert, ou ques ne avoyt maque una grant montaygne et au pie de cele montaygne aveit un arbre mout *meravillous.* En cel arbre aveit *cinc branches* que estoyent *totes seches* et *totes enclinavunt ver terra. Et es fueylles de la premere branche avoyt escrit: visu, en la seconde avoyt escrit: auditu, en la tierci avoy escrit: gustu, en la quarta avoyt escrit: odoratu, en la cinquiesma avoyt escrit: tactu.* Sus la cime de l'arbre avoyt un grant rondel, come se fut un fonz de vayssel, si que li arbres estoyt toz clos par desus en tel maneri que li selouz ne la rosee ne poyent ferir per desus. 146. En tant quant ele o *regarda* l'arbre *diligiament, ele leva ses euz* sus la montaygne et *vit* un grant ruysel qui descendit *a si tres grant forci* que co semblavet una mer. *Cele yeve chisi si tres duremant* au pie de cel arbre que les ragies se viraront totes desus et la cime se metit en terra et les branches que enclinavont ver terra furont *totes drecies ver lo ciel,* et les foylles que erant totes seches furont *totes reverdies,* les ragies que erant devant fichies en terra furont *totes espandues et drecies ver lo ciel* et foront *totes reverdies* et follyes en maneri de branche (*Let* 145–146).

19. R. Howard Bloch, *Medieval Misogyny and the Invention of Western Romantic Love* (Chicago and London: University of Chicago Press, 1991), 34.

20. Readers will have noticed that in the original text the strong impact of expressions like "drecies ver lo ciel" and "totes reverdies," repeated

twice in one sentence, is further increased by the use of the synonyms "totes espandues" and "follyes" as well as the six occurrences of the quantifier "totes."

21. Tu es dulce electuarium in quo sunt omnes boni sapores et de cuius bonitate vivunt anime sancte in paradiso. . . . Tu es gloriosa rosa in qua sunt omnes boni odores et colores (Med 23, 25). For more examples see Med 22–27.

22. Citi creatura, per la graci de Nostre Seignor, aveit escrit en son cor la seinti via que deus Jhesu Criz menet en terra et sos bons exemplos et sa bona doctrina. E aveyt illi meis lo douz Jhesu Crit en son cor que oy li eret semblanz alcuna veis que il li fut presenz e que il tenit un livro clos en sa mayn per liey ensennier. 3. Ciz livros eret toz escriz per defor de letres blanches, neyres et vermeylles; li fermel del livro erant escrit de letres d'or. 4. En les letres blanches eret escrita li sancta conversations al beneit fil Deu, li quaus fut tota blanchi per sa tres grant innocenti et per ses sainctes ovres. En les neyres erant escrit li col et les tenplees et les ordures que li Jue li gitavont en sa sainti faci et per son noble cors, tant que il semblevet estre meseuz. En les ver-melles erant escrite les plaes et li pretious sans qui fut espanchies per nos. 5. Et puis y aveit dos fermeuz qui closant lo livro, qui erant escrit de letres d'or. En l'un aveyt escrit: "Deus erit omnia in omnibus." En l'autre aveit escrit: "Mirabilis Deus in sanctis suis" . . . 7. Quant illi aveyt ben regarda cet livro, illi comencavet a liere el livro de sa concienci, lo qual illi trovavet tot plen de fouceta et de menconges. Quant illi regardavet la humilita Jhesu Crit, illi se trovavet tota pleyna d'eguel. Quant illi pensavet qu'il volit estre mesprisies et persegus, illi trovavet en se tot lo contrayrio. Quant illi regardavet sa poureta, illi ne trovavet pas en se que illi volit estre si poure, que illi en fut mesprisie. Quant illi regardavet sa pacienti, illi non trovavet point en sei. Quant illi pensavet coment il fut obediens tan que a la mort, illi ne trovavet pas si bien obediens coment mestiers li fut. 8. Co erunt les letres blanches, en que eret escrita li conversations al beneit fil Deu. Apres quant aveit bein regarda totes ses defautes, illi se perforsavet de l'emendar tan come illi puet a l'essemplayre de la via Jhesu Crist. 9. Apres illi se estudievet en les letres neires, en les quauz erant escriptes les viutinances que on fit Jhesu Crist: en celes apreneit a sofrir les tribulations en patienci. 10. Apres illi se estudiavet en les letres roges, en les quauz erant es-criptes les plaes et li espanchimenz del pretious sanc Jhesu Crist. En celes apreneit non pas tan soulament les tribulations sofrir en patienci, mays si apreneit a deleitier en tal maneri que tuit li confort de cet mundo li tornavont a grant haine, essi que oy li eret semblanz que en cet mundo non eret ci digna chosa ne si douci come sofrir les peynes et les tormenz de cet seglo per l'amour de son creatour. 11. Apres illi se estudiavet en les letres del or. En celes illi apreneit a desirrar les choses celestiauz. 12. En cet livro trovavet escripta la via que Jhesu

        Criz menet en terra, dey da nativita tan que li montiet en ciel (*Sp* 2–5, 7–12).

23.   In her *Meditations* as well the author calls Jesus a perfect mirror without stains: "[T]u eras speculum sine macula" (*Med* 21).

24.   Ciz douz chanz s'en vait per toz les ordenz des angels et de sayns dey lo primyer tant que au derrier. E ycis chanz no est plus tot fenis que il en fant un autre tretot novel. Et ciz chanz durera seins fin (*Sp* 18).

25.   Certes jo crey qui metrit bein son cor en la tres grant beuta Nostron Seignour et coment il appareyt glorious en sos sains, hel dyroyt bein que so erant dreites mervilles, e crey que oy lo convindrit a defalir, e bein porreit *dire* que Deus lor aveit bein rendu co que il lour promet per lo propheta David: "Ego dixi, dii estis." Quar oy sera semblanz a chascun que il seit uns petiz deus, quar il seront si fil et si heyr (*Sp*. 37).

26.   Concerning the male/female paradigm, one should mention that Marguerite d'Oingt insists on the importance of the female, not only when she addresses Christ as her mother (*Med* 33, 36)—which, as Caroline Walker Bynum has shown, is a *topos* in male and female mystical writings (see her well-known *Jesus as Mother*)—but also when she specifically adds the grammatically feminine forms after the masculine in her Latin prose: "illi et ille" (*Med* 66, 77), "discipuli nec discipule" (*Med* 66). Furthermore, the prioress states in the same *Pagina Meditationum* that one of the greatest gifts God has bestowed upon her was to allow her to be free, that is, as she puts it, not under male domination: "Domine dulcis, si non fecisses mihi aliam gratiam nisi istam quod non permisisti quod sim in servitute et subiectione hominis, satis mihi fecisti" [Sweet Lord, if you gave me no other grace than that you won't permit me to serve and be subject to [a man], I would be satisfied] (*Med* 102).

27.   This is Margaret Whitford's translation of "une transcendance sensible." See Whitford's *The Irigaray Reader* (Oxford and Cambridge: Basil Blackwell, 1991), 160. This work contains a good discussion on Irigaray's concept of the flesh made word and on her vision of the divine in general.

28.   The *topos* of what Michael E. Sells has named *Mystical Language of Unsaying* (Chicago and London: The University of Chicago Press, 1994) is abundantly present in Marguerite's works.

29.   For an interpretation of Marguerite's strategic use of subject and object in reference to her Self, readers may refer to "L'enjeu de la spéculation chez Marguerite d'Oingt" at the end of the third chapter of my *Marguerite Porete et Marguerite d'Oingt de l'autre côté du miroir*.

30.   Je n'ay escrit ces choses manque por ce que quant mes cuers seroyt espanduz parmi le munde que je *pensaso* en cetes choses, por ce que puisso *retorner mon cuer a mon creatour et retrayre* du mundo (*Let* 136).

Bibliography

Austin, J. L. *How to Do Things with Words*. Ed. J. O. Urmson. London: Oxford University Press, 1962.

Bloch, R. Howard. *Medieval Misogyny and the Invention of Western Romantic Love*. Chicago and London: University of Chicago Press, 1991.

Blumenfeld-Kosinski, Renate, trans. *The Writings of Margaret of Oingt, Medieval Prioress and Mystic (D. 1310)*. Newburyport, MA: Focus Information Group, 1990.

Certeau, Michel de. *The Mystic Fable*. Trans. Michael B. Smith. Chicago: University of Chicago Press, 1992.

Duraffour, Antonin, Pierre Gardette and Paulette Durdilly, eds. *Les Œuvres de Marguerite d'Oingt*. Paris: Les Belles Lettres, 1965.

Müller, Catherine. *Marguerite Porete et Marguerite d'Oingt de l'autre côté du miroir*. Currents in Comparative Romance Languages and Literatures 72 ed. Tamara Alvarez-Detrell and Michael G. Paulson. New York: Peter Lang Publishing, 1998.

Searle, John R. *Speech Acts: An Essay in the Philosophy of Language*. Cambridge: Cambridge University Press, 1970.

Sells, Michael E. *Mystical Language of Unsaying*. Chicago and London: University of Chicago Press, 1994.

Whitford, Margaret. *The Irigaray Reader*. Oxford and Cambridge: Basil Blackwell, 1991.

CHAPTER THREE

"More Than I Fynde Written": Dialogue and Power in the English Translation of *The Mirror of Simple Souls*

Laurie A. Finke

In *Women Writers of the Middle Ages*, Peter Dronke calls Marguerite Porete "the most neglected of the great writers of the thirteenth century."[1] Author of a book of poetic prose, dialogues, and lyrics written around 1285–1295 called *Le mirouer des simples ames anienties et qui seulement demourent en vouloir et desir d'Amour*, this French visionary was condemned at Valenciennes in the last years of the thirteenth century, and, when she persisted in her heresy, was imprisoned, tried, and publicly burnt as a heretic in Paris on June 1, 1310. Copies of her book were also ordered destroyed and to possess one was itself considered an act of heresy, punishable by excommunication.[2] Despite the inquisitorial ban, surviving copies of *The Mirror of Simple Souls* in French, Latin, Italian, and English testify to the life of this visionary text long after its author's ignominious death. The English translation that is the subject of this essay was made sometime during the fifteenth century by a Carthusian monk. It survives in three manuscripts: MS Bodley 505 in the Bodleian Library, British Library MS Additional 37790 (which contains, among other things, the sole surviving copy of the short text of the

Revelations of the fifteenth-century English mystic Julian of Norwich), and St. John's College MS 71. Today the *Mirror* is significant not only because its author was a woman writer, but also because it is one of the only documents to offer evidence independent of inquisitorial testimony of the beliefs that marked the heresy known as the Free Spirit (*secta spiritus libertatis*).

What high drama mystics like Porete must have afforded their contemporaries. Or more precisely, how dramatic the clash must have been between these religious visionaries and an orthodox church anxious to safeguard its power and authority based on its institutional claim to be the only and authoritative conduit to the divine. Sometimes, as in the case of Porete, these conflicts between unruly individuals claiming divine inspiration and clerical authority erupted publicly into the carefully scripted performances of trial and execution, but they are present no less visibly in the texts produced by mystics. Robert E. Lerner describes *The Mirror of Simple Souls* as "less a treatise than a happening" (Porete, 1). Karma Lochrie argues that we misread mystical utterances if we approach them solely as constative utterances through a text-bound hermeneutic: "The mystic is more interested in the word as event, rather than in a textual relic of an ancient truth."[3] Mystical utterances are not "statements of truth but . . . speech acts, dialogues which are located at the place of the speaking subject. The question which underlies all mystical utterance is not whether it is true or not but whether the mystic occupies the place of the other's speech and who that Other which speaks through the mystic is" (Lochrie, 64). This essay explores what it would mean to approach a mystical text like the *Mirror* as an event rather than a set of propositions. More specifically, however, I am interested in how this "event"—this clash over the authority to represent God's will on earth—was re-enacted after her death in subsequent iterations of the text, especially in its English translations.

Lochrie's characterization of mystical utterance suggests that a hermeneutic based on something like J. L. Austin's speech act theory, in which language is situated within a general theory of action, might illuminate the performative aspects of a mystical text like the *Mirror*. In such a theory, language does not refer to something that exists outside of and prior to it; rather "it produces or transforms a situation, it effects."[4] Like most church rituals, say, for instance, the sacraments, the mystical utterance requires that its readers be attuned not to what the text *says* but to what it *does*. If the priest's words absolve sins or transform bread and wine into the Body and Blood of Christ, the words of the *Mirror* "scholde perfet tho devout saules. that schalle rede it"(f. 131).[5]

To understand the performative nature of Porete's text, however, we must push considerably beyond Austin's formulations, which tend rather rigidly to wed the efficacy of the performative speech act to institutional authority.[6] For Austin, a performative speech act (let us take, by way of example, the confession of sins) can be effective only if there is a conventional procedure which has a conventional effect. It must include the uttering of certain words by certain persons in certain circumstances (in the confessional, the priest utters certain ritual words of absolution).[7] The persons and circumstances must be appropriate for the procedure invoked (only a priest can absolve sins, 34). Finally, it must be executed by all participants correctly (35) and completely (including, in the case of confession, the penitent's performance of penance, 36). Austin's analysis of performative language, Derrida remarks, recognizes that "the possibility of the negative (in this case, of infelicities) is in fact a structural possibility, that failure is an essential risk of the operations under consideration"; at the same time, however, he "excludes that risk as accidental, exterior, one which teaches us nothing about the linguistic phenomenon being considered" ("Signature," 188).

Mystical discourse is a perfect example of the kind of instability Derrida wants to introduce into the discussion of performative language, speech acts whose efficacy cannot be guaranteed by recourse to conventional procedures. The Eucharistic visions of the thirteenth-century German mystic Mechtild of Hackeborn are a case in point. On more than one occasion, when she desires to receive communion, but had not confessed herself, Mechtild claims she has confessed her sins directly to God, substituting her own performance for that of the confessional.[8] By its very nature, as Lochrie suggests, mystical discourse cannot claim institutional authority even when the mystic uses the same ritualistic language that is conventionally reserved for the priest. This is especially true of women mystics because women, by reason of their sex, were excluded from most religious ritual of the period. Yet instances in which female mystics appropriate the institutionalized language of the Church cannot be so easily dismissed as "non-serious" or infelicitous speech acts (Austin, 104, 121). The mystical text's iteration of the Church's performative language outside of the conventional procedures and places marked out for such speech, and uttered by individuals not authorized to perform such speech acts, does not invalidate the speech act; instead it marks the utterance as a site in which such institutional authority is being contested. These unstable performatives, as Derrida suggests, are analytically much more interesting than those governed by established conventions of time, place, and person because they interrogate the very mechanisms by which performative utterances become meaningful.

For this reason, I think the notion of the dialogic articulated by the Russian cultural theorist Mikhail Bakhtin and members of his circle is more useful than Austin's speech act theory for understanding the performative nature of a mystical text like Porete's *Mirror*. In essays like "Discourse in the Novel," "Speech Genres," and "Discourse in Life and Discourse in Art,"[9] Bakhtin covers much the same semiotic ground as Austin. He is interested in speech not simply as an inert and passive code for communication, but as a social action and interaction. "Far more often, behavioral utterances actively continue and develop a situation, adumbrate a plan for future action, and organize that action" ("Discourse in Life," 100). He is interested in the conventional procedures that regulate (and render meaningful) performative utterances. Unlike Austin, however, Bakhtin is also interested in the ways in which individuals can appropriate performative utterances outside of, and even in resistance to, conventional procedures, shaping them to their own ends. And he is interested in the ongoing processes of appropriation and reappropriation of utterance that dialogue enables.

Let me make clear what I mean by the dialogic and what I do not. When Bakhtin uses the term dialogue, he is not referring simply to alternating lines in a script in which one speaker follows another (Morson and Emerson, *Mikhail Bakhtin*, 138), though Marguerite's text is, in fact, structured as a series of dialogues among the personifications of Love, Reason, and the Soul. This sort of dialogue is the most basic formal feature of theatrical performance, of the drama. Critics are fond of pointing out, however, that despite his interest in dialogue, Bakhtin usually dismisses the drama as a monologic genre, though these critics rarely attempt to ascertain why the novel rather than the drama should be for Bakhtin the dialogic genre par excellence.[10] Robert Markley has suggested that perhaps because the dramaturgical is, for Bakhtin, so much more than a metaphor, because it is so epistemologically central to Bakhtin's theoretical program, drama as a genre occupies a thoroughly ambivalent position in his writing. Bakhtin wants to argue that generic features usually associated with the drama—such as dialogue, performance, or spatial purview—occur in most nondramatic genres and, in fact, in almost all meaningful language. Classical drama seems, to him, an inert crystallization of language's potential for the dramatic.[11]

What Bakhtin attempted to describe in his formulations on the dialogic is at once more complex and messier than a simple exchange of lines; it challenges tidy generic classifications. The dialogic or double-voiced word, as Bakhtin writes in "Discourse in the Novel," involves "the intense interaction and struggle between one's own and another's word, . . . in which [these words] oppose or . . . interanimate one another" (354). This opposition and struggle, however, is not simply binary (self/other). Because every word comes to us already dialogized, already spoken, spoken about, and evaluated in advance, the dialogic text is, in reality, what I will call heterodialogic, marked by multiple, concurrent, and sometimes contradictory dialogues that have become sedimented in the text through the process of iteration. However, and this is my second caveat, this multiply dialogic approach to the text does not promise, as some critics have implied, a kind of discursive anarchy or relativism in which all voices are equally regarded in a free, natural, and spontaneous conversation.[12] Such a condition would require that discourse be located outside of history in some utopic (in both senses of the world) and amnesiac space in which the word could be invented anew every time it is used. This kind of ahistoricism is the very error with which Bakhtin charged the linguistic schools of individualistic subjectivism and not one he would be likely to repeat.[13] Instead, Bakhtin's point is precisely that words carry sedimented in them their histories of dialogue, struggle, and conflict, including their own histories of power relations.

The English translation of *The Mirror of Simple Souls* is a compelling example of what Bakhtin would call a dialogic text, a text in which neither the voice of the translator nor that of the original author is assimilated to a single style, in which there is no single controlling authorial "voice."[14] It is a site of struggle over authority that in many ways re-enacts Marguerite's own struggle to articulate her beliefs in the face of inquisitorial intimidation. An English Carthusian's fifteenth-century translation of the French of a thirteenth-century heretical beguine marks this text as a site, one of many such sites, that establishes, maintains, and polices power relations, as well as one in which power relations are challenged, resisted, and modified. The text's many dialogues can perhaps most clearly be read in the frequent instructions to readers on the proper way to read the text. Porete simultaneously carries on dialogues with her imagined readers, with God (through the personifications of Love, Reason, and Soul), and with the Church authorities who condemn her. In a prologue that prefaces the Old French manuscript, but is not included in the English translation, Porete addresses her readers while glancing anxiously at those authorities who might condemn her book:

> You who would read this book,
> If you indeed wish to grasp it,

Think about what you say,
For it is very difficult to comprehend; . . .

Theologians and other clerks,
You will not have the intellect for it,
No matter how brilliant your abilities,
If you do not proceed humbly. . . .

Humble, then, your wisdom
Which is based on Reason,
And place all your fidelity
In those things which are given
By Love, illuminated through Faith.

And thus you will understand this book
Which makes the Soul live by love. (Porete, 79)

In his analysis of what makes a performative utterance meaningful, Vološinov stresses the relationship between participants rather than established conventional procedures: "the behavioral utterance always joins the participants in the situation together as *co-participants* who know, understand and evaluate the situation in like manner"; that is they share a common purview, common knowledge, and common evaluation ("Discourse in Life," 100). The conventional procedures of which Austin speaks would provide a mechanism to link participants together, but they are not essential to the creation of meaningful performatives; that can be accomplished by other means as well. In the absence of established procedures, Porete's prologue attempts to establish a common purview within which a reading of her text will make sense, at the same time she attempts to head off critical response.[15] She simultaneously attempts to challenge her readers to read in unaccustomed ways and to neutralize those who have the power to silence her. She warns potential readers that they will not be able to understand her writing by rationally evaluating it as a series of logical propositions. That is the purview of "theologians and other clerks," who are excluded from participation unless they can adopt the appropriate stance of humility. The shift Porete asks of her readers is from a constative evaluation of the text to a performative one. She asks them to subordinate reason to humility. To adopt the common purview of humility is to choose a position that is, interestingly, defined as much spatially by one individual's relation to another as by an internal state of mind. Humility is almost indistinguishable from the performance of humility, usually indicated by spatial relations (one is beneath another) and physical gestures (kneeling, bowing, lowering one's head). Even textual discussions of humility are generally couched in terms of spatial relations and gesture.

In another prologue attributed to Porete that appears in the English translation but not in the Old French, Porete models for her readers this posture of humility:[16]

> I creature made of the makere. bi me. that the makere hase made of hym this book. why it is I knawe nouȝt. nor I kepe noȝt witt. For why I awe it noȝt. it suffies me yᵗ it is. wher ynne I may knawe the diuine wisedom. And in hope. here I thame salue by the love of the pees of charite: (BL MS Add. 37790, f. 138v)[17]

In these lines Porete seems indifferent, almost dismissive of her readers; she does not care who they are, so long as they are worthy of direction. In fact, however, her words function less to establish her relationship with readers than her status as an annihilated or "nouȝted" soul in relation to God. Before God, the soul ought not to know. Knowledge is presumably the outcome of reading, but here Porete reverses that expectation, arguing that the outcome of reading this text should be an emptying out of knowledge in a posture of abjection before the divine.

What I have called elsewhere the politics of sanctity, the very temporal process by which the Church evaluated an individual's often audacious claims of divine inspiration (Finke), requires that Porete establish some sort of relation with her official audience. The prologue goes on to glance sideways at Church authorities in an apparent effort to head off charges that her book's contents are heterodox. She constructs an elaborate pedigree for her text, a "record of clerkis yᵗ hane redde þis boke"[18] and who testify to its doctrinal soundness:

> The first was a frere iohn of Querayn. þat seide we sende you þis by these lettres of loue. receyves it for curtesie. for love prayes it ȝou: to the worship of god and of þome that be made fre of god. and to the profite of tham that noȝt be. . . . He saide soþli yᵗ þis boke is made be the holi goste hand And þowȝ alle the clerkes of the worlde herde it. but ȝif þey vnderstonde it. yᵗ is to seye. but ȝif þey hafe hie gostly felynges and this same wyrkynge. they schalle noȝt witt whate it menes: And he prayed for the loue of god that it be wisely kept: and that fewe schulde se it. And he saide thus.that it was so

hie: that hym self my3t not vnderstand it. And after hym a monke
of Cisetyns red it that hi3t Daun Franke. Chauntour of the Abbay of
villiers. and he saide that it proved welle by the Scripture: that it is
alle trowthe that thys boke says. and after hym redde it a maister of
diuinity: that hi3t. Maister. Godfrey of ffountaynes. and he blamed
it nou3t: no more than did ye o þer. but he seide thus. that he con-
seylede no3t: that fewe schould se it. and for this cause. ffor they
myght leue þer awne wurkyng: and folow this callynge to þ^e which
they shulde neuer come: and so thay my3t deceyue þam selfe. ffor it
is made of a spiritt so stronge. and so kuttynge: y^t þer be but few
such or none. (138^v-139^r)

[The first was a Friar John of Quaregnon, who said, "We send you
this [book] by these words of love. Receive it with courtesy, for love
asks it of you to the honor of God and of those who are made free
by God and for the profit of those who are not [yet free]. . . ." He
said truely that this book was made by the Holy Ghost and even if
all of the clerks of the world heard it unless they understood it, that
is to say, unless they have the same high spiritual feelings and work-
ings, they shall not know what it means. And he prayed for the love
of God that it be closely kept and that few should see it. And he said
thus, that it was so lofty that he himself might not understand it.

    And after him a Cistercian monk by the name of Don Frank
of the Abbey of Villiers read it and he said that the book was well
proven by Scriptures, that everything this book says is truth.

    And after him a master of divinity who was called Godfrey of
Fountaines read it and he did not find any fault any more than any
of the others did. But he said thus, that he counselled that few should
see it because they might leave their own life and follow this calling
to which they should never come and so they might deceive themselves, for this book is made of so strong a spirit and so incisive that
there are few or none to be found like it.]

In the second prologue, Porete (if indeed she herself wrote this prologue)
engages in an elaborate dialogue with these authorities, appropriating for
her own words whatever prestige might accrue to their positions as master
of theology at the University of Paris (Godfrey), Cistercian of Villiers-en-
Brabant, and minor friar. Not content simply with increasing the authority
of the text through "symple kunnynge," someone—either Porete or her
translators—constructs a textual lineage for the *Mirror* much different from

those contemporary historians might compose. A twentieth-century feminist historian might group this text alongside those of other prominent medieval women mystics such as Hadewijch of Brabant, Beatrice of Nazareth, Marie d'Oignes, or Christina Mirabilis. A church historian might portray Marguerite as part of a long line of Free Spirit rebels and heretics that stretches from Amaury of Bené in the early thirteenth century to Bentivenga of Gubbio in the late thirteenth, Heilwige Bloemardine and Sister Katrai in the early fourteenth, the Men of Intelligence in the late fourteenth to the Reformation and beyond.[19] But this prologue allies the text not with heretics or women, but with the authorities of the Church whose word is sufficient to provide testimony of the text's orthodoxy. These authorities do not simply silently approve the text, however; they also attempt to limit its reading to the chosen few who are "discerning" enough not to read it too literally. Both Friar John and Godfrey of Fountaines argue that the text should be read only by a very select few, only those who have "hie gostly felynges and this same wyrkyng." Friar John is not sure that even he can understand it. Godfrey fears that the text could harm a reader who does not share Porete's purview, "ffor they myght leue þer awne wurkyng: and folow this callynge to þᵉ which they shulde neuer come: and so thay my3t deceyue þam selfe."

In this passage, Porete uses direct discourse when she wishes most to highlight the authenticity of her authorities' testimonies—she directly quotes Friar John and Godfrey of Fountaines—and indirect discourse when she wishes to merge her own voice more completely with theirs.[20] Yet this is an instance in which examination of the manuscript's punctuation yields significant insights into the dialogics of the text that would be obliterated by modern editorial practices of normalization. Because medieval manuscripts did not use the formal apparatus of punctuation and quotation marks to set direct discourse off from its quoting context—to distinguish between two different "voices"—the distance between her own words and those of her allies is elided; their words (and their authority) merge with those of the writer.

Porete's English translator carries on a different and competing set of dialogues with Marguerite, with his fifteenth-century readers (who are very different from the readers Marguerite envisions for her text), and with the Church authorities he wishes to appease and with whom he wishes to ally Marguerite's words. The manuscript copies of the English *Mirror* are nearly identical, suggesting that they were produced under strict clerical supervision. The translator appears not to have known that the *Mirror* was written by a woman nor that it had been condemned as heretical. But he is nevertheless very anxious about the doctrinal soundness of the text he is reproducing. That anxiety displays itself throughout the translator's prologue where he attempts to recuperate the text for orthodoxy. He begins:

> This boke the which is called þe myrroure of symple saules. I moste unworthy creature and. oute cast of alle oþers. many ʒeeris goone wrote it oute of ffrenche into englisch after my lewyd konnnge in hope that by þe grace of god it scholde perfet tho devout saules. that schalle rede it. This was forsoth myne entente. But now I am stirryd to labore it aʒene newe ffor by cause. I am enfourmed. that som wordes þerof hafe bene mystaken. þerfore ʒif god will. I schalle declare þoo wordes more openly. ffor þouʒ loue declare þo poyntes in the same boke. it is but schortly spoken. and maye be taken oþerwise than it is mente of thaym þᵗ rede it sodeynly and takis no forther hede. (BM Add. 37790, f. 137ʳ)

> [This book, which is called *The Mirror of Simple Souls*, I, most unworthy creature and outcast of all others, for many years have translated out of French into English as best I could in the hope that by the grace of God it should perfect those devout souls who shall read it. This was my intention. But now I am stirred to labor at it again because I am informed that some of its words have been mistaken. Therefore, if God wills, I shall declare those words more openly, for, although Love declares those points in this book, it is done briefly and may be taken otherwise than it is meant by those who read it quickly and superficially.]

Curiously the translator, in his prologues, also gestures toward the stance of humility Porete requires of her readers by including references to himself as an "unworthy creature" and "oute cast of alle oþers," yet he seems supremely confident that careful and scholarly reading (reason) rather than divine grace will enable his readers to understand the text's significance.

How does the translator understand the nature of his work? He does not see himself, as a modern translator might, as simply "carrying over" the sense of the French words into the English language. He is not simply the passive conduit of the author's original style and sense, but rather functions as an active participant in the text's construction. Because the text is so elusive, so difficult—it "is of hye deuyne maters and of hie gostely felyngis and kunnyngly and fulle mystely it is speken"[21]—it may easily be misunderstood by its readers. Presumably an earlier (though now

lost) translation has produced what he feels are misreadings. The translator, then, cannot simply mediate between two mutually incomprehensible
languages and cultures; he does not simply receive passively an already
constituted text. Rather he must actively intervene in the readers' reception
of the text; he must constitute his own dialogue with both the text and
the text's readers. At times, he adds his more authoritative voice as cloistered monk to the author's as a form of choral support praising the text's
"high gostely felyngis" and cunning language; at other points, he rejects
the author's sense altogether and attempts a counterargument. At such
moments the text most clearly reveals its dialogic qualities, its struggles
around issues of authority and orthodoxy.

The translator's anxiety is perhaps most clearly marked by his attempt to gloss those passages that seem to him doctrinally questionable.
Because the translator has marked his rather lengthy glosses of Marguerite's
text with his own initials (M.N.), physically setting off his glosses as if
they were responses in a formal dialogue, we are able to reconstruct the
text as an actively double-voiced text in which two powerful and contradictory voices struggle for recognition.

> Bot ʒit as I sayde afore. it hase bene mystaken of sum persones that
> hase red the boke. Therfore at siche places there me semes. moste
> nede. I wylle write mo werdes þerto in maner of glose. aftir my
> symple kunnynge as me semes best. And in these fewe places that I
> put in more than I fynde written. I wole be gynne with the ferste
> letture of my name. M. and ende with the letter N. the first of my
> vnc name. (138ʳ⁻ᵛ)

> [But as I said before, the book has been mistaken by some persons
> who have read it; therefore at such places where it seems to me most
> necessary I will write more words in the manner of a gloss after my
> own simple knowledge as I see fit. And in these few places where I
> put in more than I find written, I will begin [the gloss] with the first
> letter of my name, M., and end with the letter N, the first letter of
> my last name.]

What emerges from a reading of the English translation are two equally
forceful voices or styles, one male with the full backing of ecclesiastical
authority, the other, as it turns out, female, attempting to align itself with
the authority of God against that of her clerical accusers. Neither is able
to drown out the other. While it is possible to read this translation, as

Raoul Vaneigem does in *The Movement of the Free Spirit* (129), as an appropriation of the *Mirror* that serves the ends of a conservative Christian doctrine, eradicating the call for radical freedom and pleasure that marks the
original, it is my belief that such a reading would itself be monological.
Such a reading would misunderstand the extent to which the translator
fails to domesticate the *Mirror* for orthodoxy. The translator is not willing
to allow Marguerite's words simply to be relayed to even the most pious
and discriminating reader without comment. But neither is he able to erase
the radical import of those words; they actively resist such appropriation.
The translator's method of marking his textual interpretations of the *Mirror*
with his initials at the beginning and end sets the two styles, or, to use
Bakhtin's term, "accents," into sharp relief.

   This strategy results in a text that Bakhtin would call a hidden polemic, in which the author's (or, in this case, the translator's) discourse is
only partially directed towards its referent. At the same time, it seems to
"cringe in the presence of a listener's word, to take a 'sideward glance' at
a possible hostile answer" (Morson and Emerson, *Mikhail Bakhtin*, 155). It
responds by striking a "polemical blow . . . at the other's discourse on the
same theme" (Bakhtin, *Dostoevsky's Poetics*, 195). This double orientation is
realized in the text's style, intonation, and syntax. Or in this case the text's
two styles, intonations, and syntaxes. In the English *Mirror* the double
orientation is redoubled because the cited text—Marguerite's—is also itself
a hidden polemic. If the translator's language reveals an anxious glance in
the direction of possible clerical superiors, in Porete's style and syntax we
can also note "sideward glances" at the hostility of the Church. This is
especially prominent in her appropriation—or iteration—of the style and
intonation of biblical discourse, especially the gospels and St. Paul's epistles, as in the following passage:

> charite obeyeth to no thynge yᵗ is made: but to loue./ Charite has
> nothynge proper: not so muche yᵗ sche wille aske thynge yᵗ is hirris./
> Charite leues her awne werke: and gose to do otheres./ Charite askis
> none alowance of creature:/ for thynge that sche hase done:/ Charite
> hase no drede. ne disese. sche is so ryȝtwys:/ that sche may nat flitte
> for nothynge that fallis:

> [Charity obeys nothing that is made except Love. Charity possesses
> nothing; she will not even ask for anything that is hers. Charity leaves
> her own work and goes to do others. Charity asks no payment from
> anyone for anything she has done. Charity has no dread nor discom-

fort. She is so righteous that she will not be inconstant for anything that happens.]

Porete borrows the intonations of biblical style, drawing on the power of its balanced repetition and anaphora, but substituting words of her own choosing, words that allow for a more radical interpretation of the text. The manuscript's punctuation helps to highlight the performative nature of the prose; it signals accent and intonation in a text designed to be read aloud.[22] The virgules indicate how the text should be performed, stressing the anaphora in the several clauses beginning with "charity." The lyricism that the translator imparts to Porete's French contrasts sharply with his own rational, even prosaic language in the glosses.

Space allows for only one example of the dialogically agitated style of the English *Mirror*, of the struggle between its two competing voices. Discussing the nature of love and the perfected soul, Marguerite writes that the annihilated (or "nouȝted") soul has no need of the virtues.

> The saule of suche loue says loue hym selfe:may saye thus to vertues: / I take leue of yow./ to the which vertues þis saule many a day hase be seruant to./ I assente lady loue sais this saule. so was than but now is thus: that your curtesy hase throw me oute of her daungere. Therefore I saye vertues. I take leue of yow: and more in pees than it hase bene: /ffor soth I wete welle. youre seruyse is to travelous:/ Summe tyme I laide myn herte in you with owtyn any disseueryng: ȝe wote welle this. I was in alle thynges to you obeyinge./ O I was then your seruant. but now I am delyuered out of your thraldome. welle I wote I leyde alle myn herte in yow./ so hase I lange endured in grete seruage in whiche I hase suffred many greuous tormentis. and many paynes endured. It is mervayle that I am scapid with the lyfe: But nowe I make no forse sithen it is thus. that I am departed fro you/ and therfore in pees I dwelle. (ff. 143)

> ["The soul by such love," says Love himself, "may say thus to vertues: 'I take leave of you.' To which vertues this soul has many days been a servant." "I assent Lady Love," says this soul. "So it was then, but now it is thus, that your courtesy has brought me out of their *daunger*. Therefore I say, 'Vertues, I take leave of you, and more in peace than it has been. For truly I know well your service is too laborious. Once I placed my heart in you, without any deception. You know well that I was in all things obedient to you. Oh, I was

then your servant but now I am delivered out of your servitude. Well I know I placed all my heart in you. Thus I have long endured in bondage in which I have suffered many grievous torments and endured many pains. It is a marvel that I am escaped with my life. But now I no longer care because it is thus: I am departed from you and therefore I dwell in peace.]

This passage illustrates the skill with which M.N. has adapted Porete's lyrical French to take advantage of the stylistic possibilities of Middle English prose. The first thing the modern reader will note is the lack of the modern conventions of punctuation that separate sentences and set dialogue apart, enabling us to distinguish narrative and dramatic voices. In the Middle English text, voices run together, they truly "interanimate" one another, as for instance, the repetition in the first clause of "love" as both a speaker and an abstract object of speech. As Malcolm Parkes has pointed out, medieval punctuation served the ends of the spoken rather than the written text (45). In medieval manuscripts, punctuation serves as a kind of pragmatics of writing, offering guidelines on intonation, pausing, and other extralinguistic dimensions of the spoken language. Porete's style draws on the rhetorical power of highly wrought liturgical language that cries out to be performed rather than read silently. The punctuation in this passage serves to highlight its highly wrought aural patterning, including alliteration ("The saule of such loue says loue him self: may say thus to vertues"), parallelism ("so was then but now is thus"), and repetition (of key words like "this saule," for instance, or "love" in my example above). It divides clauses into balanced phrases: "O I was then your seruant. But now I am delyuered out of your thraldome." Finally, it sets phrases off for special emphasis, as for instance, the climax of the passage—"I take leue of yow." The terseness of this phrase is highlighted by setting it off from the rest of the text using a combination of colon and virgule (/) at the beginning of the phrase and a punctus (.) with a virgule at the end.

In this elegant passage, Porete expresses one of the tenets most frequently associated with Free Spirit sects—and the one most noxious to spiritual authorities—that the annihilated soul has no need of virtue "ffor loue may do alle with outen any mysdeynge"(fl. 40ᵛ).[23] The *Determinatio de novo spiritu*, attributed to Albertus Magnus and written toward the end of the thirteenth century, attributes to heretics of the Free Spirit the belief that "Man can be united with God in such a way that he no longer sins, whatever he does" (Vaneigem, 118). The inquisitor Ubertino of Casale writes around 1305 of similar beliefs: "They say that men who have the grace of God and charity cannot sin" (Vaneigem, 128). In this passage, Marguerite's rejection of virtue is expressed through metaphors of feudal servitude, metaphors that already carry sedimented within them political relations of power, as well as traditional descriptions of Adam's fall into sin and the subsequent bondage of the human race. Like all dialogic language, Porete's words are already "overlain with qualification, open to dispute, charged with value" ("Discourse," 276). Words like "thralldom" and "servage," for instance, often appeared in popular narratives of the fall (see, for instance, Langland's *Piers Plowman*). Terms like "paynes" and "travelous," which would have been appropriate to describe the pains of hell, are here attributed to the virtues. It is interesting to speculate to what extent such metaphors expressed resistance not only toward the restrictions imposed by spiritual authority, but resentment toward temporal authority as well, toward the "servage" inherent in feudal relations.

The translator is all too aware of the conventional uses of these figures. At this point in the text, he interjects a gloss, marking his dialogue with the text carefully, not only with his initials, but also by addressing his audience, "ȝee auditours of this boke,"[24] with phrases like "Towchynge these words that this saule says." He restores the "proper" tenor of the metaphor, claiming that when the soul gives itself to perfection it labors day and night to "get vertues by counsel of reason" and strives with vice at every point.

Thus the vertues ben maystresses: and every vertue makes her to werre with his contrarye. the whiche be vices:/ many scharpe paynes and bitternes of conscience: felis the saule in this werke: and these paynes and passions be not only in exercise of yᵉ spirit. by puttynge away vices in getynge of vertues: But þai be also of bodely exercise by commandementis of vertues. and bi conseyle of resoun. to faste. and wake. and to do penaunce in many diuerse wises. and to forsake alle hyr plesaunces and alle lustes and likynges. [f. 143]

[Thus the virtues become mistresses and every virtue wars upon her contrary, which are vices. In this work, the soul feels many sharp pains and bitterness of conscience. And these pains and passions come not only from the exercise of the spirit, by avoiding vices in the attainment of virtues, but also by bodily exercise and by the counsel of reason, in fasting and waking, in doing penance in many different ways, and in forsaking all her pleasures, lusts, and delights.]

M.N. restores an orthodox reading to the passage, reinstating the traditional substance of its metaphors of servitude. The "vertues" are once again the "maystresses," who impose both spiritual and physical suffering on the soul. But he can achieve this interpretation only by doing severe violence to the sense of Porete's text. Notice also that M.N. punctuates his own writing logically rather than rhetorically, calling attention not to the performative dimensions of his text but to its precision. For instance, the phrase "the whiche be vices" is set apart from the previous clause not for any rhetorical effect; rather it is set in apposition to "contrarye," logically defining that term.

These tactics are repeated throughout the English *Mirror*. When Marguerite proclaims that the "nouȝted soule" should give "to nature alle þt he askis. wttoute grucchynge of conscience,"[25] M.N. at least suspects that she is expressing the heretical belief that (again the words of the *Determinatio*), "Whoever is united with God, can assuage his carnal desire with impunity and in any way, with either sex, and even by inverting the roles" (Vaneigem, 118). He counters with a shocked reply:

> Now god forbede that any be so fleschly to thenke þᵗ it schulde mene to giffe to nature any luste that drawis to fleshly synne ffor god knowes welle it is not so mened. [146ʳ]

> [Now God forbid that any be so carnal as to think that this means to give to nature any desire that inclines toward the sins of the flesh, for God knows well that it is not meant that way.]

When she argues that "this saule no desires despite. ne pouert. ne tribulacioun. ne disese. ne masses. ne sermones. ne fastynges. ne orisouns,"[26] she again expresses sentiments that are attributed to Free Spirit heretics, that, in the words of the *Determinatio*, "Man [sic] united with God . . . is not bound to accord honor or respect to the saints, nor to observe fasts and similar things on the day of the Lord" (Vaneigem, 118). Her words, for M.N., "semes fable or erroure. or harde to vnderstande."[27]

> for I am sikyr that who so redes ouer this boke by good avisemente twies or thries and be disposed to the same felynges: they schalle undirstonde it welle ynouȝ: And þowȝ þay be nat disposed to the felynges ȝitt they schalle thynk it is alle wele I sayde: But who so takes þe naked wordes of Scriptures and leues the sentence: he in aye lyghtly erre.

[for I am certain that whoever reads this book two or three times with proper counsel and who is disposed to the same feelings shall understand it well enough. And even those who are not disposed to such feelings shall think it is all right as I explained it. But whoever takes the naked words of Scriptures and leaves the sentence errs in all.]

M.N. argues that the "nouʒted" souls in fact really do "desire for goddis sake" despite tribulation, disease, masses, sermons, fastings, and orisons. When love says that these souls don't desire masses or sermons, fastings, or orisons, we shouldn't take her to mean that they should leave these things undone: "He were to blynde that wolde take it in yᵗ wyse."[28] Rather these souls simply cannot will or desire; instead God wills or desires in them. Love's statement that annihilated souls don't desire these things provokes in him a two and one-half page commentary designed to demonstrate that the author of the text meant exactly the opposite of what her text quite plainly says.

In a purely textual reading, such diatribes might seem, and no doubt were intended as, a heavy-handed reassertion of monologic authority designed to "correct" a flawed reading and save it for orthodoxy. Such a reading approaches the text as a constative utterance, one that can only be either true or false. Yet as a monologic reading, the translation fails utterly. Even as the translator attempts to assert his control, and that of the institutional Church, over the text's statements, even as he tries to manipulate those utterances for his own purposes, because he is so clearly enamoured of the text's performative dimensions, it resists appropriation and disputes his intentions. If M.N. attempts to gloss Porete's "misty" text, that text itself glosses the translator's words. M.N.'s fascination with the text conflicts with his role as representative and guardian of Christian orthodoxy. Two voices and two accents compete within the text for supremacy, but they also clearly interanimate one another. The English *Mirror of Simple Souls* brings together in a single text the rebel and the conformist, the powerless and the powerful, the heretic and the monk, but not as two distinct individuals or actors. The actively dialogical text collapses such neat binaries, so that "the author's thought no longer oppressively dominates the other's thought, discourse loses its composure and confidence, becomes agitated, internally undecided, and two-faced" (Bakhtin, *Dostoevsky's Poetics*, 198). In this loss of composure, we can begin to imagine alternative readings of visionary texts, readings that transform dry treatises into events, and static religious devotions into dynamic performances that speak from sites not necessarily sanctioned by the institutional Church, but which nonetheless speak to us from the past with a certain elegant power.

Notes

1. Peter Dronke, *Women Writers of the Middle Ages: A Critical Study of Texts from Perpetua (c. 203) to Marguerite Porete (c. 1310)* (Cambridge: Cambridge University Press, 1984), 202.
2. For a description of the events surrounding Porete's trial and execution see Ellen L. Babinski, introduction to Marguerite Porete, *The Mirror of Simple Souls*, Ellen L. Babinski, trans. (New York: Paulist Press, 1993), 20–26.
3. Karma Lochrie, *Margery Kempe and Translations of the Flesh* (Philadelphia: University of Pennsylvania Press, 1991), 64.
4. Jacques Derrida, "Signature Event, Context," *Glyph* 1 (Baltimore: Johns Hopkins University Press, 1977), 186.
5. should perfect those devout souls that read it. (All citations to the English translation of *The Mirror of Simple Souls* will be to the British Library manuscript Additional 37790, hereafter referred to parenthetically as BL MS Add. 37790. All translations from the Middle English are my own).
6. For a critique of Austin that examines the iterability of performative language in contexts that fall outside of conventional procedures see Derrida, "Signature," and "Limited Inc. a.b.c. . . ." *Glyph* 2 (Baltimore: Johns Hopkins University Press, 1977), 162–254.
7. J. L. Austin, *How to Do Things with Words* (Cambridge: Harvard University Press, 1962), 26.
8. See the Middle English edition by Theresa Halligan, ed. *The Book of Ghostly Grace* (Toronto: Pontifical Institute, 1979). For a discussion of the ritualistic dimensions of Mechtild's visions see Laurie A. Finke, *Women's Writing in English: Medieval England*. London: Longmans, 1999.
9. Mikhail Bakhtin, "Discourse in the Novel," in *The Dialogic Imagination*, trans. Michael Holquist and Caryl Emerson (Austin: University of Texas Press, 1984); Mikhail Bakhtin, *Speech Genres and Other Late Essays*, ed. Michael Holquist and Caryl Emerson, trans. Vern W. McGee, (Austin: University of Texas, 1986), and Mikhail Bakhtin (attributed), "Discourse in Life and Discourse in Art (Concerning Sociological Poetics)," in *Freudianism: A Critical Sketch*, trans. I. R. Titunik (Bloomington: University of Indiana Press, 1976), 93–111. This last essay is signed by V. N. Vološinov but attributed by some to Bakhtin. A full discussion of the Bakhtin authorship controversy is outside the scope of this essay. Because Bakhtin had a difficult time getting his works published in Soviet Russia, at least two members of his circle, V. N. Vološinov

and P. N. Medvedev, signed their names to texts that some argue were actually written by Bakhtin. Whether or not the allegations are true, the works that bear Vološinov's and Medvedev's signatures are heavily influenced by Bakhtin and for the purposes of this essay I will treat them as one. While I do not agree with all of their conclusions, Morson and Emerson provide a useful account of the authorship controversy; see Gary Saul Morson and Caryl Emerson, *Mikhail Bakhtin: The Creation of a Prosaics* (Stanford: Stanford University Press, 1990), 104–118.

10. Jody L. H. McQuillan, "Dangerous Dialogues: The *Sottie* as Threat to Authority," in Thomas Farrell, ed., *Bakhtin and Medieval Voices* (Gainesville: University of Florida, 1995), 63; see Mikhail Bakhtin, *Problems of Dostoevsky's Poetics*, Caryl Emerson, ed. and trans. (Minneapolis: University of Minnesota Press, 1984), 19.

11. Robert Markley, *Two-Edg'd Weapons: Style and Ideology in the Comedies of Etherege, Wycherley and Congreve* (Oxford: Clarendon Press, 1988), 22–23. In "Discourse in the Novel," Bakhtin writes that "pure drama strives toward a unitary language, one that is individualized merely through dramatic personae who speak it" (405). Yet, his position is inconsistent. In the very next sentence he can acknowledge that "to a certain extent comedy is an exception to this," while, in a note on the very same page, he distinguishes between "pure classical drama . . . as the ideal extreme of the genre" and "realistic social drama [which] may, of course, be heteroglot and multi-languaged" (405, n. 62), thus opening up a space for critics like McQuillan and Markley to examine the dialogics of dramatic texts.

12. A common criticism of Bakhtinian dialogics; see Gary Saul Morson and Caryl Emerson, eds., *Rethinking Bakhtin: Extensions and Challenges* (Evanston, IL: Northwestern University Press, 1989), 173–196 and 197–223. For a discussion of this criticism see Laurie A. Finke, *Feminist Theory, Women's Writing* (Ithaca, NY: Cornell University Press, 1992), 15–18.

13. On the individualistic subjectivism of such linguists as von Humboldt, Vossler, Spitzer, and Croce see V. N Vološinov and M. M. Bakhtin, *Marxism and the Philosophy of Language*, trans. Ladislav Matejka and I. R. Titunik (Cambridge: Harvard University Press, 1973), 48–52.

14. Robert Sturges has argued that the material practices of manuscript production—the "additions, deletions, revisions, and errors that constitute *mouvance* and variance"—are as responsible for the polyphony of the medieval text as authorial intention; see "Medieval Authorship and the Polyphonic Text: From Manuscript Commentary to the Modern Novel," in Farrell, *Bakhtin and Medieval Voices*, 123.

15. As Bakhtin notes, dialogues are shaped not only by previously spoken words, but by anticipated responses as well.

16. This prologue also appears in the Latin manuscript and is appended

to the end of Babinski's translation; see Porete, *Mirror*, 221–222. We can only guess as to whether it is Porete's or a later addition designed to make a heretical text more acceptable.

17. I will retain in all my quotations the manuscript's punctuation for stylistic reasons that I hope will become clearer below. Babinski's translation makes clearer Porete's relation to her imagined readers: "I [am] a creature from the creator by whose mediation the Creator made this book of Himself for those whom I do not know nor do I desire to know, because I ought not to desire this. It is sufficient for me if it is in the secret knowledge of divine wisdom and in hope. I greet them through love of the peace of charity. . . ." (Porete, *Mirror*, 221).

18. Record of the clerks who have read this book.

19. See Raoul Vaneigem, *The Movement of the Free Spirit* (New York: Zone Books, 1994), 95–201; Vaneigem constructs just this lineage.

20. For a discussion of direct and indirect discourse see Vološinov, *Marxism*, 125–140.

21. It is of high divine matters and of high spiritual feelings and is spoken cunningly and obscurely.

22. For a discussion of the role of punctuation in religious manuscripts see Malcolm B. Parkes, *Pause and Effect: An Introduction to the History of Punctuation* (Berkeley: University of California Press, 1993), 76–80. As Parkes notes, punctuation, especially of liturgical texts, was primarily designed to serve as a guide to the text's performance.

23. For love may do anything without any misdoing.

24. The translator's continual use of the term "auditors" suggests that he imagines his audience as listening to the text rather than silently reading.

25. The annihilated soul should give to nature all that he asks without any complaining.

26. This soul has no desire for spite, nor poverty, nor tribulations, nor discomfort, nor masses, nor sermons, nor fasting, nor orisons.

27. This seems a lie or an error or hard to understand.

28. He is too blind who would take it in that way.

Bibliography

Austin, J. L. *How to Do Things with Words*. Cambridge: Harvard University Press, 1962.

Bakhtin, Mikhail. *The Dialogic Imagination*. Trans. Michael Holquist and Caryl Emerson. Austin: University of Texas Press, 1984.

———— (attributed). *Freudianism: A Critical Sketch*. Trans. I. R. Titunik. Bloomington: University of Indiana Press, 1976.

————. *Problems of Dostoevsky's Poetics*. Ed. and trans. Caryl Emerson. Minneapolis: University of Minnesota Press, 1984.

————. *Speech Genres and Other Late Essays*. Ed. Michael Holquist and Caryl Emerson. Trans. Vern W. McGee. Austin: University of Texas, 1986.

British Library manuscript Additional 37790, *The Mirror of Simple Souls*. See also MS Bodley 505, Bodleian Library.

Derrida, Jacques. "Limited, a b c." In *Glyph* 2. Baltimore: Johns Hopkins University Press, 1977.

————. "Signature Event, Context." In *Glyph* 1. Baltimore: Johns Hopkins University Press, 1977.

Dronke, Peter. *Women Writers of the Middle Ages: A Critical Study of Texts from Perpetua (c. 203) to Marguerite Porete (c. 1310)*. Cambridge: Cambridge University Press, 1984.

Farrell, Thomas, ed. *Bakhtin and Medieval Voices*. Gainesville: University of Florida, 1995.

Finke, Laurie A. *Feminist Theory, Women's Writing*. Ithaca, NY: Cornell University Press, 1991.

————. *Women's Writing in English: Medieval England*. London: Longmans, 1999.

Halligan, Theresa, ed. *The Book of Ghostly Grace*. Toronto: Pontifical Institute, 1979.

Lochrie, Karma. *Margery Kempe and Translations of the Flesh*. Philadelphia: University of Pennsylvania Press, 1991.

Markley, Robert. *Two-Edg'd Weapons: Style and Ideology in the Comedies of Etherege, Wycherley and Congreve*. Oxford: Clarendon Press, 1988.

Morson, Gary Saul, and Caryl Emerson. *Mikhail Bakhtin: The Creation of a Prosaics*. Stanford: Stanford University Press, 1990.

Morson, Gary Saul, and Caryl Emerson, eds. *Rethinking Bakhtin: Extensions and Challenges*. Evanston, IL: Northwestern University Press.

Parkes, Malcolm B. *Pause and Effect: An Introduction to the History of Punctuation*. Berkeley: University of California Press, 1993.

Porete, Marguerite. *The Mirror of Simple Souls*. Trans. Ellen L. Babinski. New York: Paulist Press, 1993.

Vaneigem, Raoul. *The Movement of the Free Spirit*. New York: Zone Books, 1994.

Vološinov, V. N. (Bakhtin, M. M.). *Marxism and the Philosophy of Language*. Trans. Ladislav Matejka and I. R. Titunik. Cambridge: Harvard University Press, 1973.

CHAPTER FOUR

Preaching and Prophesying: The Public Proclamation of Birgitta of Sweden's Revelations

Claire L. Sahlin

> May Mary diligently take heed that she opens her mouth for preaching.[1]
>
> —Birgitta of Sweden

In his classic study of ritualized speech, Maurice Bloch asserts that "the performance of religion" establishes and sustains authority. In formal religious settings, the leader's words—frequently repetitive and limited in their mode of expression—must adhere to fixed patterns in order for them to be perceived as sacred and authoritative in a ritual context. The authoritative leader who delivers a public address or intones the words of the gods abandons linguistic originality and conforms to accepted rules of formalized religious speech. Paradoxically, the religious leader asserts power by relinquishing individual expression; the ritual orator compels acceptance as a legitimate envoy of the supernatural by remaining within the bounds of acceptable patterns of speech.[2]

In this essay I will extend Bloch's insight about the performance of religion to the case of St. Birgitta (Bridget) of Sweden (1302/3–1373), a celebrated visionary who felt called by God to deliver apocalyptic messages about the imminent judgment of God. Like other authoritative religious leaders, who employ conventional patterns of speech in ritual settings, Birgitta established authority by relinquishing her personal expression. However, in her case she did not compel audiences to accept her messages simply by restricting the content and style of her speeches; rather, she usually relinquished her public speaking voice altogether. Since only ordained clergymen were conventionally recognized as legitimate religious orators, Birgitta engaged clerical supporters to proclaim/perform messages on her behalf. These men, who were invested by the church with the authority to preach, frequently functioned as her mouthpieces, using her revelations to exorcise demons and to proclaim the imminent judgment of God from church pulpits. Even when Birgitta herself occasionally faced public assemblies, clerical disciples mediated between her and her audiences by serving as interpreters and addressing crowds on her behalf. Enlisting clerical officials to "perform" her revelations in formal settings enhanced Birgitta's legitimacy and compelled acceptance of her claims to mediate the Word of God at a time when women were generally prohibited from exercising a public speaking voice, especially from the pulpit.

For Birgitta of Sweden, mystical contemplation and comminatory preaching were inextricably linked. This charismatic widow, who recorded a collection of revelations more voluminous than that of any other medieval mystic, saw preaching as a direct outgrowth of mystical rapture.[3] She believed that Christ mandates those who achieve the heights of contemplation to proclaim God's will to the world. In one passage of her *Liber celestis reuelacionum* (Celestial Book of Revelations), Christ exhorts his friends to go forth into the world like the apostles Peter and Paul, in order to share the "sweetness" of his spirit with others, instead of keeping their personal experiences of God's comfort to themselves.[4] Another passage describes the contemplative life chosen by Mary of Bethany (identified with Mary Magdalene in medieval sources) as necessarily joined with preaching.[5] Comparing the Holy Spirit to the warmth of fire, this revelation states that

> whenever a fire is lit in a closed vessel that does not have any opening, it is soon extinguished and the vessel becomes cold. So is it also

with Mary [the model of contemplation]. For if she wishes to live for nothing else but conferring honor to God, it is fitting for her that her mouth be opened and the flame of her love go forth. Her mouth, moreover, is opened, when she produces spiritual children for God by speaking from burning love. But may Mary diligently take heed that she open her mouth for preaching [predicacionis], wherever the good might be made more fervent and the bad might become better, and wherever justice can be increased and an evil custom be destroyed.[6]

Birgitta's conception of the contemplative Mary included moral exhortation, which she understood as comparable to the missionary activity of the apostle Paul.

Commanded to preach justice and repentance, Mary of Bethany symbolizes Birgitta's own vocation to proclaim God's will throughout the world. Birgitta's *Revelations* offer occasional glimpses of her intense prayer life and bodily asceticism, which culminated in experiences of intimate union with the Divine.[7] Rather than representing the goal of her religious life, however, mystical rapture inspired Birgitta to labor for the salvation of others. Understanding her mission to be founded on her experiences of spiritual grace and intimacy with God, Birgitta believed that God authorized her to speak as a prophet of moral reform.

During her lengthy career as God's messenger—from the time she was widowed in the mid-1340s until her death in 1373—she claimed to receive communications directly from Christ, the Virgin Mary, and many saints. These revelations instructed her to advise and castigate Christians throughout most of western Europe, including several popes (Clement VI, Innocent VI, Urban V, and Gregory XI), many high-ranking clerics, kings, and queens, as well as aristocratic ladies and lowly servants. In her northern homeland as well as in Rome, throughout Italy, and during her pilgrimage to the Holy Land, Birgitta sought to transform her church and society by denouncing moral corruption and exhorting Christians to rekindle their love for God.[8]

Birgitta's mandate to speak on God's behalf is ubiquitous in her books of *Revelations*. Scattered throughout the *Revelations* are numerous statements enjoining Birgitta to serve as God's mouthpiece. *Rev.* 7.27, for example, reports Jesus Christ commanding her to serve as his messenger:

Hear, O you to whom it has been given to hear and see spiritual things; and listen carefully; and in your mind beware in regard to those things that you now will hear and that *on my behalf you will announce to the nations,* lest you speak them to acquire for yourself honor or human praise. *Nor indeed are you to be silent about these things* from any fear of human reproach and contempt; for these things that you are now going to hear are not being shown to you only for your own sake. (Emphasis added.)[9]

In another passage, Mary summons her to impart what she sees and hears through the Holy Spirit, regardless of whether or not others heed her messages.[10] Repeatedly, Christ, the Virgin Mary, or other heavenly beings direct her to proclaim their words to others. The *Revelations* are replete with such hortatory statements as "Hear what I say and speak what I instruct you!" (*Rev.* 8.56.1), "Say to the bishop . . ." (*Rev.* 3.2.1), and "Through you the words of God ought to be poured forth into others" (*Rev.* 4.66.1).

While Birgitta was enjoined regularly to speak on behalf of God, her initial and most significant commission to proclaim God's word to the world occurred a few days after the death of her husband, when she was anxious about her new state in life.[11] According to accounts of this event in her *Revelations* and *vita,* the "spirit of the Lord inflamed her and enveloped her" while she was praying in her chapel [in sua capella sua]. After becoming "rapt in spirit," a voice spoke to her from a bright cloud, saying: "I am your God and I wish to speak with you." Then as Birgitta reportedly was greatly terrified, fearing that it was an "illusion of the enemy," she heard the voice saying to her again:

Do not be afraid. For I am the creator of all and am not a deceiver. *You should know that I do not speak to you for your sake alone, but for the sake of the salvation of all Christians. Therefore, hear what I say. For you shall be my bride and channel* [sponsa mea et canale], and you shall hear and see spiritual things and heavenly secrets, and my Spirit shall remain with you even to your death. Therefore, believe firmly that I am he who was born from the pure virgin, who suffered and died for the salvation of all souls, who also rose from the dead and ascended into heaven, who even now with my spirit speaks with you. (Emphasis added.)[12]

This call to serve as God's mouthpiece, which resembles the callings of prophets in the Hebrew Bible, represents the fulfillment of Birgitta's longing to be filled with the Holy Spirit and to speak the words of God like the ancient apostles and evangelists. Earlier during her childhood and marriage, she reportedly had received ecstatic visions and auditions, but these were imparted to her primarily for her own spiritual edification—to awaken her compassion for Christ's crucifixion, to encourage the dedication of her children to the Virgin Mary, to exhort her to intensify her ascetic practices, or to console her during the illness of her husband.[13] However, a surviving meditation, dating from the period of her married life, indicates her ardent desire for the gift of inspired speech: "Pray for me, apostles and evangelists and all those who were enclosed in the house on the day of Pentecost when you received the Holy Spirit, for what you felt when you received courage to speak. . . . Help me, that by your prayer the same spirit is worthy to visit my heart and come alight in it and never cease or be quenched. Then I would receive words and deeds to do and speak according to his blessed will."[14]

While calling her to serve as a vessel of revelation, God bestowed on Birgitta the title "bride" [sponsa]. This title was applied to her more frequently than any other appellation in the *Revelations*. According to various passages, her identification as "bride" signifies her exclusive devotion to Christ and wholehearted commitment to fulfilling the will of God in the world. Rather than emphasizing a passionate, mystical union between her soul and God, as bridal imagery in medieval ecstatic texts most frequently does,[15] most references to Birgitta as the bride of Christ stress her obedience to God's will and burning desire to fulfill God's work in the world.[16] In a revelation received shortly after Birgitta's initial prophetic call, Christ explains why he received her as his bride and what he expects from his marriage to her:

> I have chosen you and taken you as my bride, so that I might show my secrets to you, because it thus pleases me. And you also were justly made mine, when at the death of your husband, you assigned your will into my hands. Even at his death you thought about and asked how you could be poor for me, and you desired to forsake everything for me. And therefore you are justly made mine. And it was proper for me to care for you by virtue of such love. Therefore, I take you as my bride and into my own delight, of which kind it is proper for God to have with a chaste soul. . . .
>
> The bride ought to do the will of the bridegroom. What is my will, except that you wish to love me above all things and to desire nothing except me? . . . Now you, my bride, if you long for nothing except me and if you despise all things for me—not only children and kin, but also honors and riches—I will give you the most

precious and sweetest stipend. Not silver or gold, but I, who is the king of glory, will give you my very self as your bridegroom and reward.[17]

According to this passage and others, Birgitta becomes the bride of Christ by desiring nothing but him, conforming her own will to his, and forsaking her longings for worldly goods and her biological family. Birgitta's love for her heavenly bridegroom replaced love for her fleshly husband and superseded all attachments to her family. By becoming the bride of Christ, Birgitta abandoned her desires and determined to fulfill the will of God. Although she physically was not a virgin like many other medieval holy women who envisioned themselves as "brides" of Christ, her chaste widowhood and exclusive devotion to God accorded her privileged status as a spiritual virgin wedded to Christ.[18]

Occasionally, Birgitta's *Revelations* mention marital intercourse or a close embrace between her soul and the Divine. In one recorded instance, Christ, for example, tells Birgitta: "You will rest in the arms of my deity, where there is no carnal pleasure but joy and delight of the spirit."[19] A few passages also refer to the meeting place between her soul and God as a bed—a commonplace motif in medieval Christian mystical texts.[20] However, the *Revelations* rarely use erotic language to describe experiences of mystical union. In fact, very few passages in the entire Birgittine corpus explicitly narrate any unitive encounters between her soul and God.[21]

Instead of referring to mystical experiences, the title "bride" is used throughout the *Revelations* to denote Birgitta's obedience and submission to God. For example, *Extrav.* 62.7 states that "it is proper for the bride to obey and to humble herself to her God."[22] The *Revelations* also stress that Birgitta, as the bride of Christ, was to labor actively for the spiritual welfare of others. She—like the contemplative Mary in the revelation quoted above—was called to be fruitful for Christ by bearing "spiritual children." In a revelation exhorting Birgitta to place love for Christ above her love for her biological family, she is enjoined to produce spiritual offspring:

> You are joined in spiritual marriage. . . . You shall be fruitful from spiritual seed for the benefit of many. For just as a dry trunk begins to flower, if a twig is inserted into it, so through my grace you ought to bear fruit and flower. . . . I say to you for certain, that just as Zechariah and Elizabeth inwardly rejoiced with unspeakable joy for the future promise of a child [cf. Luke 1:14], so also will you rejoice for my grace, which I desire to do to you, and furthermore, others even

will rejoice on account of you. To those two, namely Zechariah and
Elizabeth, one angel spoke. But I, God and the creator of the angels
and your God, speaks with you. Those two produced my dearest
friend John for me. But through you I desire to produce many children
for me—not fleshly but spiritual ones.[23]

According to this passage and others, Birgitta's task was to inspire others
to become faithful sons and daughters of Christ through the divine revelation specially granted to her.[24] As Anders Piltz observes, the portrayal
of her role as Christ's bride resembles less the passionate bride of the Song
of Songs than it does the bride of John's Apocalypse, who in conjunction
with the Holy Spirit calls all who are thirsty to receive the waters of life:
"And the spirit and the bride say, 'Come.' And let everyone who hears say,
'Come.' And let everyone who is thirsty come. Let anyone who wishes
take the water of life as a gift" (Apoc. 22:17).[25]

Furthermore, Birgitta's initial prophetic call summoned her to be not
only the bride of Christ, but also the "channel" [canale] of revelation. As
"channel of the Holy Spirit" [canalis Spiritus Sancti], as she was also named
(Rev. 3.30.8), her task was to transmit living waters of salvation from God
to humanity. The Revelations indicate that Birgitta was called to function
like a conduit that transports water from one place to another, or like a
vessel that is filled with liquid and then emptied. The metaphorical liquid
that she conveyed to others represented the salvific word of God. In one
passage, for example, Christ declares to Birgitta: "My words—which you
hear from me frequently in spiritual vision—like the good drink, satisfy
those who thirst for true charity, . . . warm those who are cold, . . . gladden
those who are disturbed, . . . and heal those who are weak in soul."[26] Using
similar imagery, Mary tells her in another revelation: "Through you the
words of God ought to be poured forth into others."[27] Birgitta's use of the
image "channel" closely resembles its use by Rupert of Deutz (d. ca. 1130),
who wrote that the mouths of the prophets and apostles are like channels
through which mindfulness of Christ's Passion flows to the church.[28]

Although they are the earliest and most conspicuous titles bestowed
on her, "bride" and "channel" are not the only epithets used in the Revelations. These writings delight in devising and embellishing images for her
vocation as God's chosen medium. Some of the images are entirely conventional; others appear to be original. As God's intermediary, Birgitta is
likened to a musical instrument (Rev. 4.100; 6.31.5), a vessel of wine (Rev.
2.16), a pipe through which liquids flow during the process of making
wine (Rev. 8.48), a servant carrying precious gold for the master (Rev. 2.14),

and a daughter-in-law who carries out the wishes of her husband's aging parents (*Rev.* 6.88.6–7). Such images and many others emphasize God's use of Birgitta as an instrument of revelation.

As God's bride and channel, Birgitta saw herself as a new apostle with a vocation parallel to the preaching ministry of the earliest Christian apostles. In several recorded revelations Christ, encouraging her to persevere in her task of conveying the divine word, likened her to the early apostles and evangelists. For instance, when she was distressed that many did not favorably accept the divine words that she proclaimed, the examples of the disciples and the Gospel writers reassured her (see *Rev.* 8.48.237–238; 1.32.5). In *Rev.* 8.56 Christ informs her, "I sent my Holy Spirit to the apostles and spoke through their tongues just as even daily I speak by spiritual infusion through those whom it pleases me."[29] In *Rev.* 6.8 Christ draws the parallel between Birgitta and the apostles more directly, telling her that "just as the apostles preached to many, although not all were converted . . . so also shall it be with you. Because even if not all will hear you, nevertheless, there will be some who will be edified and healed from your words."[30] According to Christ's words, preaching—the public proclamation of the Word of God—is an essential aspect of the vocation to which Birgitta was called.

In one of her lengthiest and most spectacular revelations, Birgitta sees an immense, tricolored lectern, or pulpit (pulpitum), upon which an open book rests. There is no writing with ink in this book, which shines most brilliantly like gold; rather, each word of the book is alive and speaks by itself (*Rev.* 8.48.54–56).[31] In Birgitta's vision, this book, the eternal embodiment of divine justice and wisdom, rests symbolically on the Triune God, the lectern, and promises damnation for the unrighteous and mercy for faithful Christians. The vision interprets the book as the eternal Word of God, which visibly spoke to humanity through Jesus—the Word made flesh. The Word now speaks through Birgitta, so that "human beings . . . might hear the words that proceed from the mouth of God" (*Rev.* 8.48.236).[32] As the revelation indicates, Birgitta believed that her mission was analogous to the open, speaking book on the pulpit; she—and by extension, her book of *Revelations*—was the instrument through which the living Word of God becomes visible and resounds throughout the world.

Like other women throughout Christian history, however, Birgitta encountered formidable obstacles to exercising her religious calling to serve as an instrument of divine communication. Whereas, as Bloch's theory suggests, authoritative religious orators such as medieval preachers would have been somewhat limited by cultural expectations in the style and content of their sermons, social norms ordinarily restricted women in later medieval Europe from speaking publicly at all, especially in church or to assemblies in which men were present. Although exceptional women such as Hildegard of Bingen (d. 1179) and Rose of Viterbo (d. 1252) sometimes expounded the Word of God in public without censure, ecclesiastical legislation and theological writings generally forbade women, who were considered intellectually inferior and subordinate to men, to preach or to teach assemblies.[33] The twelfth-century *Decretum Gratiani* prohibited women from publicly addressing men, and in 1234 Pope Gregory IX banned the laity, which included women, from preaching.[34]

Because of the presence of female prophets in the Bible, ecclesiastical leaders could not deny the theoretical possibility that women could speak on God's behalf; yet from the time of the apostle Paul they attempted to regulate and limit the disclosures of divinely inspired women. In the later Middle Ages, when theologians were increasingly skeptical about women's suitability for mediating God's Word, many stressed that female recipients of the gift of prophecy should divulge their revelations only in private. Thomas Aquinas's prohibition against women's public religious speech typified the limitations placed upon women's religious speech. "Speech," he wrote, "can be used in two ways. In one way privately, to one or a few, in familiar conversation. In this way the grace of speech becomes a woman. The other way publicly, addressing oneself to the whole Church. This is not conceded to women. . . . Women if they have the grace of wisdom or of knowledge, can impart these by teaching privately but not publicly."[35] Aquinas based his statements not only on New Testament injunctions against women's authority over men (for example, 1 Tim. 2:12), but also on the widespread belief that women, lacking in wisdom, are naturally subject to men and the common fear that women might entice the minds of men to lust.

In an age of heightened skepticism about women's suitability to mediate the Word of God and proclaim it publicly to assembled audiences, patriarchal restrictions constrained Birgitta of Sweden's ability to exercise her commission to speak widely. In fact, her *Revelations* and records from her canonization proceedings indicate that she did not customarily deliver revelations orally to a public audience. She frequently imparted many messages privately to individuals in need of advice, comfort, moral guidance, or theological resolution. Many individuals, believing that she could provide powerful access to God, beseeched her to obtain specific answers from God for them. Birgitta's confessors Prior Petrus of Alvastra (d. 1390) and Master Petrus of Skänninge (d. 1378) report in her *vita* that "when any person asked her about some doubt in his conscience and sought from her advice and a special remedy that would be very good . . . after three days or so and sometimes on the very same day . . . she gave him the words that she had had from Christ or from the Blessed Virgin Mary as the response in this matter."[36]

Many examples of such revelations transmitted privately to individuals who consulted her for advice are scattered throughout the corpus of Birgitta's *Revelations*. Birgitta, for instance, prayed for answers to the grave doubts of Archbishop Bernard de Rodes of Naples (d. 1379) and offered detailed instructions—obtained in a revelation—about how he should conduct himself in his ecclesiastical office. She not only exhorted him to guard against clerical concubinage among priests under his authority, but she also told him precisely how many material possessions he should own and revealed how souls in purgatory could be consoled.[37] The archbishop had requested Birgitta to pray for resolutions to his questions, after questioning her closely about the manner in which she received visions and becoming convinced of the authenticity of her oracular abilities.[38]

Similarly, Birgitta's confessor Canon Mathias of Linköping (d. ca. 1350), who enthusiastically praised and defended the veracity of God's disclosures to Birgitta, relied on her oracular abilities to resolve questions that his academic training could not. Persuaded by her exemplary life, orthodox teachings, and miracles attributed to her revelations,[39] Mathias requested Birgitta on more than one occasion to petition God for insight into exegetical problems. While writing his highly-regarded commentary on the Book of the Apocalypse, he asked Birgitta to help him resolve the question of its authorship and the meaning of the seven thunders in Apoc. 10:3. Serving as Mathias's personal channel to God, Birgitta reportedly divulged the answers he requested, after praying to God and receiving divinely-revealed understanding.[40]

Many of Birgitta's revelations were also sent to individuals as letters. Birgitta's *vita* reports that "like the apostles . . . at God's instruction, she sent letters to the major personages of the whole of Christendom: namely, to the supreme pontiffs; to the emperors; to the kings and queens of France and of England, of Sicily and of Cyprus; to princes and princesses; to various prelates; to seculars and to religious; to kingdoms, and to lands and to cities."[41] Many of these letters, advising and admonishing individuals such as Queen Joanna I of Naples (d. 1382), Pope Gregory XI (d. 1378), and unknown masters of theology, were gathered and recorded in Birgitta's book of *Revelations*.[42]

Still other revelations—perhaps the majority—were kept hidden until they were collected and edited after her death for their widespread circulation and presentation to papal examination committees. Birgitta's *vita* reports that three years before her death, her Spanish confessor, Alfonso Pecha of Jaén (d. 1389), the chief editor of the *Revelations*, was instructed "to write down and copy the books of the revelations that had been divinely given to her and which indeed until then *had been kept secret.*" When Birgitta was dying, Christ—or Birgitta—also directed her Swedish confessors Petrus of Alvastra and Petrus of Skänninge, who assisted her in recording revelations and translating the revelations into Latin, to hand "all the secret revelations" [omnes reuelaciones secretas] over to Alfonso, so that he "might publish them to the nations for the honor and glory of God."[43]

Yet, Birgitta—like other Christian women who received calls to prophesy—employed creative strategies for gaining a wide hearing. Although she did not customarily deliver her revelations publicly, she frequently established her authority as an authentic prophet by voicing her messages through the mouths of male supporters. For example, Birgitta's clerical devotees, who relied on her for direct contact with the celestial world, served as her mouthpieces by using her words to exorcise demons. Several surviving accounts report that Birgitta received formulas of exorcism directly from Christ and the Virgin Mary, which Prior Petrus of Alvastra then used to exorcise demons in spectacular displays of the authenticity of Birgitta's revelations. The *vita* states that several Swedish demoniacs were cleansed "in the presence of two trustworthy witnesses [Master Mathias and Bishop Thomas of Växjö],[44] at the words from the mouth of the aforesaid religious [Prior Petrus]—words whose form this lady heard from Christ and which the brother said to the demon according to Christ's instruction."[45]

Book 6, chapter 34, of the *Revelations* recounts one formula, based on traditional creedal materials, that the Virgin Mary revealed to Birgitta for Petrus's use in casting out demons:

> God the Father is one with the Son and the Holy Spirit, the creator of all things and judge of those things, which were made. With his very self God sent his blessed son, into the womb of the Virgin Mary for the sake of our salvation. I command you, unclean spirit, for his glory and on account of the prayers of the Virgin Mary to withdraw from this creature of God in the name of him, Jesus Christ, born from the virgin, one God, who is the Father and the Son and the Holy Spirit.[46]

Book 6, chapter 78, narrates an incident of exorcism in much fuller dramatic detail, describing the scene in which Birgitta's revealed words were proclaimed through her confessor. It relates that Birgitta was staying one night in a certain demon-possessed house, in which the devil spoke aloud and made predictions of the future for the inhabitants. A voice spoke to Birgitta while she was praying and explained that the devil ruled the dwelling-place, since the people who previously and presently lived in the house worshipped household gods (penates) and did not listen to God's word or attend church. The voice then gave Birgitta a lengthy statement, which her confessor was to pronounce over a gathering of all the household members and their neighbors, in order for the devil to be expelled. The statement included formulas of faith (for example, "God is one and three"; "Through God all things were made and without God nothing can be done"; and "The devil is God's creature") as well as exhortations to trust in God, to renounce curious, non-Christian practices (for example, putting out milk for serpents and making offerings of bread and wine to household gods), and to accept traditional Christian teachings about the Eucharist and the other sacraments. After Birgitta's confessor—presumably Prior Petrus—uttered these pronouncements over the people, they pledged to change their ways and assented to his teachings. Then the devil immediately withdrew from the oven from which he was accustomed to speak and did not trouble anyone in the house again.[47]

Although Birgitta did not perform this exorcism directly herself, it engendered widespread amazement and awe toward her as a living conduit of divine revelation. To bystanders and others who heard reports, the public spectacle dramatically exhibited the veracity and efficacy of Birgitta's revelations. Interpreted as proof of Birgitta's authenticity, the exorcism helped to attract numerous lay and clerical disciples to Birgitta.[48] In addition, the manner in which the exorcism was conducted also exemplified the gender-conditioned partnerships in which Birgitta worked. Hand-in-hand with clerics, she labored to restore her audience to right belief and proper Christian devotion without transgressing gender norms. Behind the scenes, while Birgitta prayed alone, she received the Word of God, while religious men—the visible actors—pronounced it over the people.

Similarly, priests sometimes preached her messages of divine judgment from church pulpits. Testimonies on behalf of her canonization mention that in many parishes of Sweden, priests threatened their congregations with Birgitta's predictions of imminent famine, plagues, and widespread death. Petrus Johannis, a priest from Norrköping, for example, relates that "prior to the Jubilee Year [1350], when the . . . kingdom [Sweden] and all its inhabitants were taking pleasure in peace and prosperity, it was preached before the people in many parish churches that the blessed Birgitta prophesied and predicted great tribulations, namely persecution, hunger, destruction, and pestilence, in the near future in the said kingdom of Sweden," unless the people turned from their sins.[49] Alfonso Pecha also reports that a theologian preached one of her revelations in the cathedral of Naples. He states that the master of theology delivered her message of God's judgment to the entire population of Naples, which had been called by the queen and the archbishop to attend.[50]

Remarks in Birgitta's *Revelations* and other sources even suggest that she at least occasionally intended preachers to proclaim her revelations from the pulpit and also arranged for them to do so. For instance, at the conclusion of one revelation, Christ tells her that "the revelation is completed, when it is spoken from the pulpit."[51] Another revelation addressed to priests belonging to the religious order that she founded—the *Ordo Sanctissimi Salvatoris*, commonly known as the Birgittine or Bridgettine Order—instructs them to preach not only from the Bible, the lives of the Fathers, and other traditional material, but also from her *Revelations*.[52] Two surviving letters to Pope Urban VI from leading clerics and politicians of Sweden state that "she predicted and *caused to be preached publicly* the terrible evils that were to befall the kingdom of Sweden.[53] In fact, as several scholars have observed, her recorded revelations frequently employ rhetorical techniques—similitudes, *exempla*, numerical divisions—that are characteristic of later medieval sermons.[54] By enlisting priests to preach her revelations, Birgitta could ensure that her revelations would gain a hearing; the traditional authority of the priesthood and the pulpit lent credence to the words that were mediated through her and increased the likelihood of their acceptance among the populace.

Although surviving sources do not disclose exactly how she was able to engage priests to preach her revelations, it is likely that her strong familial ties to the Swedish ecclesiastical hierarchy were beneficial. More significantly, Birgitta's visions received formal approbation from an assembly of Swedish bishops, which must have paved the way for her revelations to be proclaimed by Swedish priests from their pulpits. Fearing delusion, desiring to dispel the criticisms of others, and driven to broadcast the revelations widely, Birgitta had turned her early revelations over to the scrutiny of Swedish bishops and theologians. After analyzing her revelations and conferring with each other, the Swedish ecclesiastical examiners verified that "all [the revelations] had been revealed to [Birgitta] . . . from heaven by the good spirit of truth and light by the special grace of the Holy Spirit."[55] This official stamp of approval is likely to have attracted enthusiastic followers to her message and certainly provided the sanction she needed to enlist clerics to serve as her voices in the pulpit.

Toward the end of her life, when the intensity of her messages increased, Birgitta's proclamations became bolder and can be characterized as public preaching, in the sense that she faced large gatherings and exhorted them on behalf of God. Canonization documents indicate that at least one of her ardent devotees, Magnus Petri (d. 1396), even identified her proclamations as preaching. His testimony states that "he . . . heard the lady Birgitta divulge, declare, and *preach* [predicare] judgments and tribulations, particularly in the kingdom of Cyprus and in Naples as well as in many other places."[56] Other depositions by eyewitnesses report that on the island of Cyprus, she addressed the kingdom's rulers on two separate occasions, warning them of God's impending punishment for their sins.[57] Reportedly speaking in the name of Christ, Birgitta harshly proclaimed:

> O people of Cyprus, my adversary, listen and be diligently attentive to what I say to you! . . . O people of Cyprus, I now announce to you that if you will not correct yourself and amend your life, then I shall so destroy your generation and the progeny in the kingdom of Cyprus that I shall spare neither the poor person nor the rich. Indeed, I shall so destroy this same generation of yours that in a short time, your memory will thus slip away from the hearts of human beings as if you had never been born in this world. . . . Nevertheless, know for a certainty that if any one of you wills to correct himself, amend his life, and humbly turn back to me, then like a loving shepherd, I shall joyfully run out to meet him, lifting him onto my shoulders and personally carrying him back to my sheep.[58]

Still, her confessor Alfonso mediated between her and the Cypriots, serving as her interpreter (interpres), presumably because her audience spoke mostly Greek or could not understand her Latin spoken with a Swedish accent.[59] Alfonso's translation functioned, in effect, to minimize and sanction Birgitta's transgression of the standard prohibitions against women's public speech.

Moreover, testimonies for her canonization indicate that she disclosed a terrifying prediction of divine wrath to a large assembly in Naples, which was specially gathered to hear it. Prior to this convocation, Birgitta had received ecclesiastical approval for her visions by leading figures in Naples: the archbishop, a Dominican inquisitor, theologians, and other distinguished characters.[60] Her prophecy to the Neapolitan people, which Christ reportedly revealed directly to Birgitta, foretold God's damnation of recalcitrant sinners:

> I am the Creator of all and Lord over the devils as well as over all the angels, and no one will escape my judgment. . . . What are those human beings who are my enemies doing to me now? In truth, they have contempt for my precepts; they chase me out of their hearts like a loathsome poison; indeed, they spit me out of their mouths like something rotten; and they abhor the sight of me as if I were a leper with the worst of stenches. But the devil and his works they embrace in their every affection and deed. For they bring him into their hearts, doing his will with delight and gladness and following his evil suggestions. Therefore, by my just judgment they shall have their reward in hell with the devil eternally without end.[61]

This time, however, Birgitta was silent while Alfonso read the revelation aloud to the crowd, which included Archbishop Bernard of Naples, several masters of theology, canon lawyers, religious men, and notable laymen and women. When he was finished, Birgitta handed a written copy of the revelation over to the people and responded to the archbishop's interrogations about her manner of receiving visions from God. The sources state that Birgitta described her visionary experiences with her own mouth as Archbishop Bernard had requested.[62] Several spectators observed that she showed remarkably little fear during the examination, even though, as Alfonso, points out, she "realistically could have feared death or imprisonment or other tribulations."[63]

These vignettes from the *Revelations* and canonization documents thus indicate that Birgitta pushed the limits of women's normative behavior by occasionally exhorting assemblies of political and ecclesiastical leaders. She also sometimes enlisted clerics to use her words to drive out demons and to serve as her mouthpieces in church pulpits, although she herself never preached in that venue. To fulfill her mission as a prophet of moral reform, Birgitta often walked and sometimes slightly overstepped the thin line drawn between public address and moral instruction. However, the mediation and sanction of clerics, who addressed audiences on her behalf and sometimes ordered her to speak directly, tempered the impropriety of her occasional—and rather dramatic—public proclamations.

Paradoxically, Birgitta's authority as an authentic spokesperson for
God was never greater than when she relinquished her public speaking
voice. As Maurice Bloch observed, religious orators who are accepted as
legitimate generally exercise conformity to culturally acceptable patterns
of speech. Illustrating this insight, Catherine Bell notes that an invited
speaker's decorous sermon to a specially-assembled audience is more likely
to elicit positive responses in our society than the informal, unconventional
oratory of a street preacher who preaches damnation to pedestrians on a
city corner.[64] For Birgitta, as for many other female prophets in the Christian tradition, this observation does not simply mean that her speech was
required to conform to a prescribed, formal oratorical style; rather, it
meant that she could not even do the speaking herself, if her messages
were to be taken seriously. As far as we know, Birgitta never directly
challenged prescriptions against women's public speech even while she was
undeterred by the limitations placed upon her activities. Instead, she cir-
cumvented the prohibitions through legitimate means; by relinquishing her
public speaking voice, Birgitta's voice of prophecy could resound loudly
through her willing and faithful mouthpieces.

Notes

1. Diligenter attendat Maria, quod ibi aperiat os predicacionis sue. Birgitta
    of Sweden, *Revelaciones, Book 6*, ed. Birger Bergh, SFSS, ser. 2, Latinska
    skrifter 7:6 (Stockholm: Almqvist and Wiksell International, 1991),
    chapter 65, verse 54.
        Portions of this essay appeared previously in Claire L. Sahlin, "The
    Prophetess as Preacher: Birgitta of Sweden and the Voice of Prophecy,"
    Medieval Sermon Studies 40 (Autumn 1997): 29–44; and Claire L. Sahlin,
    "Birgitta of Sweden and the Voice of Prophecy: A Study of Gender
    and Prophetic Authority in the Later Middle Ages" (Ph.D diss., Har-
    vard University, 1996).
2. Maurice Bloch, "Symbols, Song, Dance and Features of Articulation: Is
    Religion a Form of Traditional Authority?" *Archives europeénes de sociologie*
    15 (1974): 55–81.
3. With the assistance of no less than four confessors, Birgitta of Sweden
    recorded more than seven hundred revelations, which circulated widely
    throughout Western Europe in Latin and vernacular languages until
    well into the seventeenth century. Over two hundred Latin manu-
    scripts of her *Liber celestis reuelacionum* can be found today in European
    and North American libraries. My examination of Birgitta's *Revelations*
    is based on the following editions: *Revelaciones, Book 1 with Magister Ma-
    thias' Prologue*, ed. Carl-Gustaf Undhagen, SFSS, ser. 2, Latinska skrifter
    7:1 (Uppsala: Almqvist and Wiksell, 1978); *Revelaciones, Book 3*, ed. Ann-

Mari Jönsson, SFSS, ser. 2, Latinska skrifter 7:3 (Uppsala: Almqvist and Wiksell Tryckeri, 1998); *Revelaciones, Book 4*, ed. Hans Aili, SFSS, ser. 2, Latinska skrifter 7:4 (Göteborg: Graphic Systems, 1992); *Revelaciones, Book 5, Liber Questionum*, ed. Birger Bergh, SFSS, ser. 2, Latinska skrifter 7:5 (Uppsala: Almqvist and Wiksells Boktryckeri, 1971); *Revelaciones, Book 6*, ed. Birger Bergh, SFSS, ser. 2, Latinska skrifter 7:6 (Stockholm: Almqvist and Wiksell International, 1991); *Revelaciones, Book 7*, ed. Birger Bergh, SFSS, ser. 2, Latinska skrifter 7:7 (Uppsala: Almqvist and Wiksells Boktryckeri, 1967); *Revelaciones Extravagantes*, ed. Lennart Hollman, SFSS, ser. 2, Latinska skrifter 5 (Uppsala: Almqvist and Wiksells Boktryckeri, 1956); *Opera minora*, vol. 1, *Regula Saluatoris*, ed. Sten Eklund., SFSS, ser. 2, Latinska skrifter 8:1 (Lund: Berlingska Boktryckeriet, 1975); *Opera minora*, vol. 2, *Sermo Angelicus*, ed. Sten Eklund, SFSS, ser. 2, Latinska skrifter 8:2 (Uppsala: Almqvist and Wiksells Boktryckeri, 1972); *Opera minora*, vol. 3, *Quattuor Oraciones*, ed. Sten Eklund, SFSS, ser. 2, Latinska skrifter 8:3 (Stockholm: Almqvist and Wiksell International, 1991). For Books 2 and 8, whose critical editions have not yet been completed, I make use of the Latin texts on computer diskettes provided by Professor Birger Bergh of Lund University's Department of Classical Languages. These texts, while corrected for some obvious errors, are based on the first printed edition, *Revelationes S. Birgitte* (Lübeck: Bartholomeus Ghotan, 1492). References to Birgitta's *Revelations* will be made to the book, chapter, and sometimes verse numbers of the Latin texts. English translations from Latin are mine, unless indicated otherwise.

4. *Rev.* 2.14.61–64, 74; cf. *Rev.* 4.128.

5. See Luke 10:38–42. Birgitta's understanding of Mary Magdalene as both an exemplar of contemplation and a model of preaching accords with the portrayal of Mary Magdalene in Jacobus de Voragine's *The Golden Legend*. For analysis of medieval interpretations of the story of Mary and Martha, see Giles Constable, *Three Studies in Medieval Religious and Social Thought: The Interpretation of Mary and Martha, the Ideal of the Imitation of Christ, the Orders of Society* (Cambridge: Cambridge University Press, 1995), 3–141.

6. *Rev.* 6.65.52–54: . . . vbi ignis accensus est in vase clauso non habens exitum, cicius extinguitur et vas frigescit. Sic est et cum Maria. Si enim ipsa ad nichil aliud velit viuere, nisi vt possit facere honorem Deo, expedit ei, vt os eius aperiatur et flamma caritatis eius egrediatur. Tunc autem aperitur os, quando ex feruenti caritate loquendo filios spirituales Deo generat. Sed diligenter attendat Maria, quod ibi aperiat os predicacionis sue, vbi boni fiant feruenciores et mali efficiantur meliores, vbi iusticia possit augeri et praua consuetudo aboleri.

7. See, for example, *Rev.* 6.88.

8. Accounts of Birgitta's activities and thought in non-Scandinavian languages include the following: Ingvar Fogelqvist, *Apostasy and Reform in*

the Revelations of St. Birgitta, Bibliotheca Theologiae Practicae 51 (Stockholm: Almqvist and Wiksell International, 1993); Tore Nyberg, "Birgitta/Birgittenordern," in Theologische Realenzyklopaedie, 2nd ed., vol. 6 (New York: Walter de Gruyter, 1980), 648–652; Barbara Obrist, "The Swedish Visionary: Saint Bridget," in Katharina M. Wilson, ed., Medieval Women Writers (Athens, GA: University of Georgia Press, 1984), 227–251; Claire L. Sahlin, "Gender and Prophetic Authority in Birgitta of Sweden's Revelations," in Jane Chance, ed., Gender and Text in the Later Middle Ages (Gainesville: University Press of Florida, 1996); James Hogg, ed., Studies in St. Birgitta and the Brigittine Order, 2 vols., Analecta Cartusiana 35:19 (Lewiston, NY: Edwin Mellen Press, 1993); and Saint Bridget: Prophetess of New Ages, Proceedings of the International Study Meeting, Rome, October 3–7, 1991 (Santa Brigida: Profeta dei tempi nuovi, Atti dell'incontro internazionale di studio, Roma, 3–7 ottobre 1991) (Rome: Tipografia Vaticana, 1993).

9. Rev. 7.27.2–3: Audi tu, cui datam est audire et videre spiritualia, et attende diligenter et in mente tua caue, quod ea, que modo audies, que tu ex parte mea annunciabis gentibus, non loquaris ea pro acquirendo tibi honorem aut humanam laudem. Nec eciam ea sileas propter aliquem timorem humani improperii et contemptus, quia non propter te tantum, sed eciam propter preces amicorum meorum hec tibi ostenduntur, que modo es auditura; based on the translation by Albert Ryle Kezel in Birgitta of Sweden: Life and Selected Revelations, ed. Marguerite Tjader Harris, trans. Albert Ryle Kezel (New York: Paulist Press, 1990), 207–208.

10. Rev. 8.56.100–101.

11. Cross-cultural observations of prophets, mediums, and other intermediaries between the divine and human realms indicate that individuals often assume their vocations when they are uncertain about their social roles or are experiencing a life crisis. For Birgitta—as for many other Christian women of the Middle Ages who assumed religious vocations—widowhood provided the opportunity to dedicate herself to a heavenly bridegroom. Widowhood also signified the authenticity of her calling; from early Christian times, sexual purity—usually virginity or chaste widowhood—was regarded as a precondition for the acceptance of women as legitimate prophets. See Robert R. Wilson, Prophecy and Society in Ancient Israel (Philadelphia: Fortress Press, 1980), 47–48; I. M. Lewis, Ecstatic Religion: A Study of Shamanism and Spirit Possession (1971; reprint 2nd ed., New York: Routledge, 1989), 71–77; Clarissa W. Atkinson, The Oldest Vocation: Christian Motherhood in the Middle Ages (Ithaca, NY: Cornell University Press, 1991), passim; and Karen King, "Prophetic Power and Women's Authority: The Case of the Gospel of Mary (Magdalene)," in Women Preachers and Prophets through Two Millennia of Christianity, ed. Beverly Mayne Kienzle and Pamela J. Walker (Berkeley: University of California Press, 1998), 28–31.

12. *Extrav.* 47: Transactis aliquibus diebus post mortem mariti, cum beata Birgitta sollicita esset de statu suo, circumfudit eam spiritus Domini ipsam inflammans. Raptaque in spiritu vidit nubem lucidam, et de nube audiuit vocem dicentem sibi: "Ego sum Deus tuus, qui tecum loqui volo." Conterrita illa, ne forte hostis esset illusio, audiuit iterum: "Noli timere. Ego enim sum omnium conditor, non deceptor. Scias, quia non loquor propter te solam sed propter salutem omnium Christianorum. Audi igitur, que loquor. Tu quippe eris sponsa mea et canale meum, audies et videbis spiritualia et secreta celestia, et spiritus meus remanebit tecum vsque ad mortem. Crede igitur firmiter, quia ego ipse sum, qui de pura virgine natus, qui passus et mortuus sum pro salute omnium animarum. Qui et resurrexi a mortuis et ascendi in celum, qui et nunc cum spiritu meo loquor tecum." Cf. *Acta et processus canonizacionis beate Birgitte* (hereafter abbreviated *AP*), ed. I. Collijn, SFSS, ser. 2, Latinska skrifter 1 (Uppsala: Almqvist and Wiksells Boktryckeri, 1924–31), 80–81 (*Vita b. Brigide prioris Petri et magistri Petri*).

13. See, for example, *AP*, 76, 79, 80 (*Vita b. Brigide prioris Petri et magistri Petri*); *Extrav.* 53; and *Extrav.* 92.

14. Bidhin for mik appostoli oc ewangeliste oc alle the ther jnnelukte j the huseno varin a pingizdagha dagh tha j tha kändin tha j fingin thwru at tala. . . . hiälpin mik til, at for idhra bön then sami ande värdhoghas mit hiärta sökia ok sik siäluan i thy tända oc aldre aflata älla släkkia. Tha finge jak ordh ok gerninga til at göra oc tala äptir hans signadha vilia. I thank Bridget Morris for calling my attention to this meditation and for providing me with her translation from *Heliga Birgittas Uppenbarelser* (St. Birgitta's Revelations), ed. G. E. Klemming, SFSS 14 (Stockholm: Almqvist and Wiksell, 1857–1884), vol. 2: *Rev.* 4.144, 263, lines 2–11. On the basis of internal and linguistic evidence, Dr. Morris argues that the meditations can be dated to a time prior to the death of Birgitta's husband and her calling vision; "Four Birgittine Meditations in Medieval Swedish," *Birgittiana* 1, no. 2 (1996).

15. See Jeffrey Hamburger, *The Rothschild Canticles: Art and Mysticism in Flanders and the Rhineland Circa 1300* (New Haven: Yale University Press, 1990), 105–117; Bernard McGinn, *The Growth of Mysticism: Gregory the Great through the Twelfth Century*, vol. 2 of *The Presence of God: A History of Christian Mysticism*, (New York: Crossroad, 1994), 158–224; E. Ann Matter, *The Voice of My Beloved: The Song of Songs in Western Medieval Christianity* (Philadelphia: University of Pennsylvania Press, 1990); Wolfgang Riehle, *The Middle English Mystics*, trans. Bernard Standring (London: Routledge and Kegan Paul, 1981), 34–55; and Denys Turner, *Eros and Allegory: Medieval Exegesis of the Song of Songs*, Cistercian Studies Series 156 (Kalamazoo: Cistercian Publications, 1995).

16. On bridal imagery in the *Revelations*, see Peter Dinzelbacher, "Die hl. Birgitta und die Mystik ihrer Zeit," in *Saint Bridget: Prophetess of New Ages*, 267–302; Birgit Klockars, "S. Birgitta and Mysticism," in Hogg, ed.,

Studies in St. Birgitta and the Brigittine Order, vol. 1, 296–305; and K. B. Westman, *Birgitta-studier,* 1 (Uppsala: Akademiska Boktryckeriet, 1911), 116–129.

17. *Rev.* 1.2.3–4, 7–8: Ego elegi te et assumpsi te michi in sponsam, ut ostendam tibi secreta mea, quia michi sic placet. Tu eciam quodam iure facta es mea, cum in morte mariti tui voluntatem tuam in manus meas assignasti, cum eciam eo defuncto cogitasti et rogasti, quomodo pauper pro me esse posses, et voluisti omnia pro me relinquere. Et ideo de iure facta es mea. Et oportuit me pro tanta caritate tibi prouidere. Propterea assumo te michi in sponsam et in meam propriam delectacionem, qualem Deum decet habere cum anima casta. . . . Sponsa debet eciam facere voluntatem sponsi. Que est voluntas mea, nisi quod velis diligere me super omnia, nichil velle aliud nisi me? . . . Tu autem, sponsa mea, si nichil nisi me desideraueris, si omnia pro me contempseris, non solum filios et parentes, sed eciam honores et diuicias, ego dabo tibi stipendium preciosissimum et dulcissimum. Non aurum et argentum sed me ipsum dabo tibi in sponsum et premium, qui sum rex glorie.

18. The case of Birgitta illustrates Clarissa Atkinson's observation that between the thirteenth and the fifteenth centuries holiness was increasingly perceived to be compatible with chaste marriage and widowhood. See Clarissa W. Atkinson, *The Oldest Vocation: Christian Motherhood in the Middle Ages* (Ithaca, NY: Cornell University Press, 1991), chap. 5; and Clarissa W. Atkinson, *Mystic and Pilgrim: The Book and the World of Margery Kempe* (Ithaca, NY: Cornell University Press, 1983). See also Barbara Newman, *From Virile Woman to WomanChrist: Studies in Medieval Religion and Literature* (Philadelphia: University of Pennsylvania Press, 1995), 28–32.

19. *Rev.* 1.1.12: Requiesces in brachiis deitatis mee, ubi nulla voluptas carnis sed gaudium et delectacio spiritus.

20. Riehle, *Middle English Mystics,* 38. In *Rev.* 1.30.9 Christ addresses the bride: "In your heart, which is my dwelling-place, ought to be . . . a bed on which we may rest" (In corde, quod est habitaculum meum, debent esse . . . lectus, in quo requiescamus).

21. Dinzelbacher, "Die hl. Birgitta," 293; Westman, *Birgitta-studier,* 118–119.

22. *Extrav.* 62.7: Decet sponsam obedire et humiliare se Deo suo.

23. *Rev.* 1.20.10–12: Coniugio spirituali copulata es. . . . Eris enim fructifera semine spirituali multis profuturo. Sicut enim, surculus si inseritur trunco arido, truncus incipit florere, sic gracia mea fructificare et florere debes. . . . Dico tibi pro certo, quod sicut Zacharias et Elizabeth ineffabili gaudio gaudebant interius de promissione prolis future, sic et tu gaudebis de gracia mea, quam tibi facere volo, et insuper et elii gaudebunt per te. Illis duobus, scilicet Zacharie et Elizabeth, loquebatur unus angelus, ego autem, Deus et creator angelorum et Deus tuus, loquor tecum. Illi duo genuerunt michi amicum meum carissimum Io-

hannem, et ego per te volo generare michi multos filios, non carnales sed spirituales.

24. Some medieval clerics similarly understood effective preaching to produce spiritual sons. See John H. Van Engen, *Rupert of Deutz* (Berkeley: University of California Press, 1983), 272.

25. Anders Piltz, "Uppenbarelserna och uppenbarelsen: Birgittas förhållande till Bibeln," ed. Tore Nyberg, *Birgitta, hendes værk och hendes klostre i Norden*, Odense University Studies in History and Social Sciences 150 (Odense: Odense University Press, 1991), 451. In this regard Birgitta may have been heavily influenced by her confessor Mathias, who wrote and discussed his commentary on the Apocalypse with her around the same time that she received her early revelations. See *Rev.* 6.89; *Rev.* 6.110; and Ann-Marie Billing-Ottosson, "Magister Mathias' apokalypskommentar: Edition av kap. 1 och 2 med inledande anmärkningar, handskriftsklassificering och kommentar till texten" (Master's thesis, Uppsala University, 1960).

26. *Rev.5. rev.* 11.10: Verba mea, que tu in spirituali visione frequenter a me audis, saciant bonus potus sicientes veram caritatem; . . . calefaciunt frigidos, . . . turbatos letificant . . . debiles in anima sanant.

27. *Rev.* 4.66.1: Per te verba Dei diffundi debent in alios.

28. Anders Piltz, "Revelation and the Human Agent: St. Birgitta and the Process of Inspiration" (unpublished manuscript), 5; Rupert of Deutz, *Liber de divinis officiis* 5.1, ed. Hrabanus Haacke, *Corpus Christianorum, Continuatio Mediaevalis* 7 (Turnholt: Brepols, 1967), 147.

29. *Rev.* 8.56. 38: Ego eciam misi spiritum sanctum apostolis et loquebar per linguas eorum sicut et quotidie, quibus michi placet, infusione spirituali loquor.

30. *Rev.* 6.8.6: Sicut enim apostoli multis predicabant, quamuis non omnes conuertebantur . . . , sic erit et tibi, quia et si non omnes audierint te, erunt tamen aliqui, qui ex verbis tuis edificentur et sanentur.

31. *Rev.* 8.48.55: "Post hec autem in ipso pulpito vidi librum resplendentem quasi aurum fulgentissimum et habentem formam libri. Qui quidem liber apertus erat et scriptura eius non erat scripta atramento sed vnumquodque verbum in libro erat viuens et se ipsum loquebatur.

32. *Rev.* 8.48.236: . . . quod homines . . . audirent verba, que procedunt de ore dei.

33. For a nuanced treatment of female preaching in the Middle Ages, see Alcuin Blamires, "Women and Preaching in Medieval Orthodoxy, Heresy, and Saints' Lives," *Viator: Medieval and Renaissance Studies* 26 (1995): 135–152. See also Carolyn Muessig, "Prophecy and Song: Teaching and Preaching by Medieval Women," 146–148; and Darleen Pryds, "Proclaiming Sanctity through Proscribed Acts: The Case of Rose of Viterbo," 159–172, in Beverly Mayne Kienzle and Pamela J. Walker, eds., *Women Preachers and Prophets Through Two Millennia of Christianity* (Berkeley, CA: University of California Press, 1998).

34. Nicole Bériou, "The Right of Women to Give Religious Instruction in the Thirteenth Century," in Beverly Mayne Kienzle and Pamela J. Walker, eds., *Women Preachers and Prophets*, 137–139.

35. Thomas Aquinas, *Summa theologiae*, vol. 45, ed. and trans. Roland Potter, *Prophecy and Other Charisms*, 133: 2a, 2a, q. 177, art. 2 (New York: Blackfriars in conjunction with McGraw-Hill, 1970), 133.

36. *AP*, 84: Quando aliqua persona requirebat eam de aliquo dubio consciencie sue petens ab ea consilium et remedium optimum speciale . . . post tres . . . dies uel aliquos dies et aliquando eadem die . . . dabat ei verba, que habuerat a Christo uel a beata virgine maria, responsura ad illam materiam; translated by Kezel, in *Birgitta of Sweden*, 81.

37. See *Rev.* 7.12.

38. *AP*, 265–66, 325, 373–74, 518, 562–63.

39. See Mathias of Linköping, *Prologus magistri Mathie*, in *Revelaciones*, Book 1, 229–240.

40. *Rev.* 6.89, 110. For another example of Birgitta's private revelations to individual clerics, see *Rev.* 7.7–8 (to an unnamed Franciscan friar). For discussion of the significance of saintly women to Dominican and Franciscan friars in the later Middle Ages, see John Coakley, "Friars as Confidants of Holy Women in Medieval Dominican Hagiography," in *Images of Sainthood in Medieval Europe*, ed. Renate Blumenfeld-Kosinski and Timea Szell (Ithaca, NY: Cornell University Press, 1991), 222–46; John Coakley, "Gender and the Authority of Friars: The Significance of Holy Women for Thirteenth-Century Franciscans and Dominicans," *Church History* 60 (1991): 445–60; and John Coakley, "Friars, Sanctity, and Gender: Mendicant Encounters with Saints, 1250–1325," in *Medieval Masculinities: Regarding Men in the Middle Ages*, ed. Clare A. Lees with the assistance of Thelma Fenster and Jo Ann McNamara, Medieval Cultures 7 (Minneapolis: University of Minnesota Press, 1994), 91–110.

41. *AP*, 86: Sicut apostoli . . . ex precepto Dei epistolas ad tocius christianitatis maiores personas, videlicet ad summos pontifices, ad jmperatores et reges et reginas Francie et Anglie, Cecilie et Cipri, ad principes et principissas, ad prelatos diuersos et ad seculares et religiosos et regna et terras ac ciuitates transmittebat; translated by Kezel, in *Birgitta of Sweden*, 83.

42. For examples of revelations sent to individuals in writing, see *Rev.* 7.11 (to Queen Joanna); *Rev.* 7.18 (to the king of Cyprus and the prince of Antioch); *Rev.* 7.28 (to Archbishop Bernard of Naples); and *Rev.* 4.139–140, 142–143 (to Pope Gregory XI). See also *Rev.* 3.8–9 (to an unknown master), which is examined by Ann-Mari Jönsson in Excursus B of her edition of *Revelaciones*, *Book III*.

43. *AP*, 98: . . . ipse scriberet et copiaret libros reuelacionum, que sibi date fuerant diuinitus, que quidem reuelaciones vsque tunc secrete tenebantur. . . . Quod in morte eiusdem domine Christus confirmauit preci-

piens eidem domine Brigide, quod ipsa diceret suis confessoribus, vt ipsi traderent dicto heremite [Alfonso] omnes reuelaciones secretas . . . , vt idem heremita eas . . . ad honorem et gloriam gentibus publicaret; translated by Kezel, in *Birgitta of Sweden*, 95.

44. *AP*, 539.

45. *AP*, 90: . . . presentibus duobus fidedignis testibus ad verba oris predicti religiosi, quorum formam hec domina a Christo audiuit et frater secundum Christi preceptum ad demonem dixit.

46. *Rev.* 6.34.20–21: Deus Pater, qui est cum Filio et Spiritu Sancto creator omnium rerum et iudex eorum que facta sunt, qui misit benedictum filium suum cum se ipso in viscera virginis Marie propter nostram salutem, precipio tibi, immunde spiritus, vt ad gloriam eius et propter preces Marie virginis exeas ab ista creatura Dei in nomine eius, qui natus est de virgine Ihesus Christus vnus Deus, qui est Pater et Filius et Spiritus Sanctus.

47. On the "spectacle" of exorcism in the later middle ages, see Nancy Caciola, "Discerning Spirits: Sanctity and Possession in the Later Middle Ages" (Ph.D. diss., University of Michigan, 1994).

48. See Mathias of Linköping, *Prologus magistri Mathie*, in *Revelaciones, Book 1*, 239.

49. *AP*, 460: . . . predicabatur coram populo in multis parrochialibus ecclesijs ante pace gaudebant et prosperitate, quod beata Brigida prophetauerat et predixerat magnas tribulaciones, scilicet persecucionem, famem, stragem, et pestulencias in proximo futuras super dictum regnum Swecie. Cf. *AP*, 466 (deposition of Johannis Petri of Leksberg).

50. Alfonso of Jaén, *Epistola solitarii ad reges* 6.12: . . . immo quedam reuelacio . . . per vnum dictorum magistrorum ex precepto domine regine et archiepiscopi coram toto populo ciuitatis ad hoc vocato specialiter fuerit in ecclesia cathedrali publicata et solempniter predicata; in Arne Jönsson, ed., *Alfonso of Jaén: His Life and Works with Critical Editions of the "Epistola Solitarii," the "Informaciones" and the "Epistola Serui Christi,"* Studia Graeca et Latina Lundensia 1 (Lund: Lund University Press, 1989), 153.

51. *Rev.* 4.32, *declaracio* 8: Et ista reuelacio completa est, ubi loquitur de pulpito.

52. *Extrav.* 23.3: Ideo, si est dominica, predicantes in ista religione proponant euangelium diei et eius exposiciones, Bibliam et *ista verba mea et dilecte matris mee sanctorumque meorum*, Vitas patrum et miracula sanctorum, simbolum fidei, remedia quoque contra temptaciones et vicia secundum vniuscuiusque capacitatem. Recent studies of extant sermons from Vadstena Abbey (the mother house of the Birgittine Order) indicate the brothers' preaching displayed extremely high regard for the authority of the *Revelations*. Dr. Monica Hedlund finds that "the Revelations are cited in the Vadstena sermons in an extraordinarily authoritative manner, almost on the same level as the Bible and in any case as the church

fathers. . . . The Revelations *are* quite simply the words of God." Monica Hedlund, "Vadstenapredikanter om Birgitta," in *Heliga Birgitta—budskapet och förebilden: Föredrag vid jubileumssymposiet i Vadstena 3–7 oktober 1991,* ed. Alf Härdelin and Mereth Lindgren, Kungl. Vitterhets Historie och Antikvitets Akademien, Konferenser 28 (Stockholm: Almqvist and Wiksell International, 1993), 321.

53. *AP,* 58: . . . predixit et publice predicari fecit . . .; the same remark is made in *AP,* 60.

54. Bengt Strömberg, *Magister Mathias och Fransk Mendikantpredikan,* Samlingar och studier till Svenska kyrkans historia 9 (Stockholm: Svenska Kyrkans Diakonistyrelse, 1944), 163–78; Eva Odelman, "Uppenbarelsernas retorik," in *Heliga Birgitta—budskapet och förebilden,* 15–21; and Undhagen, "General Introduction," in *Revalaciones, Book 1,* 20.

55. *RS* π-text 1.8–10: Que . . . archiepiscopo Vpsalensi vna cum alias tribus episcopis et cuidam magistro deuotissimo, qui magnus theologus habebatur, atque vni abbati Deo deuoto et valde religioso eadem persona cum magna reuerencia et timore Dei humiliter propalauit timens illud sub specie angeli lucis ab illusore angelo tenebrarum. Et hii omnes et multi amici Dei hec audientes et super hoc . . . adinvicem conferentes, diuinitus a spiritu bono veritatis et lucis ex speciali Spiritus Sancti gracia omnia eidem persone reuelata fuisse comprobarunt. The key ecclesiastical examiners of Birgitta's revelations in Sweden were likely to have been Archbishop Hemming Nilsson of Uppsala, Bishop Hemming of Åbo, Bishop Thomas Johansson of Växjö, and Bishop Petrus Tyrgilsson of Linköping, along with Master Mathias and Prior Petrus. Their meeting probably took place in Uppsala in the spring of 1346. See Undhagen, "Special Introduction," in *Revelaciones, Book 1,* 46–50.

56. *AP,* 260: Audiuit . . . ipsam dominam Brigidam diuulgare, indicare et predicare judicia et tribulaciones et maxime in regno Cypri et Neapoli et alijs pluribus locis.

57. *AP,* 429–30 (deposition of Charles Malansel of Genoa) and 431–32 (deposition of William Williamson of England). See *Rev.* 7.19.

58. *Rev.* 7.19.12, 24–25, 27: O, popule Cypri michi aduersarie, ausculta et attende diligenter, que tibi dico. . . . Popule Cypri, annuncio tibi, quod, si tu noueris te corrigere et emendare, tunc ego generacionem et progeniem tuam ita delebo in regno Cypri, quod nec pauperi parcam persone neque diuiti; ita eciam delebo eandem generacionem tuam, quod in breui tempore ita labetur memoria tua a cordibus hominum, ac si numquam fuissetis nati in hoc mundo. . . . Sed tamen sciatis pro certo, quod, quicumque vestrum voluerit se corrigere et emendare et ad me cum humilitate reuerti, ego ei gaudenter occurram vt pius pastor, leuando ipsum super humeros meos et ad oues meas eum personaliter reportando; translated by Kezel, in *Birgitta of Sweden,* 198.

59. *AP,* 266 (deposition of Magnus Petri), 326 (deposition of Birgitta's daughter Katarina), 372–73, 383 (deposition of Alfonso), 429–30 (dep-

osition of Charles Malansel of Genoa), 431–32 (deposition of William Williamson of England). In personal correspondence Dr. Bridget Morris suggested the difficulties posed by Birgitta's Swedish accent. Many scholars have discussed Birgitta's abilities in Latin. It appears that she studied Latin grammar seriously for many years, beginning during her married years. When she first went to Rome, she probably could not converse in Latin, but eventually she could understand and speak the language adequately. See *AP*, 393 (testimony of Alfonso), 420 (testimony of Lorenzo Angeleri), and other passages in the canonization documents. See also Eric College, *"Epistola solitarii ad reges*: Alphonse of Pecha as Organizer of Birgittine and Urbanist Propaganda," *Medieval Studies* 18 (1956): 23–25; and Arne Jönsson, "Birgitta i Birgittalegenderna," in *Heliga Birgitta—budskapet och förebilden*, 35–45.

60. *AP*, 562–63.

61. *Rev.* 7.27.6, 11–13: Ego sum creator omnium et dominus tam super dyabolos quam super omnes angelos, et nullus effugiet iudicium meum . . . Sed quid faciunt michi nunc illi homines, qui sunt inimici mei? Vere ipsi contempnunt precepta mea, eiciunt me de cordibus suis tamquam virus abhominabile, expuunt eciam me de ore ipsorum velut rem putridam, et abhorrent me videre quasi leprosum pessime fetentem. Dyabolum vero et eius opera amplectuntur toto suo affectu et opere. Hunc enim introducunt in cordibus suis, faciendo delectabiliter et gratanter eius voluntatem et sequendo eius immissiones malignas. Ideo iusto iudicio meo remunerabuntur in inferno cum dyabolo eternaliter sine fine; translated by Kezel, in *Birgitta of Sweden*, 208.

62. *AP*, 100 (*Vita b. Brigide prioris Petri et magistri Petri*), 260, 265 (deposition of Magnus Petri), 325 (deposition of Katarina), 373–374 (deposition of Alfonso), 518 (deposition of Prior Petrus of Alvastra), 562–563 (deposition of Cardinal Nicolaus Misquini). See also Alfonso, *Epistola solitarii ad reges* 6.11–12; and *Rev.* 7.27.

63. *AP*, 374: . . . verisimiliter . . . potuit timere mortem uel capcionem uel alias tribulaciones. . . .

64. Catherine Bell, *Ritual: Perspectives and Dimensons* (New York: Oxford University Press, 1997), 68–72, 139–144.

Bibliography

Editions of Birgitta's Revelations:

Aili, Hans, ed. *Revelaciones, Book 4*. SFSS, ser. 2, Latinska skrifter 7:4. Göteborg: Graphic Systems, 1992.

Bergh, Birger, ed. *Revelaciones, Book 5, Liber Questionum*. SFSS, ser. 2, Latinska skrifter 7:5. Uppsala: Almqvist and Wiksells Boktryckeri, 1971.

———, ed. Birgitta of Sweden, *Revelaciones*, Book 6. SFSS ser. 2, Latinska skrifter 7:6. Stockholm: Almqvist and Wiksell International, 1991.

————, ed. *Revelaciones, Book 7*. SFSS, ser. 2, Latinska skrifter 7:7. Uppsala: Almqvist and Wiksells Boktryckeri, 1967.

Eklund, Sten, ed. *Opera minora*. Vol. 1, *Regula Saluatoris*. SFSS, ser. 2, Latinska skrifter 8:1. Lund: Berlingska Boktryckeriet, 1975.

————, ed. *Opera minora*. Vol. 2, *Sermo Angelicus*. SFSS, ser. 2, Latinska skrifter 8:2. Uppsala: Almqvist and Wiksells Boktryckeri, 1972.

————, ed. *Opera minora*. Vol. 3, *Quattuor Orationes*. SFSS, ser. 2, Latinska skrifter 8:3. Stockholm: Almqvist and Wiksell International, 1991.

Hollman, Lennart, ed. *Revelaciones Extravagantes*. SFSS, ser. 2, Latinska skrifter 5. Uppsala: Almqvist and Wiksells Boktryckeri, 1956.

Jönsson, Ann-Mari, ed. *Revelaciones, Book 3*. SFSS, ser. 2, Latinska skrifter 7:3 Uppsala: Almqvist and Wiksell Tryckeri, 1998.

Undhagen, Carl-Gustaf, ed. *Revelaciones, Book 1 with Magister Mathias' Prologue*. SFSS, ser. 2, Latinska skrifter 7:1. Uppsala: Almqvist and Wiksell, 1978.

Other Works Cited:

Aquinas, Thomas. *Summa Theologiae*. Vol. 45, *Prophecy and Other Charisms*. Ed. and trans. Roland Potter. New York: Blackfriars in conjunction with McGraw-Hill, 1970.

Atkinson, Clarissa W. *Mystic and Pilgrim: The Book and the World of Margery Kempe*. Ithaca: Cornell University Press, 1983.

————. *The Oldest Vocation: Christian Motherhood in the Middle Ages*. Ithaca, NY: Cornell University Press, 1991.

Bell, Catherine. *Ritual: Perspectives and Dimensons*. New York: Oxford University Press, 1997.

Billing-Ottosson, Ann-Marie. "Magister Mathias' apokalypskommentar: Edition av kap. 1 och 2 med inledande anmärkningar, handskriftsklassificering och kommentar till texten." Master's thesis, Uppsala University, 1960.

Blamires, Alcuin. "Women and Preaching in Medieval Orthodoxy, Heresy, and Saints' Lives." *Viator: Medieval and Renaissance Studies* 26 (1995): 135–152.

Bloch, Maurice. "Symbols, Song, Dance and Features of Articulation: Is Religion a Form of Traditional Authority?" *Archives europeénes de sociologie* 15 (1974): 55–81.

Caciola, Nancy. "Discerning Spirits: Sanctity and Possession in the Later Middle Ages." Ph.D. diss., University of Michigan, 1994.

Chance, Jane. ed. *Gender and Text in the Later Middle Ages*. Gainesville: University Press of Florida, 1996.

Coakley, John. "Friars as Confidants of Holy Women in Medieval Dominican Hagiography." In *Images of Sainthood in Medieval Europe*, ed. Renate Blumenfeld-Kosinski and Timea Szell. Ithaca, NY: Cornell University Press, 1991.

————. "Friars, Sanctity, and Gender: Mendicant Encounters with Saints, 1250–1325." In *Medieval Masculinities: Regarding Men in the Middle Ages*, ed. Clare A. Lees with the assistance of Thelma Fenster and Jo Ann McNamara, Medieval Cultures 7. Minneapolis: University of Minnesota Press, 1994.

————. "Gender and the Authority of Friars: The Significance of Holy Women for Thirteenth-Century Franciscans and Dominicans." *Church History* 60 (1991): 445–60.

College, Eric. "*Epistola solitarii ad reges*: Alphonse of Pecha as Organizer of Birgittine and Urbanist Propaganda." *Medieval Studies* 18 (1956): 23–25.

Collijn, I., ed. *Acta et processus canonizacionis beate Birgitte*, SFSS, ser. 2, Latinska skrifter 1. Uppsala: Almqvist and Wiksells Boktryckeri, 1924–31 (*Vita b. Brigide prioris Petri et magistri Petri*).

Constable, Giles. *Three Studies in Medieval Religious and Social Thought: The Interpretation of Mary and Martha, the Ideal of the Imitation of Christ, the Orders of Society.* Cambridge: Cambridge University Press, 1995.

Fogelqvist, Ingvar. *Apostasy and Reform in the Revelations of St. Birgitta.* Bibliotheca Theologiae Practicae 51. Stockholm: Almqvist and Wiksell International, 1993.

Hamburger, Jeffrey. *The Rothschild Canticles: Art and Mysticism in Flanders and the Rhineland Circa 1300.* New Haven: Yale University Press, 1990.

Hedlund, Monica. "Vadstenapredikanter om Birgitta." In *Heliga Birgitta—budskapet och förebilden: Föredrag vid jubileumssymposiet i Vadstena 3–7 oktober 1991*, ed Alf Härdelin and Mereth Lindgren, Kungl. Vitterhets Historie och Antikvitets Akademien, Konferenser 28. Stockholm: Almqvist and Wiksell International, 1993.

Hogg, James, ed. *Studies in St. Birgitta and the Brigittine Order*, 2 vols. Analecta Cartusiana 35:19. Lewiston, NY: Edwin Mellen Press, 1993.

Jönsson, Arne, ed. *Alfonso of Jaén: His Life and Works with Critical Editions of the "Epistola Solitarii," the "Informaciones" and the "Epistola Serui Christi,"* Studia Graeca et Latina Lundensia 1. Lund: Lund University Press, 1989.

Kezel, Albert Ryle, trans. *Birgitta of Sweden: Life and Selected Revelations.* Ed. Marguerite Tjader Harris. New York: Paulist Press, 1990.

King, Karen. "Prophetic Power and Women's Authority: The Case of the *Gospel of Mary* (Magdalene)." In *Women Preachers and Prophets through Two Millennia of Christianity*, ed. Beverly Mayne Kienzle and Pamela J. Walker. Berkeley: University of California Press, 1998.

Klemming, G. E., ed. *Heliga Birgittas Uppenbarelser* (St. Birgitta's Revelations). SFSS, 14, vol. 2. Stockholm: Almqvist and Wiksell, 1857–1884.

Lewis, I. M. *Ecstatic Religion: A Study of Shamanism and Spirit Possession.* 1971. Reprinted 2nd ed. New York: Routledge, 1989.

Matter, E. Ann. *The Voice of My Beloved: The Song of Songs in Western Medieval Christianity.* Philadelphia: University of Pennsylvania Press, 1990.

McGinn, Bernard. *The Growth of Mysticism: Gregory the Great through the Twelfth Century.* Vol. 2 of *The Presence of God: A History of Christian Mysticism.* New York: Crossroad, 1994.

Morris, Bridget. "Four Birgittine Meditations in Medieval Swedish." *Birgittiana* 1, no. 2 (1996).

Muessig, Caroline. "Prophecy and Song: Teaching and Preaching by Medieval Women." In *Women Preachers and Prophets through Two Millennia of Christianity*, ed. Beverly Mayne Kienzle and Pamela J. Walker. Berkeley: University of California Press, 1998.

Newman, Barbara. *From Virile Woman to WomanChrist: Studies in Medieval Religion and Literature*. Philadelphia: University of Pennsylvania Press, 1995.

Nyberg, Tore. "Birgitta/Birgittenordern." In *Theologische Realenzyklopaedie*, 2nd edition, vol. 6. New York: Walter de Gruyter, 1980.

Piltz, Anders. "Uppenbarelserna och uppenbarelsen: Birgittas förhållande till Bibeln." In *Birgitta, hendes værk och hendes klostre i Norden*, ed. Tore Nyberg. Odense University Studies in History and Social Sciences 150. Odense: Odense University Press, 1991.

———. "Revelation and the Human Agent: St. Birgitta and the Process of Inspiration." Unpublished manuscript.

Pryds, Darleen. "Proclaiming Sanctity through Proscribed Acts: The Case of Rose of Viterbo." In *Women Preachers and Prophets through Two Millennia of Christianity*, ed. Beverly Mayne Kienzle and Pamela J. Walker. Berkeley: University of California Press, 1998.

Riehle, Wolfgang. *The Middle English Mystics*. Trans. Bernard Standring. London: Routledge and Kegan Paul, 1981.

Rupert of Deutz. *Liber de divinis officiis* 5.1. Ed. Hrabanus Haacke, *Corpus Christianorum, Continuatio Mediaevalis* 7. Turnholt: Brepols, 1967.

Sahlin, Claire L. "The Prophetess as Preacher: Birgitta of Sweden and the Voice of Prophecy." *Medieval Sermon Studies* 40 (Autumn 1997): 29–44.

———. "Birgitta of Sweden and the Voice of Prophecy: A Study of Gender and Prophetic Authority in the Later Middle Ages." Ph.D diss., Harvard University, 1996.

Saint Bridget: Prophetess of New Ages. Proceedings of the International Study Meeting, Rome, October 3–7, 1991 (*Santa Brigida: Profeta dei tempi nuovi*, Atti dell'incontro internazionale di studio, Roma, 3–7 ottobre 1991). Rome: Tipografia Vaticana, 1993.

Strömberg, Bengt. *Magister Mathias och Fransk Mendikantpredikan*. Samlingar och studier till Svenska kyrkans historia 9. Stockholm: Svenska Kyrkans Diakonistyrelse, 1944.

Turner, Denys. *Eros and Allegory: Medieval Exegesis of the Song of Songs*. Cistercian Studies Series 156. Kalamazoo: Cistercian Publications, 1995.

Van Engen, John H. *Rupert of Deutz*. Berkeley: University of California Press, 1983.

Westman, K. B. *Birgitta-studier*, 1. Uppsala: Akademiska Boktryckeriet, 1911.

Wilson, Katharina M., ed. *Medieval Women Writers*. Athens, GA: University of Georgia Press, 1984.

Wilson, Robert R. *Prophecy and Society in Ancient Israel*. Philadelphia: Fortress Press, 1980.

CHAPTER FIVE

A Performance Artist and Her Performance Text: Margery Kempe on Tour

Nanda Hopenwasser

Religion, like art, *lives* in so far as it is performed. . . .
　　　　—Victor Turner, *The Anthropology of Performance*, 48[1]

Performance implies always an audience/performer or ritual participant relationship—a reciprocity, a practice in the constructions of cultural reality relative to its effects. As such the study of performance and the trope of performativity have become integral to a cultural critical analysis which wants to explore the dynamic two-way street, the "space between" self and others, subjects and objects, masters and slaves, or any system of social signification.
　　　　—Rebecca Schneider, *The Explicit Body in Performance*, 22[2]

Prelude: Meet Margery Kempe, Performance Artist

Margery Kempe, protagonist of *The Book of Margery Kempe*, is a master performance artist. Like such modern performance artists as Carolee Schneeman, Karen Finley, Annie Sprinkle, and Ann Magnuson, Kempe uses her body to elicit strong responses from her audiences.[3] Her self-expression manifests itself through acts that often criticize the social and religious hypocrisy of her society. As a spiritual gadfly, Kempe fits squarely into the hagiographic tradition she emulates.[4] Like St. Birgitta of Sweden, she presents herself as a heroine in her theater of belief. Her visionary performances also resemble those of her near contemporary, St. Theresa of Avila. Moreover, Kempe's self-presentation in *The Book of Margery Kempe* makes her a transitional figure, a mother of Renaissance autobiography and a direct antecedent to the self-fashioners described by Stephen Greenblatt.[5] Kempe also draws strongly from the performance tradition of her native East Anglia, and although she never overtly acknowledges it in her *Book*, it informs her textual performance.[6]

Although she occasionally attempts to appear ordinary, her self-expressive gifts often scuttle this desire.[7] Rather, she almost always appears theatrical and charismatic. Beneath the glittering image resides a gifted writer who has fashioned a mobile, resilient model of herself that permits her to lasso her reading audience with the skill of a trained cowgirl. Her performance text, her *Book*, allows her to transcend the confines of time and space, and use her self-representation as a life lived in service of her God.[8] For the purpose of clarity, I will for the remainder of this paper distinguish between Margery Kempe, historical figure and author, and Margery Kempe, fictional creation and "creatur," by calling the former Kempe and the latter Margery. I will also refer to the authorial/editorial older voice in the text as Kempe in opposition to the younger, acting, reconstructed voice, which I shall call Margery. The distinction between the two is complicated by the assumption that although Kempe bases her character on what she believes is an accurate representation of her earlier self, her religious agenda colors her writing, creating a framework within which she chooses to recreate herself as a religious pilgrim. I will use the full name, Margery Kempe, when character and writer intertwine so closely that their functions are difficult to unravel.

Kempe's text finds its grounding in her belief in the primacy of God's love. Her faith allows her to create a visionary self who converses easily with the religious figures who inhabit her visions. Margery also finds earthly helpers, often in the strangest of places and in the darkest of times. Her courage, verbal fluency, and "chutzpah" endear her to many of the *Book*'s readers, but her self-centeredness and stubbornness irk others. But like the best of the performance artists examined in Rebecca Schneider's book *The Explicit Body in Performance,* Margery Kempe's enthusiastic activities rarely put her audience to sleep (1–25).[9]

The pilgrimage chapters of the *Book* are significant because they follow Margery's transition from apprentice visionary to mistress of her craft, from neophyte improvisationalist to master performance artist. Many of the performance patterns recorded in the later sections of the *Book* begin here. This is why I have chosen to emphasize this portion of Kempe's text. Self-dramatization is at a height.[10] These exciting chapters serve to trace Margery Kempe's development into the consummate actress and playwright she becomes in her maturity.

My analysis of this section, based on my approach to performance theory, is eclectic, for like Margery, I draw my inspiration from multiple traditions. I employ biological, psychological, psychoanalytic, anthropological, sociological, and mythic approaches, but primarily perceive the visionary act as an act of personal creation. Therefore, performance theory lends itself to my intuitive methodology. The works of Mircea Eliade and later mythographers retain a hold on a mythic consciousness fashioned, in part, by a childhood spent reading myriad folk tales, myths, and fantasy and science fiction stories (Bell, *Ritual,* 10–16). Early adulthood readings of psychoanalytical and anthropological texts contributed to my framework.[11] However, readings in Freud's works appear to have left me unscathed, and I have found most structuralist texts, including those by Claude Lévi-Strauss, too binary for my taste. But performance theory models, particularly those of Victor and Edith Turner and Richard Schechner, have proven very helpful in framing my understanding of Margery's public and private performances (Bell, *Ritual,* 72–76).[12] My performance model derives rather closely from my study of autobiography and theories of creativity and self-expression. I agree with James Olney that all creative human endeavors are "metaphors of self."[13] This does not mean that the "self" is an easily defined isolate, totally separate from its interactions with its environment; but I do believe that the biological construct of human self-consciousness allows us to perceive ourselves as separate selves embedded in time, space, and society. Therefore, even the most repetitive of actions, the most structured ritual, must reveal a measure of individual human activity. I, therefore, choose to privilege the individual creative elements of the performative act with the understanding that all such acts arise out of the rich matrix of biology and culture. Moreover, in keeping with the performance art of Margery Kempe and her *Book,* this chapter approaches the subject from the perspective of performance: I intend to explore Kempe's artistry by creating my own analytical textual performance consisting of a prelude, two acts, and an epilogue.

Act I. Margery Kempe: Neophyte Performance Artist

Margery Kempe begins by introducing herself as she is in her maturity, but almost immediately she returns to her younger self and we begin to hear the dual voice Elizabeth Petroff noted in her analysis of medieval female visionary authors.[14] Kempe leads her self-creation through progressive stages to explain how she became spiritually mature. She presents the past as a continuing narrative, interrupted, at times, by interjections of her mature editorial voice. The first section of Kempe's *Book* traces Margery's initial halting steps. Haunted by an unnamed sin and overcome by feelings of unworthiness, Margery undergoes a spiritual crisis after the birth of her first child.[15] Obsessively concerned about what others think, she cannot alleviate her sense of guilt through confession, and, for once, cannot speak.

Margery's characteristics manifest themselves even at this early stage. Like many bright women without formal education, Margery frequently cannot express herself directly. Her actions appear reactive; a desire to win the approval of others remains one of her fundamental character traits even after she matures.[16] Spiritual pride, tactlessness, and an occasional inability to empathize with others are also some of Margery's less savory characteristics. Kempe, like Schneider's performance artists who expose their nakedness for all to see, exhibits herself body and soul to the scrutiny of observers. But in doing so she humanizes her self-creation so that her audience can sympathize and identify with her as a woman valiantly doing the best she can to improve herself but often failing in the attempt.

Kempe uses Margery's inability to rise to the Christian ideal of sexual purity as a psychological motivation for Margery's actions in this initial scene.[17] Instinctive sexuality wars with her desire to remain chaste, and she feels that she is unable to live up to her ideals.[18] Kempe makes her character's insecurities concrete by having Margery take to her bed in a fit of postpartum depression, graphically describing her self-destructive actions (6–7). Margery's illness reflects her conflicted emotions.

Jesus' initial appearance sets the stage for later appearances. His assumption of the traditional roles of father and physician include the possibility of later broadening his character to incorporate the roles of husband, advisor, mentor, and friend. Jesus heals Margery of her initial malady, but she is not yet ready to commit herself to a more spiritual life. Therefore, her recovery is incomplete. She can fend for herself in the quotidian but cannot yet negotiate the larger spiritual world because she has not yet accepted her calling.

Succeeding chapters follow Margery's progress as she undergoes many trials in preparation for her mature vocation. The culmination of this primary phase occurs when she is finally allowed to embark on the long, grueling pilgrimage to Jerusalem and Rome. Her journeyman voyage blends psychological ordeals with visionary heights and results in increased cosmopolitan experiences and a new maturity of belief.

Margery's internal voyage parallels her geographical journey, encompassing multiple levels as she travels from England to the Holy Land, to Rome, and finally returns home. She begins her pilgrimage in the spirit of an eager convert. Prior to her embarkation, she has already engaged in spiritual healing, conversed with Jesus, and prophesied to the local community. But she is still a neophyte. She tries too hard to be holy and shows herself insensitive to the needs of others. Because she is a comic figure, the audience need not judge her too harshly even though her actions might well have proven grating in real life. Indeed, Kempe creates characters who respond normally, if somewhat harshly, to Margery's irritating self-absorption and religious fanaticism. So although readers remain sympathetic to Margery's travails, they also understand her companions' motivations.

Margery's character needs tempering; the hardships of her pilgrimage weather her and mold her later sense of self. Her painful experiences endow her with spiritual hardihood and humility; they permit her to arrive at the holiest sites in Christendom with the perspective to gain most profitably from them. Her prior visions prepare her for the numinousness of these sites. Because experience stimulates the visionary imagination, her visits to the places where religious history occurred deepens her identification with the holy family and their travels, making concrete what was previously imaginatively amorphous.

Margery's character grows in proportion to her capacity to internalize the patterns of religious pilgrimage. She discovers that Christological history can be used to create good theater (Harris, *Theater*, 1–17) and that traditional pilgrimage sites are endowed with great spiritual power.[19]

Kempe makes Margery a seer. Her character draws its depth from its ability to intuit what spiritual truths lie below the surface of commonplace events. Her sensitivity causes her to react strongly to places of spiritual power; the *omphalos* of her world is both a place of origins and a source of personal strength.[20] For Margery, God frequents sites, and she can draw inspiration from them. Her dramatic capacity produces a vessel for her inspiration, a script that draws upon the constructs of the pilgrimage, allowing her to create in accordance with her multifaceted vision.[21] Her special gifts allow her to maintain contact with the present while living both a mythic and a reconstructed historical past, melding all three into an active theater of the mind. Her spiritual intensity forces her viscerally to experience events that took place at salient pilgrimage sites, directly leading to her externally manifested emotional responses.

The Jerusalem pilgrimage allows Margery to understand emotionally the events leading to the crucifixion, lending the historical figures of Jesus and Mary a poignant reality. Following the footsteps of the tortured Christ along the *via dolorosa* provides Margery with a holistic experience that serves as the foundation for her reconstruction of the crucifixion drama. Her visit to Bethlehem produces visions replete with images of pregnancy, childbirth, and parturition, emphasizing the Virgin's motherly healing power and providing Margery with an accepting mother figure. Margery's experiences in Rome strengthen her ties to Jesus and Mary and provide a concrete basis for her reconstruction of the spirit of St. Birgitta.

Margery's spiritual gifts set her apart from ordinary religious women, bothering her and comforting her in turn. She will implicitly refer to the pilgrimage each time she manifests her holy cries and publicly acknowledges her special relationship with Jesus. These performative actions will remind her of the great heights she reached during this period, but they will also serve as painful reminders of the less pleasant parts of the journey, particularly on occasions when her cries elicit responses that mirror the negative responses of her fellow pilgrims. The events of the pilgrimage section train Margery under the most difficult of circumstances to survive the effects her gifts produce on others. The established pattern will persist for the remainder of her life, giving way only in old age, when her physical frailty undermines her ability to perform her theatrical duties in service of her God.

Margery Kempe perceives herself as God's "creature," but although she does her best to follow his direction, she is an inveterate improvisationalist. Like all great actresses, she interprets her given role in its maximum dramatic capacity. In choosing the part of visionary writer and actress she becomes a guide to her internal audience and those who read her *Book* in service of their own spirituality. Her self-depiction implies a belief that her life's drama unfolds on Christ's eternal stage. It also implies a belief that her audience shares that stage with her and that failure to act well loses the actor the right to Christian immortality.

Act II. Margery Kempe on Tour

Scene 1: The Pilgrimage Begins

Kempe prepares us for Margery's voyage well before its inception by presenting the pilgrimage idea indirectly.[22] Margery's confidant, the anchor of the Friar Preachers in Lynn, "by the spirit of prophecy told her that when she would go to Jerusalem, she should have much tribulation with her maid and how our Lord should assay her sharply and prove her full strictly" (Kempe, *cap.* 18: 44).[23] Margery, living through the text, although privy to the same prophecy as her audience, is wary and fearful. She protests: "Ah, good sir, what shall I then do when I am far from home and in strange countries and my maiden be against me? Then is my bodily comfort gone, and spiritual comfort of any confessor such as you know I not where to find."(44)[24] The anchor reassures her in words that recall earlier dialogues with Jesus and his earthly representatives: "Daughter, dread you not, for our Lord, whose comfort surpasses all others, shall comfort you himself, and when all your friends have forsaken you, our Lord shall make a broken-backed man lead you forth where you will be" (44).[25]

The anchor acts as a holy prophet. Paralleling Kempe's prophetic function for her reader, he predicts the outcome of Margery's decision. He particularizes his prophecy by telling Margery that she will have trouble with her maid and she will be rescued by a hunchback. This foreknowledge creates a sense of dramatic irony. Readers expect Margery to suffer but also to learn from her experiences, knowing full well that she will win out over her hardships. They also learn of specific actions that occur on the pilgrimage.

This is the first complete dialogue to present the pilgrimage idea.[26] Kempe establishes a dramatic conflict that occurs many times in this section. A member of the clergy advises Margery. She protests the action or decision. Jesus or one of his human representatives settles the conflict, often siding with Margery but sometimes instructing her to follow the advice of the cleric. The sequence follows the pattern of the typical conflict: action, reaction, then resolution. Margery learns from her experi-

ences, good triumphs over evil, and the audience learns its lesson. Kempe
then plants a memorandum for the future. Insisting on the holiness of the
anchor, she writes, "And so it befell as the anchor had prophesied on every
point, and, as I trust, shall be written more plainly afterward" (44).[27] But
the time is not ripe for the completion of the prophecy. Several more
years and *capitula* separate the prediction from its fulfillment.[28]

Margery's desire for pilgrimage is translated into action in *capitulum*
26 when she suddenly understands that the time is right to undertake the
journey.[29] Knowing that many do not return from such a trek, she fulfils
all of her personal obligations so that she can leave with a clear conscience
(60). Margery first travels to Norwich and then goes to the port city of
Yarmouth to board a ship to the European mainland and the Holy Land.[30]
Her first sea voyage is short. She lands in "a great town called Seryce,
where our Lord in his high goodness visited this creature with abundant
tears of contrition for her own sins and sometimes for other mens' sins
also" (60–61).[31]

Here Margery embarks on her first public performance of the journey.[32] She enacts the ritual of a woman overcome by contrition.[33] Placing
herself in the midst of the holy space, she diverts attention away from the
priest performing mass and captures her audience by interrupting the service with her weeping, maintaining an alternate ritual inspired by the drama
of Christ's crucifixion.[34] The Christian tradition of penitence dictates her
role; her audience understands her actions because they share her tradition.[35] Her weeping is a token of her love for God, but it also signifies
that she is beloved by God.[36] Even before she receives the special gift of
holy crying in Jerusalem, Margery's proof of her special relationship to
God takes the form of weeping:[37] "And especially she had tears of compassion in mind of our Lord's Passion. And she was given the Eucharist
each Sunday at that time and at a place convenient to it with great weeping and violent/boisterous sobbing so that many men marveled and won-
dered about the great Grace that God wrought in his creature" (61).[38]

Several items make this selection remarkable. First, Margery's performance takes place in public in the presence of a large audience. Second,
it is repeated.[39] Third, Kempe, employing the word "wonder" to express
audience reaction, creates an ambiguity concerning how the performance
is greeted. Some observers feel uncomfortable about the intensity of her
reaction and her use of dramatic movement in response to the liturgy. Her
actions appear inappropriate. Margery, however, believes that the audience
response is predominantly positive. But whereas Margery is naive, the
writer Kempe is more sophisticated. Conscious of the outcome of later

events, she again creates a sense of irony by portraying Margery as overly enthusiastic about her early performances. A close reading of the text suggests that Kempe understands the ambivalence of Margery's audiences. Early on in the narrative Kempe wants her readers to understand that the audience's initial responses to Margery's performances are mostly positive until some negative force shifts opinions to ones of distrust.

Nevertheless, it is clear that Margery does feel some discomfort with her show of emotion. Although she likes the affirmation such a performance can elicit, she understands that her display makes her a disturbing center of attention. In this Margery resembles the participants in shamanic rituals which emphasize trance or possession. Participants, most particularly the shaman or *hungan,* can often feel uncomfortable because they become the foci for divine messages expressed in flamboyant actions and project a sense of the uncanny.[40] Such rituals are often deeply disturbing to less involved observers who tend to misunderstand the activities and construe them as pathological. Therefore, Kempe must keep reassuring her readers that Margery is divinely inspired, not subject to an illness nor an egoistic desire to call attention to herself. In this instance, she relates that in preparation for her pilgrimage Margery has eaten no meat nor drunk no wine since her departure from England and had been in the habit of such fasts for three years. Margery, therefore, appears a sincere pilgrim, whereas the other English pilgrims seem mere voyagers in search of "curiositas."[41]

Conflict is the root of all good dramatic performance. Kempe now introduces personal conflict in the person of a cleric who shadows her namesake with the tenacity of Javert tracking Jean Valjean in *Les Misera-bles.*[42] This character provides the source of the most flagrant and continuous conflict in the pilgrimage chapters. Kempe presents him as the representative of an authoritarian church that promotes the letter of the law over its spirit. He rejects dramatic expressions of holiness, discards visionary experience, and seeks to discredit Margery's followers. But in championing the social construct of pilgrimage over its spiritual components, he proves himself no match either for God's power or Margery's. Kempe's depiction of him borders on social satire.[43]

The prelate's first bid for control is to order Margery to give up her fast, promising that she will be excused, suffering "her to do for a time as he pleased" (61).[44] He ostensibly wishes to teach her the virtues of obedience. Actually, he fears her fervor and does not wish her to exhibit behavior deviant from that of her companions. At first Margery agrees to his demands as an exercise in humility. But her decision disturbs her conscience. Kempe implies that Margery, despite her desire to follow the rules, cannot do so, so she practices deception, appearing to comply but avoiding meat and wine whenever possible.

Her abstemious behavior is noticed. Both the routine travelers and the confessor are frightened by Margery's orthodoxy and fear that it reveals their lack of spiritual commitment, "And they were most displeased, for she wept so much and spoke always of the love and goodness of our Lord as well at the table as in any other place" (61).[45] Although Margery displays proper religious feeling, she displays poor table manners: "And, therefore, shamefully they reproved her and severely chided her and said they would not suffer/put up with her as her husband did when she was at home and in England" (61).[46]

Kempe characterizes Margery's detractors as a bunch of spiteful gossips. Her depiction of their speech proves this, for they exhibit her personal history publicly, lowering their status by their behavior. Kempe stresses the distinction between Margery and her adversaries by presenting the accusations indirectly, whereas Margery's retort appears in direct speech.

Margery then draws the discourse to a higher level, effectively deflecting the argument from personal issues to morality and theology. But her companions are not pleased with her wit. Unable to win verbally, their animosity shows itself first as avoidance and then as violence. Nevertheless, Margery tries to excuse them, although she is hurt by their behavior (61). Rather than continue the quarrel, she addresses the ringleader, " 'You do me much shame and great grievance' " (61).[47] Her words are gentle but unfortunately do not sway the angry man. He answers harshly, cursing her for her pains and wishing her a miserable death.

Others follow his example, and her maid, as earlier prophesied, abandons her. People abscond with her money; the whole company tells her that she can no longer abide with them (61–62). Margery has now suffered the first major setback of her journey.[48] She attempts to emulate Christ in her reaction to adversity, but because she has also drawn her fate upon herself by her antisocial actions, the audience may laugh at her.

Comic performers rarely sink to the depths of overt tragedy. This time, one of the English pilgrims comes to her rescue. "Then, the next morning there came to her one of her company, a man who loved her well, praying/asking her that she to go to his fellows and humble herself before them and pray/ask them if she might still go in their company till she comes to Constance" (62).[49] But respite is temporary. Margery, ill and uncomfortable, receives similar treatment to that she received before. The violence and humiliation escalate: "They cut her gown so short that it came but a little beneath her knee and made her don/wear a white canvas in the manner of a sackcloth garment, for she would be held a fool and the people should not make much of her nor to have much repute. They made her sit at the table end beneath all the others so that she dared hardly ever to speak a word" (62)[50]. Margery can be bowed but not broken: "and not withstanding all their malice, she was held in more respect than they where-that-ever they came" (62).[51]

But Margery's special powers prove useful when the company is threatened with illness. Her prayer of supplication becomes the public salvation. Because the Lord wishes to save Margery, he saves the whole company. Jesus tells her, " 'Dread not, daughter, your fellowship shall not incur harm while you are in their company" (62).[52] Margery temporarily becomes a heroine because of her intercessory powers, but that still does not make her a desirable traveling companion.

Now another rescuer arrives, this time a person with spiritual authority: the pope's legate. She tells him her problems, but more importantly, his acceptance of her activities serves as authorization for the unorthodox intercessory behavior she has actively displayed, proving her a proper Christian woman who serves God and receives her special powers as gifts of grace.

The next scene reconfirms Margery's position and transfers the prelate's private approval to the public arena. The fellowship invites the "worthy doctor to dinner" (63). They seat Margery at the lowliest, and the doctor, as befits his station, at the highest place. A rehearsed scene, recounted in dialogue, follows. " 'Why are you no nearer?' " the legate asks. Margery, proving her humility "sat still and answered not, as he had commanded her to do" (63). The company sets out its complaints about Margery's behavior. They wish her to eat meat, to cease weeping and crying, and to refrain from talking about holiness and God. The expected happens. Margery is vindicated; the papal legate delivers a long speech favoring her activities. He provides a moral example to the assembled company by refusing to give into their demands; worse still, he asserts that they are not worthy of Margery's speech nor her attention. The religious audience of the *Book* can bask in Margery's vindication. The conflict with her unholy company has come to a satisfactory conclusion with Margery on top. But this is only one battle in a whole campaign. The conflict with Margery's cohort continues throughout this section; the pattern persists throughout her long life. Margery must continually learn patience and prove her willingness to suffer for the sake of her God.

Scene 2: Jerusalem

Margery's sojourn in Jerusalem is a significant component of the complete pilgrimage narrative (*capitulum* 28). Kempe relates that prior to their arrival in the holy city, Margery's fellow pilgrims persist in their unchristian behavior. Again they cast her away from the table, order a ship solely for themselves, refuse her provisions, and ostracize her from their company. But again she gains special knowledge from God, who assigns her another ship, warning her that the ship her former company has chosen might prove unsafe. She again performs as seer; the group heeds her warning, shifts plans, and chooses to accompany Margery on her ship.[53]

Trouble still follows. The cleric steals her sheet and proclaims that "she was as false as she might be and despised her and so rebuked her" (67).[54] Their company's reaction proves that Margery's *via dolorosa* has already begun. She again returns unkindness with kindness, asking members of the company to forgive her inadvertent transgressions, and presents others with the opportunity to do the same. Again Margery plays the part of the penitent woman, ritually cleansed for her entrance to the holy city and prepared for the spiritual experiences to follow.

Like Jesus, Margery enters Jerusalem on a donkey. Overcome by the beauty of the holy city, she gives thanks for the opportunity she has been given to enter. Margery, conscious of the symbolic significance of her action, marks her transition from secular to holy space by including a reference to the heavenly city of Jerusalem in her prayer of thanksgiving. Her entrance, however, is hardly understated. Her great emotion and unfamiliarity with her means of transportation cause her to lose her balance. Unlike her ideal, she, a comic figure, does not enter the city gracefully but nearly falls from her ass onto her ass. Two German pilgrims keep her from falling; one, a priest, administers salubrious spices, in essence, blessing her as she makes her entrance. Again Margery's rescuers come from beyond the borders of Britain. Readers may blame her weakness on her overwhelming emotion, but they may also notice that her entrance parallels the aged Birgitta's ride into Jerusalem with a northern entourage that included family members and a priest.[55]

Conscious that she is likely to cry loudly, Margery warns her compatriots in advance, preparing both them and her readers for what follows (67). Almost immediately, they visit the Temple in Jerusalem.[56] Here ceremony and symbolism combine to produce in Margery and the other pilgrims an atmosphere conducive to their mental replaying of the horrors of Jesus' trials, his painful journey to Calvary, ending with his torture, death, and resurrection. "Then the friars lifted up a cross and led the pilgrims about from [one] place to another where our Lord had suffered his [pains] and his passions, every man and woman bearing a wax candle in their hand. And the friars always, as they went about, told them what our Lord suffered in every place" (68).[57]

Margery's reaction is immediate, called forth by the tragedy of the last hours of Jesus' earthly life, a virtual reality shared by the more imaginative of her fellow pilgrims. Kempe explains that "the forsaid creature wept and sobbed so plentiously as though she had seen our Lord with her bodily eye suffering at that time" (68).[58] This, the beginning of the most powerful scene in this section, culminates when Margery, following in the footsteps of Jesus, finally arrives at the Church of the Holy Sepulcher. Here she reacts emotionally at the Calvary chapel, making changes in her theatrical performance that will be retained for many years afterwards.[59] She attributes the reason for the change to Jesus' gift at the foot of the cross and explains the difference between her holy tears and other forms of theatrical crying. Copying the cruciform position, Margery lies prone on the pavement before the altar of the crucifixion; her emotional responsiveness to the power of the site causes her to yowl, scream, and ululate loudly.

Margery's dramatic model can be traced back at least as far as Jerome's account of his acolyte Paula's personal reconstruction of the events of the Passion and the crucifixion:

> [I]n visiting the holy places so great was the passion and the enthusiasm she exhibited for each that she could never have torn herself away from one had she not been eager to visit the rest. Before the Cross she threw herself down in adoration as though she beheld the Lord hanging upon it: and when she entered the tomb which was the scene of the Resurrection, she kissed the stone which the angel had rolled away from the Sepulcher. . . . What tears she shed there, what groans she uttered, and what grief she poured forth, all Jerusalem knows.[60]

Ellen Ross explains that Paula's dramatic reaction to these holy sites reveal that for her "they are not located in the distant past, but happening in the present, before her eyes" (100). This is likewise true for Margery; "historical places as bearers of the sacred have the power to transport the spiritual significance of the past to the present, and to enable someone centuries removed to remember and reunderstand what happened" (100).

Kempe attempts to do the same thing for her audience by describing her experience graphically: "And when they came up to the mount of Calvary, she fell down because she could not stand nor kneel, but wallowed and wrested with her body, spreading her arms abroad, and cried with a loud voice as though her heart would have burst asunder, for in the city of her soul she saw verily and freshly how our Lord was crucified"(69).[61]

She identifies with the Virgin, Saint John, Mary Magdalene, and the other saints whose mourning she "saw in her spiritual sight" (68). All those she mentions by name are members of Jesus' immediate family or close friends. Her experience threatens to overwhelm her, so much so that "she could not keep herself from crying and roaring even though she might die therefore" (68).

Margery's gift for dramatic recreation leads to her standard activity— emotional weeping. But this time her tears are accompanied by loud screams and cries. She tells us specifically that "this was the first cry that ever she cried in any contemplation" (68). Her cries and writhing reveal her inner pain, signaling her identification with female members of the holy family. But they may also express publicly similar visions occurring more quietly among other members of the group. So she acts as their representative, performing a private ritual publicly, translating into action the private thoughts of others and taking upon herself their painful emotions, embarrassing though it might be to the members of the group who are unable to identify with her actions. Reactions to her activity make the divisions clear. Those who are committed to the pilgrimage empathize with Margery, calling her a holy woman because she can feel so strongly the power of the site; those who are tied to worldly pursuits remain unmoved by her display of emotion. Margery performs as she has done formerly, astonishing those in her audience who have heretofore not seen her performance. She tells us that "the crying was so loud and so wonderful that it made the people astonished unless they had heard it before and or else that they knew the cause of the crying" (68).[62]

Emotional triggers that remind Margery of her traumatic crying at the Calvary chapel cause her to repeat this experience for many years afterward. For example, Kempe tells us that Margery would feel weak in the knees when she heard someone speak of the Passion, when she saw a crucifix, when she saw a man with a wound, or if a man beat a child or even a horse or another beast with a whip (68). As a result of her experience, Margery becomes capable of translating the pains of Jesus' torture into an empathy for the pain of others on all levels. Moreover, Margery feels the pain of such cruelty every time it occurs; acts of cruelty cause her to call attention to them by means of her performative action of crying. She asserts, "first when she had her cryings at Jerusalem, she had them oftentimes, and in Rome also" (69). Her mention of both holy places in one sentence links the two sites and reminds the audience of the sacred relationship between the two. One is the seat of holy power deriving from the generalized Christian tradition; the other is the seat of the orthodox Western Roman Catholic tradition. The third site mentioned is England, her homeland. Kempe also keeps track of the temporal component of Margery's gift:

> And when she came home to England, first at her coming home it came but seldom, as it were once in a month, then once in the week, afterward daily, once she had nine on one day, and another day she had seven, and so as God would visit them on her, sometimes in the church, sometimes in the street, sometimes in the chamber, sometimes in the field then God would send them, for she knew never the time nor hour when they would come. (69)[63]

Margery feels powerless in presence of such awesome power. She informs her audience that she is not master of herself as she undergoes this most holy and difficult of experiences. God presents her with "great sweetness of devotion and high contemplation" (69). God controls her performance, making his creature act in such an unseemly manner. She is his puppet and, therefore, cannot be held responsible for her embarrassing actions. Her passivity allows her to act as the best vehicle for God's word, conveying his message in an active form without directly promoting herself despite her flagrant self-dramatization.

Kempe feels the need to explain that this uncomfortable, antisocial behavior is maintained not out of any maladjustment to society nor out of illness but as a manifestation of God's love. She does this by addressing the problem directly, naming the ills that can cause similar behavior. Her detractors receive a voice in her text, but her emphasis on God's voice drowns out the more rational possible reasons for her eccentric behavior and counter the objections of the detractors; her ability to mention all the choices possible proves her sanity and her good faith. "For some said it was a wicked spirit vexed her; some said it was a sickness; some said she had drunk too much wine; some cursed her; some wished she had been in the haven; some would she had been in the sea in a bottomless boat; and so each man as he thought" (69).[64] Her list proves that she is conscious of what others think and is cognizant of her surroundings. However, she is confident that she can prove that her actions are not signs of moral failings or physical illness and gain sympathy by admitting her powerlessness in the face of such behavior. Attempts at suppression of the gift, in order to spare the feelings of the others, result in heavier crying and more unseemly behavior. She writes that those who would suppress her "knew full little what she felt, otherwise they would not believe but that she might have abstained from crying if she had wanted to" (69).[65]

Scene 3: Rome

Suddenly God commands Margery to leaves Jerusalem and travel to Rome.

> And then our Lord commanded her for to go to Rome, and so forth home to England, and said unto her, "Daughter, as oftentimes as you say or think, 'Worshipped be all the holy places in Jerusalem that Christ suffered bitter pain and passion in,' you shall have the same pardon as if you were there with your bodily presence both to yourself and to all those that you will give it to." (75)[66]

Now, having creatively replicated the torment and Passion of Jesus so that she and her loved ones will be spared the pains of hell, Margery must go forth and learn the advanced lessons her God has prepared. Reluctantly she leaves Jerusalem to travel further both geographically and spiritually. She embarks on a ship for Venice; many of the returning pilgrims fall ill on the voyage, but Margery is assured that none shall die (75). Again at landfall her company abandons her, and again Jesus reassures her: "Dread you not, daughter, for I shall guide you right well and bring you in safety to Rome and home again into England without any shame of your body if you will be clad in white clothes and wear them as I said to you while you were in England" (76).[67]

White clothes, which become a bone of contention between Margery and her various confessors, set her apart from ordinary pilgrims; they also exhibit her commitment to a costume symbolizing her internal spiritual purity. She believes that God has designated her an honorary virgin despite her marriage and motherhood, and her costume signals men that she should not be approached sexually despite her age and marital status. It also marks her as a visionary and an intercessor with heavenly powers. Therefore, white clothing acts as a red flag to prelates who are resentful of Margery's special status. Throughout this section, Margery's dress serves as an obvious flash point in the conflict between earthly religious authorities and Margery's heavenly directors. Margery's costume shifts from white to black and black to white depending upon whether or not she is permitted to display publicly her intimate relationship with God. When wearing black clothes, Margery signals her humility, her desire to progress, her thoughtfulness of others. When she is clothed in black she is often in the process of learning new matters of faith or reaching new levels of understanding. Once she moves to another level, however, she is rewarded for a time with white clothes, a temporary but meaningful costume change that reassures her of God's love as much as do her ubiquitous visions.

Margery, ever the bargainer, promises to wear white clothes in Rome if she arrives there safely; immediately thereafter she is provided with a guide, "a poor man sitting who had a great hump on his back" (76). Margery learns that "his name was Richard and he was from Ireland" (76). Margery, remembering the prophecy of the anchor, feels reassured. Dialogue between the two follows, and Margery "with a glad spirit said unto him 'Good Richard, lead me to Rome, and you shall be rewarded for your labor' " (77). After some initial reluctance, he agrees to do so and remains her faithful servant for most of the remainder of her journey.

Margery and Richard travel next to Assisi, the home of Saint Francis, where again Margery meets an approving prelate and where she weeps copious tears upon seeing her Lady's veil (79). On Lamas Day, Margery again performs, playing the part of intercessor for all those in need of grace, employing her holy tears "for to purchase grace, mercy, and forgiveness for herself, for all her friends, for all her enemies, and for all the souls in Purgatory" (79).[68] Lamas eve, August first, is traditionally a day to say prayers for the dead; it is a time when the boundaries become more fluid and ghosts travel the worlds. Margery's actions reveal her belief in her performative capacity to help people at various levels of closeness to her: first, herself; next, those who have befriended her; third, those who have reviled her; and, finally, unknown souls in need of Margery's intercessory power.

These exercises prepare Margery for the highest honor accorded her during her long spiritual life. But, since Margery is a comic character as well as a serious seeker of spiritual wisdom, her mystical marriage cannot go forward without a measure of uncertainty and backsliding. Unsure of her spiritual potential, she wishes to remain at a comfortable earthly level of visionary activity. She knows that she feels comfortable with the manhood of Jesus. The Godhead, on the other hand, is an awesome unknown quantity. In her reluctance to marry the unknown she reveals the audience's own fears of the heights of mystical experience. The human characteristics of Jesus and Mary can serve good Christians in ways that the more remote Father cannot; and Margery reveals the intrinsic fear of the unknown unknowable God by balking at her prospective marriage to him. But since she is a comic figure, she can present herself dragged "kicking and screaming" to the altar by a brotherly figure who reassures her that all will be well and that she shouldn't fear marriage to his Father. Fear becomes resignation and then finally joy as Kempe provides a detailed description of the marriage in terms that allow her readers to reconstruct an entire royal high church wedding scene complete with heavenly witnesses, flowers, perfume, and music.

Kempe begins this important scene by setting it in place and time.[69] God the Father tells Margery that he is well pleased with her spiritual progress, but especially appreciates her attention to his Son. "As this creature was in the Apostles Church at Rome on Saint Laterans Day, the Father of Heaven said to her, 'Daughter, I am well pleased with you inasmuch as you believe in all the Sacraments of Holy Church and in all faith that belongs thereto, and especially for that you believe in the manhood of my Son and for the great compassion that you have of his bitter Passion' " (86).[70]

He then requests her hand in marriage, saying, " 'Daughter, I will have you wedded to my Godhead, for I shall show you my secrets and my counsels, for you shall dwell with me without end' " (86).[71] Margery's immediate reaction to the Father's approach is to feel an awesome fear. She responds meekly but firmly by her thoughtful silence. Her honesty is manifest in her unique response to this request. Sensitive to the limitations of her mystical capabilities, she understands her shortcomings as a prospective saint and fears to tread where others more worthy than herself have not been invited to go. Yet she cannot tell the Godhead that she refuses his offer of greater power and spiritual wisdom. So she remains silent, paralyzed in thought and tongue by the request, which to her appears entirely beyond her human comprehension. She explains to her audience her mixed emotions by telling them she "answered not thereto, for she was sorely afraid of the Godhead and she had no skill of dalliance with the Godhead, for all her love and all her affection was set in the manhood of Christ and because of that had she good skill and she would for nothing be parted from that" (86).[72]

Kempe then digresses to an explanation of her understandable devotion to the manhood of Christ, describing her attraction to babies and young children who remind her of the infant Jesus. Her explanation mirrors the time she is silent before God the Father and serves as a minute gap in the narrative while the audience waits to see what will happen. But Jesus does not allow Margery to escape her responsibility to grow spiritually, which can only happen by her total acceptance of God's will. Jesus gently goads her, " 'What say you Margery, daughter, to my Father of these words that he speaks to you?' "(87). Margery does not answer verbally, yet she does answer in making her discomfort clear in the only way her kind can—she weeps "wonderfully sore, desiring still to have himself and in no wise to be departed from him" (87). Like the preverbal child, she can only react to this unique request as an infant reacts to the possibility of loss of the mother. Jesus has been a mother to her as well as father, brother, husband, lover, friend, and mentor. Her realization that he has been all this to her is sudden and devastating. And Margery is not yet mature enough to understand that the gaining of the Father does not mean the loss of the Son. Jesus, understanding this explains this to his Father saying, " 'Father, have her excused, for she is yet but young and has not fully learned how she should answer' " (87). The Father's response, therefore, is both reassuring and nonverbal. He makes an active physical movement towards Margery, claiming her as his bride, leading her before the assembled company.

> And then the Father took her by the hand in her soul before the Son and the Holy Ghost and the Mother of Jesus and all the twelve apostles and Saint Katherine and Saint Margaret and many other saints and holy virgins with great multitudes of angels, saying to her soul, "I take you, Margery, for my wedded wife, for fairer, for fouler, for richer, for poorer, so that you be gentle and promise to do what I bid you do. For, daughter, there was never child so kind to the mother as I shall be to you both in well and in woe,—to help you and comfort you. And thereto I make you surety." (87)[73]

Margery, motherless child that she is, promises to obey her husband, following his will and speaking his word forever. The Mother of God and all the saints give the union their blessing. And Margery, still feeling unworthy of the honor she has received, feels great comfort both spiritually and physically. She smells sweet odors, hears beautiful melodies, and sees white things flying around her for years afterwards (87–88). Again her religious state has improved. Her ability to see the unseen and know the unknown proves that she has become, finally, a master shaman, a mistress of her visionary trade. This last dramatic scene provides the culmination of her visionary experience and makes her capable of repeating such experiences even though she need not explain the details in such graphic terms ever again in her text. Her mystical marriage to the Godhead, described by Kempe in dramatic terms comprehensible to an audience used to the mystery plays and the moralities, allows them to understand that Margery, our everywoman, is capable of ascending the ladder, step by step, until she finally achieves a mystical marriage worthy of the highest female saints.

Epilogue

In her *Book,* Margery Kempe provides a step-by-step practicum that will appeal to the medieval middle-class woman who wishes to lead a balanced mixed life. Although she never overtly states that religious women should emulate her activities, she presents herself as a believable exemplum, entertaining yet serious, pious yet human. She creates a character with whom her audience can identify both in triumph and in failure. Here Margery Kempe is also like a whole host of modern performance artists who use self-satire in their one-woman performances. Like them, she criticizes the moral flaws of her society, directing her textual spotlight particularly on the spiritual hypocrisy of many members of the clergy. Margery Kempe, in revealing her personal relationship with Jesus, the Virgin Mary, and God the Father exposes herself to the same kind of humiliation as do many of these artists. Like them, she displays a picaresque persona and emphasizes her survival capabilities. Like them, she is often confrontational as a function of her difficult personality and social criticism. Like them, she shows her audience that high moral principles and a rich spiritual life can lead to discomfort but also to the heights of spiritual knowledge and understanding. Most of all, Margery Kempe expresses her creativity through her performance art; as conscious author of her self-referential autobiographical construct, she conveys her spiritual message in forms most likely to capture her textual audience. She re-creates herself as a unique personality capable of mesmerizing most audiences, her theater amuses and edifies, and her performance elicits strong responses from all who come in contact with her through her art.

Notes

1. Victor Turner, *The Anthropology of Performance* (New York: Performing Arts Journal Publications, 1986), 48. In this work, Turner explores the

relationship between ritual and religion. Also see his *From Ritual to Theatre: The Human Seriousness of Play* (New York: Performing Arts Journal Publications, 1982) and, with his wife, Edith Turner, *Image and Pilgrimage in Western Culture* (New York: Columbia University Press, 1978).

2. See Rebecca Schneider, *The Explicit Body in Performance* (New York: Routledge, 1997) for an extensive study of female performance artists and postmodern explicit performance. Her analysis of the use of the body in performance informs my analysis of Margery Kempe's performance art.

3. Schneider describes the responses of audiences to the explicit performances of these artists. Like Margery, the female artist in the twentieth century has often been reviled, humiliated, and ignored by the male bastions of an elite art world. Schneider begins her study of female performance artists by describing the actions of the Guerrilla Girls, women who protested the exclusion of female artists from major galleries by donning gorilla masks and staging performative events (1–2). Karma Lochrie emphasizes Kempe's use of the body in *Margery Kempe and the Translations of the Flesh* (Philadelphia: University of Pennsylvania Press, 1991).

4. See John Hirsh, *The Revelations of Margery Kempe: Paramystical Practices in Late Medieval England* (New York: E.J. Brill, 1989). St. Birgitta, whose life and writings also conform to performance patterns, sets the example for Margery to follow: both marry and bear children, engage in continent marriages, embark on pilgrimages, heal the spiritually ill, receive messages from heavenly figures, brave the displeasure of traditional prelates, and produce written texts of their revelations. See Claire Sahlin's essay, "Preaching and Prophesying: The Public Proclamation of Birgitta of Sweden's Revelations," in this collection. See also St. Birgitta, *Himmelska Uppenbarelser*, ed. and trans. Tryggve Lunden, vols. 1–4 (Malmo: Allhems Forlag, 1957); *The Liber Celestis of St Bridget of Sweden*, ed. Roger Ellis, EETS 291 (London: Oxford University Press, 1987); *The Revelations of Saint Birgitta*, ed. William Patterson Cumming, EETS 178 (London: Oxford University Press, 1928). Also, Aron Andersson, *St. Birgitta and the Holy Land*, trans. Louise Setterwell (Stockholm: Museum of National Antiquities, 1983); Johannes Jørgensen, *Saint Bridget of Sweden*, trans. Ingeborg Lund (New York: Longman, Green & Co., 1954). Many critics have noted Margery Kempe's debt to St. Birgitta, beginning with Hope Emily Allen in the notes to the EETS critical edition of the *Book*. Of particular interest are Clarissa Atkinson's study of the relationship in *Mystic and Pilgrim: The Book and the World of Margery Kempe* (Ithaca, NY: Cornell University Press, 1983) and Julia Bolton Holloway, "Bride, Margery, Julian and Alice: Bridge of Sweden's Textual Community in Medieval England," in *Margery Kempe: A Book of Essays*, ed. Sandra McEntire (New York: Garland, 1992), 215–222. Signe Wegener and I have also explored the way St.

Birgitta's motherhood has influenced Margery's in "Autobiography and Domesticity: Margery Kempe and St. Birgitta as Wives and Mothers," a paper presented at the 31st International Congress on Medieval Studies, Western Michigan University, Kalamazoo, MI, May 1996. For a developmental biography of St. Theresa which includes her capacity for drama see: Francis L. and Toni Perior Gross, *The Making of a Mystic: Seasons in the Life of St. Teresa of Avila* (Albany: State University Press of New York, 1993).

5. Stephen Greenblatt, *Renaissance Self-Fashioning: More to Shakespeare* (Chicago: University of Chicago Press, 1980).

6. Many recent works have explored the performance tradition of the English cycle plays. The most relevant to this article is Gail McMurray Gibson, *The Theater of Devotion: East Anglian Drama and Society in the Late Middle Ages* (Chicago: University of Chicago Press, 1989), 47–65. Gibson, defending Margery Kempe against critics which charge her with hypocrisy and hysteria, writes that "It would be far more accurate, however, to say that Margery Kempe of Lynn possessed an unswerving sense of devotional theater and that she embraced her martyrdoms deliberately and self-consciously" (47). See also V. A. Kolve's *The Play Called Corpus Christi* (Stanford: Stanford University Press, 1966).

7. Margery most often presents herself as a simple sinner. Her youthful self displays her social pretensions by telling us that she comes from worthy kindred. The historical Kempe was the daughter of the mayor of King's Lynn, the wife of a prominent alderman John Kempe, and the mother of 14 children. See Clarissa Atkinson, *Mystic and Pilgrim*, 67–102; Anthony Goodman, "The Piety of John Brunham's Daughter of Lynn," in *Medieval Women*, ed. Derek Baker (Oxford: Blackwell, 1978), 347–358; Deborah Ellis, "Margery Kempe and King's Lynn," in *Margery Kempe: A Book of Essays*, ed. Sandra McEntire (New York: Garland, 1992), 139–163, for more information on Kempe's family life.

8. One resource helpful in understanding this work is the theory of autobiography. Two excellent books on the theory of autobiographical writing are Janet Varner Gunn, *Autobiography: Towards a Poetics of Existence* (Philadelphia: University of Pennsylvania Press, 1982) and James Olney, *Metaphors of Self: The Meaning of Autobiography* (Princeton, NJ: Princeton University Press, 1979).

9. See Schneider (1–25). Modern authors have found Kempe's text fascinating; dramatists and novelists have referred to her works from time to time. At least two have based whole works on her story: Roger Howard's "Margery Kempe," in *The Tragedy of Mao in the Lin Pao Period and Other Plays* (Colchester, England: Theater Action Press, 1989), 56–71, wrote a one-act ballad play based on her *Book*; Robert Glück wrote a novel, *Margery Kempe* (New York: High Risk Books, 1994).

10. See Laurelle Levert's paper presented at the International Medieval

Congress at Kalamazoo, May 1997, entitled "Margery Kempe and the Theatre of Her Imagination."

11. Margery Kempe shares many characteristics with the shaman who is chosen by the spirit (or spirits) through great illness to become an otherworld interpreter and spiritual healer. See Mircea Eliade, *Shamanism: Archaic Techniques of Ecstasy*, trans. Willard Trask (New York: Pantheon, 1964) and Joan Halifax, *Shaman: The Wounded Healer* (London: Thames and Hudson, 1982) for discussions of how spiritual and physical crises are frequent prerequisites to the shamanic vocation. For good analyses of the relationship between cosmic drama and shamanism see Dwight Conquergood, "Performance Theory, Hmong Shamans and Cultural Politics," in *Critical Theory and Performance*, ed. Janelle G. Reinelt and Joseph R. Roach (Ann Arbor: University of Michigan Press, 1992), 41–64, and Richard Schechner, *Performance Theory* (New York: Routledge, 1988), 41–3, 65–6 nn. 4, 5, 92, 103, 122, 135–6, 143, 145–6, 150 n. 17. See Youngsook Kim Harvey, *Six Korean Women: The Socialization of Shamans*, (St. Paul, MN: West, 1979), and Michele Jamal, *Shape Shifters: Shaman Women in Contemporary Society*, (London: Penguin, 1987) for capsule personal histories of female shamans.

12. Catherine Bell's *Ritual Theory, Ritual Practice* (New York: Oxford University Press, 1992) is a valuable theoretical work analyzing the interface between performance and ritual. Also see her more recent book, *Ritual: Perspectives and Dimensions* (New York: Oxford University Press, 1997), for a comprehensive study of the history of ritual theory.

13. See Olney, *Metaphors of Self*, 3–50.

14. Elizabeth Alvida Petroff, in her introduction to *Medieval Women's Visionary Literature*, (New York: Oxford University Press, 1986), presents many characteristics of the female visionary author and her work.

15. See Janette Dillon, "Margery Kempe's Sharp Confession," *Leeds Studies in English*, new series, 27 (1996): 131–38, and Hope Phyllis Weissman's article "Margery Kempe in Jerusalem: *Hysterica Compassio* in the Late Middle Ages," in *Acts of Interpretation: The Text in Its Contexts, 700–1600. Essays on Medieval and Renaissance Literature in Honor of E. Talbot Donaldson*, ed. Mary Carruthers and Elizabeth Kirk (Norman, OK: Pilgrim, 1982), 201–217, for varied interpretations of this crisis that results in Margery's depression.

16. This is true, at least, for Book I. Dhira Mahoney has made an excellent case for Margery's overcoming such a need in her cronage. In "Margery Kempe's Tears and the Power over Language," in *Margery Kempe: A Book of Essays*, ed. Sandra McEntire (New York: Garland, 1992), she asserts that in Book II, the elderly Margery is secure in herself and in God's support of her spiritual calling (45–49).

17. Margery Kempe's ideal wife and mother, St. Birgitta, has often been presented as wishing to retain her virginity. According to the testimony of her daughter Katarina, her marriage to Ulf Gudmarsson was

engineered by her father despite her wishes. According to the tales that developed around Birgitta, the marriage was originally chaste; only when the couple decided to bring more souls into the world for the sake of Christ was the marriage supposed to have been consummated. See Nanda Hopenwasser and Signe Wegener, "Does Mother Know Best? Saint Birgitta of Sweden: A Study in Spiritual and Secular Motherhood," paper presented at the Fourth International Medieval Conference at Leeds, Leeds, England, July 1997; and Johannes Jørgensen, *Saint Bridget of Sweden*, 46–50.

18. See Anneke B. Mulder-Bakker's introduction to *Sanctity and Motherhood: Essays on Holy Mothers in the Middle Ages*, ed. Anneke B. Mulder-Bakker (New York: Garland, 1995), 3–30, for an explanation of late medieval ideas concerning holy motherhood.

19. See Mircea Eliade, *The Myth of the Eternal Return*, trans. Willard Trask (New York: Pantheon, 1954) and "Sacred Places: Temple, Palace, 'Centre of the World'," in *Patterns in Comparative Religion* (New York: World Publishing Co., 1963). Margery's preoccupation with event recreation appears to be a particularly Roman Catholic experience according to Glenn Bowman in "Christian Ideology and the Image of the Holy Land: The Place of Jerusalem Pilgrimage in the Various Christianities," in *Contesting the Sacred: The Anthropology of Christian Pilgrimage*, ed. John Eade and Michael Sallnow (New York: Routledge, 1991), 112–116. However, Margery appears to take the recreation experience well beyond the borders of "normal." Nevertheless, extreme emotions, including weeping and prostration, still occur at Calvary. I personally was witness to such an encounter while visiting the Church of the Holy Sepulcher in 1996. A young Italian woman broke into impassioned crying at the Chapel of the Crucifixion.

20. See Eliade, *The Myth of the Eternal Return*.

21. See Victor Turner "Are There Universals of Performance in Myth, Ritual, and Drama?" 8–18; and Richard Schechner, "Magnitudes of Performance," in *By Means of Performance: Intercultural Studies of Theater and Ritual*, ed. Richard Schechner and Willa Appel, 19–49 (Cambridge: Cambridge University Press, 1990) to explore the interrelatedness of theater, myth, and ritual. The pilgrimage partakes of all these.

22. Margery's pilgrimage is alluded to earlier in the *Book*. From the preface we learn that pilgrimage was one manifestation of her holy calling and later on in the text, but entering into the discussion as a future event, we learn that Jesus promises that he will call on her to undertake a pilgrimage to Rome and Jerusalem (in *emulatio Birgittae*).

23. þe þe spyrit of prophecye teld hir, whan sche xuld gon to-Ierusalem-ward, sche xuld haue mech tribulacyon wyth hir amyden and how owyr Lord xuld asayn hir scharply and preuyn ful streytly (Kempe, *cap.* 18: 44). All passages quoted in this chapter are taken from the EETS edition: *The Book of Margery Kempe*, ed. Sanford Brown Meech and

Hope Emily Allen, EETS 212 (London: Oxford University Press, 1940). All translations into modern English are my own, but I did consult the notes in *The Book of Margery Kempe*, ed. Lynn Staley (Kalamazoo: Western Michigan University, 1976).

24. A, good ser, what xal I þan do whan I am fer fro hom & in strawnge cuntreys & my mayden be a-ʒens me? Þan is my bodily comfort a-go, & gostly comfort of any confessowr as ʒe beth wot I not wher to haue (44). Birgitta also appears to have protested, citing her advanced age as her reason to avoid the journey. But like Margery she is given reassurance that all will be well and that she will survive the journey and return to Rome again (Andersson, 10).

25. Dowtyr, drede ʒe nowt, for owyr Lord schal comfort ʒow hys owyn self, hoose comfort passyth alle oþeris, &, whan al ʒowr frendys han forsakyn ʒow, owyr Lord schal makyn a brokyn-bak man to lede ʒow forth wher ʒe wyl be (44).

26. See Elizabeth Alvida Petroff's introduction to *Medieval Women's Visionary Literature* (New York: Oxford University Press, 1986), 23–30, for a discussion of the role of dialogue in medieval women's visionary writing.

27. & so it be-fel as þe ankyr had prophecyed in euery poynt, and, as I trust, xal be wretyn more pleynly aftyrward (44). Note how extremely conscious Kempe is of the written nature of her text here—hardly the comment of an "illiterate" woman. For a recent article arguing for Margery's literacy in the vernacular see Josephine Tarvers, "The Alleged Literacy of Margery Kempe: A Reconsideration of the Evidence," *Medieval Perspectives* 11 (1986): 113–24. Kempe, here, appears to be dictating her work to an amanuensis and is commenting as the work is being written. So again, her voice seems strangely double. She is telling the tale, guiding its progress, yet cannot be actually sure that it will be written because the fuller explanation of events lies in hers and the reader's future.

28. The audience is reminded of the Jerusalem trip once more before Margery proceeds to describe it in detail when at the beginning of *capitulum* 19, she says "Be-forn þis creatur went to Ierusalem, owyr Lord sent hir to a worshipful lady þat sche xuld spekyn wyth hir in cownsel & do hys eraend vn-to hir" (46).

29. Discussions of the pilgrimage chapters focusing on the pilgrim's spiritual progress can be found in Clarissa Atkinson, *Mystic and Pilgrim*, 51–65, and Marion Glasscoe, *English Medieval Mystics: Games of Faith* (London: Longman, 1993), 292–298.

30. Yarmouth was a common port of embarkation for English pilgrims. See Christian Zacher, *Curiosity and Pilgrimage: The Literature of Discovery in Fourteenth-Century England* (Baltimore: Johns Hopkins University Press, 1978). For a short introduction to the pilgrimage route see Ronald Musto, Introduction to *Guide to the Holy Land*, by Theoderich, trans. Aubrey Stewart (New York: Italica Press, 1996), xxvi-xxi. Although

the route was familiar, pilgrimage routes had to be modified from time to time during Margery's and Birgitta's lifetimes because of political conflicts. Moslem rulers were often more interested in making money from trade than in preventing Christians (and sometimes Jews) from traveling in the Holy Land. But the trip was expensive: much *baksheesh* (bribes) had to be paid by pilgrims who wanted to see their holy sites. See Benjamin of Tudela, *The Itinerary of Benjamin of Tudela: Travels in the Middle Ages*, ed. and trans. A. Asher, intro. Marcus Nathan Adler and Michael Signer (Malibu, CA: Pangloss Press, 1993) for a peek into Jewish settlement in the Middle Ages.

31. a gret town hyte Seryce, wher owyr Lord of hys hey goodnesse vysited þis creatur wyth abundawnt teerys of contricyon for hir owyn synnes and sumtyme for oþer mennysynnes also (60–61). According to note 60/37–38 in the EETS edition, the town is Zierikzee in Zealand, the Netherlands, a Hansa town (285). According to Hope Emily Allen, "At the time when Margery was in Holland, St. Lydwine must have been exhibiting there the miraculous visitation of tears, . . ." (286). Margery, therefore, had a tangible performative model.

32. Of course, the public leave taking from King's Lynn might "count" as a performance. Certainly, her public settlement of her debts, her taking leave of husband and spiritual advisors, her giving donations to the churches in Norwich and in Yarmouth are all part of the great pilgrimage rite as part of ritual theater. See Victor and Edith Turner, *Image and Pilgrimage in Christian Culture* (New York: Columbia University Press, 1978). This performance, however, is a conscious theatrical action; Margery has a ready audience ready to witness her activity in a ritual framework.

33. For thoroughgoing studies analyzing Margery's compunction and contrition see Sandra McEntire, "The Doctrine of Compunction from Bede to Margery Kempe," in *Medieval Mystical Tradition in England: Exeter Symposium IV*, ed. Marion Glasscoe (Cambridge: Brewer, 1987), 77–90, and "Walter Hilton and Margery Kempe: Tears and Compunction," in *Mysticism: Medieval and Modern*, ed. Valerie Lagorio (Salzburg: Institut für Anglistik und Amerikanistik, 1986), 49–57. For more information on public performance see Conquergood, and Mary Suydam, "Writing Beguines: Ecstatic Performances," *Magistra* 2:1 (Summer 1996): 137–69.

34. In this way Margery acts very much like theater groups who protest political actions or social foibles in versions of plays that undercut traditional theater. See David McDonald, "Unspeakable Justice: David Hare's *Fanshen*" (129–45) and Jim Carmody, "Alceste in Hollywood: A Semiotic Reading of *The Misanthrope*" (117–28). Also note the religious and political disruptions of people in carnival and political demonstrations. See Richard Schechner, "Invasions Friendly and Unfriendly: The Dramaturgy of Direct Theater" (88–106). All three of these references

can be found in *Critical Theory and Performance*, ed. Janelle G. Reinelt and Joseph Roach (Ann Arbor: University of Michigan Press, 1992).

35. See Max Harris, *Theater and Incarnation* (London: Macmillan, 1990), 57–73. For a detailed explanation of the religious use of symbols with regard to pilgrimage and other religious rituals see "Appendix A: Notes on Processional Symbolic Analysis" in Turner and Turner, 243–55.

36. See Joseph Parry, "Margery Kempe's Inarticulate Narration," *Magistra* 1:2 (Winter 1995): 292–298; also Karma Lochrie, *Margery Kempe and Translations of the Flesh* (Philadelphia: University of Pennsylvania Press, 1991), 177–193; Dhira B. Mahoney, "Margery Kempe's Tears and the Power over Language," in *Margery Kempe: A Book of Essays*, ed. Sandra McEntire, 37–50. Mahoney suggests that Margery's tears are "physical markers that would perform the same function as enclosure" of anchorites such as Julian of Norwich, and "would announce her separation from society, her holiness and her link with God" (38). Other markers are "continence and white clothes" (39).

37. David Colt in *The Theatrical Event: A Mythos, A Vocabulary, A Perspective* (Middletown, CT: Wesleyan University Press, 1975) emphasizes the intercessor role in his chapter on the actor (12–57).

38. And specyaly sche had terys of compassyon in þe mende of owyr Lordys Passyon. And sche was howselyd eche Sunday wher þat tyme was & place convuenient þerto wyth gret wepyngys & boystows sobbyngs þat many men meruelyed & wonderyd of þe gret Grace þat God wrowt in hys creatur (61).

39. Meech and Allen believe that "Margery is probably referring to her custom throughout her journey, rather than only her experience in the 'great town' of Zealand' (n. 61/1). Their conclusion makes sense and argues for repetitive performance rituals.

40. See Eliade, *Shamanism*; Halifax, *Shaman: The Wounded Healer*; and Harvey, *Six Korean Women*; but especially David Cole, *The Theatrical Event: A Mythos, A Vocabulary, A Perspective* (Middletown, CT: Wesleyan University Press, 1975) on the performance as a shamanic experience taking place in the *illud tempus* and the actor as shaman and *hungan* (the divine vehicle in a possession ritual) (12–57).

41. For such distinctions see Christian Zacher, *Curiosity and Pilgrimage: The Literature of Discovery in Fourteenth-Century England* (Baltimore: Johns Hopkins University Press, 1976).

42. Dhira Mahoney points out that Margery's antagonists are frequently friars who, according to Jill Mann, *Chaucer and Medieval Estates Satire* (Cambridge: Cambridge University Press, 1973, 37–40, were a "familiar theme for medieval satirists "because of their persuasive and deceptive tongue" (50). Kempe, therefore, creates "worthy" opponents for Margery's own persuasive rhetoric.

43. With a little more filling out, this prelate would be worthy to attend to Chaucer's Canterbury lot. Lynn Staley in chapter 2, "Sacred Biog-

raphy and Social Criticism," of *Margery Kempe's Dissenting Fictions* (University Park, PA: Pennsylvania State University Press, 1994), 39–82, discusses Margery as social critic.

44. hir to do as sche wold for a tyme as hym lykyd (61).

45. And þei wer most displesyd for sche wepyd so mech & spak alwey of þe lofe & goodnes of owyr Lord as wel at þe tabyl as in oþer place (61).

46. & þerfor schamfully þei repreuyd hir & alto-chedyn hir & seyden þei wold not suffren hir as hir husbond dede whan sche was at hom & in Inglond (61).

47. & þan sche seyd to oon of hem specyaly, '3&e do me meche schame & gret greuawns' (61). The implication remains that this tormentor is the same priest who gives her a great deal of trouble throughout the pilgrimage, but since he remains unnamed and since she implies rather than says it, other implications can be drawn also. This gives us a bit of room to vary our interpretations of Margery's drama of conflict.

48. Like the picaresque heroine, Margery's fortunes rise and fall; she has varied adventures and actions repeat. This is but the first of such encounters on the pilgrimage. See Anne Kaler, *The Picara: From Hera to Fantasy Heroine* (Bowling Green, OH: Bowling Green State University Popular Press, 1991).

49. Þan on þe next morwyn þer com to hir on of her company, a man whech louyd hir wel, preying hir þat sche wold go to hys felaws & mekyn hir on-to hem & preyn hem þat sche myth go stylle in her cumpany tyl sche come at Constawns (62).

50. Þey cuttyd hir gown so schort þat it come but lytil be-nethyn hir kne & dedyn hir don on a whyte canwas in maner of a sekkyn gelle, for sche xuld ben holdyn a fool & þe pepyl xuld not makyn of hir ne han in reputaeyon. Þe madyn hir to syttyn at Þe tabelys ende be-nethyn alle oþer þat sche durst ful euyl spekyn a word (62).

51. & not-wythstondyng al her malyce, sche was had in mor worshep þan þei wher-þat-euyr þei comyn (62).

52. 'Drede þe nowt, dowtyr, þi felawshep xal non harm han whyl þu art her cumpany' (62).

53. We hear nothing of the fate of the former ship; so we cannot judge the value of Margery's prophecy as a guarantee of protection. See Thomas Overholt, *Channels of Prophecy: The Social Dynamics of Prophetic Activity* (Minneapolis: Fortress Press, 1989) for an excellent explanation of the nature of the prophetic process and the public politics of prophecy.

54. sche was as fals as sche mytgth be & dispysed hir & so-rebukyd hir (67).

55. Birgitta made her pilgrimage to the Holy Land when she was an elderly woman. She was accompanied by her daughter Katherina, Petrus

Olafsson, Alfons of Jaen and others according to Tryggve Lunden, "Den Heliga Birgittas Liv och Skrifter," in *Himmelska Uppenbarelser*, ed. Tryggve Lunden (Malmo: Allhems Förlag, 1957), 1: 11. For a detailed monograph about the pilgrimage see Andersson, *St. Birgitta and the Holy Land*.

56. Notes written by Meech and Allen explain Margery and companies movements in detail (289).

57. Þan þe frerys lyftyd up a cros & led þe pylgrimys a-bowte fro[on] place to an-oþer wher owyr Lord had sufferyd hys [peynys] and hys passyons, euery man and woman beryng a wax candel in her hand. & þe frerys alwey, as þei went a-bowte, teld hem what owyr Lord sufferyd in euery place (68).

58. þe forseyd cretur wept & sobbyd so plentyvowsly as þow sche had seyn owyr Lord wyth hir bodyly ey sufferyng at þat tyme (68).

59. She writes, "And þis maner of crying enduryed many ȝerys aftyr þis tyme for owt þat any man myt do, & þerfor sufferyd sche mych despyte & mech reprefe" (68).

60. Ellen Ross quotes this passages in "Diversities of Divine Presence: Women's Geography in the Christian Tradition," in *Sacred Places and Profane Spaces: Essays in the Geographies of Judaism, Christianity, and Islam*, ed. Jamie Scott and Paul Simpson-Housley (New York: Greenwood Press, 1991), 100, 112, citing her source as Jerome, *Epistolae*, in *Corpus Scriptorum Ecclesiasticorum Latinorum*, ed. I. A. Hilberg (Vienna, 1912), Letter 108:8–14; English translation in *Nicene and Post-Nicene Fathers*, ed. Philip Schaff and H. Wace (Grand Rapids, Michigan: William B. Eerdmans, 1892), 6: 198–202.

61. &, whan þei cam vpon-to þe mount of Caluarye, sche fel down þat sche mygth not stondyn ne knelyn but walwyd & wrestyd wyth hir body, spredyng hir armys a-brode, & cryed wyth a lowde voys as þow hir hert vulde a brostyn a-sundyr, for in þe cite of hir sowle sche saw veryly & freschly how owyr Lord was crucifyed (69).

62. the cryeng was so lowde & so wondyrful þat it made þe pepyl astoynd les þan þei had herd it be-forn & er ellys þat þei knew þe cawse of þe crying (68).

63. & whan sche com hom in-to Inglonde, fyrst at hir comyng hom it comyn but seldom as it wer onys in a moneth, sythen oncys in þe weke, aftyrward cotidianly, oncys sche had xiiij on o day, & an-oþer day sche had vij, & so as God wolde visiten hir, sum tyme in þe cherch, sumtyme in þe strete, sumtym in þe chawmbre, sumtyme in þe felde whan God wold sendyn hem, for sche knew neuyt tyme ne owyr whan þei xulde come (69).

64. For summe seyd it was a wikkyd spiryt vexid hir; sum seyd it was a sekenes; sum seyd sche had dronkyn to mech wyn; sum bannyd hir; sum wisshed sche had ben in þe hauyn; sum wolde sche had ben in þe se in a bottumless boyt; and so ich man as hym thowte (69).

65. knewyn ful lytyl what sche felt, ne þei wolde not beleuyn but þat sche myth an absteynd hir fro crying yf sche had wold(69).

66. And þan owyr Lord comawyndyd hir for to gon to Rome, & so forth hom in-to Inglond, & seyd vn-to hir, "Dowtyr, as oftyn-tymes as þu seyst or thynkyst, 'Worshepyd be alle þe holy placys in Ierusalem þat Crist suffyrde bittyr peyn & passyon in,' þu schalt haue þe same pardon as ȝyf þu wer þer wyth þi bodily presens bothyn to þi-selfe & to alle þo þat þu wylt ȝeuyn it to" (75).

67. "Drede þe not, dowtyr, for I xal ordeyn for þe ryth wel & bryng þe in safte to Rome & home a-geyn in-to Inglond wuth-owtyn ony velany of þi body ȝyf thow wilt be clad in white clothys & weryn hem as I seyd to þe whil þu wer in Inglond" (76).

68. for to purchasyn grace, mercy, & forȝeuenes for hir-selfe, for alle hir frendys, for alle hir enmys, & for alle þe sowlys in Purgatory (79). Here Margery is following the tradition of Saint Francis. Meech and Allen explain, "the Portiuncula Indulgence, which according to tradition, was granted to St. Francis himself by Pope Honorius III, originally gave plenary remission of sins to all people who came to the Chapel of the Portiuncula from the Vespers of 1 Aug. to those of 2 Aug." (n. 79/25–26, 298). They also assign the date Margery's sojourn in Assisi to Lamas day 1414 and her departure from Rome to the spring of 1415 (298–99).

69. Meech and Allen write "this was almost certainly the feast of the dedication of St. John Lateran, 9 Nov., and probably it was in the year 1414" (n. 86/10, 301).

70. As þis creatur was in þe Postelys Cherch at Rome on Seynt Laterynes Day, þe Fadyr of Hevyn seyd to hir, "Dowtyr, I am wel plesyd wyth þe in-as-mech as þu beleuyst in alle þe Sacramentys of Holy Chirche & in al feyth þat longith þerto, & specialy for þat þu beleuyst in manhode of my Sone & for þe gret compassyon þat þu hast of hys bittyr Passyon." (86).

71. "Dowtyr, I wil han þe weddyd to my Godhede, for I schale schewyn þe my preuyteys & my cownselys, for þu xalt wonyn wyth me wyth-owtyn ende" (86).

72. answeryd not þerto, for sche was sor aferd of þe Godhed & sche cowde no skylle of dalyawns of þe Godhede, for al hir lofe & al hir affeccyon was set in þe manhode of Criste & þerof cowde sche good skylle & sche wolde for no-thynge a partyd þerfro (86).

73. And þan þe Fadyr toke hir be þe hand in hir sowle be-for þe Sone & þe Holy Gost & þe Modyr of Ihesu and alle þe xij apostelys & Seynt Kateryn & Seynt Margerete & many oþer seyntys & holy virgynes wyth gret multitude of awngelys, seying to hir sowle, "I take þe, Margery, for my weddyd wyfe, for fay rar, for fowelar, for richar, for powerar, so þat þu be buxom & bonyr to do what I byd þe do. For, dowtyr, þer was neuyr childe so buxom to þe modyr as I xal be to þe boþe in wel

& in wo,—to help þe and comfort þe. And þerto I make þe suyrte"
(87).

Bibliography

Andersson, Aron. *St. Birgitta and the Holy Land.* Trans. Louise Setterwell. Stockholm: Museum of National Antiquities, 1983.

Atkinson, Clarissa. *Mystic and Pilgrim: The "Book" and the World of Margery Kempe.* Ithaca, NY: Cornell University Press, 1983.

Bell, Catherine. *Ritual: Perspectives and Dimensions.* New York: Oxford University Press, 1997.

———. *Ritual Theory, Ritual Practice.* New York: Oxford University Press, 1992.

Benjamin of Tudela. *The Itinerary of Benjamin of Tudela: Travels in the Middle Ages.* Ed. and Trans. A. Asher. Intro. Marcus Nathan Adler and Michael Signer. Malibu, CA: Pangloss Press, 1993.

Birgitta of Sweden. *Himmelska Uppenbarelser.* Ed. and trans. Tryggve Lunden. Vols. 1–4. Malmo: Allhems Forlag, 1957.

———. *The Liber Celestis of St Bridget of Sweden.* Ed. Roger Ellis. EETS 291. London: Oxford University Press, 1987.

———. *Revelationes Extravagantes.* Ed. Lennart Hollman. Stockholm: Kungl. Vitterhets Historie och Antikvitetsakademien, 1956.

———. *Revelationes S. Birgittae.* Ed. Elias Wessen. Hafnia: E. Munksgaard, 1952–56.

———. *Revelationes S. Birgittae: Translatio Suecana.* Ed. Marta Wessen. Hafnia: E. Munksgaard, 1949.

———. *The Revelations of Saint Birgitta.* Ed. William Patterson Cumming. EETS 178. London: Oxford University Press, 1928.

Bowman, Glenn. "Christian Ideology and the Image of the Holy Land: The Place of Jerusalem Pilgrimage In the Various Christianities." In *Contesting the Sacred: The Anthropology of Christian Pilgrimage,* ed. John Eade and Michael Sallnow. New York: Routledge, 1991.

Carmody, Jim. "Alceste in Hollywood: A Semiotic Reading of *The Misanthrope,*" in *Critical Theory and Performance,* ed. Janelle G. Reinelt and Joseph Roach, 117–28. Ann Arbor: University of Michigan Press, 1992.

Colt, David. *The Theatrical Event: A Mythos, A Vocabulary, A Perspective.* Middletown, CT: Wesleyan University Press, 1975.

Conquergood, Dwight. "Performance theory, Hmong Shamans and Cultural Politics." In *Critical Theory and Performance,* ed. Janelle G. Reinelt and Joseph Roach, 41–64. Ann Arbor: University of Michigan Press, 1992.

Dillon, Janette. "Margery Kempe's Sharp Confession." In *Leeds Studies in English,* new series, 27 (1996): 131–38.

Eade, John. and Michael Sallnow, eds. *Contesting the Sacred: The Anthropology of Christian Pilgrimage.* New York: Routledge, 1991.

Eliade, Mircea. *The Myth of the Eternal Return*. Trans. Willard Trask. New York: Pantheon, 1954.

———. "Sacred Places: Temple, Palace, 'Centre of the World'." In *Patterns in Comparative Religion*. New York: World Publishing Company, 1963.

———. *Shamanism: Archaic Techniques of Ecstasy*. Trans. Willard Trask. New York: Pantheon Books, 1964.

Ellis, Deborah. "Margery Kempe and King's Lynn." In *Margery Kempe: A Book of Essays*, ed. Sandra McEntire, 139–63. New York: Garland, 1992.

Flaherty, Gloria. *Shamanism and the Eighteenth Century*. Princeton, NJ: Princeton University Press, 1992.

Fogelqvist, Ingvar. *Apostasy and Reform in the Revelations of St. Birgitta*. Bibliotheca Theologicae Practicae, Kyrkovetenskapliga Studier, 51. Stockholm: Almquist and Wiksell International, 1993.

Geertz, Clifford. *The Interpretation of Culture*. New York: Basic Books, 1973.

Gibson, Gail McMurray. *The Theatre of Devotion: East Anglian Drama and Society in the Late Middle Ages*. Chicago: University of Chicago Press, 1989.

Glasscoe, Marion. *English Medieval Mystics: Games of Faith*. London: Longman, 1993.

Glück, Robert. *Margery Kempe*. New York: High Risk Books, 1994.

Goodman, Anthony. "The Piety of John Brunham's Daughter of Lynn." In *Medieval Women*, ed. Derek Baker, 347–57. Oxford: Blackwell, 1978.

Greenblatt, Stephen. *Renaissance Self-Fashioning: More to Shakespeare*. Chicago: University of Chicago Press, 1980.

Grim, John. *The Shaman: Patterns of Siberian and Ojibway Healing*. Norman, OK: University of Oklahoma Press, 1983.

Gross, Francis L. and Toni Perior Gross. *The Making of a Mystic: Seasons In the Life of St. Teresa of Avila*. Albany: State University Press of New York, 1993.

Gunn, Janet Varner. *Autobiography: Towards a Poetics of Existence*. Philadelphia: University of Pennsylvania Press, 1982.

Halifax, Joan. *Shaman: The Wounded Healer*. London: Thames and Hudson, 1982

Harner, Michael. *The Way of the Shaman*. San Francisco: Harper and Row, 1990.

Harris, Max. *Theater and Incarnation*. London: Macmillan, 1990.

Harvey, Youngsook Kim. *Six Korean Women: The Socialization of Shamans*. St. Paul, MN: West, 1979.

Hirsh, John. *The Revelations of Margery Kempe: Paramystical Practies in Late Medieval England*. New York: E.J. Brill, 1989.

Hogg, James, ed. *Studies in St. Birgitta and the Brigittine Order*. 2 vols. Analecta Cartusiana, 35/19; Spiritualität Heute und Gestern, 19. Salzburg: Institut für Anglistik und Amerikanistik; Lewiston, NY: Edwin Mellen Press, 1993.

Holloway, Julia Bolton. "Bride, Margery, Julian and Alice: Bridget of Sweden's Textual Community in Medieval England." In *Margery Kempe: A Book of Essays*. Ed. Sandra McEntire. New York: Garland, 1992, 215–222.

Hopenwasser, Nanda and Signe Wegener. "Autobiography and Domesticity: Margery Kempe and St. Birgitta as Wives and Mothers." Paper presented at the

31st International Congress on Medieval Studies, Western Michigan University, Kalamazoo, MI, May 1996.

———. "Does Mother Know Best? Saint Birgitta of Sweden: A Study in Spiritual and Secular Motherhood." Paper presented at the Fourth International Medieval Conference in Leeds, Leeds England, July 1997.

Howard, Roger. "Margery Kempe." In *The Tragedy of Mao in the Lin Pao Period and Other Plays*, Colchester, England: Theater Action Press, 1989: 56–71.

Jamal, Michele. *Shape Shifters: Shaman Women in Contemporary Society*. London: Penguin, 1987.

Jørgensen, Johannes. *Saint Bridget of Sweden*. Trans. Ingeborg Lund. New York: Longman, Green & Co., 1954.

Kaler, Anne. *The Picara: From Hera to Fantasy Heroine*. Bowling Green, OH: Bowling Green State University Popular Press, 1991.

Kempe, Margery. *The Book of Margery Kempe*. Ed. Sanford Brown Meech and Hope Emily Allen. EETS 212. London: Oxford University Press, 1940.

———. *The Book of Margery Kempe*. Ed. Lynn Staley. Kalamazoo, MI: Western Michigan University, 1996.

Kendall, Laurel. "The Shaman's Apprentice." *Natural History*, 6:2 (March 1997): 39–40.

Kolve, V.A. *The Play Called Corpus Christi*. Stanford: Stanford University Press, 1966.

Levert, Laurelle. "Margery Kempe and the Theatre of Her Imagination." Paper presented at the International Medieval Congress at Kalamazoo, May 1997.

Lévi-Strauss, Claude. *The Raw and the Cooked*. Vol. 1 of *Introduction to a Science of Mythology*, trans. John and Doreen Weightman, New York: Harper and Row, 1969.

Lochrie, Karma. *Margery Kempe and Translations of the Flesh*. Philadelphia: University of Pennsylvania Press, 1991.

Mahoney, Dhira. "Margery Kempe's Tears and the Power over Language." In *Margery Kempe: A Book of Essays*, ed. Sandra McEntire, New York: Garland, 1992. 45–49.

Mann, Jill. *Chaucer and Medieval Estates Satire*. Cambridge: Cambridge University Press, 1973.

McDonald, David. "Unspeakable Justice: David Hare's *Fanshen*." In *Critical Theory and Performance*, ed. Janelle G. Reinelt and Joseph Roach, 129–45. Ann Arbor: University of Michigan Press, 1992.

McEntire, Sandra. "The Doctrine of Compunction from Bede to Margery Kempe." In *Medieval Mystical Tradition in England: Exeter Symposium IV*, ed. Marion Glasscoe, 77–90. Cambridge: Brewer, 1987.

———. "Walter Hilton and Margery Kempe: Tears and Compunction." In *Mysticism: Medieval and Modern*, ed. Valerie Lagorio. Salzburg: Institut für Anglistik und Amerikanistik, 1986, 49–57.

Mulder-Bakker. Anneke. Introduction to *Sanctity and Motherhood: Essays on Holy Mothers in the Middle Ages*, ed. Anneke Mulder-Bakker. New York: Garland, 1995.

Musto, Ronald. Introduction to *Guide to the Holy Land*, by Theodorich, i–xxi. Trans. Aubrey Stewart. New York: Italica Press, 1994.

Olney, James. *Metaphors of Self: The Meaning of Autobiography*. Princeton: Princeton University Press, 1979.

Overholt, Thomas. *Channels of Prophecy: The Social Dynamics of Prophetic Activity*. Minneapolis: Fortress Press, 1989.

Parry, Joseph. "Margery Kempe's Inarticulate Narration." *Magistra* 1 (1995): 292–98.

Petroff, Elizabeth Alvida. *Medieval Women's Visionary Literature*. New York: Oxford University Press, 1986.

Ross, Ellen. "Diversities of Divine Presence: Women's Geography in the Christian Tradition." In *Sacred Places and Profane Spaces: Essays in the Geographies of Judaism, Christianity, and Islam*, ed. Jamie Scott and Paul Simpson-Housley, New York: Greenwood Press, 1991.

Schechner, Richard. "Invasions Friendly and Unfriendly: the Dramaturgy of Direct Theater." In *Critical Theory and Performance*, ed. Janelle G. Reinelt and Joseph Roach, 88–106. Ann Arbor: University of Michigan Press, 1992.

———. "Magnitudes of Performance." In *By Means of Performance: Intercultural Studies of Theater and Ritual*, ed. Richard Schechner and Willa Appel, 19–49. Cambridge: Cambridge University Press, 1990.

———. *Performance Theory*. New York: Routledge, 1988.

———. and Willa Appel. *By Means of Performance: Intercultural Studies of Theater and Ritual*. Cambridge: Cambridge University Press, 1990.

Schneider, Rebecca. *The Explicit Body in Performance*. New York: Routledge, 1997.

Staley, Lynn. *Margery Kempe's Dissenting Fictions*. University Park, PA: Pennsylvania State University Press, 1994.

Suydam, Mary. "Writing Beguines: Ecstatic Performances." *Magistra* 2 (1996): 137–69.

Tarvers, Josephine. "The Alleged Literacy of Margery Kempe: A Reconsideration of the Evidence." *Medieval Perspectives* 11 (1986): 113–24.

Theodorich. *Guide to the Holy Land*. Trans. Aubrey Stewart. New York: Italica Press, 1994.

Turner, Victor. *The Anthropology of Performance*. New York: Performing Arts Journal Publications, 1986.

———. "Are There Universals of Performance in Myth, Ritual and Drama?" In *By Means of Performance: Intercultural Studies of Theater and Ritual*, ed. Richard Schechner and Willa Appel, 8–18. Cambridge: Cambridge University Press, 1990.

———. *From Ritual to Theatre: The Human Seriousness of Play*. New York: Performing Arts Journal Publications, 1982.

Turner, Victor and Edith. *Image and Pilgrimage in Christian Culture: Anthropological Perspectives*. New York: Columbia University Press, 1978.

Walsh, Roger. *The Spirit of Shamanism*. Los Angeles: Jeremy P. Tarcher, 1990.

Weissman, Hope Phyllis. "Margery Kempe in Jerusalem: Hysterica Compassio in the Late Middle Ages." In *Acts of Interpretation: The Text in Its Contexts, 700–1600. Essays on Medieval and Renaissance Literature in Honor of E. Talbot Donaldson*, ed. Mary Carruthers and Elizabeth Kirk, 201–217. Norman, OK: Pilgrim, 1982.

Zacher, Christian. *Curiosity and Pilgrimage: the Literature of Discovery in Fourteenth Century England*. Baltimore: Johns Hopkins University Press, 1978.

Zaleski, Carol. *Otherworld Journeys: Accounts of Near-Death Experience in Medieval and Modern Times*. New York: Oxford University Press, 1987.

CHAPTER SIX

Thomas of Cantimpré: Performative Reading and Pastoral Care

Robert Sweetman

Introduction: Scholarly and Performative Reading as Self-Expression

I confess that I am most familiar with four kinds of reading and that I engage in these to the exclusion of any others. In the first place, I earn my bread in scholarly examination of texts. But, often, when my own writing has begun to sag under the gathered weight of a prolix pedantry, I read literary texts for the mimetic effect their fluidity and elegance work upon my belabored pen. Then there is the hedonistic consumption of texts for pleasure and entertainment, and finally devout absorption with and by sacred texts.

It is all well and good to announce distinctions in kind. After all, *bene distinguere bene philosophare est.* Moreover, the distinctions one makes are often durable, maintaining their personal cachet no matter how idiosyncratic and insubstantial they appear to others. But if distinctions are to acquire the gravitas required for truly communal service, they must, at the least, be described in ways that prove suggestive, evoking recognition in others. "Oh," one hopes the reader will say, "I know exactly what you mean; except what you call 'x', I call 'y'."

I distinguish within my own experience four kinds of reading because I am aware of assuming four discrete attitudes or postures, of constructing four "selves" vis-à-vis texts. This assumption of attitude or construction of self corresponds, in turn, to different dynamics moving me to read. It would not do to dwell overly long on this modest effort at philosophical introspection. Nevertheless, it is worth noting that the four attitudes, postures, or selves I have distinguished can be ranged along conceptual continua construed in terms of different qualities: mobility/immobility, permeability/impermeability, priority/posteriority, and surely others that escape me. Generally speaking, scholarly and hedonistic or consumptive reading tend toward the one pole of these continua, while mimetic and devotional reading tend toward the other. In other words, scholarly and consumptive reading assume postures vis-à-vis texts that are relatively more immobile, impermeable, and prior, while mimetic and devotional readings assume postures that are relatively more mobile, permeable, and posterior. Moreover, scholarly and devotional readings tend furthest toward the poles of these continua, while consumptive and mimetic readings tend toward the mean.

I can perhaps illustrate what I have in mind in these introductory remarks by considering briefly scholarly and devotional reading in terms of their permeability, that is, the reader's openness to allow what she reads to get under her skin, to change her essential posture towards the text at hand, or perhaps even in life. The scholarly reader whose research questions determine her reading is relatively impermeable. She asks questions of texts to which they answer "yes" or "no." For example, she asks: "Do you, o texts, exhibit the motif of the jaws of hell? If so, are they depicted in classical terms? If not, do they owe their divergence to the language of biblical apocalyptic?" In such an approach, the text's impact upon the scholarly reader is controlled. It can only really confirm or refute the scholar's a priori guesses or hypotheses. The scholar goes where the text leads but only grudgingly, preferring rather to have it go where she wills, never more so than when looking to uncover what is hidden, as it were, between the lines. Of course, scholars do not always approach texts in so rigid a fashion; there is an appropriate play in deed. There are even exceptional instances in which scholars have been converted by the texts they read: evangelical Sinologists taking up the *Tao*, or lifelong agnostics finding Julian of Norwich's sweet Jesus, Son of the Father and Mother of us all. Nevertheless, I view controlling chains of questions such as those in our illustration to be paradigmatic. Seldom do we, as scholars, go to texts and read out of unfocused curiosity. One can use even stronger language. We never go, as scholars, to texts to be interrogated but to inter-rogate. Devotional readers of a sacred text, on the other hand, are self-consciously permeable.[1] The devotee is in search of the "Words of Life." By implication, he does not have them or at least has them only in part. Hence, he does not know what exactly he hopes to find. Of course this last description can work for scholars too, but what devotional readers have that differentiates their reading from the scholarly enterprise is that they know in their bones where to look: there in the Good Book, in the *Summa*, in the *Lives* of the saints—there one will encounter those words and patterns that transform life, that is, that enter, possess, and make one anew. Moreover, one can calibrate the devotion of the devout reader by the degree to which sacred locution transcribes itself onto the reader's subsequent body, tongue, and heart.

In general, scholars have given most thought to the structure and character of scholarly reading, and each scholarly discipline has developed its own descriptions and traditions. Now, if I reflect upon my formation to scholarly life among North American historians and medievalists, I recall a number of claims made about scholarly reading. For example, it was often said that scholarly reading was to map the patterns implicit in a text; to break texts down into their significant elements, whether these be in-tertextual or originary; to bring out meanings hidden, as it were, between the lines: hidden political, economic, psychological, gender, aesthetic mat-ters, and so on.[2] Such claims are all founded upon the assumption that scholarly reading is something self-assured. By that I mean that the schol-arly reader approaches her text in a determined posture, which determi-nation effects a unidirectional movement outward toward texts. In other words, scholarly reading is the act of a self essentially formed and stable. It is a causal operation such a self carries out upon texts, an operation by which they are effected meaningful, that is, present, to it. It is I who control what the text is and can mean to me. To be sure, I might expe-rience myself edified or titillated by a text I have read. I might feel that I am no longer quite the same, even that I have been profoundly affected by what I have read. Nevertheless, such change, however important, is only ever accidental, for the scholarly self remains essentially identical thoughout. In other words, a formed or essential self is presupposed by any such change as its very condition of possibility.[3]

The present essay, however, seeks to examine scholarly reading in the light cast by another way of reading, one arising from a different, less self-assured relation to texts. I will call this way of reading "performative" for reasons that will become clear as we go along. I will suggest that there is a connection between medieval "performative" reading and the type of devotional reading we have just considered, and will do so ominously in terms of a story of demon possession, acknowledging thereby that possession, like cholesterol, comes in good and bad kinds.[4] In the meantime, since the body of the essay concentrates upon exceptionally arcane instances of scholarly and performative reading, I propose to illustrate what I mean by the latter term in a way that prepares for, even as it eases, the historical vertigo to be endured through extended examination of a strange vignette or *exemplum* included in what is itself a sprawling curiosity, the *Bonum universale de apibus* or *Book of Bees*, of the thirteenth-century Dominican Thomas of Cantimpré.[5] I draw my opening illustration from that wildly successful (if less often read than displayed) piece of medievalism, Umberto Eco's *The Name of the Rose*.[6]

You may or may not remember that Adso, novice monk of the Benedictine house of Melk, is brought by his warrior uncle to Italy in the military train of Louis of Bavaria. As Louis's Italian campaign grinds on interminably, Adso is assigned a *socius*, or religious companion, the English Franciscan and sleuth William of Baskerville. Together they proceed to a North Italian monastery where a crucial ecclesiastical convocation is to take place. Once arrived, they undertake a series of researches, including several clandestine nocturnal wanderings in hopes of solving the mystery surrounding a rash of deaths plaguing the resident monastic community.

After Compline on the third day of their sojourn, Adso is nearly discovered at his secret perambulations and hides in the monastery's spacious kitchens, where he meets another stowaway, a certain village girl who has come to trade sexual favours to the establishment's corpulent cellarer in return for an ox heart and lungs for her hungry family. At first Adso and the girl approach each other tentatively but soon they are copulating with considerable energy, in his case imaginative quite as much as glandular.

His experience of the event is expressed in an outpouring of words flowing with the phraseological oil of monastic *lectio divina*, that is, in hymnody resounding with the music of the Song of Songs:

> And she kissed me with the kisses of her mouth, and her loves were
> more delicious than wine and her ointments had goodly fragrance,
> and her neck was beautiful among pearls and her cheeks among ear-
> rings, behold thou art fair, my beloved, behold thou art fair; thine
> eyes are as doves (I said), and let me see thy face, let me hear thy

voice, for thy voice is harmonious and thy face enchanting, thou hast
ravished my heart, my sister, thou hast ravished my heart. . . . [7]

In and through his verbal effusion Adso re-collects liturgical reading of
the sacred text performed in service of God. This reading, in turn, "performs" him in the sense that it forms him as, in the educational jargon of
the day, a "liberally formed" (articulate) intellect "free" (able) to "invent"
(discover and represent) the sense of his experience.[8]

Adso begins his sexual adventure as a dumb brute, little different
from the ox whose heart had originally drawn the girl hither. As Eco has
him tell it: "What did I feel? What did I see? I remember only that the
emotions of the first moment were bereft of any expression, because my
tongue and my mind had not been instructed in how to name sensations
of that sort."[9] Directly, however, the constitutive features of a liberally
articulate, that is, truly human self emerge from appropriated *enarrationes
sanctorum*: "I recalled other inner words, heard in another time and in other
places, spoken certainly for other ends, but which seemed wondrously in
keeping with my joy in that moment, as if they had been born consub-
stantially to express it. Words pressed into the caverns of my memory rose
to the (dumb) surface of my lips, and I forgot that they had served in
Scripture or in the pages of the saints to express quite different, more
radiant realities."[10] That is to say, words uttered by the saints form Adso
so that he experiences himself allegorically re-membered from their verbal
relicta.

The more perfect Adso's submission to authoritative texts, the more
he is formed in their image such that he no longer experiences their difference: "But was there truly a difference between the delights of which
the saints had spoken and those that my agitated spirit was feeling at that
moment? At that moment the watchful sense of difference was annihilated
in me."[11] To be sure, Adso appropriates *enarrationes sanctorum*, that is, in his
own way and to his own ends. Consequently, he factually pre-exists his
formation or determination as articulate mind. Nevertheless, such pre-
existence is but brute fact; full human subjectivity and the meaning it
construes[12] emanates from the agency inherent within those texts he has
submitted to. Of course, in such reading, the meaning of the text is not
immediately present. Rather the reader's subsequent (and consequent) performance *(moralitas)* "exegetes" the text *moraliter*, that is, via its application
to the concrete exigencies of life.[13]

Adso is, of course, a fictional character, and Umberto Eco, his creator, is a noted semiologist whose theoretical work has been instrumental in conceptually expanding the play of meaning inherent within texts at the expense of authorial intention, an expansion crucial to the project of "de-centering" the subject within contemporary literary criticism.[14] It is at times hard to avoid suspecting Eco of having endowed his characters with disproportionately semiotic proclivities.[15] Still, Eco is an accomplished medievalist; he knows well the pioneering work of Jean Leclercq. One thinks especially of *L'amour des lettres et le désir de Dieu*.[16] The Solomonic rhetoric of Adso's passion parodically evokes that form of monastic study called *ruminatio* (literally, chewing the cud) and its "performative" effects upon the ruminator's subsequent self. Here one does catch a glimpse, however carnivalesque, of a recognizably medieval textuality, one far removed, it would seem, from its modern scholarly successor.

But modern scholarly examination of a text has historical roots in the Middle Ages. For it was in the twelfth and thirteenth century that the technologies of the page necessary for this kind of reading were developed and disseminated: subject indices, principles of subdivision (for example, the verse divisions of Scripture), alphabetization, cross-referencing systems within the layout of the page, a more elaborate and considered system of punctuation.[17] The Dominicans of St. Jacques in Paris and the stationers whom they patronized were heavily implicated in this transformation. Dominican involvement leads me to ask the following question: How might a thirteenth-century alumnus of St. Jacques' *studium generale* read texts? Is he likely to have read in ways that are closer to the long monastic tradition of "performative" reading sent up by Umberto Eco? Or is such a reader more likely to have adumbrated the self-assurance of the modern scholar in her or his study?

The Case of Thomas of Cantimpré

1. The Man and the Book

Thomas of Cantimpré provides us just the sort of case study called for by these questions. He was born to a knightly family of Brabant in 1199 or 1200. At the age of six or seven (1206) his father sent him to the episcopal see of Cambrai to study "letters and the chaste life" at its cathedral school.[18] After eleven years of such instruction he entered religion among the Augustinian canons of Cantimpré (1217). He remained a canon there until 1232, when he was "translated to a stricter Rule," that is, to the community of Friars Preachers newly established at Louvain. He remained a member of this community until his death (ca. 1270).

In 1237 or 1238, Thomas was sent by his prior to the Order's *studium generale* at the above mentioned St. Jacques' in Paris. He studied there for two or possibly three years. It is this period of study above all that qualifies Thomas of Cantimpré's reading for consideration as apposite case study, for he was a student at St. Jacques' when it was a crucial player in several of the technological innovations mentioned above.[19]

Thomas returned to Louvain in 1240, where he was elected subprior by 1246. In 1250–1251, he seems to have followed Albert the Great's lectures on Aristotle's *libri naturales* in the Order's three-year-old *studium generale* at Cologne (he would have been a "classmate" of that other Thomas, the large Sicilian from Aquino).[20] Shortly thereafter, he was, in all probability, appointed a preacher general by his provincial prior.[21] Such an appointment at any rate explains his freedom to travel widely throughout the Order's province of Teutonia, and his expansive network of friends and acquaintances from many places, orders, and walks of life. For years he compiled the stories he gleaned from his travels and contacts into the *Book of Bees*, a work designed to lay bare the norms for prelates and subjects within religious communities from analogical consideration of the apian society of the beehive.[22]

The work is divided into two books, dealing with prelates and subjects respectively. The last half of the second book is given over to the norms regulating the life of officeholders among a religious community's subjects. Much of this group of chapters is given over to the pastoral care such officeholders are to exercise within the convent of subjects at large.

The last three chapters of the work bespeak the agency of demons among the faithful and the genera of harm (*nocumenta*) they are capable of.[23] Thomas identifies five such genera, three of which can be associated with four species of demon, allegorically signified by the wasp, the cockroach, the hornet, and the oxviper.[24] The last of these signifiers calls for some explanation. Thomas had in mind an incendiary insect reportedly given to hiding in meadowlands until ingested by grazing oxen, only to ignite upon reaching the entrails of their luckless bovine hosts.[25]

Thomas amply illustrates the powers of illusion that demons possess. He also illustrates their ability to plague even Christians in good standing with two distinct sets of *exempla* or narrative appeals to experience. The first three *exempla* narrate events in the life of King Louis IX of France. Another three involve demon possession, the first two of devout women under Thomas's own pastoral care.[26] It is to the last of the two *exempla* about the demon possession of devout women that I wish to call your attention.

2. The Text

Here is the story as Thomas tells it:

> In the same land [Brabant], I saw another woman, one rich and of excellent life, who was possessed by a demon. I visited her at the request of a religious priest. We found her undisturbed by demonic torment. She was able to speak coherently as if of sound mind. I secretly repeated three times that verse of the Canticle of Moses found in Deuteronomy which goes, "You have abandoned the God who produced you and have forgotten the Lord your Creator." In this I acted in accordance with what I had heard from a certain holy man, and so as to call forth the demon who had possessed the woman. Directly, the woman's face and lips began to grow pallid and the two veins in her neck began to swell until they were as thick as thumbs. I then addressed the demon, "Why, O worst of all beings, have you dared to take possession of this woman?"
>
> The demon answered, "She had such compassion for her dead husband that she credited to him in aid of his soul all the good which she did in this life. Thus, an opportunity presented itself to me and I entered directly 'an empty vessel.'"
>
> I addressed it again, "You are lying, O most wretched of beings, for her giving, since it was mediated by charity, would only accrue to her account."
>
> He chuckled, saying, "I am a liar. Therefore, it is small wonder that I am lying."
>
> I responded forthwith, "Is she so beautiful that she recalls the heavenly Home which you have lost?"
>
> He answered, "Heaven is infinitely more beautiful than what she can possibly call to mind."
>
> I then said, "Do you wish to return to that Place, if you are able?"
>
> And he said, "Would that I could undergo every imaginable punishment from now until the Judgment Day, [and merit thereby to return]."
>
> I responded, "And I promise you upon danger of losing the

salvation promised me if I am lying that you can regain glory if only you say this: 'O Lord God, I have sinned; forgive me.' "

Straightaway, the woman's neck began to contort, and the demon called out in a horrible voice, "O Lord . . . O Lord . . ." And when he had sounded these words over and over again with great clamour and could not proceed further (for I knew that it was not possible for him to profess that God was his Lord and confess that he had sinned and to beg to be forgiven), he finally added, "Lord God of Margaret (for that was the possessed woman's name) I am offended to have to profess [You], God, as my Lord."

Then I said, "O most unfortunate of all creatures, pride has crushed you and has cast you from Heaven; inexpiable pride does not permit you to return."

Thwarted, the demon fell silent without delay, and, even still, he did not leave the woman for a few days.[27]

The narrative is divisible into three parts. The first segment consists in Thomas's *mise en scène*, in which he introduces his characters and the exorcistic context in which their interaction will take place. The second segment encompasses an opening series of verbal parries by which exorcist and demon take the measure of each other. The third and final segment is the narrative's dénouement: the exorcist delivers his masterstroke, the demon is thwarted and the victim finds her blessed if anticlimactic release.

a. Thomas as Performative Reader

The exorcist of this narrative is, of course, none other than Thomas of Cantimpré. In other words, he narrates his own textual persona (subjectivity) via this *exemplum* (among others). Moreover, his subjectivity, like that of Umberto Eco's Adso, is formed in large measure by allegorically re-membered texts. In this *exemplum* remembered texts perform Thomas as an exorcist as is clear from an examination of the rite of exorcism.

The rite as promulgated by Benedict XIV is divided into three chapters.[28] The first chapter assembles 21 articles in which exorcists are admonished to right action in the performance of the rite. Something like this early modern compilation of *admonitiones* must have already accompanied the rite in Thomas of Cantimpré's day, for our *exemplum* conforms to the strictures articulated in a number of them.[29] The *admonitio* found in the fifth article warns the exorcist to be vigilant in the face of demonic arts and deceptions; in particular it warns that demons try to make their victims appear free of demonic vexation.[30] The *admonitio* of the next article further elaborates the demonic penchant for hiding itself as if relinquishing the demoniac's body and exhorts the exorcist not to cease the rite until he has observed the "signs of liberation."[31] In our *exemplum* Thomas does, in fact, find the woman, Margaret, quiescent, as if in her right mind, and refuses to be taken in.[32]

The *admonitiones* published in articles 15 to 17 and article 20 are also reflected in Thomas's story. Article 15 lists the kinds of questions exorcists are to restrict themselves to. They are to ask after the number and name(s) of the possessing spirits, as to when the spirit(s) entered the demoniac, the reasons why, and the circumstances surrounding demonic entry.[33] Article 16 admonishes the exorcist to command with authority, great faith, and humility, and to be swift to follow up the advantage when he observes the demon in torment, a torment manifested in somatic phenomena convulsing the body of the possessed. Swelling of body portions is specifically mentioned.[34] Article 17 admonishes exorcists to keep track of those words that spark demonic response.[35] Article 20 advises the exorcist to use the words of Scripture above all.[36]

The ways in which these articles come to expression in our *exemplum* are clear enough, as we shall see. Thomas is single-minded in his pursuit of the demoniac's liberation. Moreover the questions he asks at the beginning of his inquiry reflect the prescribed list.[37] The demon is spurred to create swelling contortions in the body of its host, and the spur is provided by scriptural words that had previously been observed to effect the desired demonic response.[38] Finally, Thomas wastes no time in pressing his advantage, once he is aware of it.[39]

The most telling and complex allusion of all, however, refers to the text of the rite of exorcism itself. In the prayer that constitutes the heart and soul of the rite, the offending demon is abjured to give way to Christ, "in whom you find nothing of your works, who has despoiled you, who has destroyed your kingdom, who has bound you captive and who has overturned your vessels."[40] The first three clauses of the passage list major achievements of Christ's triduum (the time between crucifixion and resurrection): the Old Testament saints were led out of hell, the kingdom of hell was laid waste, the devil was enchained. The fourth clause, then, ought also to be associated with the infernal events of Christ's harrowing of hell.[41] One must imagine him upsetting, in righteous anger, the bulging containers of Hades' treasuries. In addition, however, the overturning of hellish vessels has a secondary scriptural association: Christ's cleansing of the temple and the overturning of the tables of the moneychangers. Now, the term "vessel" [vas] also occurs in Thomas's story. The demon explains its entry into its victim by calling her an "empty vessel" [vas vacuum]. This might have been safely passed over in silence but for the fact that her putative emptiness was the result of spiritual moneychanging, that is, the woman's investment of her spiritual goods on her husband's behalf. Consequently, in a complex allusion, the demon of Thomas's *exemplum* itself refers to the rite of exorcism and its coming defeat in and through Christ's overturning of its vessel, that is, the freeing of its victim.

Once we have established the exorcistic elements within Thomas's narrative subjectivity, however, we confront a difficulty that suggests that these elements no less than Adso's *enarrationes sanctorum* are appropriated *moraliter*. We read that the "demoniac" in question was a woman "of excellent life" [honestam] and was nevertheless "possessed by a demon" [possessam a daemone]. But how could a demon possess a person who lived a pre-eminent life?

It should be noted that this is not the only story of the demon possession of virtuous women to be included within the *Book of Bees*. The dissonance between the presence of active virtue and demonic power to command is even more intense in the story that immediately precedes ours. There the possessed woman is identified as a Cistercian nun, one who was "intensely religious and pure in life" [religiosam valde et vita puram].[42]

Theologians of the thirteenth century were as one in emphasizing the limits of demonic power with respect to human beings.[43] All demonic activity took place, according to them, under the watchful forebearance of God. Demons were permitted wide powers with respect to the world of bodies in keeping with their spiritual natures. They were, however, impotent to change human nature. Consequently, they stood before the human will as before what was simultaneously their greatest obstacle and their greatest hope, for it was a Janus-like entity, conduit to as well as adamant guardian of the inner recesses of the human person.

Since demons were helpless in the face of sustained repudiation, they perforce acted in stealth. They wheedled and coaxed, hoping to recruit willing compliance with their suggestions. But in our *exemplum* and in its immediate predecessor, whatever Thomas may have meant by "mulierem honestam" and "monialem vita puram," he does not seem to have imagined the women as having voluntarily opened the citadel of their souls to demonic occupation [possessio]. The question then returns: Is the Thomas of this *exemplum* in fact an exorcist? It returns because it is not at all clear how Thomas understands the demon possession of exemplary women.

In the *exemplum* immediately preceding ours, the word "possession" is

never actually used. Rather, the demon is said to have been hiding within
the nun in question: "in ea latebat." The demon clearly had a distressing
level of control over her body, for Thomas describes how it responded to
the prospect of an hour's worth of what he laconically called the "words
of salvation." The woman's body began to bark like a dog with mouth
agape and neck contorted. It turned away from all sources of light and
began to blaspheme. Consequently, it would appear that in this story the
phrase "in ea latebat" indicates that the demon had access to the nun's
body without a corresponding access to the inner recesses of her person.

Our *exemplum* speaks of some of the same somatic manipulations just
described. One thinks in particular of the demon's ability to contort its
host's neck. Indeed, in the first segment of the story the woman's jugular
veins swell unimaginably, whereas in the third segment her neck is again
said to have been contorted as the demon struggled with the invitation to
confess before God. Here, too, demonic access to the woman's body seems
clear.

The demon in this *exemplum*, however, would also seem to have had
access to the inner recesses of its host's person, for she is explicitly identified as possessed in the course of the narrative. Thomas uses two words
to indicate possession: "possessa" [twice] and "obsessa" [once]. The words
are, of course, perfect participles derived from the verbs "possidere" and
"obsidere." In classical usage, the verbs shared a semantic field of military
meaning.[44] "Possidere" indicated the military occupation of what had been
assaulted and captured, while "obsidere" indicated laying seige to what one
hoped to capture. While the latter verb maintains its classical significance
in medieval usage, the former verb expands. While it can be and is used
in its classical sense, "possidere" also comes to be used as a synonym for
"obsidere."[45] In other words, these verbs, when used interchangeably, denote a laying seige to what one hopes to capture. Since, in the present
story, Thomas of Cantimpré uses their passive participles interchangeably,
they are best viewed as synonyms.

Consequently, the virtuous woman of our *exemplum* is possessed, not
in the sense that the demon has acceded to the inner recesses of her being.
Rather, she is possessed in that the demon is laying seige to her spiritual
core. It is not yet victorious, and, given the woman's mode of life, is not
likely ever to be so. In this story, then, demon possession has another
meaning altogether. It indicates a pestiferous and malicious plaguing, an
invidious nuisance-making. It constitutes a distinct species of the genus
"temptation," a genus that is itself subject to misunderstanding, particularly
regarding the temptation of saints (and, in medieval tellings, of Jesus).[46]

Temptation in its generic sense indicates something broader than the attempt to allure and entrap, that is, the common experience of the ordinary or mediocre faithful. It indicates rather quite simply the attempt to make life difficult. Medieval demons tempt the saints (as they were understood to have tempted Jesus) not because they really hope that the saints (or Jesus) will be defeated by the difficulties placed before them. Rather, demons tempt out of sheer cussedness. Why should the saints have it easy? Demonic "crucifixion" of a saint may only serve to make her more Christlike. Nevertheless, it also causes her suffering and pain. The enormous effort expended in causing such ineffectual, even counterproductive pain may seem vain and wasted. And so it is. But, it is a vanity and a waste entirely fitted to the kind of beings demons were believed to be.

At this point it is clear that Thomas's citation of the rite of exorcism performs him exorcistically. We also see Thomas reading in a way that is far closer to the *lectio divina* of the monk and nun than the research of the modern scholar. He reads the rite of exorcism *moraliter*; he reads it for performance, that is, with an eye upon subsequent, active service of God, in this instance via pastoral care of the faithful. Thus, we might say that we have caught him out in the act of reading "clerically," not inasmuch as "clericus" had come by his day to refer to a "university student," but inasmuch as it continued to refer to a pastor of the faithful. In other words, the light cast upon the religious culture of the High Middle Ages by Jean Leclercq's luminous distinction between monastic and scholastic learning has acted simultaneously to obscure an equally important distinction between religious and secular practice of performative reading. That is, secular clerics also learned to read performatively but not as part of a contemplative and penitential regime. Rather their reading was active in that it was motivated by their ordination and investiture as curates of the faithful.[47] But if we have managed to tease out an interesting example of Thomas of Cantimpré's performative reading, it should be added that it is not the only indication of Thomas's reading we encounter in this *exemplum*.

b. Thomas as Scholarly Reader

The first segment of our *exemplum* ends when the vexing demon makes its presence known in and through its manipulation of the woman's body. The second segment begins when Thomas asks the demon the reason it has come to "possess" the woman.

The demon responds in characteristically demonic fashion with a sophism. Its reply centers upon the woman's sufferages on her husband's behalf. She invested her goodness in her husband's spiritual profit.[48] As the demon has it, the investment of her merits elsewhere renders her empty of merit and, thus, open to any demon willing to fill her void. The demon's argument hinges upon the properties of physical natures also being proper to *spiritualia*. To be sure, if merits are like coins or other physical media of exchange, their investment elsewhere entails their actually being elsewhere. Moreover, the movement of capital from investment to return necessarily takes time. Consequently, if merits are like coins, there would be a vacuity, that is, a window of opportunity to an enterprising spirit.

Merits, however, are spiritual things.[49] As such, they are not constrained by time and space. They can exist in more than one place simultaneously, and the movement of spiritual capital from investment to return is instantaneous. The demon's argument, while cunning in its way, falls short of true intelligence. To the trained scholastic eye, it is patently fallacious, and Thomas sees the fallacy instantly.

The demon cheerfully admits its lie and adds cheek by framing its admission as an allusion to the words of John 8:44. The citation of Scripture provides Thomas a complex piece of information. While it reveals the characteristically deprecating and devious demeanour of his opponent, paradoxically, it also gives warrant to the demon's self-identification. All things being equal, a demon's disposition is simply incredible. Since it is a liar, how can it be believed? Scripture, however, can always be believed; it can be cited perversely but it cannot itself lie. As a result, Jesus's identification of the devil as a liar and the father of lies transforms the demon's word into what can be believed.

This exchange teaches Thomas much about his foe: it is a deceiver that uses art and duplicity in order to escape full disclosure. Thomas has now measured his opponent and is prepared to wrest control of the interchange so as to effect the woman's release.

He embarks on a new line of inquiry. He asks whether the woman's beauty conjures up memories of lost paradise, whether the spell of such reminiscence spurs the demon to the assault. The demon denies the charge implied in Thomas's question. However, since, as already noted, the demon is a liar, its denial functions only to confirm Thomas's guess. He presses his advantage, asking whether the demon regrets its loss of bliss. The demon admits that it would gladly undergo any and all imaginable punishments if it could thereby return to heaven. But this reply puts Thomas in a delicate hermeneutical way.

How is he to understand this admission? Is it a lie or the naked truth? In this instance, Thomas views the demon as telling the truth, but willy-nilly in confusion, that is, in an inadvertent way appropriate to an inveterate liar. We are fortunate in being able to reconstruct the criteria by which Thomas establishes the truthfulness of this demonic admission. His criteria are textual, rooted in scholarly reading, as can be seen by an examination of a strikingly similar demonic admission to be found in Caesarius of Heisterbach's *Dialogus miraculorum*. Again, I cite the pertinent passage *in extenso*:

> One demon said to another, "O wretched one, why did we hurry so from eternal glory when we sided with Lucifer?"
> The other replied [in amazement], "Why are you doing this?" And then when the first demon persisted with what almost amounted to words of penitence, it added, "Be silent! This penitence comes too late; you cannot return." . . . This same evil spirit [however,] when questioned . . . concerning [the possibility] of returning to glory responded in my hearing with a word which strongly contradicted what it had said earlier. For now he said, "Were there to be erected between heaven and earth an iron and fiery column, inlaid with the sharpest edges and with blades, I would wish to shinny up it and slide down it from now until Judgment Day, even had I flesh whereby I suffered horribly, if only I could return to the glory I once had."[50]

Caesarius's story shares much with Thomas's. Both assume a huge demonic longing for heaven, and a wistful desire to earn readmittance by their own efforts. Moreover, both express the conviction that such a demonic return cannot take place. These parallels urge consideration of the nature of the relationship between the two stories.

It is possible, of course, that all similarities are coincidental and point to nothing more than a broad demonological consensus that both compilers appropriate in their own separate ways. Such a possibility is, however, unlikely. Thomas knows Caesarius's *Dialogus*.[51] Consequently, it seems far more likely that Thomas has read Caesarius of Heisterbach's account of demons conversing nostalgically about heaven and, consequently, that his own narrative echos Caesarius's.

But one must still ask how Thomas is using his source? Nothing could be simpler than to say that Thomas is cribbing from Caesarius. The problem, however, is that he claims his story to be autobiographical. If he is cribbing from a work as widely known as Caesarius's[52] and passing vicarious experience off as his own, he undermines his whole treatise, for he explicitly founds its credibility on his and his circle of acquaintances' narrative trustworthiness.[53] Cribbing from what is the equivalent of a "best seller" is, at the very least, egregiously dull-witted. I suggest a different scenario.

Thomas has read Caesarius's story and believes it to illumine the demonic mind. He appropriates the tale's lesson, however, to his own ends. Whereas Caesarius presents his story as an example of demonic self-contradiction, that is, as a variation on the theme of demon as liar, Thomas sees it as revealing an exploitable demonic weakness. Our *exemplum*, then, shows Thomas putting the lesson into practice. He plays on demonic longing for heaven so as to sow the seeds of doubt and hesitation. In so doing he brings about precisely the contradictory confusion Caesarius's story illustrates.

What is significant in this trace of Thomas's past reading is that it is scholarly in something like the way we identified above. He reads a monastic work designed to confirm Cistercian novices in their religious calling as a source of scientific information about demons, for it is information he needs above all as he casts about for a way of easing the burden of temptation among his pastoral charges. In other words, he comes to the text as a subject essentially formed and stable and acts upon it such that a work of spiritual formation assumes the lineaments of a scientific *tractatus de daemonibus*. In this way, he effects it meaningful in a specified context by controlling for all concerns outside the determination of present, subjective need. Thus, in this *exemplum*, we find evidence of scholarly as well as performative reading.

We do well, however, to delineate precisely how Thomas's performative and scholarly reading differ. Both kinds of reading bespeak the reader's existential priority with respect to the text he is reading, and in both the reader affects the meaning of his text. While Thomas the scholar acts upon a text until a work of spiritual direction manifests the qualities of a scientific treatise *de daemonibus*, Thomas the pastor appropriates the rite of exorcism or specific passages of Scripture, establishing their meaning analogically within a concrete situation of demonic temptation. Thus, in both his performative and scholarly reading, he exceeds his textual engagement and exercises agency with respect to the present meaning of the text(s) to hand.

These forms of reading differ, however, in the way Thomas relates to texts. As performative reader, Thomas approaches his text in such a way that his essential subjectivity is manifestly on the line.[54] He enters into a reciprocal relationship with the text in the sense that the text forms his subjectivity even as he appropriates the text. Moreover, this reciprocity is not symmetrical. Thomas approaches the rite of exorcism or passages of Scripture as subject in a second sense; he subjects himself to the text such that it "performs" him. By contrast, Thomas as scholarly reader, because he prescinds from all concerns outside of the horizon of present scientific need, cannot be subject to the text in this way. Indeed, by definition, such a reader can only approach a text in the imperative mode.[55]

It is in the imperative mode that Thomas of Cantimpré finds within Caesarius of Heisterbach's *Dialogus miraculorum* an exploitable weakness in the spiritual eminence of his demonic foe. And so it does, at least after Thomas reframes the meaning of Caesarius's *exemplum*. Thomas uses the weakness he has "invented" to create a moment of confusion and uses it to deflate the demon so that it is diminished, too diminished to maintain its grip on its victim. He does so by promising the demon that heaven is within its grasp if it would only make contrite confession. He adds weight to his appeal by pledging his own salvation as surety. The demon's efforts to confess end in failure and defiance. Its failure gives Thomas the occasion to entone the grim reality of its spiritual predicament. Faced with the magnitude of its folly, the demon indeed shrinks and grudgingly, over the course of days, loosens its grip on the woman. It must be said, however, that Thomas is honest enough to record something of his disappointment and wonder at the length of time the woman's liberation still took. But in fact there is no need to wonder; the reason lies to hand: why should the saints have it easy?

Thomas's appeal for demonic conversion is, of course, troublingly disingenuous. It lacks the excessive charity of, for example, the Dominican tertiary Catherine of Siena's desire to be used as a spiritual stopper to cork the mouth of hell from now until the Last Days.[56] He reveals the merely strategic character of his concern by saying, "I knew that he could not acknowledge God as his Lord, and confess himself a sinner, and pray that he be forgiven."

But how is it that Thomas's masterstroke is a ruse, a beating of the demon at its own game? After all, the rite of exorcism demands that "an exorcist be pre-eminent in piety, prudence and integrity of life."[57] What integrity is there in deception?

However easily such questions come to mind to the modern reader, they are foreign to medieval pastoral sensibilities. Rather, a properly medieval question, one explicitly asked in inquisitorial manuals, is: how is one to deal with those who exist, so to speak, "outside" of the law of God, that is, where its norms do not hold? In that dark dale, oaths have no force; conversely, lies do no harm and, if they are effective, can do great good.[58] In short, some medieval inquisitors seem to suggest that one can only meet a demon on its own ground, beyond the river of virtue and its liquid expression in deed. No streams that emanate from virtue's font can issue forth a desirable end; such means merely provide the demon matter for further perversion. Thus, in the unique case of the devil and his minions, only demonic means will do. In this case alone, two wrongs make a right. And if it is true that we begin to shiver at this point, huddling together against the chill wind blowing off the Spanish steppes, medieval inquisitorial theory could cite in its defense the very highest precedent. For it was God himself, or so very ancient tellings of the story go, who practiced in Christ's earthly mission the Great Deception by which the Deceiver was robbed of its human booty.[59]

Thomas's Reading as Suggestive *Exemplum*

We began by describing modes of reading and the relative self-assurance demanded by each mode. Indeed, the present study suggests that we human readers are capable of constructing ourselves in relation to texts as occasion arises. At least, this is what I make of Thomas of Cantimpré's ability to move between two modes of reading, and of the different "selves" they seem to require or produce. It is possible to dismiss these reading "selves" as mere *integumenta*, as gauzy veils we need to strip away if we are to espy the "real self" beneath in all its naked determination. On the other hand, it is also possible to see them as but two of the several determinate ways in which that mystery that is the human person becomes visible to the human intellect.[60] Doubtless there are other plausible "readings" as well. But how are we to choose from among the possible explanations? Our task is made particularly delicate by the fact that the past often comes to us reticent and shy, bruised by much mishandling. It must be coaxed into entrusting us with its secrets and we, in turn, must be worthy of such trust.

Despite such limitations, the present study does allow us to claim that Thomas of Cantimpré reads both performatively and scholastically. Consequently, we can legitimately ask after the circumstances that attend his reading in these ways. We have noted that in our *exemplum* Thomas reads performatively when reading for ecclesiastical performance. In other words, he reads performatively with a view to a certain active practice (individual and communal) of faith. It must be admitted that Thomas also reads scholastically because he wishes to act, even to act pastorally; his is not a contemplative soul given to slow rumination upon texts for the subtle flavors released by unhurried mental mastication. Nevertheless, there is this difference. In contrast to his reading for ecclesiastical performance, Thomas reads scholastically when he needs to distinguish one set of things (demonic attributes of superior being and power) from another (exploitable attributes at the exorcist's disposal), that is, when he must make a logical determination of what something is or is not. Thus, it would seem that these two modes of reading and the "selves" they require or produce respond to the contours inherent within two distinguishable modes of human life and endeavor: the cultic practice of faith and the contemplative science of analysis and composition. Significantly, Thomas brings both types of reading together to effect performance of a single pastoral act.

In addition, Thomas of Cantimpré's complex practice of reading suggests that scholastic reading occurs for the sake of performative understanding, at least when scholastic reading is engaged toward religious ends. That is, in matters of religious practice, medieval readers acknowledged the priority of the performative. Such a hypothesis demands testing out; it can only remain a suggestion for now. Nevertheless, this suggestion has more going for it than Thomas of Cantimpré's narrative élan. For example, it corresponds with the privilege accorded the performative in Leonard E. Boyle O.P.'s attempt to reframe the study of medieval popular piety.[61] Moreover, both these instances of the priority of the performative are congruent with the formal priority that medieval societies ceded to religion and its obligations.

I am not arguing here for a recuperation of the Romantic cliché of the Middle Ages as "The Age of Faith." Rather, I am arguing that historians take seriously the penchant of medieval societies to acknowledge the formal priority of religion and its obligations, even while insisting that the effect of that priority differs wildly from group to group, and from person to person. The question next arises, however, as to the nature of medieval religious obligation and the imaginative impulses it inculcated. Indeed, it is precisely this concern that underlies Leonard Boyle's discussion of medieval piety.

He begins by examining the binary oppositions modern historians use to contrast the sensibilities of medieval religious elites and the people whom they lived among: popular piety/learned piety; official piety/popular piety; *foi savante/foi populaire*.[62] He then takes up the contrast between learned and popular faith, insisting that one distinguish between faith and the many modes of its expression. Faith in his view is an originary phenomenon, one that is always already anterior to its historical manifestations. In and of itself, then, it is undifferentiatable, a theoretical simple:

"one either has this faith or not." The latter assertion leads Boyle to conclude that the faith of peasants and theologians is conceptually of a piece,
that is, to be understood as individuated instances of the same phenomenon. He acknowledges that the same faith can come to expression in
many different modes; there are, to be sure, learned as well as ignorant
expressions of faith. None of these modes, however, is to be held up as
somehow in and of itself a truer expression of faith than any other. Rather,
a cultural expression associated with faith is true or false to the degree
that it points to the "real presence" of faith or belies its absence.

Boyle works with the couplet "learned" and "popular piety" similarly.[63] But here a second objection arises. For if it is true that learned
expressions of faith can legitimately be distinguished from ignorant expressions, it is not, according to Boyle, possible to distinguish popular and
learned piety. That is, for Boyle, "piety is, of its very nature, 'popular,' no
matter where it is found." This claim precipitates his working definition:
"[p]iety . . . is simply a grateful and respectful acknowledgement of one's
relationship, generally of dependence, sometimes of admiration, to someone or something above one, whether mother, father, older brother or
sister, church, country, minister, teacher, leader, God." Medieval Christian
piety, then, takes at its most general "the form of obedience to [God's]
commandments, and, at its more specific Christian level, takes on as well
the singular form of Thanksgiving proposed by his Son: the Eucharist."

Boyle proceeds to argue that the Eucharist is the paradigmatic act
of medieval Christian piety, even as its outrageous corporeality identifies
it as flagrantly "popular." Indeed, he argues that Eucharistic piety is to
other manifestations of piety as, in medieval theology, the Eucharist is to
the other sacraments, namely "the hub around which [they all] revolve."
Since Eucharistic piety was consistently named The Liturgy, Boyle argues
that one classify expressions of piety by their proximity to or remoteness
from The Liturgy, in the manner that other acts of formal worship are
referred to it, as in "the Liturgy of Baptism," "Liturgy of Confirmation,"
"Liturgy of Hours," etc.

Thus, the liturgy of the Eucharist forms the center of a whole series
of concentrically arranged categories. Those acts intimately associated
with the Eucharist and with the person of Christ are arranged in the innermost circle and can be named liturgical piety without qualification.
Boyle places the sacraments in this circle. A second circle is made up of
acts that have "a close but not necessarily intimate connection with the
Eucharist," acts he calls semiliturgical. Preaching and the Divine Office are
offered as cases in point. A third circle Boyle calls the paraliturgical and

is formed by those acts that have a connection to the Eucharist even if it is not all that close. The cult of the saints is cited as paradigmatic. Then there is the motley crew of acts that bear no connection to the Eucharist but that are also not at variance with its spirit and meaning. These acts can be called "without any negative connotation" nonliturgical. Finally, Boyle identifies a last and most remote circle of acts that run counter to the spirit and meaning of the Eucharist. These he classes under the rubric of the aliturgical.[64]

The concentric model outlined here cuts through the simple oppositions current among many medievalists.[65] Moreover, it has the considerable advantage of emerging from religious phenomena themselves rather than from social or political polarities (as if religious phenomena merely made up a field upon which other more originary forces inscribed themselves). In addition, Boyle's model has a more precise importance in the present context, for it insists that religiosity is above all an activity of the body, that is, is first a matter of performance: "[a]ll forms of piety, with the Eucharist setting the headline in the Christian context, are attempts by believers to engage the whole person and not just the mind and heart."

Boyle's language emphasizes the intellectuality of faith and the consequent need for corporeal compensation. It trades upon a hierarchical opposition of intellect and body. Nevertheless, one need not accept the opposition in order to see the value of Boyle's model, for he associates corporeal compensation with a second type, a type that trades upon a second opposition, that between the communal and the personal. While the Eucharist is paradigmatic of piety and is even thought of as a divine acknowledgement of the human need for tangible performance, still it is, in both its setting and its form, "too communal to be wholly and satisfyingly personal." Boyle goes on to elaborate that "out on the streets, in a eucharistic procession . . . [t]he medieval believer, so much an onlooker in church, could now walk behind, before, beside, perhaps even shoulder Christ the Son of God in the bread he had designated as his Body, could strew flowers, dance and make music, in a friendly, companionable, and very personal act of thanksgiving." Other historians too have noted the distinction between the communal and the personal as it came to function in the religious life of the later Middle Ages.[66] One can then gather up Boyle's several suggestions and say that medieval piety is profitably viewed as a pattern of performance by which medieval believers acted out their faith as integral selves, that is, as bodies as well as intellects, as persons as well as members of the community. In medieval piety as in Thomas of Cantimpré's practice of reading, one sees the priority of the performative, a priority that is capable of subsuming other modes of human act. This priority is consistent with what medieval societies understood by the formal priority of religion and its obligations. For the primary and secondary meanings of "christianitas" and "fides" reveal that at their most elemental and primary the terms refer to sacramental performance: the liturgy of Baptism in and through which people were given being as persons within the community of the faithful.[67]

In conclusion, we return to Thomas of Cantimpré's reading "selves" and the *exemplum* in which they appear. The priority he accorded to performative reading in the concrete pastoral situation to hand meshes well with the performative heart of medieval piety as Leonard Boyle understands it and the formal priority of religion and its obligations within medieval societies at large. Both Thomas's *exemplum* and that of Umberto Eco with which this essay began are in certain respects profoundly unsettling. I have attempted to identify at least one of the sources of our discomfort: the connection Thomas of Cantimpré makes between the exorcist and the inquisitor, and the demonizing potential of that connection for the subjects of inquisitorial attentions. But the *exempla* are also chilling in a second sense. In both, a woman is narratively present, but only as object. One feels the ice inherent within such freezing objectifications. Nevertheless, even in the presence of offense, there is more to the story; there is always more to the story. For our peek at Thomas of Cantimpré's practice of reading helps us imagine an intellectual ethos quite different from our own, an ethos in which logical determination of a text's meaning and order did not preclude the performative authority of that same text, an authority capable of receiving the reader's submission, a submission by which the text came to inscribe itself upon the reader's subsequent practice of life.

Notes

1. This permeable posture, of course, begs the question as to whether the intended quality is actually realized or ever can be. The same is true of the scholar's impermeability, as was already suggested.
2. Among North American historians, theoretical concern is still largely addressed by example, theoretical claims largely made in and through the complex language of concrete historical practice. Thus, I learned of the distinction between intertextual and originary elementa from historical writing in the tradition of Ernst Curtius's *Europäische Literatur und lateinisches Mittelalter* (Bern: A. Francke, 1948). I learned of both the potential and limits of a focus upon hidden political and economic

meaning in, among many fine studies, Ernst Werner's *Häresie und Ge-sellschaft im 11. Jahrhundert*, Sitzungsberichte der sächsischer Akademie der Wissenschaften zu Leipzig, Philologische-Historische Klasse, 117.5 (Leipzig, 1975). More recently, I have been made aware of the formative power of aesthetic sensibility by David D'Avray's *The Preaching of the Friars: Sermons Diffused from Paris Before 1300* (New York: Oxford University Press, 1985); of the usefulness of psychoanalytic models by Nancy Partner's "No Sex, No Gender," *Speculum* 68 (1993): 419–443; and of the ubiquity of hidden gender meanings by a host of suggestive studies of which I cite but one of my favorites: Caroline Walker Bynum's *Fragmentation and Redemption: Essays on Gender and the Human Body in Medieval Religion* (New York: Zone Books, 1991).

3. It will become evident why this must be so in the body of this study.

4. I want to thank G. Marcille Frederick for pointing out the affinities between the two types of possession I am juxtaposing in this study. Curiously, I had been unaware of the connection until she spoke.

5. The edition used throughout is *Bonum universale de apibus, sive, Miraculorum exemplorum memorabilium sui temporis libri duo*, ed. G. Colvenère (Douai, 1627). Henceforth *B.U.* followed by book, chapter, part, and page.

6. Umberto Eco, *The Name of the Rose* (New York: Harcourt Brace Jovanovich, 1983).

7. Eco, *Rose*, 292–293.

8. For the educational language of the day as it operated within cathedral but also monastery schools see C. Stephen Jaeger, *The Envy of Angels: Cathedral Schools and Social Ideals in Medieval Europe, 950–1200* (Philadelphia: University of Pennsylvania Press, 1994). The memorial structure of culture in which this language emerged and that gave to it its peculiar force is brilliantly described in Mary Carruthers, *The Book of Memory: A Study of Memory in Medieval Culture*, Cambridge Studies in Medieval Literature 10 (Cambridge: Cambridge University Press, 1990).

9. Eco, *Rose*, 290.

10. Ibid.

11. Ibid., 290.

12. There is no precise equivalent in medieval theory for the modern notion of subjectivity as human center or as agent of meaning. Nevertheless, the term "subjectivity," inclusive of its characteristic act of construing the meaning of its world, can be used with proper caution as pointing to aspects of the human condition that medieval theorists named differently and associated with the term *"mens,"* or mind and its cognitive power.

13. For the pedagogical theory that tropological reading of texts constitutes a *formatio morum* or *moralitas*, see Jaeger, *Envy of Angels*, 1–195. Jaeger's fine study reconstructs a pattern of literary formation native to eleventh-century cathedral schools, and describes the fate of its found-

ing insights in the following century and a half. The applicability of
the eleventh-century terminology he collates to a thirteenth-century
source such as Thomas of Cantimpré's *Book of Bees* or to Umberto Eco's
studied medievalism, however, strongly suggests that Jaeger's eleventh-
century masters were engaged in a literary practice, in particular a
reading practice, that was more persistent than his study would lead
one to believe. It was also considerably older than the eleventh century. Indeed, Brian Stock describes an analogous memorial and ethical
configuration of reading in his *Augustine the Reader: Meditation, Self-
Knowledge and the Ethics of Interpretation* (Cambridge: The Belknap Press
of Harvard University Press, 1996). I want to say that Jaeger is grap-
pling with the eleventh-century version of what is a perennial feature
of the three "religions of the Book": the necessity of a reader's essential
openness to the sacred text and its magisterial interpreters in the confidence that from them issues forth the very ichor of Life. Indeed, I
would go so far as to draw a line of continuity (not identity) between
the medieval performative reading considered in this study and devout
reading among Christians, Jews, and Muslims today.

14. For Eco's own attempt to place his oeuvre in this light (including a
partial palinode), see *Interpretation and Overinterpretation* (Cambridge:
Cambridge University Press, 1992).

15. For example, soon after the vignette we have been discussing, Eco has
his young novice muse: "What was similar in the sight of the flame
consuming him, in the desire for carnal union I felt with the girl, in
the mystic shame with which I translated it allegorically, and in the
desire for joyous annihilation that moved the saint to die in his own
love in order to live longer and eternally? Is it possible that things so
equivocal can be said in such a univocal way? And this, it seems, is
the teaching left us by Saint Thomas, the greatest of all doctors: the
more openly it remains a figure of speech, the more it is a dissimilar
similitude and not literal, the more a metaphor reveals its truth." Eco,
Rose, 295.

16. In *Initiation aux auteurs monastiques du moyen âge* (Paris: Editions du Cerf,
1957).

17. See R. H. Rouse, "L'évolution des attitudes envers l'autorité écrite: le
développement des intruments de travail au XIIIe siècle," in *Culture et
travail intellectuel dans l'occident médiéval* (Paris: Editions du CNRS, 1981),
115–144; M. A. Rouse and R. H. Rouse, *Preachers, Florilegia and Sermons:
Studies in the* Manipulus Florum *of Thomas of Ireland*, Studies and Texts,
47 (Toronto: The Pontifical Institute for Mediaeval Studies
Publications, 1979), 3–90; and now the essays gathered in M. A. Rouse
and R. H. Rouse, *Authentic Witnesses: Approaches to Medieval Texts and Manuscripts* (Notre Dame, IN: University of Notre Dame Press, 1991).

18. For the chronology of Thomas's life see A. DeBoutte C.rr.S., "Thomas
van Cantimpré zijn opleiding te Kamerijk," *Ons geestelijk erf* 56 (1982):

283–299; idem, "Thomas van Cantimpré als auditor van Albertus Magnus," *Ons geestelijk erf* 58 (1984): 192–209; A. Debroux, "Thomas de Cantimpré (v. 1200–1270): l'homme et son oeuvre écrite. Essai de biographie" mémoire de license, Université Catholique de Louvain, 1979, unpublished; and Thomas W. Grzebian, "Penance, Purgatory, Mysticism and Miracles: The Life, Hagiography, and Spirituality of Thomas of Cantimpré (1200–1270)." (Ph.D. diss., University of Notre Dame, 1990).

19. For the role of St. Jacques' in the development of search technologies like the concordance and of the *peciae* system of manuscript production see above all M.A. Rouse and R.H. Rouse, "The Development of Research Tools in the Thirteenth Century" and "The Book Trade at the University of Paris, ca. 1250–ca. 1350," in *Authentic Witnesses*, 221–338.

20. I recount Thomas's formal education here in order to establish his connection to the great Dominican *studia generalia* at Paris and Cologne which were so important to and at the dawn of modern scholarly reading. His spiritual formation, however, encompasses rather more than his formal education. One ought especially to mention the formative role played by circles or networks of holy women to which he gained access as it were in the footsteps of his boyhood hero, Jacques de Vitry. I have written elsewhere about one clear influence of holy women upon Thomas's spiritual outlook and orientation. See the bibliographical entry included in note 53 below.

21. Grzebian, 90–98, but especially 97–98.

22. For the *Book of Bees* and its several intents see A. Murray, "Confession as a Historical Source in the Thirteenth Century," in *The Writing of History in the Middle Ages: Essays Presented to Richard William Southern*, ed. R. H. C. Davis and J. M. Wallace-Hadrill (Oxford: Clarendon Press, 1982), 275–322; Henri Platelle, "Le recueil des miracles de Thomas de Cantimpré et la vie religieuse dans les Pays-Bas et le Nord de la France au XIIIe siècle," in *Actes du 97e Congrès national des sociétés savantes, Nantes 1972, Section de philologie et d'histoire jusqu'à 1610* (Paris, 1979), 469–498; but especially Robert Sweetman, "Dominican Preaching in the Southern Low Countries, 1240–1260: *Materiae praedicabiles* in the *Liber de natura rerum* and *Bonum universale de apibus* of Thomas of Cantimpré" (Ph.D. diss., University of Toronto, 1989); and idem, "Visions of Purgatory and Their Role in the *Bonum universale de apibus* of Thomas of Cantimpré," *Ons geestelijk erf* 67 (1993): 20–33.

23. *B.U.* 2.55.1: Sunt autem quinque modi secundum quod in textu considerari potest quibus vexantur apes (supple: in hac vita praesenti). These "modes" are subsequently referred to as "nocumenta" in the remainder of the chapter.

24. *B.U.* 2.57.1: Vesparum generi trium vermium species adiunguntur blacte, strabones, atque stupestres et hiis quattuor daemoniorum species figurantur.

25. Thomas is undoubtedly thinking here of the discussion of the oxviper inserted into his own book of natural history and philosophy. See *Liber de natura rerum*, ed. H. Boase (Berlin: Walter de Gruyter, 1973), 9.42.1–5.309: "Stuprestis vermis est parvus in Italia, ut dicit Ysidorus, simillus scarabeo, longos habens pedes. Decipit inter herbas latens animalia, sed bovem precipue, unde et nomen habet. Quippe cum bos eum inter herbas latenter devoraverit et fel eius tetigerit, ita inflamatur atque tumescit, ut protinus rumpatur mediis visceribus."

26. There are around a half dozen stories in the *Book of Bees* given over to Thomas's involvement with demon troubled women. There are no corresponding stories of his involvement with demon troubled men. This is not to say that there are no demon troubled men in the *Book of Bees*; they are "Legion." Nevertheless, Thomas's own pastoral care does evince an obvious tilt toward troubled women as if women are somehow more vulnerable to demonic vexation. What this tilt might betoken, however, is not clear to me. It might indicate assumptions about women and their vulnerabilities that flow from misogynist assumptions. Alternatively, it may well mean no more than that Thomas was far more involved in the *cura mulierum* than with a corresponding pastorate among men. That is, it is plausible that such a proclivity was a matter of self-conscious patterning in terms of the model of *procurator mulierum* as he would have learned it from the writings and self-projection of Jacques de Vitry. Then again, it could have arisen from the different fit with his *Book of Bees* evinced by internal Dominican pastoral responsibility for friars, on the one hand, and external apostolate among women religious (nuns and beguines for the most part), on the other. It may well be that materials drawn from his apostolate *ad extra* better suited his purposes in the *Book of Bees*. I am consequently not able at this point to account for Thomas's pastoral predilection for women. In the present context, however, one would confront a much more sinister asymmetry were Thomas only to have recognized the demonic vexation of innocent *women*. This however is not the case. In the section of the *Book of Bees* given over to demonic vexation of the innocent, four of the *exempla* deal with men (three with the saint-king of France), two with women. Moreover, one of the cases of innocent possession is also of a man. I have chosen to concentrate attention upon the stories of the possession of righteous women because Thomas is there narrating his own experience, and because he leaves us, in the most extensive of these stories, a precious trace of his own reading practice.

27. *B.U.* 2.57.67.591–593: Vidi et aliam in eadem terra mulierem divitem et honestam possessam a daemone. Quam cum, rogante religioso presbytero, visitarem, invenimus eam a vexatione daemonis quiescentem, et sensate loquentem ut sanam. Tunc occulte, nullo advertente, versum cantici Moysi in Deuteronomio, secundum quod a sancto quodam viro audieram, tertio repetivi, ad provocandum daemonium in obsessa:

"Deum, qui te genuit dereliquisti, et oblitus es Domini creatoris tui. Nec mora, mulier pallere coepit labijs atque vultu, et duae venae in collo eius ad grossitiem pollicis intumescere. Tunc ego: Quare (inquio), pessime, vexare feminam presumpsisti? Et daemon: Mortuo (inquit) viro suo compassa, in subsidium animae illius contulit quidquid boni fecerat in hac vita, et ex hoc nacta occasione, vas vacuum mox intravi. Cui ego: Mentiris, miserrime, ex hoc enim quod dedit, mediante caritate, cumulatum est bonum eius. Et ille cum cachinno: Mendax, inquit, sum, nec mirum si mentior. Mox ego: Estne illa tam pulchra, ut dicitur caelestis patria, quam perdidisti? Et respondit: In infinitum pulchrior, quam dicatur. Et ego: Vellesne redire ad illam, si posses? Et ille: Vellem, inquit, ut possem, et me usque in diem iudicij omnia excogitata supplicia pati oporteret. Cui dixi: Et ego promitto tibi in periculum promissae salutis meae, si mendax inveniar, illam perditam gloriam recuperare te posse, si tantum hoc dixeris: Domine Deus meus peccavi, ignosce mihi. Et mox ille, contorto collo, exclamat horrifice: Domine, Domine. Cumque hoc saepius cum clamore valido personaret, nec ultra in verbis procederet. (Impossibile enim sciebam illi, ut Deum suum Dominum recognosceret, et se peccasse fateretur, atque sibi precaretur ignosci) tandem subiunxit: Domine Deus Margaretae (sic enim obsessa mulier vocabatur) Deum recognoscere suum Dominum indignatus. Tunc ego: O infelicissime omnium creaturarum, superbia elisit te, et celo depulit. Te redire inexpiabilis superbia non permittit. Nec mora, confusus obmutuit, et post paucos dies, non tamen tunc, feminam dereliquit".

28. *Rituale romanum* (Boston: Benziger, 1975), 326–347.

29. As a result, I refer to the first *capitulum* of the early modern *Rituale romanum* when working with *admonitiones* addressed to the exorcist, but to the text of the tenth-century Romano-Germanic Pontifical when referring to the rite itself. See, in this regard, Cyrille Vogel and Reinhard Ilze, eds., *Le pontifical romano-germanique du dixième siècle. L text II (n.n. xcix-ccluiii)* (Vatican City: Biblioteca Apostolica Vaticana, 1963), 193–204, esp. 199–204.

30. *Rituale* 1.5.326: Advertat, quibus artibus ac deceptionibus utantur daemones ad exorcistam decipiendum: solent enim ut plurimum fallaciter respondere, et difficile se manifestare, ut exorcista diu defatigatus desistat; aut infirmus videatur non esse a daemonio vexatus.

31. *Rituale* 1.6.326: Aliquando postquam sunt manifesti, abscondunt se, et relinquunt corpus quasi liberum ab omni molestia, ut infirmus putet se omnino esse liberatum: sed cessare non debet exorcista, donec viderit signa liberationis.

32. *B.U.* 2.57.67.591: Quam cum . . . visitarem, invenimus a vexatione daemonis quiescentem, et sensate loquentem ut sanam.

33. *Rituale* 1.15.327: Necessariae vero interrogationes sunt, ex. gr. de numero et nomine spirituum obsidentium, de tempore quo ingressi sunt,

de causa, et aliis hujusmodi. Ceteras autem daemonis nugas, risus, et ineptias exorcista cohibeat. . . .

34. *Rituale* 1.16.327: Exorcismos vero faciat ac legat cum imperio, et auctoritate, magna fide, et humilitate, atque fervore; et cum viderit, spiritum valde torquere, tunc magis instet et urgeat. Et quoties, viderit obsessum in aliqua corporis parte commoveri, aut pungi, aut tumorem alicubi apparere, ibi faciat signum crucis, et aqua benedicta aspergat, quam tunc in promptu habeat.

35. *Rituale* 1.17.327: Observet etiam ad quae verba daemones magis contremiscant, et ea saepius repetat.

36. *Rituale* 1.20.328: Dum exorcizat, utatur sacrae Scripturae verbis potius quam suis, aut alienis.

37. *B.U.* 2.57.67.591–593: Quare (inquio), pessime, vexare feminam praesumpsisti?

38. Ibid.: Tunc occulte, nullo advertente, versum cantici Moysi in Deuteronomio, secundum quod a sancto quodam viro audieram, tertio repetivi, ad provocandum daemonem in obsessa . . . Nec mora, mulier pallere coepit labijs atque vultu, et duae venae in collo eius ad grossitiem pollicis intumescere.

39. One thinks, in particular, of Thomas's exchange with the demon about heaven.

40. *Le pontifical romano-germanique,* 200–201. . . . in quo nihil invenisti de operibus tuis: qui te expoliavit, qui regnum tuum destruxit, qui te victum ligavit, et vasa tua diripuit: qui te projecit in tenebras exteriores, ubi tibi cum ministris tuis erit praeparatus interitus.

41. The classic telling of Christ's harrowing of hell can be found in *The Gospel of Nicodemus,* Toronto Medieval Latin Texts, ed. H. C. Kim (Toronto: Pontifical Institute for Mediaeval Studies Publications, 1973).

42. *B.U.* 2.57.66.590–591: Vidi in Brabantiae partibus in monasterio Cisterciensi monialem quamdam religiosam valde et vita puram, quam cum visitarem et eam, ut poteram, consolarer, subito daemon pessimus, qui in ea latebat, per horam verba salutis ferre non valens, coepit latrare ut canis et hianti ore et collo contorto, eversisque luminibus blasphemare. Cui dixi: "O miserrime, qui Dei laudibus cum bonis angelis insistere noluisti, nunc canum latratus et bestias imitaris."

43. For an overview of medieval views about the Devil see Jeffrey Burton Russell, *Lucifer: The Devil in the Middle Ages* (Ithaca, NY: Cornell University Press, 1984), esp. 159–207. Many of the formulations that follow, however, are drawn from the oeuvre of St. Bonaventure as surveyed in Robert Sweetman, "When Popular Piety and Theological Learning Conjoin: St. Bonaventure on Demonic Powers and the Christian Soul," *Fides et Historia* 23 (1991): 4–18.

44. See the discussions of "obsideo" and "possideo" in Carleton T. Lewis and Charles Short, *A Latin Dictionary* (Oxford: Clarendon Press, 1975), 1243 and 1403.

45. C. F. Duchange, *Glossarium mediae et infimae latinitatis*, new edition (Paris: Librairie des sciences et des arts, 1938), 6.430.

46. See, in this regard and with respect to what follows in the subsequent paragraph, the patristic discussions of Luke 4, 1–13 (the temptation of Jesus) compiled by Aquinas in his *Catena aurea in quatuor evangelia. II. Expositio in Lucam et Ioannem*, ed. P. Angelico Guarienti O.P. (Turin: Marietti, 1953), 61–66. This commentary is full of the language of being filled and being empty, in which emptiness is associated with vulnerability to demonic vexation.

47. As regards high medieval understanding of the curates of the faithful, their identity and functions, see Joseph Avril, "A propos du 'proprius sacerdos': quelques reflections sur les pouvoires du prêtre de paroisse," in *Proceedings of the Fifth International Congress of Medieval Canon Law, Salamanca 1976* (Vatican City: Bibliotheca Vaticana Apostolica, 1980), 471–486; Leonard E. Boyle O.P., "The Inter-conciliar Period 1179–1215 and the Beginnings of Pastoral Manuals," in *Miscellanea Rolando Bandanelli, Papa Allesandro III*, ed. F. Liota (Siena: Nella Sede dell'Accademia, 1986), 45–56; idem., "The Fourth Lateran Council and Manuals of Popular Theology," in *The Popular Literature of Medieval England*, ed. Thomas Heffernan (Knoxville: University of Tennessee Press, 1985), 30–45; and M. Maccarone, " 'Cura animarum' e 'parochialis sacerdos' nelle constituzioni del IV concilio lateranense (1215): Applicazioni in Italia nel secolo XIII," in *Pievi e parrochie in Italia nel basso medioevo (sec. XIII-XV): Atti del VI Convegno di storia della chiesa in Italia (Firenza, 21–25 sett. 1981)* (Rome:Herder,1984), 81–195.

48. This religious project in which one person's acts are invested in another's welfare is well studied in Jennifer Carpenter, "A New Heaven and a New Earth: A Study of the *Vitae* of the *Mulieres Religiosae* of Liège" (Ph.D. diss., University of Toronto, 1997), especially its third chapter, "Spiritual Charity and Vicarious Suffering in the *Mulieres Religiosae*."

49. For the notion of merit as understood by Thomas Aquinas, see Michael Argus, "Divine Self-Expression Through Human Merit According to Thomas Aquinas" (Ph.D. diss., University of Toronto, 1990), esp. 338–343; and also Joseqh P. Wawrykow, *God's Grace and Human Action: Merit in the Theology of Thomas Aquinas* (Notre Dame, IN: University of Notre Dame Press, 1996).

50. Caesarius of Heisterbach, *Dialogus miraculorum*, ed. J. Strange, 2 vols. (Cologne-Bonn-Brussels, 1851), 5.10.290: Daemon daemoni dicebat: Miser, ut quid consentiendo Lucifero sic de gloria aeterna ruimus? Ad quod alter respondit: Quare fecisti? Cumque ille adhuc quasi poenitudinis verba proferret, alter subiunxit: Tace, poenitentia ista nimis est sera, redire non poteris. . . . Idem spiritus malignus de reditu ad gloriam, sicut superior, interrogatus, verbum sermoni eius valde contrarium audiente me respondit: Si esset, inquit, columna ferrea et ignita, rasoriis et laminis acutissimis armata, a terra usque ad coelum erecta, usque ad

diem iudicii, etiam se carnem haberem, in qua pati possem, me per illam trahere vellem, nunc ascendendo, numc descendendo, dummodo redire possem ad gloriam in qua fui.

51. Thomas's early modern editor marks 18 *exempla* that recall either in part or in toto stories recorded previously in Caesarius's *Dialogus Miraculorum.* In nearly all cases, the corresponding narratives relate in ways similar to the ways discussed in this essay. Some seem to relate as different redactions of a common narrative tradition. This, for example, seems to be the best explaination of the resonances between *D.M.* 6.22 and *B.U.* 2.7.4.150–152. Others seem to relate in the manner that the two narratives presently under discussion relate, namely, Thomas uses Caesarius's narrative as a source of information. In one case, however, the relationship is more direct. In *D.M.* 21.2, Caesarius tells the story of a certain Count Louis, who is a tyrant in life. Facing death, Louis arranges to have his corpse clothed in the habit of the Cistercian Order. His machinations are to no avail. A colleague describes his fate in rich, ironic tones. His soul is received as a novice in the infernal order, so to speak, in which it takes on the discipline of that school of the devil's service. In *B.U.* 1.3.5.16, Thomas also tells of a worldly sinner who seeks and is granted his dying wish to be buried, in this case, in a Dominican habit. We are not told of the otherworldly outcome, but Thomas does take the occasion to defend the practice against the disapproval of other, pastorally flint-hearted orders who see the practice as spiritually vain. It is hard to avoid the impression that Thomas's *exemplum* is designed among other things to act as a response to and criticism of Caesarius's. Of course, Caesarius is reflecting the Cistercian position on these things. Decades earlier, Cistercians were criticized on this score via an *exemplum* in Peter of Poitiers, *De miraculis.*

52. See the list of manuscripts of the *Dialogus* published in A. Meister, *Die Fragmente der Libri VIII Miraculorum des Caesarius von Heisterbach* (Rome: Spithöven, 1901), xxi-xxiv. It should be noted that Caesarius's story is itself a stock telling. However, he never claims it to be anything else as he never enters into his own text, so to speak. All narration occurs via his fictive voices of experienced monk and novice.

53. See in this regard, Robert Sweetman, "Thomas of Cantimpré, *Mulieres Religiosae,* and Purgatorial Piety: Hagiographical *Vitae* and the Beguine 'Voice,'" in *"In a Distinct Voice:" Medieval Studies in Honor of Leonard E. Boyle, O.P.,* ed. Jacqueline Brown and William P. Stoneman (Notre Dame, IN: University of Notre Dame Press, 1997), 606–628.

54. The contrast between "existential" and "essential" invoked at this point adapts the metaphysical distinction identified and argued for by Etienne Gilson in *Being and Some Philosophers* (Toronto: The Pontifical Institute for Mediaeval Studies Publications, 1952). The distinction, as I have appropriated it, implies that what is of the essence, so to speak, exists within a broader and deeper existential horizon. Thus, the es-

sential self is not a Self such as Descartes, Kant, or Husserl posited, that is, it is not a First Thing. Rather, from this vantage point, it would appear that the essential self is the determinate posture or attitude that a concrete human person assumes under a certain conceptualizable aspect. Consequently, it comes to seem that Descartes, Kant, and Husserl, each in his own way, hypostasizes the essential self of scholarly reading and raises it up to the level of metaphysical principle.

55. It is by dint of this imperative approach, this commanding posture, that the scholarly reader insulates himself, albeit willy-nilly, from any essential change.

56. For Catherine's prayer, see the passage of her *vita* cited by Barbara Newman in *From Virile Woman to WomanChrist: Studies in Medieval Religion and Literature* (Philadelphia: University of Pennsylvania Press, 1996), 129.

57. *Rituale* 1.1.326. ea qua par est pietate, prudentia, ac vitae integritate.

58. See, for example, the strategems suggested in *The Malleus Maleficarum of Heinrich Kramer and James Sprenger*, trans. M. Sumner (New York: Dover, 1971), 3.16.230–232. The same treatise can also be used to see the lack of theoretical consensus about such matters, for example, the legitimacy of using sorcery to undo sorcery. See idem 2.2.intro.155–164.

59. Gustaf Aulén, *Christus Victor: An Historical Study of the Three Main Types of the Idea of the Atonement*, trans. A. G. Hebert (London: S.P.C.K., 1953), 67–71.

60. Calvin Seerveld, "A Christian Tin Can Theory of Man," *Journal of the American Scientific Affiliation* 33 (1981):74–81; and James H. Olthuis, "Be(com)ing Human as Gift and Call," *Philosophia Reformata* 58 (1993): 153–174.

61. See, in this regard, "Popular Piety in the Middle Ages: What is Popular?" *Florilegium: Carleton University Annual Papers on Classical Antiquity and the Middle Ages* 4 (1982): 184–193.

62. Boyle treats this opposition in ibid., 184–185.

63. Piety comes under scrutiny in ibid., 186–187.

64. Boyle elaborates this typology in ibid., 187-188.

65. For a survey of current historical scholarship see the notes to John Van Engen, "The Christian Middle Ages as an Historiographical Problem," *American Historical Review* 91 (1986): 519–552, supplemented by idem, "Faith as a Concept of Order in Medieval Christendom," in *Belief in History: Innovative Approaches to European and American Religion*, ed. Thomas Kselman (Notre Dame, IN: University of Notre Dame Press, 1991), 19–67.

66. See, for example, the famous or perhaps infamous study of Colin Morris, *The Discovery of the Individual, 1050–1200*, Medieval Academy Reprints for Teaching (1972; reprint Toronto: University of Toronto Press, 1991); and its necessary complement/corrective, Caroline Walker

Bynum, "Did the Twelfth-Century Discover the Individual?" in *Jesus as Mother: Studies in the Spirituality of the High Middle Ages* (Berkeley: University of California Press, 1982), 82–109.

67. See John Van Engen, "Christian Middle Ages," esp. 551–557; and idem, "Faith as a Concept," esp. 19–31.

Bibliography

Argus, Michael. "Divine Self-Expression Through Human Merit According to Thomas Aquinas." Ph.D. diss., University of Toronto, 1990.

Aulén, Gustaf. *Christus Victor: An Historical Study of the Three Main Types of the Idea of the Atonement.* Trans. A. G. Hebert. London: S.P.C.K., 1953.

Avril, Joseph. "A propos du 'proprius sacerdos': quelques reflections sur les pouvoires du prêtre de paroisse." In *Proceedings of the Fifth International Congress of Medieval Canon Law, Salamanca 1976,* 471–486. Vatican City: Bibliotheca Vaticana Apostolica, 1980.

Benedict XIV, Pope. *Rituale romanum.* Boston: Benziger, 1975.

Boyle, Leonard E., O.P. "The Inter-conciliar Period 1179–1215 and the Beginnings of Pastoral Manuals." In *Miscellanea Rolando Bandanelli, Papa Allesandro III,* ed. F. Liota, 45–56. Siena: Nella Sede dell'Accademia, 1986.

———. "The Fourth Lateran Council and Manuals of Popular Theology." In *The Popular Literature of Medieval England,* 30–45. Ed. Thomas Heffernan. Knoxville: University of Tennessee Press, 1985.

———. "Popular Piety in the Middle Ages: What is Popular?" In *Florilegium: Carleton University Annual Papers on Classical Antiquity and the Middle Ages* 4 (1982): 184–193.

Bynum, Caroline Walker. *Fragmentation and Redemption: Essays on Gender and the Human Body in Medieval Religion.* New York: Zone Books, 1991.

———. "Did the Twelfth Century Discover the Individual?" In *Jesus as Mother: Studies in the Spirituality of the High Middle Ages,* 82–109. Berkeley: University of California Press, 1982.

Carpenter, Jennifer. "A New Heaven and a New Earth: A Study of the *Vitae* of the Mulieres Religiosae of Liège." Ph.D. diss., University of Toronto, 1997.

Carruthers, Mary. *The Book of Memory: A Study of Memory in Medieval Culture.* Cambridge Studies in Medieval Literature 10. Cambridge: Cambridge University Press, 1990.

Curtius, Ernst. *Europäische Literatur und lateinisches Mittelalter.* Bern: A. Francke, 1948.

D'Avray, David. *The Preaching of the Friars: Sermons Diffused from Paris Before 1300.* New York: Oxford University Press, 1985.

DeBoutte, C.rr.S, A. "Thomas van Cantimpré en zijn opleiding te Kamerijk." *Ons geestelijk erf* 56 (1982): 283–299.

———."Thomas van Cantimpré als auditor van Albertus Magnus." *Ons geestelijk erf* 58 (1984): 192–209.

Debroux, A. "Thomas de Cantimpré (v. 1200–1270): l'homme et son oeuvre écrite." Essai de biographie, mémoire de license. Université Catholique de Louvain, 1979.

Duchange, C. F. *Glossarium mediae et infimae latinitatis.* New edition. Paris: Librairie des sciences et des arts, 1938.

Eco, Umberto. *Interpretation and Overinterpretation.* Cambridge: Cambridge University Press, 1992.

———. *In The Name of the Rose.* New York: Harcourt Brace Jovanovich, 1983.

Gilson, Etienne. *Being and Some Philosophers.* Toronto: The Pontifical Institute for Mediaeval Studies Publications, 1952.

Grzebian, Thomas W. "Penance, Purgatory, Mysticism and Miracles: The Life, Hagiography, and Spirituality of Thomas of Cantimpré (1200–1270)." Ph.D. diss., University of Notre Dame, 1990.

Heisterbach, Caesarius of. *Dialogus miraculorum.* Ed. J. Strange. 2 Vols. Cologne-Bonn-Brussels, 1851.

Ilze, Reinhard, and Cyrille Vogel, eds. *Le pontifical romano-germanique du dixième siècle,* 193–204. Vatican City: Biblioteca Apostolica Vaticana, 1963.

Jaeger, C. Stephen. *The Envy of Angels: Cathedral Schools and Social Ideals in Medieval Europe, 950–1200.* Philadelphia: University of Pennsylvania Press, 1994.

Kim, H. C., ed. *The Gospel of Nicodemus.* Toronto Medieval Latin Texts. Toronto: Pontifical Institute for Mediaeval Studies Publications, 1973.

Leclerq, Jean. *L'amour des lettres et le desire de Dieu.* Paris: Editions du Cerf, 1957.

Lewis, Carleton T., and Charles Short. *A Latin Dictionary.* Oxford: Clarendon Press, 1975.

Maccarone, M. " 'Cura animarum' e 'parochialis sacerdos' nelle constituzioni del IV concilio lateranense (1215): Applicazioni in Italia nel secolo XIII." In *Pievi e parrochie in Italia nel basso medioevo (sec. XIII-XV): Atti del VI Convegno di storia della chiesa in Italia (Firenza, 21–25 sett. 1981),* 81–195. Rome: Herder, 1984.

Meister, A. *Die Fragmente der Libri VIII Miraculorum des Caesarius von Heisterbach.* Rome: Spithöven, 1901.

Morris, Colin. *The Discovery of the Individual, 1050–1200,* Medieval Academy Reprints for Teaching. 1972; reprinted, Toronto: University of Toronto Press, 1991.

Murray, A. "Confession as a Historical Source in the Thirteenth Century." In *The Writing of History in the Middle Ages: Essays Presented to Richard William Southern,* ed. R. H. C. Davis and J. M. Wallace-Hadrill, 275–322. Oxford: Clarendon Press, 1982.

Newman, Barbara. *From Virile Woman to WomanChrist: Studies in Medieval Religion and Literature.* Philadelphia: University of Pennsylvania Press, 1996.

Olthuis, James H. "Be(com)ing Human as Gift and Call." *Philosophia Reformata* 58 (1993): 153–174.

Partner, Nancy. "No Sex, No Gender." *Speculum* 68 (1993): 419–443.

Platelle, Henri, "Le recueil des miracles de Thomas de Cantimpré et la vie religieuse dans les Pays-Bas et le Nord de la France au XIIIe siècle." In *Actes du 97e*

Congrès national des sociétés savantes, Nantes 1972, Section de philologie et d'histoire jusqu'à 1610, 469–498. Paris, 1979.

Rouse, R. H. "L'évolution des attitudes envers l'autorité écrite: le développement des intruments de travail au XIIIe siècle." In *Culture et travail intellectuel dans l'occident médiéval*, 115–144. Paris: Editions du CNRS, 1981.

———, and M. A. Rouse. *Preachers, Florilegia and Sermons: Studies in the Manipulus Florum of Thomas of Ireland*. Studies and Texts, 47. Toronto: The Pontifical Institute for Mediaeval Studies Publications, 1979: 3–90.

———, and M. A. Rouse. In *Authentic Witnesses: Approaches to Medieval Texts and Manuscripts*. Notre Dame, IN: University of Notre Dame Press, 1991.

———. "The Development of Research Tools in the Thirteenth Century" and "The Book Trade at the University of Paris, ca. 1250–ca. 1350." In *Authentic Witnesses*. 221–338.

Russell, Jeffrey Burton. *Lucifer: The Devil in the Middle Ages*. Ithaca, NY: Cornell University Press, 1984.

Seerveld, Calvin. "A Christian Tin Can Theory of Man." *Journal of the American Scientific Affiliation* 33 (1981): 74–81.

Stock, Brian. *Augustine the Reader: Meditation, Self-Knowledge and the Ethics of Interpretation*. Cambridge: The Belknap Press of Harvard University Press, 1996.

Sumner, M., trans. *The Malleus Maleficarum of Heinrich Kramer and James Sprenger*. New York: Dover, 1971.

Sweetman, Robert. "Dominican Preaching in the Southern Low Countries, 1240–1260: *Materiae praedicabiles* in the *Liber de natura rerum* and *Bonum universale de apibus* of Thomas of Cantimpré." Ph.D. diss., University of Toronto, 1989.

———. "Visions of Purgatory and Their Role in the *Bonum universale de apibus* of Thomas of Cantimpré." *Ons geestelijk erf* 67 (1993): 20–33.

———. "When Popular Piety and Theological Learning Conjoin: St. Bonaventure on Demonic Powers and the Christian Soul." *Fides et Historia* 23 (1991): 4–18.

———. "Thomas of Cantimpré, *Mulieres Religiosae*, and Purgatorial Piety: Hagiographical *Vitae* and the Beguine 'Voice.' " In *"In a Distinct Voice:" Medieval Studies in Honor of Leonard E. Boyle, O.P.*, Ed. Jacqueline Brown and William P. Stoneman, 606–628. Notre Dame, IN: University of Notre Dame Press, 1997.

Thomas Aquinas. *Catena aurea in quatuor evangelia. II Expositio in Lucam et Ioannem*. Ed. P. Angelico Guarienti, O.P. Turin: Marietti, 1953.

Thomas of Cantimpré. *Bonum universale de apibus, sive, miraculorum exemplorum memorabilium sui temporis libri duo*. Ed. G. Colvenère. Douai: 1627.

———. *Liber de natura rerum*. Ed. H. Boase. Berlin: Walter de Gruyter, 1973.

Van Engen, John. "The Christian Middle Ages as an Historiographical Problem." *American Historical Review* 91 (1986): 519–552.

———. "Faith as a Concept of Order in Medieval Christendom." In *Belief in History: Innovative Approaches to European and American Religion*, ed. Thomas Keselman, 19–67. Notre Dame, IN: University of Notre Dame Press, 1991.

Wawrykow, Joseph P. *God's Grace and Human Action: Merit in the Theology of Thomas Aquinas.* Notre Dame, IN: University of Notre Dame Press, 1996.

Werner, Ernst. *Häresie und Gesellschaft im 11. Jahrhundert.* Sitzungsberichte der sächsischer Akademie der Wissenschaften zu Leipzig, Philologische-Historische Klasse 117.5. Leipzig, 1975.

CHAPTER SEVEN

Beguine Textuality: Sacred Performances

Mary Suydam

In this century the phenomenon of the beguine movement—groups of women desiring to live a religious life while not being confined to cloisters or involving permanent vows—has been reclaimed as part of the history of medieval mystical piety. In the past scholars often considered the extravagant ecstasies of beguine and other Flemish holy women to be less mystically pure than the refined spirituality espoused by Platonist mystics such as Meister Eckhart or the author of *The Cloud of Unknowing*. Caroline Walker Bynum has astutely analyzed the consequences of such early attitudes towards religious experiences: "Troeltsch mentions as mystics almost no medieval figures who would today be recognized as such, and he mentions no women at all. Such scholarly neglect of women's mysticism is part of a general prejudice against all religiosity with paramystical elements.... Women's mysticism was ... more fleshly and bodily, if you will—than ordinary Christian piety."[1]

Thanks to Bynum and a host of other scholars, the study of women mystics, and especially beguines, flourishes today.[2] Yet a holdover from earlier scholarship remains in the unconscious paradigm of the mysic as a solitary contemplative. Although her "more fleshly" practices may now be studied as genuine spirituality, the mystic is still considered to be an individual communing solely with God. Medieval witnesses of beguine holiness sometimes foster this impression, as in the accounts of the thir-

teenth-century writer Jacques of Vitry: "Others were drawn with such in-
toxication of spirit that in sacred silence they would remain quiet a whole
day . . . so that they could not be roused by clamor or feel a blow. I saw
another whom for thirty years her Spouse had so zealously guarded in her
cell, that she could not leave it herself. . . ."[3]

One important consequence of this individualist paradigm is that
writings deemed mystical are usually analyzed as communications authored
by one person to convey that person's experiences with or commmuni-
cations from the divine realm—that is, they are categorized as literature.
Because thirteenth-century beguine writers such as Hadewijch of Antwerp,
Beatrijs of Nazareth, and Mechthild of Magdeburg wrote powerfully about
their ecstatic revelations, their works are acclaimed as individual communications intended for a literary audience of individual readers.[4]

In contrast, Flemish holy women's hagiographies, peppered with miraculous interventions and visitations, show women whose devotional lives,
including their literary productions, were intricately connected with their
communities. A detailed analysis of these *vitae* reveals a social context that
challenges contemporary conceptualizations of beguine writings as literature and suggests that devotional performance is as much their function
as literary communication. These hagiographies present compelling evidence that Flemish women's piety and its resulting written depiction were
not acts of solitary contemplation, recorded later to edify future generations, but publicly enacted sacred performances shared and shaped by
many audiences. This chapter contends that beguine textuality was interactive and performance-oriented. Consequently, I propose a different
"reading" of beguine writings, one that applies the performance theory of
the staged text advanced by Jean Alter and Richard Schechner, as well as
Jacques Derrida's postmodern challenge to the assumption of oral/perfor-
mative versus written/literary modes of communication.

Beguine Communal Life

It is important to understand that the beguines were not recluses but
groups of women who desired to live communally, although they did not
formally profess eternal vows.[5] Beguines first appeared in northern Europe
in the late twelfth century and by 1216 had obtained papal approval for
their way of life. They were a widespread religious movement in the Low
Countries and central Europe until their "irregular" living arrangements

resulted in their persecution and finally their condemnation in 1310. In the southern Low Countries, where beguines were more conventionally organized, the movement continued to flourish long after 1310. Because being a beguine was not necessarily a permanent way of life, some women who initially lived as beguines eventually did join convents, such as Ida of Nivelles and Mechthild of Magdeburg. Others, such as Beatrijs of Nazareth, were educated as children by beguines but joined convents as adults. Some beguines lived in a house with only two or three other women, whereas others were organized in large beguinages.[6] A beguinage was a self-contained set of buildings similar to a convent, but beguines were not strictly enclosed within their walls.

Just as beguine ways and trajectories of life were extremely varied, so too were the motivations that led women to join this movement. Alcantara Mens argues that religious motives, specifically the desire to imitate evangelical poverty, were characteristic of the early days of the beguine movement, whereas the desire to escape or alleviate real poverty predominated later on.[7] The sketchy data available make any conclusions about the balance between piety and practicality very speculative. Nevertheless, although Ida of Nivelles and other "heroically holy" women of the thirteenth century left an indelible impression of extraordinary piety upon observers, it is clear that such women were also members of communities. In fact, beguine rules from the earliest dates seldom mention piety; rather, they stress practical matters such as the organization of hierarchy, receipts for the sale of property upon entry, and the annual ceremony of allegiance to the rules of the beguinage.[8] Early rules indicate that beguines were expected to be self-supporting, either from regular rents received, sale of property, or by working (usually in some aspect of the cloth industry).[9] Some rules also stipulated that beguines were expected to assent publicly to aldermanic statutes in their area.[10]

Many readers may be surprised at the degree of control, relatively independent of men, achieved by medieval beguines. This autonomy, and the growth and success of the beguine movement, may be at least partially attributed to the visibility of Low Countries women in daily life. Ellen Kittell has documented the full participation of medieval Flemish women in all aspects of public life. She has demonstrated that women routinely functioned as witnesses, participants, and adjudicants in a variety of public spaces there.[11] For example, they argued property claims, served as witnesses to such claims in aldermanic courts, governed as abbesses, and served as castellans.[12] Moreover, their participation in public life was neither unusual nor remarkable. Thus, since Low Countries women took active roles within "the world," it is not surprising that many beguine religious activities were participatory and public.

The earliest rules for *begijnhoven* (beguinages), as well as the *vitae* of medieval Low Countries beguines, clearly establish that the extraordinary holiness of some beguine women was not achieved in isolation from either their own sisters or the wider world. These early rules state explicitly that beguines were expected to spend their days communally, and that they had to ask permission to go anywhere unaccompanied.[13] Even those described as recluses received visitors, gave advice, and traveled. For example, a thirteenth-century tract by Hadewijch of Antwerp named 57 living "perfect" people, spread over a far-flung geographic area, with whom she visited or communicated.[14] Other beguine women like Marie d'Oignies and Ida of Leuven (Louvain) lived communally in some form of convent life, although less strictly enclosed than most nuns.[15] Thus, beguine women, either extraordinary or ordinary, had public lives. Sometimes their "public" was the outside world, and sometimes it was the community of sisters. Consequently, they performed in a wide variety of public roles, such as singing in choirs, reading to sisters, transacting legal business, and making and selling woolen cloth.

These facts of beguine life mean that all aspects of their devotional practices had a marked communal component. Many beguines became famous for their visions, alternatively referred to as ecstatic experiences.[16] It is striking that most of the visions written or recorded in beguine *vitae* took place in public settings, most often during Mass.[17] Thus it is a mistake to regard beguine textuality primarily as the literary record of private revelations without considering the performative and communal context in which they took place.

In Flemish beguine and religious *vitae* the ecstatic visionary is often surrounded by other people who benefit from, often participate in, and react to her experiences. An example from the *vita* of Lutgard of Aywières demonstrates this point:

> Whenever Lutgard's raptures involved mindfulness of the Lord's Passion, it seemed to her that her whole body, her whole being, was turning red, as if drenched with blood. A priest . . . had secret word of this experience of hers. . . . The season was such that he was sure that her thoughts were on the Passion, and so he crept up to watch her. . . . Behold, he saw her face and hands, the only parts of her body then visible, soaked and shining as with a recent flow of blood, her

loose hairs also were wet with blood. . . . So he secretly took a pair of scissors and cut of a snippet of hair. . . . Thereupon his awe at this enormous spectacle reached unbelievable proportions and he fell over backwards.[18]

Another example, from the *vita* of Ida of Nivelles, a thirteenth-century beguine who later became a Cistercian nun, recounts her journey with another nun to the city of Liège. That night they stayed at a Cistercian convent, and before bedtime the nun asked Ida to "expand for her edification on some of the good things with which the Lord had enriched her."[19] Ida's edifying words to this nun were not Holy Scripture, although she certainly knew many portions by heart. Neither were they prayers from the Breviary—Ida and her friend had already said those. Instead, Ida recounted one of her visionary experiences. As she told the story, Ida's face began to glow. Moreover, the story itself had an amazing effect upon her companion. The *vita* says that "the nun gazed upon her [Ida's] countenance as upon the countenance of an angel who had sat next to her. . . . She also had fears lest from so honeyed an exchange she might faint away."[20]

There are two noteworthy features of this story from Ida's *vita*. First, somehow Ida was able to re-call and re-experience a vision that had presumably happened some time ago. This re-collection had the same transformative effect as the original vision: her face glowed "with the spirit," and she appeared to another as angelic. Second, this "honeyed exchange" [collocutione tam melliflua] also transformed her companion. Subsequently, the nun was able to reassure Ida that their candle would not go out until they were finished. She, not Ida, attained second sight, through *Ida's* story. Thus the re-told vision was performed, shared, participatory, and transformative.

Ecstatic Transformation: Performer and Witnessing Audiences

The term "performance" deliberately underscores the public and audience-oriented nature of beguine and religious ecstatic life. By "performance" I mean any action, done in public before an audience, that in some way is transformative for both actor and audience.[21] In the first example, Lutgard's ecstatic manifestation occurred in a public space, a church. Not only did the priest witness and share in Lutgard's perception of bloodiness, but his behavior was affected by it. Reciprocally, his performance of the Mass transformed the elements of bread and wine into the Body and Blood of Christ, which in turn facilitated Lutgard's ecstatic response. Thus each performer was both enabled and transformed by the performance of the other. In the second example the presence of a companion enabled Ida's shared re-enactment of a previous ecstasy and transformed both of them.

It is crucial to understand that "performance" (including visions) in a sacred context does not mean an artificial or secondary event enacted for the entertainment of a passive audience.[22] Rather, ritual performances are acts intended to transform both performer and audience.[23] Acknowledged ritual performances include most liturgical and priestly actions like the performance of the Mass. One definition of the Eucharistic liturgy is that "it seeks to bring about an encounter between the worshippers and the saving mystery."[24] Moreover, liturgical performances are public actions: "Liturgy is celebrated *with* others and the relationships between the members of the worshipping community are of the highest importance. *Private* acts of *public* worship are a contradiction in terms."[25] Thus, sacred liturgical performances like the Mass are public, transformative, and shared. Without priestly action, the host remains an inert wafer of bread. Although the Mass can be performed without an audience, the presence of the audience provides a context through which priestly actions are affirmed and celebrated.[26]

However, it is not always acknowledged that women's actions *in* a church that correspond and/or compete with liturgical rituals also may have qualities of ritual performance. I propose calling such actions "sacred performances" in order to emphasize both their ritual and performative aspects. Visionary and other ecstatic acts are generally regarded as private demonstrations of exceptional individual piety rather than as communal sacred performances. However, beguine and religious holy women routinely performed efficacious acts for others during these ecstatic moments, such as exorcising demons, relieving purgatorial suffering, and intervening on behalf of individuals or communities.[27] Additionally, acts of worship performed by them often resulted in others' miraculous conversions or heightened devotion. The only religious performances in which they could not participate were those of the priestly office itself. Even without this capacity, their priestly actions (for example, forgiving sins, detecting sin or sanctity in others) were regarded in their *vitae* as routine qualities of holiness, not as astounding exceptions. Though their ecstatic piety was indeed exceptional, they were regarded by contemporaries as intermediaries between heaven and earth. They were not identified with solitary or passive piety. Moreover, actions such as exorcism were recognized by contemporaries as legitimate ritual performances. As historians of *vitae* and hagiographies know, even ecstatic manifestations often had recognizable features that could be witnessed by others. Some visionaries reported trance behaviors such as seeing with "spiritual eyes," fainting, unusual secretions including copious weeping, and singing or shouting.

Flemish women's *vitae* contain many stories in which people, on their own behalf or that of a community's, sought visions and specific actions from noted holy women. A prominent theme in such *vitae* are stories relating to the status (in heaven or purgatory) of deceased relatives.[28] One such account, from the *vita* of Ida of Nivelles, states that, at the request of another nun, Ida "poured out" prayers to God on behalf of the nun's deceased father. His placement in purgatory was revealed to Ida, not in church, but during the communal harvest. Thereafter Ida undertook to suffer his torments and was gripped with a high fever for six weeks. Finally, Ida received another vision in which she understood that the man's sufferings in purgatory were partially alleviated. Realizing the multitude of his sins, she "enlisted very many prayers for him" in order to multiply the intercessions.[29] Both of Ida's visions occurred on behalf of another nun in the community, and it took the whole community to free the nun's father from his fate.

Moreover, in this story neither of Ida's visions occurred for her private edification. Her six weeks' fever was also not a "vision" in the traditional "receptive" and episodic sense of the term. It was clearly understood to be an active divine process, like Jacob wrestling with the angel. Like her visions, Ida's fever was not a private affliction, but occurred in a context of actions designed to transform the dead man's status from purgatory to heaven.

I would like to point out another characteristic of these sacred performances: their qualities of creating, not just expressing, sacred persona. Several postmodern scholars have advanced the notion that continual performances create contingent identities. That is, rather than a single, unitary identity that is expressed through performances, postmodern theorists such as Judith Butler have argued that "there is no 'I' that precedes. . . . The repetition and the failure to repeat, produce a string of performances that constitute and contest the coherence of that 'I'."[30] This perspective depends upon the poststructuralist contention that meaning is not transparent or fixed by its referent (the sign), but contingently constructed and continually deferred: "In avowing the sign's strategic provisionality (rather than its strategic essentialism), that identity can become a site of contest and revision, indeed take on a future set of significations that those of us who use it now may not be able to foresee" (Butler, 305).[31]

In the example given above, from the *vita* of Ida of Nivelles, her ecstatic performances were also transformative in the sense that her authority as a holy woman was confirmed and renewed. Just as a priest's authority is affirmed every time he transforms the elements of bread and wine into Christ's Body and Blood, Ida's authority was likewise affirmed by a series of ecstatic actions. No one "sees" the change from bread to Body, and no one "sees" the dead man's transformation, but religious performances in a communal context guarantee that such changes have indeed occurred. However, the priest's authority resides in his office, whereas the authority of holy women like Ida is only guaranteed by continuous performances of extraordinary piety. Unlike the office of priesthood, there is no ritual that can transform Ida permanently into a holy woman. Affirmation of a priest's authenticity is an affirmation of the efficacy of the Church and not a statement about a particular individual, whereas holy women's reputations depended upon continued public performances that could demonstrate their piety to all. In that regard, the performative dimension of holy women's sacred actions were critical components of their success in being recognized as truly holy, and had to be continually repeated in order to guarantee such success.

Given the performative, active, and communal nature of beguine ecstatic devotional life, it is a modern conceit to view the texts that record such devotions purely from a reader's perspective, that is, as a private communication from one author to an unseen audience of silent, individual readers. For every visionary "taken up in the spirit" there was an immediate and involved audience. Like Lutgard's priest and Ida's companion, these audiences enabled, witnessed, and participated in shared religious performances.

Mediated Textuality: The Audience of Scribes and Copyists

John Dagenais has described a conception of literary texts underlying most studies of medieval literature as beginning with "the idea that there is a human being who intends to produce a work of literature and who is solely responsible for its shape and meaning."[32] This model is totally at odds with what we know to be the actual processes of medieval book authoring, production, and transmission.[33] The composition of medieval devotional literature was not a solitary act. Reading and writing were far more public and performance-oriented than they are now. To record a mortgage, we go to the court, sign a document silently, and have it silently witnessed by a notary. But in the medieval period, and especially in Flanders, courts were often open public halls. There, all acts of writing were records of performed public events, witnessed and spoken *aloud*. As Ellen Kittell has documented, written records were not the focus of these events, but secondary to the public and oral performance. Medieval Dutch-speaking women participated fully in this public and oral dimension of discourse.[34]

Being highly educated, or "well-read," did not mean one possessed the artistic skills of writing. Most written works were dictated to scribes, not silently written by an author. This is especially the case with religious works written by women, such as the compositions of Hildegard of Bingen, Beatrijs of Nazareth, Mechthild of Magdeburg, and Ida of Nivelles. For example, Mechthild of Magdeburg's text may have been partially written and partially dictated over many years before it was finally copied by a scribe.[35] Hildegard of Bingen and Beatrijs of Nazareth did not always have control over the written versions of their works.[36] This means that even in the case of named medieval authors, especially religious female authors, their relationship to their own texts was different than that of most modern authors.

Moreover, all books were manuscripts, that is, each text was unique to each copyist. A literary model of texts assumes that there is just one authored text. We expect that every printed copy of a book will have the same content. However, hand-copied manuscripts vary so greatly that medieval authors could not have possessed this expectation. For example, consider two different copies of a poem in the manuscripts of Hadewijch of Antwerp, a thirteenth-century beguine:

Manuscript B	*Manuscript C*
Maer sien verliesen	Maer sijn verliesen
Ende sien verkiesen	Ende sijn verkiesen
[But to lose sight	[But his loss
And to choose sight]	And his choice]

In this instance, the copyists' choice of "sien" or "sijn" changes the meaning of the poem.[37] Dagenais remarks that "this reality [of manuscripts] must alter, irremediably, our ideas about the relations among author, work, text, and reader in the Middle Ages" (*Ethics*, 16).

In fact, the degree of mediation in medieval women's texts is often so great that there is no way to recover any sense of a single author. For example, Lutgard of Aywières told stories of her remarkable life to the Dominican friar Thomas of Cantimpré. In order to write Lutgard's *vita*, Thomas also listened to witnesses' accounts of her life. The resulting *vita*

Three Lives of Lutgard of Aywières

Long Latin

The Demons had such a fear of her that they even avoided contact with the spot she used to pray, just as they would avoid a red-hot iron. Now Lutgard did not understand the Psalms, and yet she used to ruminate over the Psalm, *Deus in Adjutorum meum Intende* and certain other verses from the Psalter. And she would see the demons thus flee away, desisting from their suggestions of evil deeds.

Old French

Demons came frequently to Lutgard, announcing to her some sad or tragic event. She, however, simply spat at them, or brushed off their importunity with a Sign of the Cross. The demons had such a fear of her that they even avoided contact with the spot she used to pray, just as they would avoid a red-hot iron. Now Lutgard did not understand the Psalms, nor anything from Scriptures, and yet she used to ruminate over the Psalm, *Deus in Adjutorum meum Intende* and certain other verses from the Psalter. And she would see the demons thus flee away, desisting from their suggestions of evil deeds. Friar Bernard tells how he heard her secretly saying that she had no fear at all of the Devil, and that none of his means of deceiving were able to prevail against her, however slightly; rather, in accord with the Lord's promise, she used mightily to crush his "head", that is, his intentions, with the "foot" of her own virtues.

Second Latin Text

The demons had such a fear of her that they even avoided contact with the spot she used to pray, just as they would avoid a red-hot iron. Now Lutgard did not understand the Psalms, and yet she used to ruminate over the Psalm, *Deus in Adjutorum meum Intende* and certain other verses from the Psalter. And she would see the demons thus flee away, desisting from their suggestion of evil deeds. Hence she understood that there was a virtue in those words, even short of her having understood them, by which the demonic presence could be expelled and all their power for tempting unnerved.[39]

now exists in three very different manuscripts, two in Latin and one in Old French. Thomas's work itself has been so amended and edited by the copyists of these manuscripts, that it is difficult to determine in what sense even Thomas is an "author."[38] The following example presents three versions of an episode from Lutgard's *vita* to demonstrate the complexity of medieval manuscripts.

In a very real sense, Lutgard has three lives in these manuscripts. In the first version, Lutgard, although not fully literate, can control the actions of demons by her exceptional holiness. The second version heightens Lutgard's agency: although she is completely illiterate, she laughs and spits at demons and has no fear of them. In the third version, Lutgard understands that it is not her holiness, but the virtue of the scriptural words, that has the power to ward off demons.

I believe that there is an important performance dimension associated with this phenomenon of mediated textuality. Authors expected audiences and copyists to interact with their texts. At the very least, they assumed that their words would be performed before an audience, not silently read by an individual. That is, every medieval author and copyist knew that books, especially religious writings, were usually read aloud, often in group settings of religious communities.[40]

Thus, there is a fundamental oral, interpretative, and performance orientation to all written medieval texts. Book 8 of Bridget of Sweden's (1303–1373) visionary text captures this flavor: "This book, and the scripture thereof, was not written with ink, but each word in the book was alive and spoke itself, as if a man were to say, do this or do that, and immediately it were done with the speaking of the word. No man read the writing of that book, but whatever was contained in the writing, all of it was seen in the pulpit."[41] Bridget's "book" refers to the living Word of God as a textual performance.[42] Reading, as Karma Lochrie points out, is "akin to attending to speech-acts."[43] When one dictates one's words to an audience, there is speech and action involved as well as writing. Yet, like the words themselves, these "speech-acts" were erased or added to by numerous scribes and copyists, and performed again for different audiences by readers interacting with and creating "speech-acts" in the written texts. In both the oral performance and the act of dictating/writing, the listening/transcribing audiences have potentially greater involvement than is possible when one silently writes, alone, to an unseen audience of individuals. For example, I expect that a copy of *Hamlet* published in the nineteenth century will be virtually identical to one published currently. On the other hand, the oldest written manuscript copy of the works of Hadewijch of

Antwerp, a thirteenth-century beguine, dates from the early fourteenth century, at least one hundred years after Hadewijch lived. As demonstrated earlier, other copies, dating from subsequent centuries, differ significantly from each other. How many manuscripts and readings as "speech-acts" lie between the words that Hadewijch spoke and the copies we possess today? This fact of continuous mediation is at the heart of the textual transformations that comprise medieval devotional manuscripts as texts of performance.

Textual Transformations: The Audience of Readers

There is no doubt that generations of copyists and readers actively participated in the formation of literature in medieval manuscript culture. There is also compelling evidence that authors and audiences expected such interaction with texts. In the Middle Ages, reading audiences believed that ecstatic texts, like the visions they depicted, belonged to a genre of religious writing intended to evoke a transformative power in the listener that went beyond the emotional impact of great literature or a fascinating record of encounters with the divine. Just as Ida's companion was transformed through an evocation of a vision, and in other visions unbelievers or skeptics were converted, the texts of such experiences also were intended to convey transformative power for generations of readers. According to a thirteenth-century text written by Gertrude of Helfta, God declared to her that "If anyone with devout intention desires to read this book for the good of his soul, I will draw him to myself, so that it will be as if he were reading it in my hands, and I will take part in his reading . . . I will breathe in the desires of his soul . . . and I will breathe forth over him the breath of my divinity, and he will be renewed by my Spirit within him."[44] A century later an English monk of Farne explained his reason for writing his devotional guide: "Would that my longing might imprint its own characters on the hearts of them that hear, just as the hand that writes presents them to the eyes of readers."[45] The monk wishes not only to convey edifying words, but to imprint the actual longing of his heart into the reader's heart.

According to John Dagenais, this approach is part of a larger cultural "ethics of reading": "The medieval text must be viewed not as verbal icon, not as Letter alone, but as an "event" that actualizes the ethical behavior of a reader, absorbs the reader into its own ethical system, and stimulates, among other ethical acts, its own reenactment (and, I would add, its own retelling and recopying)" (21). Dagenais emphasizes the role of the medieval reader, rather than the author or the text. By "ethics" Dagenais means "practices," specifically engaging with and confronting texts. He has proposed a paradigm shift from "literature" to "lecturature" (22–24). Such "reading" takes us beyond literature, and to some extent beyond an authoritative written text, to a performance "more interested in the word as event, than as textual relic," to quote Karma Lochrie (64). Restoring this sense of "word as event" to beguine devotional texts and their participating audiences reinforces my sense of them as sacred performances rather than as "textual relics." It is therefore crucially important to inquire how texts meant for "reading" in this more fluid and interactive sense can be reconceived by modern scholars as vehicles for readers' performances.

The Staged Text

Jean Alter has examined the way in which a written theater piece is treated differently when it is viewed as a source for performance rather than as literature. For example, when we read *Hamlet* as a literary play, we primarily read it as a narrative. Who is Hamlet and what happens in the play? What we necessarily leave out are the spaces occupied by and surrounding the performers. Although we try to flesh out these spaces in our imagination, Alter notes that this is not the same as a theatrical reading: "A properly theatrical process, however, involves a different reading of the dramatic text. As its ties to literature are severed, the text recovers its primary function as a set of fixed notations of past and future performances. It is treated deliberately like a textual matrix of theatre, a text to be staged, a source of theatrical transformations."[46]

What does it mean to say "the walls of Elsinore"? What a reader ignores or sketchily imagines, the director envisions: how the walls will be figured on the stage and how the actors will occupy the spaces around and on them. Second, rather than asking, "who is Hamlet?" the director imagines how the character "Hamlet" can be a source for an actor's construction of him. Thus, a theatrical reading necessarily has a performative dimension.

Even this theatrical text lacks the depth of a fully staged text, that is, a performance. A staged text is created by multiple theatrical readings and preliminary enactments: "The staged text involves many complete or fragmentary readings, yielding many unstable versions of the stage. Each reading, or re-reading, brings more precision to various imaginary stage features, adding or changing them, playing with the repertory of nonverbal signs" (165). Eventually this fragmentary and unstable version, in Alter's words, "takes on the density of a virtual performance."

I propose that this contemporary model of staging and performance is a useful paradigm for understanding the performative component of medieval ecstatic literature. Consider this vision of Queen Reason from the *Visioenen* of Hadewijch of Antwerp:

> It was at Matins on the feast *In nativitate beatae Mariae*, and after the Third Lesson a little wonder was shown to me in the spirit. My heart had been moved beforehand by the words of love that one read there from the Song of Songs, whereupon I thought of a complete kiss. Shortly afterwards, in the Second Noctern, I saw in the spirit a queen come in, clad in a gold dress, and that dress was full of eyes, and all the eyes were completely transparent, like fiery flames and nevertheless like crystal. And the crown she wore on her head had as many crowns one above another as there were eyes in her dress . . . And she set her foot upon my throat and screamed with a more terrible voice and said: "Do you know who I am?"[47]

First, a theatrical reading considers the context in which the performance occurs. This vision was evoked and structured by both the performance of Matins and by the biblical lesson read for that particular office. Moreover, this particular religious performance occurred on the festival of Mary's nativity. Thus, the vision is structured within a larger public space, and fixed notations of the primary performance of Matins, as well as the particular festival day and lesson, undergird the vision itself. The medieval religious reader could easily envision the physical space and sequencing characteristic of the Divine Office of Matins.

Second, a theatrical reading imagines the physical space within the vision itself—the spaces occupied by the queen and Hadewijch. Additional biblical images from Ezekiel are used to describe the queen's strange apparel.[48] During the vision, the queen attempts to choke off Hadewijch's voice, which evokes a dramatic personal response. The queen's action is also a fixed notation of assault, because in medieval visionary and hagiographic texts demons often try to attack or choke people.[49] However, although Queen Reason acts in demonic fashion, she represents the rational faculty of the soul. In this way, the apparent incongruence of Queen Reason's rich array, her identity, and her actions theatrically demonstrate the beguine ambivalence towards reason.

Finally, Hadewijch's use of dialogue in her ecstatic description forces the reader to engage with her vision rather than passively receiving her story. Hadewijch's assertive reply fends off the assault and renders Reason subject to her: "And I said, 'Yes, indeed! You have caused me woe and pain so long. You are the Reason of my soul . . . I have confessed your power.' . . . Then Reason became subject to me, and I left her. And then Love came and embraced me, and I came out of the spirit and remained lying until late in the day, drunk with unspeakable wonders."[50] The courtly dismissal of Reason allows Hadewijch (and the believing listener/reader) to focus upon and be embraced by the transformative power of Love.[51]

Envisioning the spatial and kinesthetic dimensions within this text provides a different perspective than that of dramatic literature. Such a perspective emphasizes the particular public setting (a communal religious service in honor of Mary) from which derives the power of a religious vision in which all the characters, including the deity (Love), are female. Hadewijch's triumph over Reason is meant to be a source for performance for present and future audiences. By personally engaging with Hadewijch's encounter between Reason and Love, the reader is meant to absorb the beguine emphasis on love into one's own ethical system in a more direct manner than is possible when one merely reads of Hadewijch's encounter, long ago. With its incorporation of multiple stagings (in the medieval period, textual performances by copyists, scribes, and readers), Alter's model of the staged text allows for the ongoing mediation of performers and audiences in beguine textuality.

Before considering further the evidence that writers created their texts with this performative dimension in mind, it is important to examine and reject an unintentional corollary of separating literary from peformative perspectives: the artificial distinction between speech (performance) and writing (literature).

"Writing" and Performing the Staged Text

Unlike a composed piece of theater that culminates in an opening performance, ecstatic raptures ostensibly begin with the vision as a public and immediate enactment, that is, a performance. However, upon closer examination, this initial performance may itself have been called forth by meditation on, or reading of, other composed works, or even by other performances. As noted previously, Hadewijch's Vision 9 was evoked and structured by both the performance of Matins and by written words from the Bible that Hadewijch heard. In Vision 7, to be examined shortly, the entire ecstatic experience took place during Mass, and the Mass itself served as the organizing principle of the vision.

Thus, inspired by either composition or by performance, Hadewijch's virtual performance eventually led to the text we have today. This written text may itself have been originally a staged text such as the shared vision of Ida of Nivelles (a telling that is almost a re-enactment). Additionally, it probably underwent theatrical readings (repeated tellings, dictations to scribes, and subsequent copyings) before reaching its final written state, which re-presents both "the density of performance" *and* literature.

Often the term "performance" connotes an immediacy that seems to be lacking in written literature, one that captures the emotional power of a fully-present person rather than merely re-presenting it. Jacques Derrida has called this belief in the supremacy of performance the nostalgia for origin within the fully present moment.[52] Derrida challenges this hierarchical distinction, arguing that there are no neat dichotomies between spoken and written words; one cannot be said to come before or to be superior to the other.[53] According to Derrida, "writing" includes all acts of differentiation, spoken or written. Speech is also representative: "A sign which would take place but once would not be a sign."[54]

Derrida's critique of the romanticization of speech is well taken. It is therefore critically important to realize that beguine ecstatic texts do not progress in a linear fashion from a private, ineffable experience to a compelling oral and public performance to an abstract written composition (that is, literature that exists apart from its author). A staged text does not try to recover an original compelling performance, but to engage the participant/reader in a current performance. Alter's description of the staged text emphasizes the text as sources for performance, not performance itself. If written ecstatic literature has been privileged over its performances in the past, privileging the original speech and performance over writing (assuming that it is possible to recover what was really said) repeats the same error from a different direction.

In the above example from Hadewijch's vision of Queen Reason, the liturgical performance of Matins, written biblical words, a cultural understanding of demonic themes in saint's lives, and an understanding of the beguine concepts of reason and love are all intertextualities of the ecstatic experience that structure the text, its audiences, and its multiple possibilities for performance. The process of producing the text moves both backward and forward from performance to composition, resulting in a complex interweaving of written and performative elements at all times.[55] Moreover, Derrida's definition of speech as "writing" means that oral performance and written composition cannot really be separated or fit into a developmental scheme. "Performance" may refer to *both* the vision-enacted-in-the-here-and-now *and* to the performance (dictation) of a written work. Likewise, "composition" can refer to the written work as a product, as well as to the act (performance) of constructing and interpreting an enacted performance. The ongoing participation of, and mediation by, beguine audiences further erodes the modern assumption of linear progression from a single author's speech to writing.

This process of "writing" (in all its possible manifestations) is seen more clearly in the visions of medieval women for whom *vitae* were written. According to the *vita* of Ida of Leuven (Louvain), a thirteenth-century Cistercian nun, as a child she experienced a sacramental vision during Mass when her mother was present. Later, at home, Ida recited the vision (provided a theatrical reading) for her mother and the mother agreed with (validated) the daughter's interpretation. Thus, in this story the performance of the Mass evoked an ecstatic experience, which was later repeated and interpreted by both Ida and her mother.[56] Who knows how many more re-tellings and re-visions lie between this childhood incident and its recounting many years later by the scribe(s) who wrote the *vita?*

In another example from a *vita*, Lutgard of Aywières had a vision of a friend who had just died. She told this vision to the deceased's sister as well as to the other nuns in Lutgard's convent. Later, in her grief over her friend's death, she heard the Lord comfort her with the biblical words, "Surely I am better to have than ten sons." The *vita* explains that Lutgard did not understand Scripture enough to know the meaning of these words until they were interpreted for her by someone else.[57]

In this example, the vision and its interpretation took place in several mediated phases. Moreover, this interplay between staging and composition was complicated by language barriers. According to the *vita*, Lutgard's original language was a Dutch dialect, and she did not speak French very well even after forty years in a French-speaking monastery (Cawley, 26). Again, the two Latin texts and the Old French version each present slightly different parts or stagings of this experience.

To summarize, in these examples of ecstatic experiences the mediation of many audiences resulted in multiple "writings." Alter's model of the staged text helps the scholar to appreciate the complexity of multiple authorings and readings underlying medieval ecstatic textuality. The next section considers the evidence for this kind of complex reading and writing in medieval manuscript culture.

Listening in Order to See: Texts as Sacred Performances

We have already documented how devotional books were believed to have transformative power, and suggested that Jean Alter's model of the staged text is useful for envisioning the sources for multiple performances embedded in medieval ecstatic texts. Multiple textual performances may be considered for the following groups: (1)Ecstatic Woman (2) Immediate Audience (3) Future communal audiences (4) Author(s) (5) Tran/Scriber(s) (6) Copyist(s) (7) Readers, and (8) Listening Audiences. It is important to consider exactly what is meant by "reading" when texts, authoring, and audiences are considered from this more fluid and performative perspective. In the medieval period, the writings of St. Bernard of Clairvaux, with which most beguines and religious women were quite familiar, provided a well-known description of this method of reading/performing mystical texts. Bernard's forty-first Sermon on the Song of Songs states: "You long for the power to see, but you must first listen. To listen is to move toward vision. Listen then, bow down your ear for the pendants we are making for you, that by obedient listening you may come to the splendor of the vision."[58] Bernard elaborates upon the meaning of the biblical text for his sermon:

> I cannot see what this may mean if not the construction of certain spiritual images in order to bring the purest intuitions of divine wisdom before the eyes of the soul that contemplates . . . To me they seem to signify not merely that the angels produce these images within us, but that they also inspire the elegance of diction which so fittingly and gracefully embellishes with greater clarity and keener enjoyment our communication of them to the audience. (206–7)

According to Bernard, angels produce not only the "construction of spiritual images," but also the "elegance of diction" that communicates the images to an audience. Like the ecstatic herself, the audience (both witnessing and reading) must listen in order to see.[59]

In this description vision and speech are part of communication. Both are "produced by angels." Bernard not only spoke these words as a sermon to his monks, but wrote them for reading audiences. However, he expected that speech as well as vision would form an integral part of both kinds of reading. "Obedient listening" has more active construction associated with it than does our concept of silent reading. The reader (or "hearer") as well as the speaker/reader must construct images and elegance of diction *as part of* the text.

It is important to re-emphasize that in this context listening and seeing are both performance-oriented *and* sacred ("edifying," to quote Ida's companion). There is a transformative value attached to this kind of listening that may or may not be present in reading.[60] To understand what it means to consider devotional works from this listening perspective, let us turn to another of the visions of Hadewijch of Antwerp. Vision 7 begins:

> On a certain Pentecost Sunday, I had a vision at dawn. Matins were being sung in the church, and I was present. My heart and my veins and all my limbs trembled and quivered from desire; and as had been usual with me such madness and fear befell me that I thought I could not satisfy my love and that my Beloved did not fulfill my love, so that I, dying, would go mad, and going mad, I would die.[61]

Obedient listening means paying careful attention to the details in this scene, filling in not only Hadewijch's spaces, but her audiences. Imagine an audience responding to Hadewijch as she trembled and quivered and thought she was going insane. Recall that she was not in some darkened cell, rapturously oblivious to all, but in the choir of a public church.[62] Envision the spatial perspective of the choir and Hadewijch's immediate audience. Although this audience may not have seen what she saw, her physical behavior was disturbing to all: "I thought that I . . . would go mad." Subsequent audiences of copyists and readers have the advantage of both perspectives—Hadewijch's and her choir's. The vision is presented not as a rapturous swoon, but as an imperious call to action:

> As my mind was thus so fearful, then I saw from the altar a great eagle come flying to me, and he said to me: "Will you become one? So ready yourself." And I fell to my knees and my heart beat fearfully to worship that oneness, according to that real Truth, which I thought I was not ready for, that I know well, and as God knows, to my woe and grief. But the eagle returned, saying: "Just and powerful lord, now show your great power to unite your oneness according to your sat-

isfaction." And the eagle turned again to me and said, "The one who has come, comes again, and wherever he never came, he does not come."[63]

According to Alter, a fully staged text, severed from its ties to literature, is treated as a series of fixed notations of past and future performances. As literature, Hadewijch's vision sounds forced and clumsy: "unite your oneness." However, as performance, the space occupied by the eagle, the altar, and Hadewijch indicate the eagle's role as mystical messenger of God, and his formal commands make dramatic, if not literary, sense. Further, consider how the character of the eagle could serve as a source of theatrical transformation, keeping in mind that some of the symbols in ecstatic texts have specific meanings that can be used to facilitate meditation. The eagle, a well-known Christian iconographic symbol for mystic transport, often occurs in ecstatic texts. For example, the *vita* of Lutgard records a detailed visualization of an eagle:

> Then, too, there was the time she was calling to mind that Eagle of supremely sharp eyesight, John the Evangelist, the one who imbibed the streams of Gospel truth at their own sacred fountainhead in the Lord's bosom. The Eagle appeared to her in the spirit, and he gleamed with such a sheen on his feathers that the whole world could have been lit up by the rays of his brightness. Upon seeing him, she was awestruck beyond telling, and she just had to hang on in expectation for the Lord to temper the glory of the spectacle down to the capacity of her own best focus . . . And when she had the chance to contemplate the sight and take the measure of it more moderately, she saw that the Eagle was in the act of inserting its beak into her own mouth, and thus filling her soul with a brilliant and unspeakable light with the result that, in the measure possible to living mortals, no secrets of the Divinity any longer escaped her.[64]

In this story, Lutgard's original meditation upon the mystic symbol of the Evangelist as eagle brought forth her actual vision of the eagle. It is quite likely that Hadewijch's Vision 7 condensed such explicit processes into the fixed notation of the eagle, which was intended to evoke in the reader a plethora of religious and visual images.

Notice that Hadewijch's Vision 7 itself takes place in a ritual context—the Mass—and this sacred performance shapes the form and meaning of the visionary performance. The altar is indeed the focal point of Vision 7:

> Then he [Christ] came from the altar, showing himself as a child; and that child was in the same form as he was in in his first three years; and he turned to me and with his right hand took from the ciborium his body, and in his left hand he took a chalice which seemed to come from the altar, although I do not know where it came from. There he came to me in the form and clothing of a man, of the man that he was when he gave his body to us for the first time. As a formed human being and as a man, sweet and beautiful and with glorious face, he came to me as humbly as one does who belongs to another. Then he gave himself to me in the sacraments as one does, and thereafter he gave me to drink from the chalice, in the form and taste, as one does.[65]

Hadewijch's vision clearly reproduces the Mass that was being performed elsewhere in the church. Her vision was both shaped by this ceremonial performance and, simultaneously, an alternative to it. The vision follows the visible form of the sacramental ritual, but in the vision this ritual is performed by Christ for Hadewijch alone (or for her and her company of beguines). Through this vision Hadewijch was able to partake of the sacrament in both forms, which she would have been unable to do in real life. Furthermore, in her meditation, Hadewijch used the symbolism or fixed notation of the Mass to inspire an intense ecstatic experience. It is also quite likely that this fixed notation was intended to evoke a similar experience in her reading (or hearing) audience as well as her immediate audience. That is, I believe that the reading audience was intended to be transformed by both performances (Mass and vision)—but each performance is subtly altered by the presence of the other. Restoring the spatial and contextual components of Hadewijch's staged text enables the scholar to appreciate the sacramental dimension of this ecstatic experience, rather than focusing solely on the private, dramatic union with Christ depicted there.

It is entirely consistent with my theory of ecstatic "lecturature" experiences as sacred performances for readers that two of the four beguines who are regarded as authors of visionary literature—Mechthild of Magdeburg and Marguerite Porete—wrote in dialogue form, like a play. The other two—Beatrijs of Nazareth and Hadewijch of Antwerp—used theatrical narrative.[66] There is an interactive and audience-oriented quality to these works that makes them as theatrical as they are literary. Consider this excerpt from the writings of Marguerite Porete:

> [*Love*]: This Soul, says Love, is totally dissolved, melted and drawn, joined and united to the most high Trinity. And she cannot will except the divine will through the divine work of the whole Trinity. And a ravishing Spark and Light joins her and holds her very close. And on account of this the Soul speaks thus:
> *Soul*: O very small person, rude and poorly behaved, she says.
> *Reason*: Who are you talking to? says Reason.[67]

Although we have very little evidence about the theatrical context of these specific beguine writings, accounts of other medieval visionaries demonstrate that visions often functioned as sacred theater. For example, according to stories about the twelfth-century seer Elisabeth of Schönau, the entire religious community sometimes prayed and fasted so that she would have, not a private revelation, but a vision on their behalf.[68] Like the priest in the Mass, Elisabeth served as a public intermediary between heaven and earth. There is also evidence that visionary scenes were acted out more than once. Besides the earlier story of Ida's re-telling of a vision, it is known that Hildegard of Bingen dressed the nuns of her convent in apparel resembling characters from her visions.[69] As Joanna Ziegler has shown, the thirteenth-century beguine Elisabeth of Spalbeek repeatedly re-enacted Passion scenes for a public audience.[70]

Sometimes the intended audience for these visions-enacted-as-sacred-theater were not those physically present, as in this example from Ida of Nivelle's *vita*:

> One day, at the Cistercian monastery of Maagendaal . . . [a priest] swooned for a space, as if in ecstasy. . . . He replied [to his audience, an abbess] "The lady Ida has . . . as usual, been caught up into ecstasy and carried off to Heaven. . . . There she has devoutly poured out a prayer for me." . . . To the man of God it seemed that at that moment his spirit was inseparably linked to Ida's spirit, so as to become, by an unfeigned charity, one single spirit in the Lord. (Cawley, *Lives*, 78)

In this story, the beneficiary of Ida's ecstasy was considered to be a priest at a neighboring monastery, not the nuns at Ida's convent. Such *vitae* are replete with examples of friends or strangers from afar who were transformed through the effect of another's vision on their behalf.

When it comes to understanding the effect of ecstatic writings upon their reading audience, it is quite clear that a similar transformation from afar was the intent. Recall the words of the monk of Farne: "Would that my longing might be imprinted upon the hearts of those that hear." As noted above, Gertrude of Helfta's *Herald of Divine Love* begins with a revelation from God: "By virtue of my divinity, those who read this book for my glory with upright faith, humble devotion, and devout gratitude, seeking edification, will obtain remission of their venial sins, the grace of spiritual consolation, and what is more, they will be made more receptive to grace" (Winkworth, 48). Thus, Gertrude's *Herald* declared that reading her ecstatic text would have the same effect as an act of confession. In an earlier quote, Bridget of Sweden's words re-present the "Living Word" that "speaks itself" and is "seen in the pulpit." Hadewijch's Vision 14 declares that she has "opened the closed totality" and seen what has never before been revealed.[71] Her Vision 7 contained a personal gift of the sacraments from Christ Himself. All these works are claiming that "reading" ("hearing," "performing") their texts is on a par with or in some way re-presents official Church rituals that the visionaries themselves could not perform. Therefore, these works are alternative performances for the conveyance of grace.

Performing Christ's Body

The stated purpose of the Mass is to transform elements of bread and wine into Christ's actual Body and Blood. In beguine textual performances, the elements are not bread and wine, but performed words. There were two critical precedents for the identification of Christ's body with a textual body. First, as early as the Gospel of John, Christ was identified as the Word of God.[72] Second, the New Testament itself was represented as the revelation of Christ to humankind. In Christian tradition, the Word can designate equally Christ, the New Testament, and/or the presence of God. Again, as Karma Lochrie quotes the monk of Farne: "Study then, o man, to know Christ; get to know your savior. His body, hanging on the cross, is a book, open for your perusal"(167). The book reveals his body; his body is itself a book that can be read. Many fourteenth-century devotional texts were intended to evoke the authentic Christian text, Christ's body.

In England, in addition to the Monk of Farne, Richard Rolle and Julian of Norwich each produced detailed meditations upon Christ's Passion that were explicitly intended to inscribe Christ's broken body upon the reader's heart.[73] On the continent, Heinrich Seusse's *Little Book of Eternal Wisdom* was a devotional treatise on the Passion produced in dialogue form with the author taking an "as if I were there" perspective.[74]

Like Julian's *Showings*, inscription of Christ's body is clearly the goal of many thirteenth-century beguine ecstatic writings. However, unlike Julian, many of these texts do not focus solely upon the Passion of Christ, but also provide extremely detailed descriptions of "the whole man," that is, the rest of his existence as a human being. After Hadewijch's mystical reception of the sacraments in Vision 7, the vision continues:

> Thereafter he came himself to me, and took me altogether in his arms, and pressed me to him, and all my limbs felt his in complete satisfaction after my heart's desire and my humanity. This was outwardly enough and I was fulfilled in pleasure. And for a short while I had strength to endure this, after a shorter time I lost that beautiful outward man in his form, and I saw him become nothing and also fade and all dissolve into one so that I could not see him outside nor could I distinguish him within me. Then it was at that hour that we were one without difference.[75]

This sensual perspective is typical of Hadewijch's visions. According to Vision 1, a guiding theme in Hadewijch's life is that she must experience the "full humanity" as well as the divinity of Christ.[76] This passion for humanity includes, but is definitely not limited to, Christ's suffering on the cross.

Like Hadewijch of Antwerp, the *vita* of Ida of Nivelles contains many descriptions of union with Christ, in all aspects of his humanity. One vision of sacramental reception is very similar to Hadewijch's Vision 7:

> Thus, when the priest singing the First Mass was elevating the Host, she saw in the priest's hands a newborn Child, handsome beyond any manner of beauty in all little ones, anywhere. Upon seeing him, there came upon her a fear and trembling, since she had never desired to see him in human appearance that way . . . So now she saw the Child, but slightly bigger in stature, and coming down from the altar towards her. He gave her his embrace and his kiss, and then, in his sweet

benignity and mercy, he yielded himself to her to embrace and to kiss.[77]

Notice the difference in dramatic effect between Hadewijch's vision, written from a first person and fully staged perspective, and that of Ida's. Ida's vision was clearly written by someone else. The switch from third- to first-person dialogue in Hadewijch's vision dramatically involves the reader/hearer in the events of the vision. Even more important, the shaping perspective of the hearer/transcriber is more evident in Ida's account. For example, it is the scribe, not Ida, who stresses Ida's initial lack of desire for this form of vision. In a first-person account, this aside would be instead a direct statement from Ida. In contrast, Hadewijch's desire infuses her entire vision and interpretation, detailing her pleasurable feelings and her eventual experience of unity. Since we have no way of knowing the degree of mediation in Hadewijch's text, I would argue that the differences are due more to the fact that Hadewijch's text has achieved density of performance. Ida's reading is still fragmentary, a theatrical reading but not yet fully staged.

Hadewijch's textual performance of Christ's body omits few physical details. Ronald Grimes has written of such "modes of ritual sensibility" that encompass far more than officially sanctioned religious rites or liturgy: "Often we begin to speak of ritual in far too lofty a way by referring to ultimacy, sacredness, awe, sacrifice, or eternality . . . As a result we sometimes unwittingly disincarnate ourselves from our own bodies, our own present, and our own ordinariness. This beginning leads to pretentious ritual studies and gnostic liturgics."[78]

The physicality of Hadewijch's text strongly suggests that its performance was intended to be inscribed upon the listener's body just as it had been upon Hadewijch's own body, and that both bodies be transformed through the re-telling and re-enactment. Hadewijch's Vision 7 concludes: "Hereafter I remained in a fainting away in my beloved so that I completely melted away in him, and nothing remained of myself: and I was changed and taken up in the spirit."[79] This active form of meditation would become more marked in the succeeding century, as both male-and female-authored devotional texts attempted to graphically inscribe Christ's suffering in their audiences.[80] Although, in the text quoted earlier, Ida of Leuven's scribe downplayed her desire for physical inscription, in other sections he displayed no such reticence. According to the text, Ida was a recipient of the stigmata, and its marks are described in two pages of graphic detail (Cawley, *Life of Ida*, 11–13).

Not only did men write such devotional works presumably based upon their own experiences, they wrote down and preserved the writings of women's experiences as well. Moreover, as the many marginal notations in such manuscripts indicate, many men continued to read and value, and perhaps perform themselves, such works over the next three centuries. For example, the marginal notes of medieval monastic readers for Margery Kempe's visionary text draw attention to the crying, fainting, and other physical accompaniments of her transformation, testifying to the ongoing encounter with text as "word-event" that monks sought as they read this text (Lochrie, 209–212). I suspect that the copious marginal notes that grace Hadewijch's visionary texts have a similar focus. By *envisioning* and "bringing to life" Hadewijch's Vision 7, the medieval readers or hearers did more than *read* Hadewijch's account of transformation, they performed their own.

In summary, I see these beguine ecstatic texts as a set of fixed notations to guide past and future sacred performances. That is, the written text is a guide (and, itself a performance) that enables the performed text. Even if scholars have no desire to recreate these texts as religious performances, I believe that a theatrical approach to them will yield different readings than purely literary or historical judgments. Further, we may need to use different scholarly tools to evaluate them. We need to think both spatially and in more interactive and audience-oriented terms, as illustrated in my analysis of the following story from the *vita* of Lutgard:

> Every Friday in the monastery of St. Catherine, there were the First Vespers of the Saturday, deservedly given over to the veneration of Our Blessed Lady. Now when it came to the Responsory and its verse, Lutgard was accustomed to sing solo, prompted by devotion and by grace. . . . It seemed to her that Christ came along under the appearance of a Lamb and took his place right upon her bosom . . . and he put his mouth to her mouth and thus sucked from her lungs and drew out from them a melody which was wondrously suave. . . . The hearers perceived her voice as being more infinitely pleasing than usual; and their hearts were in the meantime moved to a wondrous devotion.[81]

In this story, Lutgard's vision occurred in a public place (Vespers service) in the process of a public act (singing a solo). "Vision" is at best a partial description of this experience, which has marked auditory and sensual components as well. Neither was it an individual revelation of piety, but a performative act that enhanced the devotion of a public audience. In such a reading, the spatial and liturgical dimensions are important too. In Flanders in the medieval period, the choir's presence was actually far more visible than that of the priest, hidden behind his screen. Vespers is an evening service, so that the sensory dimensions must have been blurred visually and perhaps sharpened aurally. Thus, Lutgard's performance was likely more visually, aurally, and theatrically compelling than that of other performers in this liturgy, simultaneously a complementary and alternative performance. These are the kind of issues generated by the theory of texts as staged.

The theory also emphasizes the fixed notation of a musical performance in addition to the written text. In the Middle Ages, music was a channel for spiritual meditation. Richard of St. Victor, a twelfth-century contemplative with whose writings many beguine audiences were familiar, declared: "It is necessary for us to summon a singer of this sort, just as it is also useful for us to hear someone singing. The spiritual soul is touched at the very core of its being because of the voice of a singer of this sort and it is spiritually affected when the spirit rushes into it" (Zinn, 342). The effect of the "spirit rushing" into Lutgard in the form of Christ as a Lamb enabled her audience to experience a transforming devotion. The audience did not need to see the lamb to be so transformed. Lutgard serves as "the voice of the singer" who has been "summoned" on her audience's behalf to open a channel between divine and human.

Finally, the context of Lutgard's performance was a service devoted to the veneration of Mary. Foregrounding the presence and response of Lutgard's audience in this "reading" results in a staging of a powerful, all-female, communal religious experience in honor of a beloved saint, Mary. Lutgard was not just an individual holy woman with great personal sanctity, but a respected performer in a female public sphere.

All of these fixed notations would have been familiar to readers of Lutgard's *vita*. By envisioning and meditatively re-enacting Lutgard's event, such readers, male and female, could perform their own works of devotion. Lutgard's song would echo in the hearts of committed readers long after her own personal performance had ceased.

I believe it is critical that modern scholars attempt to reconstruct the context of such enactments because this would have four important consequences for our understanding of medieval women's spirituality. First, scholars need to be aware of the misreadings inherent in using the assumptions of print culture to assess works produced in a manuscript culture. Medieval concepts of authorship, textuality, and audience relationship to texts and authors were quite different from our own. These differences mean that we cannot rely solely on the content of the text to illuminate meaning for us. The modern historian's suspicion of non-print cues, such as spatial sequencing and the effect of music as "nonobjective," results in a serious distortion of medieval devotional texts. Perhaps contemporary postmodern recognition of various ways in which humans construct reality allows a new receptivity to non-print factors in textuality.

Second, the realization that beguine holy women performed their ecstatic actions in front of, and on behalf of, audiences results in a different appreciation of their spirituality. They were not passive recipients of divine favor, but active participants who created sacred performances that transformed both themselves and others.

Third, the historian needs to consider the multiple audiences and authorship functions in beguine textuality. The performances recorded therein were intended to engage the reader in a continuing process of interaction with the sacred. In fact, the mediation of such texts by monastic scribes and witnesses already contain many layers of religious interaction.

Finally, beguine texts—whether composed by the ecstatic or by mediators—are as much theatrical works as they are literary pieces. As such, devices that seem clumsy or forced when read may work quite well when staged. For example, many scholars have noted the tendency of medieval women's devotional texts to be repetitive, to wander around the point, and to feature dialogues that seem forced or "stagy."[82] Yet such techniques may work perfectly well from a performance, rather than from a literary, perspective. Assessments of the impact of holy women such as Lutgard and Hadewijch should consider their effect upon multiple generations of audiences and should not be dependent solely upon a modern paradigm of literary excellence.

A theatrical engagement with Lutgard's "melody wondrous suave," emphasizing the service, the public choir, and the words that reported them, leads to a new appreciation of Flemish beguine and religious women and the significance of their performative power for the spirituality of thirteenth-century medieval Europeans. These ecstatic females were not merely individual mystics rapt by the wonder of the divine, but powerful sacred performers in a communal milieu.

Notes

*Portions of this chapter appeared earlier in "Writing Beguines: Ecstatic Performances," *Magistra* 2, no. 1 (Summer 1996).

1. Caroline Walker Bynum, *Fragmentation and Redemption: Essays on Gender and the Human Body in Medieval Religion* (New York: Zone Books, 1991), 65–66. See also 324–25 for a brief bibliography of major scholarly works that have dismissed or downplayed sensory religious experiences.

2. The list of scholars is long. In addition to works cited in this chapter, see Ulrike Wiethaus, ed., *Maps of Flesh and Light: The Religious Experience of Medieval Women Mystics* (Syracuse: Syracuse University Press, 1993); Anne Clark, *Elisabeth of Schönau: A Twelfth-Century Visionary* (Philadelphia: University of Pennsylvania Press, 1992); Barbara Newman, *Sister of Wisdom: St. Hildegard's Theology of the Feminine* (Berkeley: University of California Press, 1987); Elizabeth Petroff, ed., *Medieval Women's Visionary Literature* (New York: Oxford University Press, 1992) and *Body and Soul: Essays on Medieval Women and Mysticism* (New York: Oxford University Press, 1994); Paul Szarmach, ed., *An Introduction to the Medieval Mystics of Europe* (Albany: State University of New York Press, 1993). Additionally the proliferation of translations of women's mystical writings, such as those published by the Paulist Press, have made medieval women's writings more accessible for study.

3. Quoted in Ernest McDonnell, *The Beguines and Beghards in Medieval Culture with Special Emphasis on the Belgian Scene* (New York: Octagon Books, 1969), 330.

4. The social context of such writings is generally considered only to the extent that it affected their writing. For example, Georgette Épiney-Burgard and Emilie Zum Brunn discuss the impact of Mechthild of Magdeburg's late entry into a convent upon the content of her later writings; Mother Columba Hart considers the influence of troubador poetry and of the writings of the Church Fathers upon the structures and content of Hadewijch of Antwerp's works. See Emilie Zum Brunn and Georgette Épiney-Burgard, *Women Mystics in Medieval Europe* (New York: Paragon House, 1989), 40–42; Mother Columba Hart, *Hadewijch: The Complete Works* (New York: Paulist Press, 1980), 5–7, 19–22.

5. The standard work on beguines is still Ernest McDonnell, *The Beguines and Beghards in Medieval Culture.* More recently, Walter Simons's "The Beguine Movement in the Southern Low Countries: A Reassessment" has addressed the development of the beguine movement in that area *(Bulletin de l'institut historique belge de Rome* 59 (1989): 63–105. Additionally, Carol Neel has traced the evolution of the beguines to the earlier popularity of Augustinian Canons and Premonstratensians in the same

geographical areas. See "The Origins of the Beguines," in Judith M. Bennett, et. al., *Sisters and Workers in the Middle Ages* (Chicago: University of Chicago Press, 1989), 240–260. But see also Joanna Ziegler, "Secular Canonesses as Antecedent of the Beguines in the Southern Low Countries: An Introduction to Some Older Views," *Studies in Medieval And Renaissance History*, 13 (1991): 114–135; "Women of the Middle Ages: Some Questions Regarding the Beguines and Devotional Art," *Vox Benedictina* 3, no. 4 (1986): 338– 357; and *Sculpture of Compassion: The Pietà and the Beguines in the Southern Low Countries, c. 1300–1600* (Brussels and Rome: The Belgian Historical Institute of Rome, 1992).

6. For example, very small groups of women seemed to have been the norm in Strasbourg, while in the Netherlands and Belgium, larger and more organized Beguinages developed quite early. See Dayton Phillips, *Beguines in Medieval Strasburg: A Study of the Social Aspects of Beguine Life* (Stanford University dissertation: Edwards Brothers, 1941), 19–27.

7. Alcantara Mens, "De kleine armen van christus in de Brabants-Luikse gewesten," *Ons geestelijk erf* 38 (1964): 137–144.

8. For early rules, see F. de Ridder, "De oudste statuten van het Mechelse Begijnhof," *Handelingen van de Mechelse kring voor oudheidkunde* 39 (1934): 18–29, and L. J. M. Philippen, *De Begijnhoven: Oorsprong, Geschiedenis, Inrichting* (Antwerp: Ch. & H. Courtin, 1918), 307–342.

9. The rule of the beguinage of Mechelen (1286) states that mistresses of the beguinage may receive rents from outside the *hof* for the alleviation of poor beguines. This rule also understood that beguines would leave the *hof*, stipulating only that no beguine shall go out alone or without permission. The Mechelen beguines also ran a school and an infirmary. See F. de Ridder, "De Oudste Statuten van het Mechelsche Begijnhof," *Handelingen van de Mechelse kring voor Oudheidkunde* 39 (1934): 18–29. This rule and others like it were probably regulating current practices. Descriptions of early beguine economic practices are also detailed in Roze-Marijn Quintijn, *Normen en normering van het begijnenhoven* (Ghent: Rijksuniversiteit Gent, 1983), 51– 56.

10. Florence Koorn, *Begijnhoven in Holland en Zeeland gedurende de Middeleeuwen* (Assen: Van Gorcum, 1981), 80–81.

11. Ellen Kittell, "Audience and Female Competence: Women and Public Acts in Medieval Flanders," paper presented at the 1996 American Historical Association conference in Atlanta, Georgia. See also Ellen Kittell, Mary Suydam, and Joanna Ziegler, "The Texture of the Event: Women and Performance in Medieval Flanders," manuscript in submission, and Ellen Kittell, "Testaments of Two Cities: A Comparative Analysis of the Wills of Medieval Genoa and Douai," *European Review of History* 5, no. 1 (1998): 47–82.

12. The county of Flanders was ruled by a woman from 1206–1244. The one office women did not hold was that of alderman.

13. For example, in 1246 a rule for beguines in the diocese of Liège listed

as a "more serious fault" [graviori culpa] "going out alone without per-mission" [alleene wt te gane plach sonder orloff] (Philippen, *De Begijn-hoven*, 307). A somewhat later rule of the beguines of Mechelen (ca. 1280) stated: "No beguine will go into town without the approval of her housemistress, nor without a companion outside the gates of the [beguine] *hof* (beguinage)" [Negene beghine en sal gaen inde stat son-der orlof hare huus meestersen, noch sonder gesellinne buten der gro-ter poerten vanden hove]. This was reiterated later with the statement: "This is the desire of the [beguine] *hof*, that one will [live] communally; that no young or full-grown woman who dwells in the house, will go outside the *hof*...." [dit sijn de pointe die thoef beghert, dat men houde ghemeinlike: dat ghene joffrouwe or vrouwe, die woent inden hof, ga buten den hove....]. F. De Ridder, "De Oudste Statuten van het Begijnhof van Mechelen," 24, 28. Both rules assume that women will leave the *hof* but regulate the circumstances.

14. Among those personally known to Hadewijch are the following: "Mina, a recluse who lives far away on craggy rocks and to whom I sent Master Henry of Breda.... Oda, a woman from Cologne, also used to come and see me ... a friend who lives in Bohemia [who] is a recluse ... and a forgotten master in Paris ... [who] knows more about me than I know about myself." [Mine clusenerse die verre dore sassen lach, daer ic heren van breda ... ene vrouwe van colne waert ende hiet oede ... si plach oec te mi te comen.... Noch hebbic een vriendinne die woent int lant van biheem ende es clusenerse. Te Parijs woent een vergheten meesterken alleen in een cellekenj hi weet meer van mi dan ic goets van mi seluen weet]. See Sr. Helen Rolfson, trans., "Hadewjch of Antwerp, *The List of the Perfect*," *Vox Benedictina* 5, no. 4 (Oct. 1988): 277–287; Jozef van Mierlo, ed., *Hadewijch: Visioenen*, vol. 1 (Leuven: 1924), 189–191.

15. For a discussion of the beguinages of Oignies and Nivelles, see Ernest McDonnell, *The Beguines and Beghards in Medieval Culture*, 59–70. Ida of Leuven and Beatrijs of Nazareth both became Cistercian nuns.

16. "Visionary" is, at best, at partial description of these religious experi-ences. I believe that the term "ecstatic" more accurately describes them, because they encompass the entire sensorium. However, because "ec-static experiences" is awkward, and because women themselves referred to their experiences as "visions," I will use both terms. See Rosemary Hale, " 'Taste and See, for God is Sweet': Sensory Perception and Memory in Medieval Christian Mystical Experience," in *Vox Mystica: Essays for Valerie M. Lagorio*, ed., Anne Clark Bartlett, Thomas Bestul, Janet Goebel and William F. Pollard (Cambridge: D.S. Brewer, 1995), 3–14.

17. Examples included in this article are Ida of Nivelles, Ida of Leuven, Lutgard of Aywières, and Hadewijch of Antwerp.

18. Quoties rapta in spiritu passionis dominicae memor erat, videbatur ei

quod essentialiter per totum corpus sanguine perfusa ruberet. Hoc cum quidam religiosus presbyter secretius audivisset . . . Quo dubium non erat secundum tempus Christi fore memorem passionis, aggressus est illam videre . . . Et ecce, vidit faciem ejus et manus, quae tantum nudae patebant, quasi recenti perfusas sanguine relucere; cincinnos vero ejus quasi noctium infusos sanguine. Quod videns, clam forcipe partem illorum in partem tulit, et ad lucem eos in manu ferens . . . Qui statim ultra quam credi potest ad tam ingens spectaculum pavefactus, fere cecidit resupinus. Father Martinus Cawley, trans., *Lives of Ida of Nivelles, Lutgard, and Alice the Leper* (Lafayette: Guadalupe Translations, 1987), II 23, 46.

19. Monialis autem illa beatem virginem Idam rogavit ut de bonis Domini quibus eam ditaverat aliqua sibi panderet ad aedificationem. Cawley, 63.

20. Timebatque ne ex collocutione tam melliflua corporalem pateretur defectum. Cawley, 64.

21. Richard Schechner, *Performance Theory* (New York: Routledge: 1988), 30, defines performance as a "quality of action," emphasizing that the performer *does* something. Moreover, the performer does something in the presence of and for an audience.

22. The controversy over theatrical versus ritual performances has obscured the commonalities underlying all performances. This is not the place to enter that debate. There are many kinds of theatrical performances that do not conform to our ideas of modern theater. Here I merely wish to point out that the elements often considered crucial for modern, Western theater, namely, that it involves play or pretence, that it occurs "outside time" in delineated spaces, and that the audience understand themselves to be witnesses rather than participants, are not features of the performances I am considering. Many of these components of modern theatrical performances are derived from game theory. See Schechner, *Performance Theory*, 16.

23. Schechner separates "ritual" from "theater" by noting that ritual is efficacious (*Performance Theory*, 120–124). This definition is based upon the work of Victor Turner. For a critique of Turner's concepts regarding their applicability to medieval holy women, see Caroline Walker Bynum, "Women's Stories, Women's Symbols: A Critique of Victor Turner's Theory of Liminality," in *Fragmentation and Redemption: Essays on Gender and the Human Body in Medieval Religion* (New York: Zone Books, 1991), 27–51. For a different perspective, see also Mary Giles's essay in this collection.

24. Cheslyn Jones, Geoffrey Wainwright, and Edwin Yarnold, S.J., *The Study of Liturgy* (New York: Oxford University Press, 1978), 13. The authors add: "When Christians celebrate the liturgy they encounter Christ in his passion, death, and resurrection and are renewed by it."

25. Jones et al., 19.

26. "The Christian liturgy by its nature cannot be the monologue of a single participant." Jones et al., 22.

27. Examples are taken from Father Martinus Cawley, *Lives of Ida of Nivelles, Lutgard, and Alice the Leper,* and Cawley, *Ida of Louvain: Medieval Cicstercian Nun* (Lafayette: Guadalupe Translations, 1990). For exorcism of demons, see Lutgard, 34–5, 38. For restoration of the dead to life, see Ida of Louvain, I. 18.40–41, 28–9. For purgatorial revelations, see Ida of Nivelles, 24, 29, 40–41; Lutgard, 29, 31, 37, 53, 66–67, 70; Alice, 33, 37, 43, 47. For discovery of secret sins subsequently confessed to the holy woman, see Ida of Nivelles, 34, 36, 38, 43, 44; Lutgard, 47, 48, 50, 78 54; Ida of Louvain, 53, 54. On Ida of Louvain's miraculous ability to tell the moment of Elevation of the Host at distant Masses, see II.6.9, 40; on her enabling a priest's Eucharistic devotion, see II.19.15, 44.

28. Barbara Newman's *From Virile Woman to WomanChrist: Studies in Medieval Religion and Literature* (Philadelphia: University of Pennsylvania Press, 1995) analyzes the phenomenon of religious women as "apostles to the dead," 108–136.

29. Una de monialibus Rameyensis petiit ab ancilla Christi ut funderet preces ad Dominum pro anima patris sui . . . et eadem hora revelatum est ei quod anima illa pro qua Dominum supplicaverat purgatoriis esset deputata supliciis . . . cum in ecclesia die quadam vacaret orationi, vidit hominem illum sibi assistere, peo cujus anima sacrificium orationis . . . qui, ab umbilico et sursum, candido amictu vestiebatur. Per quod intellexit partim fuisse purgata illius, partim vero non . . . cui postmodum plurimas orationes acquisivit ut animam, multiplicatis intercessoribus, a purgatorii poenis liberatum. . . . Cawley, *Lives of Ida of Nivelles, Lutgard, and Alice the Leper,* 17–18.

30. Judith Butler, "Imitation and Gender Insubordination," in *The Second Wave: A Reader in Feminist Theory,* ed. Linda Nicholson (New York: Routledge, 1997), 304.

31. Even before the advent of poststructuralism, structuralists like Claude Lévi-Strauss argued that human beings construct symbolic systems in order to organize social relations. As a structuralist, Lévi-Strauss believed that such systems, like language, were constructed by means of binary oppositions. Poststructuralist thinkers, however, have decentered meaning more radically, demonstrating that meaning is never defined by such oppositions, but continually deferred. See Claude Lévi-Strauss, *The Elementary Structures of Kinship,* trans. James Harle Bell, John Richard von Sturmer, and Rodney Needham (Boston: Beacon Press, 1969); *Totemism,* trans. Rodney Needham (Boston: Beacon Press, 1963); and Jacques Derrida's critique of Lévi-Strauss in *Of Grammatology,* trans. Gayatri Chakravorty Spivak (Baltimore: John Hopkins University Press, 1976), 101–140.

32. John Dagenais, *The Ethics of Reading in a Manuscript Culture: Glossing the "Libro de Buen Amor"* (Princeton, NJ: Princeton University Press, 1994).

33. A good overview on the evolution of silent reading is Paul Saenger's "Silent Reading: Its Impact on Late Medieval Script and Society," *Viator* (Spring 1982), 368–444. See also Brian Stock, *Listening for the Text: On the Uses of the Past* (Baltimore: Johns Hopkins Press, 1990).

34. Ellen Kittell, Mary Suydam, and Joanna Ziegler, "The Texture of the Event." Karma Lochrie believes that medieval English women were unable to take part in such public performances, and that, consequently, their written discourses evolved differently from men's in the same period. Karma Lochrie, *Margery Kempe and Translations of the Flesh* (Philadelphia: University of Pennsylvania Press, 1994), 103. However, Kittell's research demonstrates that this was not the case in Dutch-speaking areas. Of course, there was no such entity as "Dutch," either linguistically or geographically, in the medieval period. I am using this term to refer to dialects such as Brabantine and Flemish that became the foundation of the modern Dutch languages spoken in the present-day Low Countries.

35. See Christiane Mesch Galvani, trans., *Mechthild von Magdeburg's Flowing Light of the Divinity* (New York: Garland Press, 1991), introduction and prologue, xv-xvi, 3.

36. Hildegard's works were also dictated over a long period to a variety of different secretaries, at least one of whom emended her words in accordance with his own notions of style. See Barbara Newman, *Sister of Wisdom: St. Hildegard's Theology of the Feminine* (Berkeley: University of California Press, 1987), 22–23. Beatrijs of Nazareth apparently wrote an autobiography, which served as the foundation for her *vita*, written by someone else. She also apparently wrote other works which did not survive. See Fiona Bowie, ed., *Beguine Spirituality* (New York: Cross-road, 1989), 86, and Emilie Zum Brunn and Georgette Épiney-Burgard, *Women Mystics in Medieval Europe*, 7 and 71.

37. Jozef van Mierlo, ed., *Hadewijch: Mengeldichten* (Antwerp: Standaard Boekhandel, 1952), 101 (Poem 18, lines 196–197).

38. Father Martinus Cawley, Introduction to "Life of Lutgard of Aywières," in *Lives of Ida of Nivelles, Lutgard, and Alice the Leper*.

39. Cawley, *Lives*, 38–39.

40. In his analysis of the change from an oral, monastic culture to a visual, scholastic one, Paul Saenger notes that vernacular literature continued to be published by dictation longer than did Latin texts. Of course, women's texts were primarily vernacular. See Saenger, "Silent Reading," 368–414.

41. Karma Lochrie, *Margery Kempe*, 105.

42. I am indebted to Claire Sahlin for clarifying this portion of Birgitta's revelations. See *Revelationes S. Birgitte* (Lübeck: Barthelomeus Ghotan, 1492), book 8, chapter 48, verses 54–57 and 235–236.

43. Karma Lochrie, *Margery Kempe,* 105. Lochrie refers to the concept of speech-acts (performative speech) advanced by J. L. Austin, *How to Do Things with Words* (Cambridge: Harvard University Press, 1962). For example, the phrase "I pronounce you husband and wife" effects a marriage; it does not merely describe it.

44. Margaret Winkworth, trans., *Gertrude of Helfta: The Herald of Divine Love* (New York: Paulist Press, 1993), prologue, 47.

45. Quoted in Karma Lochrie, *Margery Kempe,* 56.

46. Jean Alter, *A Sociosemiotic Theory of Theatre* (Philadelphia: University of Pennsylvania Press, 1990), 164.

47. Ic was in natiuitate beate marie te mettenen ende na de iij. lessen wart mi vertoent jn enen gheeste een lettel wonders. Mijn herte wart mi beroert te voren van woerden van minnen die men daer las in die kantiken daer mi bi ghedachte eens gheheels cussens. Corteleke daer na in dandere nocturne soe saghic inden gheeste dat quam ene coninghinne ghecleedt met enen guldenen clede; ende dat cleet was al vol oghen; ende alle die oghen waren alle doersiende alse viereghe vlammen, ende nochta ghelijc cristalle. Ende die crone diese opt hoeft hadde die hadde alsoe vele cronen diese deen bouen dandere alse oghen waren ane dat cleet . . . Die coninghinne quam te mi starkeleke snel ende sette haren voet op mine kele ende riep met eenre vreeselekere stemmen ende seide: wistu wie ic ben? J. van Mierlo, ed., *Hadewijch: Visioenen,* vol. 1, 95–96, lines 10–15, 37–40.

48. Ezekiel's vision of the chariot describes wheels "full of eyes." Moreover, the expanse over the chariot was both crystalline and fiery. See Ezekiel 1:15–28 in *Tanakh: The Holy Scriptures* (Philadelphia: Jewish Publication Society, 1985).

49. Demonic attacks are a staple of saints' lives. For a contemporary beguine example of this theme, see the *vita* of Marie d'Oignies, II:108, excerpted in Elizabeth Petroff, ed., *Medieval Women's Visionary Literature* (New York: Oxford University Press, 1986), 183.

50. Jaic wel, ghi hebt mi soe langhe wee ende leet ghedaen ende sidi die redene mijnre ziele . . . daer ic mede bekint hebbe uwe macht. . . . Doe wart mi redene onderdaen, ende omuinc mi; ende ic quam buten den gheeste ende bleef ligghende verdronken tote hoghe op den dach in onseggheleke wondere. J. van Mierlo, ed., *Hadewijch: Visioenen,* vol. 1, 97–98, lines 40–71.

51. In *Minnemystik,* Love (*Minne*) is a feminine aspect of divinity and surpasses the power of Reason. See Hadewijch of Antwerp's Letter 4 in Jozef van Mierlo, ed., *Hadewijch: Brieven,* vol. 1, 37–41 (Antwerp: N.V. Standaard Boekandel,1947). For more on Hadewijch's use of feminine pronouns in reference to divinity, see Mary Suydam, "Ever in Unrest: Translating Hadewijch of Antwerp's *Mengeldichten,*" *Women's Studies* (March 1999).

52. Jacques Derrida, *Writing and Difference,* trans. Alan Bass (Chicago: University of Chicago Press, 1978), 292.

53. Jacques Derrida's trenchant critique of Claude Lévi-Strauss's romantic privileging of speech over writing is particularly pertinent here. The point is not that present speech/performance is superior to absent writing/literature. As Derrida notes: "By radically separating language from writing, by placing the latter below and outside, believing that it is possible to do so . . . one thinks in fact to restore the status of authentic language. . . ." *Of Grammatology*, trans. Gayatri Chakravorty Spivak (Baltimore: Johns Hopkins University Press: 1976), 120.

54. Jacques Derrida, *Speech and Phenomena and Other Essays on Husserl's Theory of Signs*, trans. by David Allison (Evanston, IL: Northwestern University Press, 1973), 50.

55. Mary Suydam, "Writing Beguines: Ecstatic Performances," *Magistra* 2, no. 1 (Summer 1996), 151.

56. Cawley, *Ida of Louvain*, 3.

57. Cawley, *Lives*, II.8, 32. As explained above, this translation is based upon two Latin texts and an Old French version. Through a system of different type faces, the translator has utilized all three versions. The Old French, however, is not reproduced.

58. Bernard of Clairvaux, *On the Song of Songs II*, vol. 3, trans. Kilian Walsh (Cistercian Fathers series, no. 7) (Kalamazoo: Cistercian Publications, 1976), 206.

59. Bernard was referring to "seeing" biblical texts, but beguines and monastic audiences often equated biblical and contemporary visions.

60. Richard Schechner has noted that in ritual performances there is less separation between audience and performers, and that, unlike secular theater, the audience depends upon the performance. *Essays in Performance Theory*, 79.

61. Te enen cinxen daghe wart mi vertoent inde dagheraet, ende men sanc mettenen inde kerke ende ic was daer; ende mijn herte ende mijn aderen ende alle mine lede scudden ende beueden van begherten; ende mi was alst dicke heeft gheweest Soe verwoeddeleke ende soe vreeseleke te moede dat mi dochte ic en ware minnen lieue ghenoech ende mijn lief en uerwlde minen nyet, dat ic steruende soude verwoeden ende al uerwoedende steruen. J. van Mierlo, ed., *Hadewijch: Visioenen* , vol.1, 74, lines 1–10.

62. Beguine churches tended to be small and located in public, urban centers, especially in the mid-thirteenth century when Hadewijch is thought to have written her *Visions*. Even the presence of choir screens could not have isolated the choir from the sight or hearing of others. See Mary Suydam, "Heavenly Space in the Visionary Realm of Beguines," paper presented at the thirty-third International Medieval Conference at Kalamazoo, May 1998.

63. Doe mi aldus vreeseleke te moede was, doe versaghic vanden outare comen gheuloghen te mi enen are die groet was; ende hi seide mi; Wiltu een werden soe ghereide di. Ende ic stoent op mijn knien ende

mijn herte gheberde vreseleke dat enechleke te anebedene na sine werde werdecheit, dat doch mi onghereet ware, dat wetic wel, wet god, altoes te minen wee ende te minen sware. Ende gheen aer keerde segghende: Gherechte here ende moghende, nu tone dine moghende cracht dijnre enecheit te eneghene na ghebruken dijns selues. Ende hi keerde hem weder ende seide te mi: Die ghecomen es hi comt weder ende daer hi nye en quam, daer en comt hi niet. J. van Mierlo, ed., *Hadewijch: Visoenen*, vol. 1, 76–77, lines 42–57.

64.   Cawley, *Lives*, I. 15, 15–16: Proinde ad recordationem illius acutissimae visionis Aquilae, Joannis scilicet evangelistae, qui fluenta evangelii de ipso sacro dominici pectoris fonte potavit, apparuit ei in spiritu aquila, tanto pennarum nitore refulgens ut totus potuisset orbis illius claritatis radiis illustrari. Ad visionem ergo illius super id quod dici potest admiratione nimia stupefacta, praestolabatur ut Dominus secundum capacitatem debilis aciei tanti speculationis gloriam temperaret. Et factum est ita. Visionis ergo modum moderatius contemplata, vidit quod Aquila ori suo rostrum imponeret, et animam ejus tam ineffabilis luminis coruscatione repleret ut secundum id quod vivent ibus possibile est . . . nulla eam divinitatis secreta laterent.

65.   Doe quam hi vanden outare hem seluen toenende alse een kint, ende dat kint was wan dier seluer ghedane dat hi was in sinen yersten drien jaren; ende hi keerde hem te mi waert ende nam vter ciborien sinen lichame in sine rechte hant ende in sine slinke hant nam hi, enen kelc die sceen vanden outare comende, maer ic en weet wanen hi quam. Daer mede quam hi in die ghedane des cleeds ende des mans dat hi was op dien dach doen hi ons sinen lichame iersten gaf, also ghedane mensche ende man soete ende scoene ende uerweent ghelaet tonende ende also onderdanechleke te mi comende alse een die eens anders al es. Doe gaf hi mi hem seluen in specien des sacraments in figuren alsoe men pleghet; ende daer na gaf hi mi drinken vten kelke ghedane ende smake alsoe men pleghet. J. Van Mierlo, ed., *Hadewijch: Visioenen*, vol. 1, 77–8, lines 57–74.

66.   By "theatrical narrative," I mean that Beatrijs's and Hadewijch's *Visions* are theatrically descriptive and can be easily envisioned as fully staged texts. See also Laurie Finke's essay in this collection, " 'More than I Fynde Written': Dialogue and Power in the English Translation of *The Mirror of Simple Souls.*"

67.   Ellen Babinsky, trans., *Marguerite Porete: The Mirror of Simple Souls* (New York: Paulist Press, 1993), 143. Babinsky notes in her introduction that the *Mirror* "often seems less like a treatise than a happening" (1).

68.   Anne Clark, *Elisabeth of Schönau: A Twelfth-Century Visionary* (Philadelphia: University of Pennsylvania Press, 1992), 84.

69.   Barbara Newman, *Sister of Wisdom*, 221–2.

70.   See Susan Rodgers and Joanna Ziegler's essay in this volume. See also Joanna Ziegler, "Before the Public's Eye: The Thirteenth-Century Ec-

stasy of Elisabeth of Spalbeek," paper presented at the American Historical Association, January 1996. Furthermore, it is well-documented that beguine communities (like many other religious associations) from the sixteenth century on put on religious plays during festivals.

71. op heues ghedaen die beslotene geelheit (from Vision 14, in J. van Mierlo, ed., *Hadewijch: Visioenen*, 167, lines 172–3).

72. The opening words of John's gospel: "In the beginning was the word, and the word was with God, and the word was God."

73. See William Hodapp, "Ritual and Performance in Richard Rolle's Passion Meditation B," this volume; Richard Rolle, "Meditations on the Passion", in *Richard Rolle: The English Writings*, trans. Rosamund S. Allen(New York: Paulist Press: 1988), 90–126; Edmund Colledge and James Walsh, trans., *Julian of Norwich: Showings* (New York: Paulist Press, 1978).

74. Frank Tobin, trans., *Henry Suso: The Exemplar, with Two German Sermons* (New York: Paulist Press, 1989), 211–304.

75. Daer na quam hi selue te mi ende nam mi alte male in sine arme ende dwanc mi ane heme; ende alle die lede die ic hadde gheuoelden der siere in alle hare ghenoeghen na miere herten begherten van buten in allen vollen sade. Ende oec haddic doe ene corte wile cracht dat te draghene maer saen in corter vren verloesic dien sconen man van buten in siene in vormen ende ic sachene al te niete werdene ende alsoe sere verdoiende wereden ende al smelten in een, soe dat icken buten mi niet en conste bekinnen noch vernemen ende binnen mi niet besceden. Mi was op die vre ochte wi een waren sonder differencie. J. van Mierlo, ed., *Hadewijch: Visioenen*, vol. 1, 77–8, lines 74–88.

76. Christ declares to Hadewijch: "I wish of you to have so fully lived me on earth in all the virtues. . . ." (Jc wille van di mi also volcomelike geleeft hebben in allen dogheden in erdrike), 30, lines 351–3.

77. Cumque sacerdos primam Missam cantans hostiam elevaret vidit illa in manibus ejusdem sacerdotis puerulum tamquam recenter natum speciosum vere super omnimodam pulchritudinem omnium parvulorum. Quo viso, timor et tremor venit super eam do quod numquam eum in specie humana videre concupierat . . . vidit modicum graniusculae staturae puerulum de altari venientem ad se qui ei amplexum et osculum praebens, seipsum etiam ei ad amplexandum et osculandum sua dulci benignitate et misericordia concessit. Cawley, *Lives*, 60–61.

78. Ronald Grimes, *Beginnings in Ritual Studies* (Boston: University Press of America, 1982), 36. By "gnostic" liturgics, Grimes means the overemphasis upon mental experiences, rather than those of the whole human being.

79. Hier na bleef ic in enen veruaerne in mijn lief dat ic al versmalt in heme, ende mi mijns selues niet en bleef ende ic wart verwandelt ende op ghenomen inden gheeste, ende mi wart daer vertoent uan selker

hande vren. J. van Mierlo, ed., *Hadewijch: Visioenen,* vol. 1, 79, lines 94–98.

80. In addition to the male writers already cited, it should be noted that a twelfth-century precedent for this method of physically detailed devotional guides was Richard of St. Victor's *The Mystical Ark* (or *Benjamin Major*). Written as an allegorical account of and guide to meditation, it recounts every possible feature of the Ark of the Covenant as described in the Hebrew Bible. Richard explicitly stated that through meditation upon corporeal things, the soul would be drawn higher to meditation and contemplation. Grover Zinn, trans., *Richard of St. Victor: The Twelve Patriarchs, The Mystical Ark, Book Three of the Trinity* (New York: Paulist Press, 1979), 151–370.

81. In monasterio S. Catharinae, omni feria sexta, in vespere Sabbathi subsequentis, in venerationem beatissimae Virginis Mariae merito deputati, cum versus super responsorium cantabatur (cujus utique versum ob gratiam devotionis Lutgardis sola cantare solebat) videbatur ei interim dum cantaret, quod Christus in specie agni super pectus suum se tali modo locaret . . . et os suum ori illius poneret et sic sugendo de pectore illius mirabilis melodiae suavitatem extraheret. Nec dubitare quisdam poterat in hoc cantu divinum adesse miraculum, cum in solo verso illo vox in infinitum solito gratior audiretur. Unde et corda audientium ad devotionem interim mirabiliter movebantur. Cawley, *Lives,* I.19.

82. The woman writer most maligned in this regard is surely Margery Kempe. Paul Szarmach attempts to rehabilitate her writing by emphasizing that even though "apparently formless," it in fact *has* a form. He adds that "Margery is no philosophical mystic, no especially gifted writer. . . ." Paul Szarmach, ed., *An Introduction to the Medieval Mystics of Europe* (Albany: State University of New York Press, 1984). To correct such criticisms, Elizabeth Petroff comments about women's devotional writings in general that "oral methods of composition . . . were utilized more extensively in women's writings than in men's," and further notes that visionary writing is more "like seeing a film than it was like writing or reading." *Medieval Women's Visionary Literature,* 29–30. However, a performance perspective can actually value Margery's text as good theater. See Nanda Hopenwasser's essay in this volume, "A Performance Artist and Her Performance Text: Margery Kempe on Tour."

Bibliography

Allen, Rosamund S., trans. *Richard Rolle: The English Writings.* New York: Paulist Press: 1988.

Alter, Jean. *A Sociosemiotic Theory of Theatre.* Philadelphia: University of Pennsylvania Press, 1990.

Austin, J. L. *How to Do Things with Words*. Cambridge: Harvard University Press, 1962.

Babinsky, Ellen, trans. *Marguerite Porete: The Mirror of Simple Souls*. New York: Paulist Press, 1993.

Bernard of Clairvaux. *On the Song of Songs II*. Vol. 3. Trans. Kilian Walsh. Cistercian Fathers series, no. 7. Kalamazoo: Cistercian Publications, 1976.

Bowie, Fiona, ed. *Beguine Spirituality*. New York: Crossroad, 1989.

Butler, Judith. "Imitation and Gender Insubordination," in *The Second Wave: A Reader in Feminist Theory*, ed. Linda Nicholson. New York: Routledge, 1997.

Bynum, Caroline Walker. *Fragmentation and Redemption: Essays on Gender and the Human Body in Medieval Religion*. New York: Zone Books, 1991.

Cawley, Martinus, trans. *Ida of Louvain: Medieval Cistercian Nun*. Lafayette, OR: Guadalupe Translations, 1990.

———, trans. *Lives of Ida of Nivelles, Lutgard and Alice the Leper*. Lafayette, OR: Guadalupe Translations, 1987.

Clark, Anne. *Elisabeth of Schönau: A Twelfth-Century Visionary*. Philadelphia: University of Pennsylvania Press, 1992.

Colledge, Edmund, and James Walsh, trans. *Julian of Norwich: Showings*. New York: Paulist Press, 1978.

Dagenais, John. *The Ethics of Reading in a Manuscript Culture: Glossing the "Libro de Buen Amor."* Princeton, NJ: Princeton University Press, 1994.

Derrida, Jacques. *Of Grammatology*. Trans. Gayatri Chakravorty Spivak. Baltimore: John Hopkins University Press, 1976.

———. *Speech and Phenomena and Other Essays on Husserl's Theory of Signs*. Trans. David Allison. Evanston, IL: Northwestern University Press, 1973.

———. *Writing and Difference*. trans. Alan Bass. Chicago: University of Chicago Press, 1978.

Galvani, Christiane Mesch, trans. *Mechthild von Magdeburg's Flowing Light of the Divinity*. New York: Garland Press, 1991.

Grimes, Ronald. *Beginnings in Ritual Studies*. Boston: University Press of America, 1982.

Hale, Rosemary. "'Taste and See, for God is Sweet': Sensory Perception and Memory in Medieval Christian Mystical Experience." In *Vox Mystica: Essays for Valerie M. Lagorio*, ed. Anne Clark Bartlett, Thomas Bestul, Janet Goebel and William F. Pollard. Cambridge: D.S. Brewer, 1995.

Hart, Columba. *Hadewijch: The Complete Works*. New York: Paulist Press, 1980.

Jones, Cheslyn, Geoffrey Wainwright, and Edwin Yarnold, S.J., *The Study of Liturgy*. New York: Oxford University Press, 1978.

Kittell, Ellen. "Audience and Female Competence: Women and Public Acts in Medieval Flanders," Paper presented at the 1996 American Historical Association conference in Atlanta, Georgia.

———. "Testaments of Two Cities: A Comparative Analysis of the Wills of Medieval Genoa and Douai." *European Review of History*, 5, no. 1 (1998): 47–82.

————, Mary Suydam, and Joanna Ziegler. "The Texture of the Event: Women and Performance in Medieval Flanders." Manuscript in submission.

Koorn, Florence. *Begijnhoven in Holland en Zeeland gedurende de Middeleeuwen*. Assen: Van Gorcum, 1981.

Lévi-Strauss, Claude. *The Elementary Structures of Kinship*. Trans. James Harle Bell, John Richard von Sturmer, and Rodney Needham. Boston: Beacon Press, 1969.

————. *Totemism*. Trans. Rodney Needham. Boston: Beacon Press, 1963.

Lochrie, Karma. *Margery Kempe and Translations of the Flesh*. Philadelphia: University of Pennsylvania Press, 1994.

McDonnell, Ernest. *The Beguines and Beghards in Medieval Culture with Special Emphasis on the Belgian Scene*. New York: Octagon Books, 1969.

Mens, Alcantara. "De kleine armen van christus in de Brabants-Luikse gewesten." *Ons geestelijk erf*, 38 (1964): 137–144.

Neel, Carol. "The Origins of the Beguines." In Judith M. Bennett et. al., *Sisters and Workers in the Middle Ages*. Chicago: University of Chicago Press, 1989.

Newman, Barbara. *From Virile Woman to WomanChrist: Studies in Medieval Religion and Literature*. Philadelphia: University of Pennsylvania Press, 1995.

————. *Sister of Wisdom: St. Hildegard's Theology of the Feminine*. Berkeley: University of California Press, 1987.

Petroff, Elizabeth. *Body and Soul: Essays on Medieval Women and Mysticism*. New York: Oxford University Press, 1994.

————, ed. *Medieval Women's Visionary Literature*. New York: Oxford University Press, 1986.

Philippen, L. J. M. *De Begijnhoven: Oorsprong, Geschiedenis, Inrichting*. Antwerp: Ch. & H. Courtin, 1918.

Phillips, Dayton. *Beguines in Medieval Strasburg: A Study of the Social Aspects of Beguine Life*. Stanford University diss.: Edwards Brothers, 1941.

Quintijn, Roze-Marijn. *Normen en normering van het begijnenhoven*. Ghent: Rijksuniversiteit Gent, 1983.

Ridder, F. de. "De oudste statuten van het Mechelse Begijnhof." *Handelingen van de Mechelse kring voor oudheidkunde* 39 (1934): 18–29.

Rolfson, Helen, trans. "Hadewjch of Antwerp, *The List of the Perfect*." *Vox Benedictina*, 5, no. 4 (Oct. 1988): 277–287.

Saenger, Paul. "Silent Reading: Its Impact on Late Medieval Script and Society." *Viator* (Spring 1982): 368–444.

Schechner, Richard. *Performance Theory*. New York: Routledge: 1988.

Simons, Walter. "The Beguine Movement in the Southern Low Countries: A Reassessment," *Bulletin de l'institut historique belge de Rome* 59 (1989): 63–105.

Stock, Brian. *Listening for the Text: On the Uses of the Past*. Baltimore: Johns Hopkins Press, 1990.

Suydam, Mary. "Ever in Unrest: Translating Hadewijch of Antwerp's *Mengeldichten*." *Women's Studies* (March 1999).

————. "Heavenly Space in theVisionary Realm of Beguines." Paper presented at the International Congress of Medieval Studies at Kalamazoo, Michigan, 1998.

———. "Writing Beguines: Ecstatic Performances." *Magistra* 2, no. 1 (Summer 1996).

Szarmach, Paul, ed. *An Introduction to the Medieval Mystics of Europe.* Albany: State University of New York Press, 1984.

Tanakh: The Holy Scriptures (Philadelphia: Jewish Publication Society, 1986).

Tobin, Frank, trans. *Henry Suso: The Exemplar, with Two German Sermons.* New York: Paulist Press, 1989.

van Mierlo, Jozef, ed. *Hadewijch: Brieven.* 2 vols. Antwerp: N.V. Standaard Boekandel, 1947.

———, ed. *Hadewijch: Mengeldichten.* Antwerp: Standaard Boekhandel, 1952.

———, ed. *Hadewijch: Visioenen.* 2 vols. Leuven: 1924.

Winkworth, Margaret, trans. *Gertrude of Helfta: The Herald of Divine Love.* New York: Paulist Press, 1993.

Ziegler, Joanna. *Sculpture of Compassion: The Pietà and the Beguines in the Southern Low Countries, c. 1300–1600.* Brussels and Rome: The Belgian Historical Institute of Rome, 1992.

———. "Secular Canonesses as Antecedent of the Beguines in the Southern Low Countries: An Introduction to Some Older Views." *Studies in Medieval And Renaissance History* 13 (1991): 114–135.

———. "Women of the Middle Ages: Some Questions Regarding the Beguines and Devotional Art." *Vox Benedictina* 3, no. 4 (1986): 338–357.

Zinn, Grover, trans. *Richard of St. Victor: The Twelve Patriarchs, The Mystical Ark, Book Three of the Trinity.* New York: Paulist Press, 1979.

Zum Brunn, Emilie, and Georgette Épiney-Burgard. *Women Mystics in Medieval Europe.* New York: Paragon House, 1989.

CHAPTER EIGHT

Rocking the Cradle: Margaretha Ebner (Be)Holds the Divine

Rosemary Drage Hale

In 1344 Margaretha Ebner, a Dominican nun from the convent Maria-Mödingen, experienced miraculous lactation following a vision in which a small figure of the Christ-child asked to be nursed. She had developed an intensely maternal relationship with the carved wooden figure—embracing it, caring for it, swaddling it, placing it in a cradle and rocking it to sleep. The central feature of this experience, and countless others like it, is the imitation of Mary's role as the mother of Christ. The focus of much of the scholarship on such experiences concerns their *visionary* aspect; they are, in fact, still referred to as visionary experiences.[1] Broadly speaking, my intent, along with that of the other articles in this collection, is to expand the way in which we sense mystical texts. More specifically, focusing on the transformative relationship between the performer, the object, and the ritual actions, my interest is in examining the constellation of resident performative attributes in written accounts of mystical *imitatio Mariae* as exemplified by Margaretha's narration of miraculous lactation.[2] Margaretha's Christ-child effigy and the cradle are devotional objects. She holds and caresses the wooden figure not as a representation of the Christ-child, but *as* the Christ-child, tenderly rocking him in the cradle as religious ritual. As Margaretha performs her liturgical drama, she (be)holds[3] the divine, and through her mimetic actions she is transformed. Later, she records the experience and her spiritual transformations. The written description bears witness to the vital significance of the tactile sense for both the ritual and its transformative effect.

What follows is a passage from Margaretha Ebner's spiritual autobiography, her "Revelations,"[4] in which she narrates the nursing and cradle-rocking experiences. I present it at the outset as a frame of reference for my comments on the performance of and transformation through mystical *imitatio Mariae*.

> I have an image of the Child, our Lord, in a cradle. I was so powerfully compelled by my Lord with great sweetness, longing and desire and also by His request, because it was said to me by my Lord: "If you do not nurse me I will take myself away from you at the moment you love me the most." So I took the image out of the cradle and laid it on my bare breast with great longing and sweetness and felt then the strongest possible grace in the presence of the Lord. Afterward I wondered how our blessed Lady could ever endure the incessant presence of God. Then I was answered with the true words of the angel Gabriel, *Spiritus sanctus supervenit in te*. But my longing and desire was in nursing him, so that through His pure humanity I might be purified and set afire by Him with His burning love, and His divine essence together with all loving souls who lived in truth.
>
> But later when I began to write this little book, I felt great delight for the Child of our Lord, especially as I have written, and for His sweetest of all circumcision, so that I could be nourished by His holy blood, strongest of all and flowing with love. I stood there in longing, such that I could happily give my life for that. The desires consumed me greatly, day and night, so much so that I was frequently unable to sleep at night on account of the true divine longing and desire, which I had in the choir coming into the presence of the grace of God.
>
> Since then, whenever I sit to say my Paternoster, I am powerfully compelled by a powerful love to press him to my breast. This gives me the greatest grace and sweetness, such that I can think of nothing other than Him. I remain in this sweet delight until I arrive where the loving suffering of my Lord takes hold. Delight and grace are thus transformed from the Child into the holy suffering of my beloved Lord. I long to give myself with a mighty loving desire over to every such suffering of God, such that I would abandon my life at this time to be with Him.

I have a crucifix and was compelled by my great love and the presence of God to press this cross to my heart with all my might. From the longing and sweet grace which I have for this purpose, I might never feel it and press still so strongly, so that death-marks appear on my chest and body. My Lord often speaks to me lovingly and sweetly saying, "Spare yourself and allow us to be together in another way. This I desire out of true love for you." A certain desire and longing is very strong and mighty in me. During the day I received our Lord in an interior manner with a very strong Christian love, full of God's presence, which I there openly in my soul received directly. And I knew, on account of the love which had compelled my soul, that I had in me the living power of God, His holy blood and flesh. I allowed Him during the day to bring love and compassion alive in me. The desire which I had for the images was changed there into the holy sacrament for me.

One night as I lay sleeping and Matins was called, I was constrained by the usual vow of silence and thought that I could not get up. Then my most beloved Lord spoke to me: "Stand up and come to me in the choir. I want to do to you as nicely as I have done before." Then I stood up with great joy and said Matins and went into the choir. Then the great desire came to me for the Baby of our Lord and I took the image and pressed it to my bare breast with my power and might. Then I felt a human touch from His mouth on my bare breast. Then I received a great godly dread, so that I sat for a while and could not do anything. The fear was taken away from me with great joy and mercy and I completed my prayers. You know this, my Lord, the pure truth, namely, that I never had so great a fear for any gift which God gave me as for that one [that is], whether it was He Himself in truth or merely the great desire for my Lord. And so it was answered unto me by the true faith of my Lord: "As truly as I have bound myself to you in my holy suffering and my holy sacrament, even so it is my gift, for which I rejoice because of love from you." Now I did not have the audacity ever to say this to anyone, even to a friend of our Lord whom God had given to me.

Shortly afterwards, a sister came to me who was a confidante of mine and who wrote to me. She said to me: "I saw you last night in a dream with your figure of the child and that was a living child and you took it with great longing and you put it to your bare breast and wanted to nurse it and this amazed me that you were so unhesitant, that you were unashamed." I heard of her dream with pure joy and thought that it was given to me by the will of God. Through this joy, I attained then the courage to let her know about it and to write down this very matter, which so strongly affected me in an interior way.

On St. Stephen's Day my Lord granted me a loving gift of my desire. A beautiful image of the infant Jesus in a cradle and surrounded by four golden angels was sent to me from Vienna. And one night the Child granted to me that I could see him play in the cradle with joy and full of life. Then I spoke to Him: "Why don't you be quiet and let me get some sleep? I have laid you to sleep very nicely." Then the Child spoke: "I don't want to sleep. You must take me to you." And so I took him with longing and joy out of the cradle and put him on my lap. He was a lovely child. Then I spoke: "Kiss me so that I can forget that you have disturbed my sleep." He embraced me with His arms and held me and kissed me.

A few comments about Margaretha Ebner: Born in 1291 in Donau-wörth, near Regensburg, to a patrician family,[5] she entered the Dominican cloister of Maria-Mödingen at an early age and was buried there in 1351.[6] In 1332 Heinrich von Nördlingen, her Dominican confessor, convinced her to write a record of her spiritual journey. We know that she wrote her *Offenbarungen* (Revelations) herself, without the aid of an amanuensis.[7] It is a lengthy manuscript (over 100 folio pages) and follows a chronological description of Margaretha's spiritual life, the experiences arranged according to the liturgical calendar. The text belongs to a medieval religious genre that has been referred to as "auto-hagiography."[8]

In 1312 she became seriously ill and for three years endured a variety of afflictions described in the opening chapters of her spiritual memoirs. Suffering a severe illness for an extended period of time is a feature commonly reported in medieval hagiography or auto-hagiography and figures prominently in the religious experiences of medieval women.[9] Recovered, Margaretha undertook a rigorous program of asceticism, self-mortification, fasting, and flagellation, all performative attributes of *imitatio Christi*. She renounced all worldly pleasures—bathing, for example, and conversation with her friends. At one point she begged Mary to ask God that she be granted the miracle of stigmata. Quite in keeping with fourteenth-century piety, her devotions centered on the humanity of Christ, primarily on his birth and death. Material images of both cradle and cross are, therefore, conspicuous in her devotional exercises and performances of *imitatio Mariae*.

It is essential to note that Margaretha's experience is not an isolated event; rather, it is one of countless similar experiences described in a variety of texts and images, in both monastic and lay sources, in late medieval Europe. While distinctly pan-European, the textual and visual evidence of *imitatio Mariae* is especially rich and uniquely coherent in late medieval Germany.[10] Particularly valuable are the *Nonnenbücher* (Nuns' Books), a corpus written by cloistered women in fourteenth-century Dominican convents in southern Germany. The *Nonnenbücher*, which include seven chronicles composed of the collected *vitae* of the sisters and three spiritual autobiographies, those of Margaretha Ebner, Christina Ebner and Adelheid Langmann,[11] offer hundreds of detailed narratives evidencing mimetic behavior modeled on various aspects of Mary's motherhood. Equally important, they provide attestations of the phrase *nachfolger mariae*, a parallel to the Middle High German term for imitators of Christ—*nachfolger Christi*, indicating that worshippers like Margaretha actually intended their acts as imitative of Mary.[12] These texts attest literally hundreds of visionary experiences in which nuns give birth to the Christ-child, nurse him, bathe him, and offer him a variety of maternal affections.[13] Margaretha's experience, like those narrated by the other nuns, is not simply a description of personal devotion to Mary and the Holy Child. It is a performance of union with the divine child.

Margaretha describes her *imitatio Mariae* experience in terms of physical union with God. God's presence and grace "pour" through her. By imitating Mary's maternal role she is united with God; the performance is the spiritual route to divine union. In another case, Christina Ebner (1277–1356) gives birth to the Christ-child and carries him into the refectory in the manner of Mary herself, uniting with the divine through the imitative performance of motherhood. Such experiences reflect the same desire for *unio mystica*[14] as that expressed by the imagery of the spiritual marriage or bridal mysticism. The mystical birth, like the mystical kiss, occurs between the soul and Christ and is a metaphor for the union of the soul with Christ. The spiritual motherhood described in mystical texts such as Margaretha's and Christina's can be regarded, therefore, as examples of what I am calling "mother mysticism."[15] In contrast to the view held by many scholars that the Christ-child experiences simply provide a substitute for the children the women lack, a closer look at the evidence indicates that the motherhood experiences were presented as models of piety well within the range of orthodoxy.[16] The private devotional practice of *imitatio Mariae*, in which the individual performs as mother of the divine child, results in her union with God.

The sort of imitative practices narrated by Margaretha Ebner and other fourteenth-century women are similar to those attested in all major world religions. Religious *imitatio*, identified as imitation of the example set by the paradigm's holy behavior, is, in the main, religious behavior, and distinctly performative. Within the history of Christianity, the imitation of Christ is perhaps the most well-known example. With a long tradition, the devotional practices centered on the imitation of Christ are particularly significant in the late Middle Ages. Thomas à Kempis's fifteenth-century treatise, *The Imitation of Christ* is, outside of the Bible, one of the most widely sold and most often translated books in Western history.[17] In contrast, however, widespread imitation of Mary, or even the imitation of other paradigmatic holy figures such as saints, is less researched and not as well known by historians of Christianity. The imitation of such holy figures is, however, widely attested throughout the medieval period.

In Margaretha's episode, Mary functions as the paradigm. Mary's maternal behavior towards her son is the model Margaretha follows as an aspect of her devotion to the Christ-child. Fundamentally the performative elements are consistent with the structure of *imitatio* in other religious traditions. A holy figure represents a paradigm of devotional behavior. When a spiritual guide suggests imitation of the paradigm, or when the devotee models his or her devotional behavior on the holy figure, there is *imitatio*. The "language of performance" that constitutes the practice of *imitatio* serves as the basis for a second layer of mimetic behavior. The performances, once public through recollection and writing, are didactic in purpose, serving as spiritual instruction for the viewers and listeners.

The conceptual framework for my discussion of *imitatio* as religious behavior is built upon recent work in the area of performance theory.[18] Whether we are looking at the practice of *imitatio Mariae* inside or outside cloister walls, or whether we are examining textual or visual evidence, cultural performance is the fundamental category. The core of this focus is the meaningful action that constitutes the performance of *imitatio*. Performance theory reconstructs ritual actions, such as *rocking* the Christ-child in a cradle or *weeping* at the foot of the cross, as texts and "reads" them as cultural performances. The performance paradigm provides historians with a new and fruitful hermeneutic for interpreting religious behavior.[19] It is especially useful in attempting to understand the meaning of medieval women's spirituality or the religious practices of the "ordinary" worshiper.

Richard Schechner, one of the foremost scholars in this field, defines performance as an activity done by an individual or a group in the presence of and for another individual or group.[20] Such a definition raises the question of the intended audience for the *imitatio Mariae* phenomena as narrated by Margaretha Ebner. Are the performances themselves private or communal? The distinction between private (and here I mean individual and personal *imitatio* performances in human solitude for a divine audience) and public performances intended for a community of participating onlookers reveals significant information about the function of the imitative devotion itself. Hence, it is vital for the discussions in this collection that we also understand that the audience may well be divine. Regardless of audience, performance is a mode of communication, calling forth "a heightened awareness of the act of expression and giving license to the audience to regard the act of expression and the performer with special intensity."[21] *Imitatio* naturally falls into the descriptive category of performance. In order to imitate the behavior of a particular religious model, the worshipper must *do* something, *perform* some activity in imitation.

A medieval Christian's life, like that of Margaretha Ebner, resonated with mimetic activity, imitating the lives and virtues of a host of paradigmatic figures. Mary was a primary exemplar for nuns. She represented a perfect paradigm of humility, inwardness, obedience, and chastity. Religious women attempted to imitate not only her virtues, but also her relationships to Christ. A nun was to be a virgin (at least spiritually); she took Christ as her spouse as did Mary;[22] and she felt herself to be a spiritual mother of the child in imitation of Mary's motherhood. Late medieval women imitated characteristics drawing on all three Marian roles— wife, mother, and daughter. After the thirteenth century, a depiction of Mary drawn on a human scale brought forth images of a simple mother breast-feeding, rocking the child, singing lullabies, rearing her child. Reflecting this imagery, Margaretha's utterly tactile experience of rocking the cradle and nursing the Christ-child is a ritualized performance of *imitatio Mariae* at the level of human reality.

Equally important in any discussion of these mimetic performances is the role played by images in the medieval world, a preliterate and image-based culture. The *habitus*, both individual and communal, of medieval Christians was deeply informed and shaped by the sheer presence of religious images. By this I mean not only the ubiquitous presence of imagery, but the high valence of actuality that images carried for the medieval worshiper. Prior to the sixteenth century, there was a sense that the sacred image could lay claim to being immediate evidence of God's presence in the world revealed to the eyes and the senses. Images connected the worshiper to the absent divine. In recent years, considerable contributions on the part of art historians and religionists have illuminated the intimate bond between the image and the worshiper in medieval Christianity, making credible the claim that images were a significant feature of worship, both communally in liturgical moments and privately in acts of worship.[23] These were interactive exchanges, predominantly portraying the worshiper's sense of vision as access to the object of devotion. The worshiper concentrated on the image, and the image stimulated his or her sight by provoking either an action explicitly related to the object or a particular psychological response, that is, a devotional state implicitly drawn from the image.[24] Images, therefore, suggest something of the performative shape of late medieval Christian piety.

Images are essential elements in the performances of mystical *imitatio Mariae*. There exists in mystical experiences such as Margaretha's a tripartite relationship between the object or image, the performer or actant, and the actions performed.[25] What knits the aggregate together in relationship is the arc of movement in touching, the haptic sense[26]—that is, the tactile action of handling and caressing and rocking. Margaretha does not simply gaze upon the Christ-child effigy. She apprehends it, that is, she takes and holds the effigy and she places it in the cradle and rocks it; she takes it to her breast and nurses it.

The ritual cradle, critical to Margaretha's performative ritual, is an example of a category of image-objects I would call *performative*. Such image-objects include a variety of three-dimensional devotional artifacts that, as a part of their rudimentary structure, *require* ritualized manipulation of some sort for the devotional activity to be consummated. By virtue of their construction, they necessitate a performance-related devotion. The linguistic analysis of speech act theory provides a useful heuristic parallel in examining these artifacts. Speech act theory makes a distinction between assertions and certain utterances that in and of themselves do something, actually perform something[27]—for example, christening a ship ("I christen this ship *Anchors Away*"), marriage rituals (" I hereby pronounce you husband and wife")—and promises made ("I promise you x, y, or z"). When used under the appropriate circumstances, all these utterances constitute a performance of the relevant act and are hence efficacious. Precisely the same is true of the performance-related devotional objects. When they are used, in this case manipulated, under the right circumstances, they constitute a devotional performance and are regarded as efficacious.

The cradle, a static object in disuse, necessitates a manipulation to be efficacious. A number of other such performative liturgical objects were employed in late medieval religious ritual. These include figures of Mary designed with a removable effigy of the Christ-child for which, within the context of a Christmas ritual, the removal of the effigy constitutes a devotional performance; crucifixes with movable arms, constructed to be manipulated in paraliturgical devotions on Good Friday and Easter; and the *Palmesel*, a three-dimensional figure of Christ on an ass constructed on wheels or a trolley-cart, and used to lead Palm Sunday processions, thus recreating the entry into Jerusalem with the entire community of worshipers as performers. All these performative image-objects function as constitutive elements in re-enactments—dramatizations of scriptural history—and in each case, the object-act relationship is imbedded within the figure itself.

It is the pairing of objects—the cradle and Christ-child effigy—that has a critical function in the transformative efficacy of Margaretha's ritual drama. It is generally agreed that the use of the cradle, as opposed to the scripturally based crib, developed in the late medieval period, emerging from a remarkably profound interest in realism, an innovation predicated on devotion to the humanity of Christ.[28] An image from an early fourteenth-century illustrated Bible, popular in England and Germany, shows Mary rocking her child in a cradle. The manger is absent. Similarly, in an anonymous woodcut from a fifteenth-century block-book (*Von der gheestliker kintheyt Jesu*) that was intended for cloistered women, the images of Oratio and Mediatatio, represented as nuns, instruct the viewer on the use of the effigy and cradle for devotional practice.[29] Not only did the cradle in and of itself visually represent Christ's humanity—one placed real babies in cradles, not in mangers—but, whether imaged as in these two woodcuts or in three-dimensional reality, it elicited an expected performance—that of rocking.

The cradle and effigy were not only used by cloistered women as constitutive elements of their religious rituals; they were also used in public popular ritual performances called *Kindelwiegenfeier*, or "the ceremony of the child in a cradle." When an effigy was swaddled, placed inside the cradle, and rocked according to a prescribed ritual format, performers and audience alike had completed a devotional act. A fifteenth-century description of the ritual says that "at Christmas they celebrate the childhood of Christ and they place a cradle on the altar and inside the cradle they put a carved figure of the child and a great number of children from the town spring up and dance around the child in a ring, the old look on and sing many little songs about the new born child, and they rock the child in the cradle."[30] Likewise, in a city chronicle from Biberach it is reported that "at Christmas midnight mass they have horns blown from the church-tower and rock the little child in his cradle."[31] While we are fortunate to have extant textual sources that give shape to these ritual performances, it is the object itself—the cradle—that provides the cipher key. The performative behavior of rocking is embedded within the image-object, independent of the textual evidence.

As I have indicated, all the figures and objects in the performative category require a specific haptic manipulation that when performed properly accomplishes a devotional act. There is no question that extant written documents enrich and deepen our understanding of how, why, and under what ritual circumstances the objects were manipulated. But, equally important is the fact the objects can stand alone as fundamental evidence of a performative engagement with ritual practice. Just as a book solicits opening or a scroll invites unrolling, these artifacts exhibit an invitation to devotional performance. In the bodily movement to rock the cradle, the worshiper *enacts* the role of Mary.

The late medieval accent on realism suggests that participation reflected something of the worshipers' own experiences of family, birth, and death. They rocked their own children in cradles and at Christmas, imitating Mary and Joseph, they rocked the Christ-child in a cradle. Fully understanding the human emotion of sorrow, on Good Friday they wept as they imagined Mary to have done. Through public and private devotional activity, through the ritual manipulation of revered objects, worshipers could re-enact and perform sacred history. Through the interior expression of joy and suffering, the worshipers could realize a devotional engagement with the sacred. Personally and communally, they could participate in salvation history.

Not all scholars would interpret Margaretha's ritual behavior in this way. A noted Renaissance historian, Christine Klapisch-Zuber,[32] for example, identifies figures such as Margaretha mentions as "holy dolls" and situates the performances on the border between devotional practice and play activities. What interests me is the use of the terms, "holy dolls" and "devotional toys." The categories of "doll" and "toy" lead Klapisch-Zuber to the conclusion that "ambiguous objects, both those representing the divine and those for play activities, reveal a confusion of attitudes toward the sacred and toward play on the part of those who were to manipulate them."[33] That medieval folk simply failed to appreciate the cultural constructions of sacred and profane is a relatively common notion expressed in secondary literature focusing on medieval Christianity. I would argue that the analytical use of terms such as "doll" and "toy," suggesting that Margaretha and cloistered women who performed similar ritual devotions were simply playing house, albeit with sacred "toys," contributes to an inaccurate reconstruction of their cultural experience.

If we look at the medieval vernacular German evidence for dolls and the use of Christ-child effigies, we can see this more clearly. Vernacular romance literature abounds with attestations of two words for doll, "tocke" and "puppe," as well as a variety of compounds. The *Younger Titurel*, a thirteenth-century romance, has five occurrences of "tocke" and in each case its frame of reference is children's play—children "spil mit tocken" [play with dolls].[34] A thirteenth-century poet, one Pseudo-neidhart, uses the word "tockenwiegel" [little doll cradle].[35] The term does appear in religious texts, but only when used metaphorically. One such example occurs in a sermon by David of Augsburg where he uses the term "tockenlade" [doll chest] to mean a place where one should not hide one's love as in a shrine.[36] What is important here is that none of the textual evidence involving an effigy of the Christ-child makes reference to the wax or carved figure as a "doll." Only words such as "bild" [image] and phrases such as "ein geschnitzt kind" [a carved child] are used. Medieval Germans clearly had a historical category for doll—and they conceived of this object as a child's toy used in play. This category is not employed in conjunction with religious images of the Christ-child.

Furthermore, the material evidence relevant to the performative use of the Christ-child effigy, widespread from the fourteenth to the sixteenth centuries in the areas of present-day Germany, Austria, and Switzerland, offers no evidence that there was confusion or even ambiguity about the border between sacred and profane, between play and piety. The child effigies do have doll-like features and are manipulated in a manner calling "dolls" to mind—dressed and undressed, bathed and caressed—but they are not, in the texts, categorized as dolls. To use the term "doll," and to affix words like "sacred" or "holy" to it, is to *impose* an ambiguity or confusion regarding the borders between play and piety.

Instead of locating the meaning of the *bambini* in the context of cultural performances, Klapisch-Zuber remarks that nuns or laywomen required contact—visual or physical—with sacred images in order to have immediate access to the child Jesus to "transmute their frustrations and tensions."[37] She reads the mystical texts as psychosomatic narrations, claiming that the language of these mystics "shows that the husband so desperately absent was hidden in the baby of their dreams" and that the consequent image of the "child-husband allowed these women an experience that their secluded life condemned them never to know."[38] Building on these assumptions, Klapisch-Zuber ends the chapter and the book with an echo of the recurrent notion that the manipulation of child effigies in cloisters was a "ritualization of their desire for a child."[39]

This sort of analysis finds clarification in Clarissa Atkinson's *The Oldest Vocation: Christian Motherhood in the Middle Ages*. In her chapter on spiritual motherhood she notes that as men and women entered cloistered life, they "carried images and meanings attached to such designations as 'sister,' brother,' 'mother,' and 'father.' "[40] Arguing that the clerical class represented the dominant elite, their "special perspectives played a critical part in forming Christian attitudes toward sexuality and domesticity."[41] Such insight is essential in understanding how medieval Christians might have viewed the sort of spiritual motherhood performed by Margaretha Ebner. As Atkinson says, "as physical maternity was devalued, spiritual maternity soon took its place, so that 'motherhood,' transformed, retained a high status in medieval Christian ideology."[42] This line of argumentation provides a more useful perspective for viewing the practice of maternal *imitatio Mariae*.

The women who wrote the *Nonnenbücher* narrate and describe hundreds of the performances of mother mystical experiences, most of which involve images of the Christ-child. Although devotions to the Christ-child occur throughout the year, quite unsurprisingly, they peak on Christmas Eve. There are frequent accounts of sisters who (be)hold the child on Christmas Eve "as if he were just born."[43] Heiltrut von Bernhausen, for example, was said to have had special devotion to the childhood of Christ and one Christmas Eve remained in her cell the entire night. When another sister came in the morning to wake her, shouting, "Get up. The son has been born," Heiltrut responded, "Why do you want to tell me that? I have had him in my arms all night."[44]

Nativity visions do not always involve the imitation of Mary and examining these makes clear the distinction with regard to explicit performances of *imitatio Mariae*. The visions are described in the mode of the *tableau vivant*; the nativity events unfold dramatically as an apparition and the visionary is only an observing beholder of the scene. Ite von Holloway, a lay sister, for example, had a nativity vision on Christmas Eve that was clearly inspired by Scripture and image. "She saw our Lady as she gave birth to our Lord and laid the child in the manger and she saw Joseph, the ass and the ox by the manger and this vision gave her great joy."[45] Others embellished the scene with realistic details. One chronicler tells of the nativity vision of Gertrud von Rheinfelden:

Suddenly she began to see a most beautiful bed placed in the middle of the choir, decorated with the best ornaments in which was resting alone a woman in labor and her face shone with so much beauty and so much brilliance, that from the splendor emanating from her the entire choir was miraculously bright. She fondled her child in her lap, the blessed fruit of her womb, swaddled her child in cloth, who appeared to Gertrud so small, as if he had just been born at that very moment.[46]

Such narrations differ profoundly and substantively from the episodes of performative *imitatio Mariae*. Margaretha Ebner embarks upon a transformative performance of *imitatio* when she is compelled to treat the effigy as if it were the living Christ-child and thus assumes the role she would have envisioned as Mary's. Upon responding to his request to be nursed, Margaretha miraculously lactates, assuming and imitating the role of the absent Mary. In so doing she achieves her spiritual goal—union with "divine essence." By nursing and later nurturing the child, swaddling and caressing, as if he were her own, she is afforded profound intimacy with God. Tactile nursing visions are an important feature of the mother mystical narratives. Typically, Mary is present in these visions and offers the child to be held and/or nursed by one or more of the sisters. In each instance the visionary expresses ineffable joy over the unity with the divine. Adelheid Langmann, who narrates several experiences of mother mysticism, recounts a typical proprioceptive experience of nursing the infant Christ. She says,

after Christmas she saw our Lord in the form of a small child and he appeared in size and form as he was just born from our Lady and from his feet to his shoulder he was only a hand's length. And he lay on her lap and was so beautiful and so lovely that he could not have been more beautiful. . . . At the same time our sweet Lady, the sweet queen Maria, came one night as she lay in her bed and carried the child on her arm and gave her the child on her arm while she was in bed. He was so beautiful that it was unspeakable and he suckled her little breast and stayed with her until they sounded matins and from this she had such great joy. . . . [47]

Whether with a tactile vision or in apparition, Mary rarely appears unaccompanied by Christ in the convent literature.[48] The context of these dramatic performances and the representation of Mary correspond to images known to have existed in convent settings.[49] They are those that by virtue of narrative elements engage the tactile sense. Small sculpted images such as Mary in her childbed; life-size figures of Mary holding the infant as if to hand him to the beholder; altar paintings of bathing the infant Christ; sculptures and paintings of Mary holding the child in the folds of her mantel and those of her weeping at the foot of the cross; the widespread sculpted image of the Pietà—all are narrative images that evoke the touching, holding, apprehending of Christ and all are significantly represented in the religious experiences narrated in the convent literature.

Recent scholarship has begun to take note of the importance of imagery in the narration of ecstatic experience as described by medieval mystics. Jeffrey Hamburger and Elizabeth Vavra, for example, have focused attention on the interplay between vision and image in late medieval Germany.[50] Both provide further proof that imagery has an indirect influence on the construction of performative action in the religious practice of *imitatio*. A case in point: imitation of a narrative element resident in the image of the *Shutzmantlemadonna* [Madonna of the Protective Cloak].[51] Several sisters experience seeing the Christ-child and as they lovingly gather him up, they take him under the protection of their cloaks. In one such instance the Christ-child appears to Güde von Winzel on Christmas Eve and she keeps him under her mantel throughout the Mass, receiving immeasurable grace and joy.[52] Likewise, a sister named Wila (von Wilburgis) sees the child one night as she makes her way to her dormitory in the darkness. "Then she saw our Lord Jesus Christ as the most beautiful little child . . . and the little child went under her mantel and sat on her lap and they had great joy with one another."[53]

The core element in mother mystical experiences has roots in the realism required to depict a human Christ and a human Mary, and the texts testify to a direct and explicit connection with the image culture. A tactile vision occurs while meditating in front of or embracing a particular iconographical image-object, which becomes an essential component of the performative experience.[54] Anna von Constance, for example, meditates in front of an image of Mary holding the child: "She went to the image of our Lady who had our Lord in her arms and took the child's tiny feet into her hands with great devotion and the little feet became flesh and blood in her hands."[55] Inspired by her devotional interaction with an image, Anna's tactile vision mirrors the sacerdotal performance of transubstantiation. In her hands the figure is transformed into body and blood. Just as in Margaretha's account of the effigy come to life, the experience alters the fabricated nature of the image changing it into a "flesh and blood child." And, like Mary herself, the nuns become the vessel for the transformation.

Another common tactile motif is that of the playful Christ-child.[56] The child appears with or without Mary and stays for a while playing with the nun. Christina Ebner narrates eight *vitae* in which a nun has an experience of playing with the infant Christ. Normally the experience occurs during or immediately following a performative devotion the nun has made to the childhood of Christ. In one instance, while at private prayer in the choir, a sister sees a vision of the Christ-child. Later, when she goes into the refectory, she is joined by the same child, who sits by her and plays.[57] Again, the descriptions, while theologically-centered, draw on realistic childlike characteristics. Ita von Holoway at Katarinenthal has a vision in which the Christ-child turns the image of the orb into a child's toy and plays catch with her: "One day when she wanted to dry the herbs she made a ball and our Lord appeared to her and took the ball from her hand and threw it to her again. Then they played catch with one another and she was thoroughly involved with him."[58] The sisters envision a playful infant or toddler and engage with him on human terms. The authors of the *Nonnenbücher* narrate an array of Eucharistic visions, where, upon the elevation of the host, the child appears and runs about, leaping and jumping in the manner of a flesh and blood child. Invariably, the vision concludes with a tactile engagement with the Christ-child, a mutual embrace.

Performative experiences of bathing the infant Christ also reveal a realistically playful infant and exemplify the visionary's tender affection for the child. Heinrich von Nördlingen writes to Margaretha Ebner referring to the ritual of bathing the newborn child eight days after birth.[59] Elsbeth Stagel recounts the convent custom of an Advent ritual that also suggests bathing an effigy of the Christ-child. First, all the items one might imagine necessary for taking care of a newborn are assembled and placed in a small "house" or crèche.[60] On one occasion, Margaret von Zürich, who had the "gift of tears," weeping often for hours at a time, was awarded the opportunity of preparing the bath for the Christ-child:

> To comfort her because she wept so deeply she was permitted one advent to prepare the bath of our Lord (as we usually made a spiritual house with all things on earth of use to him), and one time because of her heartfelt tears our Lord appeared to her so lovingly as if he were a little baby and sat in the bath before her and when one of her tears fell into the bath it was transformed into a little gold button

and the tender baby smacked it about in the bath with his little hands
and he was so lovingly beautiful that she received great comfort from
it.[61]

Throughout the convent literature, as with Margaretha's revelation, we see
expressions of affection toward the Christ-child. The performers or ac-
tants, while they assume the role of Mary, create the devotional exercise
with an understanding of human experience. The narrative descriptions
indicate the likelihood of life experiences of holding children on their laps,
playing with them, caressing and taking delight in them. The parallel mystical experiences, although influenced by religious imagery, were also inspired by the vivid memory of real-life experiences. We know, for example,
that infants and little children were present in the cloister environment.
Not only did women who entered the convent late in life frequently bring
their children with them, but many of the *vitae* indicate that women were
oblated as infants.[62] Consequently, the women would have had opportunities to experience children in their midst. We can also assume that those
women who entered the cloister as adults may well have had direct experience with infants in home settings. Mystical motherhood performances, however ritualized and transformative, were created out of the
drama of human experience.

The features common to the narrations of tactile *imitatio Mariae* performances from fourteenth-century Dominican convent literature reflect a
pattern. In all cases, the actant or performer assumes the role of Mary,
engages in a tactile relationship with a figure or image of Christ, and is
thereby transformed as she experiences an intimacy or union with the
divine. Margaretha moves from imitation to the real thing; she *becomes*
Mary. The transformation is evidenced by her lactation necessary for nursing an effigy, transformed to the human Christ-child by her performance.
When Margaretha embraces the effigy, she is privately imitating the maternal behavior of Mary. And, although her subsequent revelations would
become public by virtue of being read aloud as spiritual guidance for others, initially her performance was intended for a divine audience only. She
is not simply impersonating or portraying the mother of Christ; the drama
she performs blurs the boundary between imitation and becoming.

However we might constrain the meaning of Margaretha's performance with categories of reference, along with its concomitant context, it
will inevitably constitute a problem for the historian of medieval Christianity attempting to (re)construct devotional behavior of a silent informant.
Nevertheless, paltry as the textual materials are, we do have an extraor-

dinarily wide range of visual sources—images and three-dimensional arti-facts produced for and sometimes by the common worshipper—which offer a substantial corpus of evidence for examining the fundamental cat-egory of performance. Certainly, whether we harvest our evidence from the textual or visual, we are faced with the perennial question of how accurately we can discern something of the intentional fabric of those living in cultures or historical periods remote from our own.[63]

Notes

This research was supported by grant of a *Fonds pour la Formation de Chercheurs et l'Aide à la Recherche*. I am also indebted to the untiring efforts of two graduate research assistants, Rose Ftaya and Sandra Boutros.

1. Although I challenge the accuracy of the terms "vision" and "visionary," I use them throughout my work. Nonetheless, it is necessary, I believe, in our attempts to apply new approaches to the study of mystical experience, to be aware that so many of the experiences utilize the full sensorium.

2. While it is beyond the scope of this article, it should be noted that mystical performances of *imitatio Mariae* also include assuming the role of the sorrowful Mary at the foot of the cross or holding the dead Christ in one's lap as portrayed in the image of the Pietà. The textual evidence would indicate that there is a similar relationship between actant, image-object, and actions as in those tactile experiences that involve the Christ-child.

3. "Behold" is a transitive verb. It is a performative verb that requires an object. Etymologically, the word comes from OE "behealden" and ME "biholden," both of which mean "to grasp" or "to hold firmly." These historical meanings, taken along with the modern English usage ("to gaze upon"), contribute to the use of "(be)hold" in this article; it is used to signify my efforts to grasp something of the meaning of Mar-garetha's experiences.

4. From Philipp Strauch, *Margaretha Ebner und Heinrich von Nördlingen: ein Beitrag zur Geschichte der deutschen Mystik*. (Freiburg i. Br: Mohr, 1882), 87–91. The translation first appeared in my "Two Selections from Mar-garetha Ebner's *Offenbarungen*," *Vox Benedictina* 4 (1987): 320–337. For an alternative translation see *Margaret Ebner: Major Works*, trans. Leonard Hindsley (New York: Paulist Press, 1993). Marginal notes date the narrative passage to December 27, 1344, making Margaretha 53 years old at the time of the lactation experience. The dating cannot be verified, however, and it is also conceivable that Margaretha is recol-lecting an experience of some years past.

5. See Strauch, xxxi. His introduction includes an overview of Margare-

tha's life. Also see Ludwig Zoepf, *Die Mystikerin Margaretha Ebner*, Beiträge zur Kulturgeschichte des Mittelalters und der Reniassiance, Bd. 16 (Leipzig: Teubner, 1914), 1–5, for a discussion of what is known of Margaretha's life; C. Jedelhauser, *Geschichte des Klosters Maria-Medingen* (Leipzig: Vechta, 1936); and Bauerreiss Romuald, *Kirchengeschichte Bayerns*, vol. 4 (St. Ottlilien: EOS Verlag, 1954), 69–71.

6. Margaretha's grave is located in the cloister chapel of Maria-Mödingen and is positioned at the foot of the altar facing the enshrined effigy of the Christ-child.

7. It is possible that she had some help with the actual writing from Elizabeth Scheppach, the prioress of Mödingen in 1345. See Letter XL, Philipp Strauch, *Margaretha Ebner*, 61–62: "die wil wir so gar ain geträwe helferin und schriberin haben an unserm lieben kind in got Elzbet Schepach."

8. See Richard Kieckhefer, *Unquiet Souls: Fourteenth-Century Saints and their Cultural Milieu* (Chicago: University of Chicago Press, 1984), 6, where he uses the term to refer to the genre of spiritual autobiography. Referring to the broad range of medieval spiritual autobiographies, he says, "these works are far from containing unrelieved self-glorification, yet they present their authors as such fervently devout souls that one might speak of the genre as auto-hagiography."

9. See Donald Weinstein and Rudolph Bell, *Saints and Society* (Chicago: University of Chicago, 1982), 156 and 234–235, where they indicate the marked role played by chronic illness in the lives of holy penitents. See also Caroline Walker Bynum, *Holy Feast and Holy Fast* (Berkeley: University of California Press, 1987), 199–200, where she discusses how and why women's spiritual illness were represented as something which needed to be "endured"; whereas the illnesses of male penitents were described as something to be "cured."

10. Throughout this study I will use the geographical designation of Germany to refer to that area of medieval Europe that shared the language or dialects of German.

11. The term "convent" [convent, covënt, kofent] is widely attested in these texts and hence I will use it throughout my discussion. However, it should be noted that contemporary Dominican women refer to their cloisters as monasteries, not as convents. Also, I do not differentiate between the terms "Nonnenbücher" and "Schwesternbücher". This corpus includes the following texts: "Die Nonnen von Kirchberg bei Haigerloch," ed. Anton Birlinger, *Alemannia* 11 (1883): 10–20; "Die Nonnen von St. Katharinenthal bei Diessenhofen," ed. Birlinger, *Alemannia* 15 (1887): 150–183; "Les *Vitae Sororum* d'Unterlinden," ed. Jean Ancelet-Hustache, *Archives d'Historie Doctrinale et Littéraire du Moyen Age* 5 (1931): 317–517; "Die Chronik der Anna von Munzingen," ed. J. König, *Freiburger Diözesan Archiv* 12 (1980); "Der Nonnen von Engelthal Büchlein von der Genaden Überlast, ed. Karl Schröder, *Bibliothek des Litterarischen*

Vereins in Stuttgart 108 (1871): 1–44; *Die Offenbarungen der Adelheide Lang-mann: Klosterfrau zu Engelthal* ed. Phillip Strauch (Strassburg,1878); *Of-fenbarungen der Margaretha Ebner* ed. Strauch (Freiburg, 1882); and *Das Leben der Schwestern zu Töss beschrieben von Elsbet Stagel* ed. Ferdinand Vetter, *Deutsche Texte des Mittelalters*, vil. 6 (Berlin, 1906). For a bibliography on a particular author or convent see Gertrud Jaron Lewis, *Bibliographie zur deutschen Frauenmystik des Mittelalters* (Berlin: Schmidt, 1989), which is remarkably complete for materials up until 1988. The only compre-hensive discussion of the *Nonnenbücher* in English is Gertrud Jaron Lewis's *By Women, For Women, about Women: The Sister Books of Fourteenth-Century Germany* (Toronto: Pontifical Institute of Medieval Studies, 1996).

12. See Letter XXI from Heinrich von Nördlingen to Margaretha Ebner (Philipp Strauch, *Margaretha Ebner*, 204): "der diemütigen gotz und Mar-ien selige nachfolgerin . . ."

13. The use of the term "maternal" is used with recognition that it is cul-turally constructed. Suffice it here to say that textual and visual evi-dence portrays Mary swaddling her child, nursing him, holding him in her arms and on her lap. The visions necessarily reflect a picture of the world as it was actually observed and experienced by the visionary. In this sense the visions represent cultural facts. There is no doubt that the nuns regarded maternal response as a natural aspect of gender. This point is also made by P. Burke, "L'Histoire sociale des rêves," *Annales* 28 (1973): 223–234. See also the discussion of medieval notions of motherhood in Clarissa W. Atkinson's *The Oldest Vocation: Christian Motherhood in the Middle Ages* (Ithaca, NY: Cornell University Press, 1991).

14. With the term "unio mystica" I am referring to the experience of "mys-tical union"—an immediate apprehension and intuitive knowledge of God. It should be noted that while the visionaries sought union with God, the term "mystical" is not attested in their texts. They do, how-ever, frequently employ the term "unio" to refer to this experience. In addition to the word "unio," they also use nouns such as "vereinunge" or "einbaerunge" and verbs such as "einbaeren" or "vereinen." For fur-ther discussion of this issue see Hester Gehring, "The Language of Mysticism in South German Dominican Convent Chronicles of the Fourteenth Century" (Ph.D Diss., University of Michigan, 1957), 311–320. For further discussion of the meaning of this term as applied to medieval texts in general, see Paul Szarmach, ed., *An Introduction to the Medieval Mystics* (New York: New York University Press, 1984), espe-cially 2–4, where he notes that the term "mysticism" is a construct useful for facilitating the understanding of a variety of unitive experi-ences. It is clear that when we regard the term as such it does not require a static definition. The distinctions between scholastic and practical mysticism are also clearly drawn in Szarmach's introduction

(3–6). Useful comments are also woven throughout the essays in Jill Raitt, ed., *Christian Spirituality: High Middle Ages and Reformation* (New York: Crossroad, 1987). For a helpful discussion of the term as it relates generally to religious experience see Ninian Smart, "Understanding Religious Experience," in Stephen Katz, ed., *Mysticism and Philosophical Analysis* (Oxford University Press: New York, 1978), 10–22. Peter Dinzelbacher in *Vision und Visionliteratur im Mittelalter* (Stuttgart: Hiersmann, 1981), 54–55, also provides a useful definition of "mystic" as it applies to medieval texts. He separates the term from "visionary" by virtue of the experience of *unio mystica*. When the visionary experience includes unmediated union with God, he categorizes it as mystical. The problem, of course, is that the experience is often narrated in terms of cultural metaphors—such as bridal and maternal images—and it requires a sensitive hermeneutic to distinguish between a vision that was unitive and one that was not. Mary is the representative of union with and separation from the divine. This is important for assessing the *imitatio Mariae* present in the Margaretha episode and for examining similar cases in other mystical texts written by women. In these texts there is a strong mystical impulse—union with the divine is the ultimate goal; and, consequently, the role played by Mary is the primary model.

15. The discussion of mother mysticism and *imitatio Mariae* as it applies to the convent literature also appears in my earlier publication "*Imitatio Mariae*: Motherhood Motifs in Devotional Memoirs," in *Medieval German Literature: Proceedings from the 23rd International Congress on Medieval Studies* (Göppingen: Kümmerle, 1989), 129–147 reprinted in *Mystics Quarterly* 16 (Dec. 1990): 193–204.

16. There are several proponents of this view. Quoting Oskar Pfister, Ludwig Zoepf says "die Nonne suchte sich eben Ersatz für die versagte natürliche Mutterschaft und schwelgt als Mutter des göttlichen Kindes." *Die Mystikerin Margaretha Ebner* (Leipzig: Teubner, 1914), 129. In the same vein, Michael Goodich, in *Vita Perfecti: The Ideal of Sainthood in the Thirteenth Century* (Stuttgart: Anton Hiersmann, 1982), 118, claims that the maternal image of Mary represents a mother substitute for the abandoned child. There is no evidence in the texts that the women regarded either the practices of *imitatio Mariae* or the apparitions of Mary as substitutes for absent children or an absent mother.

17. See John van Engen's introduction to *Devotio Moderna: Basic Writings* (New York: Paulist Press, 1988), 8, where he notes that *The Imitation of Christ* exists in 750 handwritten copies and from its first edition in 1472 to the twentieth century it appeared in over 3,000 editions, 50 of these prior to 1500.

18. This is a rapidly growing area of scholarly interest, but there are several noteworthy contributions that form the theoretical basis of this study. Richard Bauman, *Verbal Art as Performance* (Prospect Park, Il: Waveland

Press, 1984); Catherine Bell, *Ritual Theory, Ritual Practice* (Oxford: Oxford University Press, 1992); James Clifford and George Marcus, *Writing Culture: The Poetics and Politics of Ethnography* (Berkeley: University of California Press, 1986); Dell Hymes, "Breakthrough into Performance" in *Folk-lore: Performance and Communication*, ed. Dan Ben-Amos and Kenneth Goldstein (The Hague: Mouton, 1975), 11–74; John MacAllon, *Rite, Drama, Festival, Spectacle: Rehearsals Toward a Theory of Cultural Performance* (Philadelphia: Institute for the Study of Human Issues, 1984); Richard Schechner, "From Ritual to Theatre and Back: The Structure/Process of the Efficacy-Entertainment Dyad," *Educational Theatre Journal* 26 (1974): 455–481, *Performance Theory* (New York: Routledge, 1977), *By Means of Performance: Intercultural Studies of Theatre and Ritual* (Cambridge: Cambridge University Press, 1989), and *The Future of Ritual: Writings on Culture and Performance* (New York: Routledge, 1993); Lawrence Sullivan, "Sound and Sense: Toward a Hermeneutics of Performance," *History of Religions* 26 (1986): 1–33; Stanley Tambiah, "A Performative Approach to Ritual," *Proceedings of the British Academy* 65 (1979): 113–169; Randy Martin, *Performance as Political Act: The Embodied Self* (New York: Bergin and Garvey, 1990); and Janelle G. Reinelt and Joseph R. Roach, eds., *Critical Theory and Performance* (Ann Arbor: University of Michigan Press, 1992).

19. Dell Hymes and others make a significant distinction between behavior and performance. See his "Breakthrough into Performance," ed. Dan Ben-Amos and Kenneth Goldstein, *Folk-lore, Performance and Communication*, 11–74. The distinction is based upon the quality of knowledge necessary for performance and upon the notion of intentionality. Certainly, with regard to *imitatio Mariae*, there is a recognizable distinction between rocking one's own child as behavior and ritually rocking an effigy of the Christ-child or between weeping at the death of one's own son and the stylized weeping of a Marian lament. As Hymes makes clear, the difference is largely due to intent. For additional comments on the distinction see Sullivan's "Sound and Sense: Toward a Hermenetuics of Performance," in *History of Religions* 26 (1986): 1–33.

20. See Richard Schechner, *Performance Theory*, 30, n. 10.

21. 21 See Richard Baumann's *Verbal Art as Performance*, 11.

22. See Jeffrey Hamburger, *The Rothschild Canticles: Art and Mysticism in Flanders and the Rhineland circa 1300* (New Haven: Yale University Press, 1990), 26; and Helga Sciurie, "Maria-Ecclesia als Mitherrscherin Christi. Zur Funktion des Sponsus-Sponsa Modells in der Bildkunst des 13. Jahrhunderts," in *Maria Abbild oder Vorbild?* ed. Opitz and Röcklein (Tübingen: Diskord, 1990), 110–146. Both discussions include visual evidence that Mary was represented as spouse of Christ and that this image interacted with ritual marriage imagery. The ritual of placing the garland (crown) on the head is the primary example. See John

Bugge, *Virginitas: An Essay in the History of an Ideal* (The Hague: Nijhoff, 1975), 59 and 149, where he demonstrates that as early as Tertullian a woman who had pledged virginity was regarded as the bride of Christ. He also indicates that in the twelfth century Mary was transformed from being the bride of the Holy Spirit to the bride of Christ.

23. See Margaret Miles, *Image as Insight: Visual Understanding in Western Christianity and Secular Culture* (Boston: Beacon Press, 1985), 15.

24. Ibid., 97.

25. See Alice Raynor, *To Act, To Do, To Perform: Drama and the Phenomenology of Action* (Ann Arbor: University of Michigan Press, 1994), 5–6, where she discusses this complex relationship and its impact on the identity of the performer.

26. For an in-depth discussion of the haptic sense as it relates to beholding art objects, see Jennifer Fisher, "Aesthetic Contingencies: Relational Enactments in Display Culture" (Ph. D. Diss., Concordia University, Montreal, Quebec, 1995).

27. See John Austin, *How to Do Things with Words* (Cambridge: Harvard University Press, 1962).

28. See Louise Berthold, "Die Kindelwiegenspiele," *Beiträge zur Geschichte der deutschen Sprache und Literatur* 56 (1932), 220, where she says, "Lässt man die ansicht gelten, dass die kindelwiegenfeier so aus dem spätmittelalterlichen realismus herauswächst. . . ."

29. See discussion and illustration in Henk van Os, *The Art of Devotion in the Late Middle Ages in Europe* (Princeton: Princeton University Press, 1994) 102.

30. From Sebastian Franck's *Weltbuch* (Tübingen, unedited, 1534): zu wehenacht begehn sy die kindheit christi also sy sitzen wiegen auff den altar darein ein geschnitzt kind gelegt diss wiegen die statt kind ein grosse menge springen und dantzen umb das kind in einem ring darzu die alten zu sehen und mit singen mit vil selzamen liedlin von neuwgebornen kindlin.

31. From A. Shilling, "Die religiösen und kirchlichen Zustände der ehemaligen Reichsstadt Biberach unmittelbar vor Einführung der Reformation," *Freiburger Diöcesan Archiv*, 19 (1887): 1–191, 112: Zue mitternach haben die blaser uff dem Khürchenthurn und das Khindlin gewüeget.

32. See Christine Klapisch-Zuber, *Women, Family, and Ritual in Renaissance Italy* (Chicago: University of Chicago Press, 1985), especially chapter 14, "Holy Dolls: Play and Piety in Florence in the Quattrocento," 310–331.

33. Ibid., 311.

34. *Der Jüngere Titurel*, ed. Karl August Hahn (Leipzig, 1842), line 1203: "daz ich dich herre wagete nach kindes tocken ziere," 1370: "fur in den satel sin alsam die kinder spilent mit den tocken," 1548: "saz ist ein spil mit tocken," 3480: "Sust wart uf in geurleuget einem halben

geren des ein kleine tocke," 4533: "Und sin gesellen ander wie dirre strit ein spil tocken were, Du hiez mich zu dem grale ein tocke wunschelbernde."

35. See *Niedhart's Lieder*, ed. Moriz Haupt and Edmund Weisser, 2nd ed. (Leipzig: S. Hirzel, 1923), I, s. 26, 22, lines 17–18: "der het ir genomen in schimphe ein tockenwiegel."

36. See *Deutsche Mystiker des vierzehnten Jahrhunderts* ed. Franz Pfeiffer, vol. 1 (Göttingen, 1907) 337.34: "daz waere ungevellic der dar uzmachte eine tockenlade."

37. See Klapisch-Zuber, *Women, Family, and Ritual*, 326.

38. Ibid., 327.

39. Ibid., 328.

40. See Clarissa W. Atkinson, *The Oldest Vocation*, 65. Especially significant here is chapter three, "Spiritual Motherhood: Extraordinary Women in the Early Middle Ages," 65–100.

41. Ibid., 66.

42. Ibid., 67.

43. From Töss, 48: "als es erst geboren wer." This is how Elsbeth Stagel described an anonymous sister's vision. Also in Kirchberg, 170: "das si unsern Herren gern hette gesechen als er was da er erste geborn wart."

44. From Weiler, 74: "Zu einen weihnachten in der heiligen cristnacht, da lag si an irem pett, da kom ein ander heilig swester, dy ir heimlich was, zu ir und sprach: 'wez ligestu talang? hie? Ste auf, der sun ist geporn!' Da sprach sie: 'wiltu mir daz erst sagen? Ich han yn heint lang hie an meinem arm gehabet.'"

45. From Katharinenthal, 160–161: "Disu schwester kam och in die gnad heiligen tag ze wihenehten in der mett, do man anvieng Kristus natus, das sy unser frowen sah als do si unsern herren gebar und dz kindli ligen in der krippe, und sah s. Josephen der esel und dz rind bi dem kripplin und was in grosser frod von dir gesicht. . . ."

46. From Unterlinden, 431–432: Inchoato uero responsorio misse in nocte illa secundum motem celebrande uidere cepit repente lectum pulcherrimum in medio chori positum ornamentis obtimus decoratum in quo residebat singularis illa puerpera et tanta uenustate tantque claritate uultus et habitus radiabat ut ex fulgore de ipsa procedente totus chorus mirabiliter choruscaret. Fouebat quoquo in gremio paruulum suum, benedictum fructum uentris sui pannis infantibus inuolutom qui ita corpore exiguus apparebat quasi eadem hora nuperrime esset natus.

47. From *Die Offenbarungen der Adelheid Langmann*, 66–67: Do noch zu weihenahten do sah si unsern herren in eins clein kindleins weis und er was in aller der grözz und in aller der gestalt als er von unser frawen geporn wart, und von sein füzzen untz an di ahseln was er neur einer spannen lank, und er lag ir uf der schoz und was als schön und als minneclichen daz er nit schöner könd sein gewesen. . . . In den selben zeiten kom unser frau, di suzze kunigin Maria, aines nahtes do si in irem pet lak,

und trug ir kint an arm und gab ir ir kindelein an daz pette an irn arm, und er was als schon daz unsegleichen waz und er sog ir prustlein und was pei ir untz daz man metten leutet, und si het als groz freud mit im daz da von lank ze sagen wer.

48. As a matter of fact, even when Mary appears in visions to join in the convent processions, she does so carrying the infant. From Kirchberg, 125: "One time when we celebrated the mass on Purification Day . . . and when the convent began the procession, our Lady came and brought her loving child and she walked with the convent. . . ." [Es was auch ze einem mal an unser frauen tag der liechtmess . . . da der convent procession ging, da kom unser frau und brachte ir liebes kint und ging sie mit dem convent. . . .]

49. See Jutta Eissengarthen, *Mittelalterliche Textilien aus Kloster Adelhausen im Augustinermuseum Freiburg* (Aldelhausen Frieburg im Breisgau: Karl Schillenger, 1985), 50–56 and *Kunstschatten uit Freiburg* (Utrecht, 1987) for discussions of images present in the fourteenth-century convent of Adelhausen.

50. Elizabeth Vavra, "Bildmotiv und Frauenmystik—Funktion und Rezeption," in *Frauenmystik im Mittelalter*, ed. Peter Dinzelbacher and Dieter Bauer (Stuttgart: Schwaben, 1985), 201–231; and Jeffrey Hamburger, *The Rothschild Canticles: Art and Mysticism in Flanders and the Rhineland circa 1300* (New Haven: Yale University Press, 1990); and "The Use of Images in the Pastoral Care of Nuns," in *Art Bulletin*, 71 (1989): 161–82. In "The Visual and the Visionary: The Images in Late Medieval Monastic Devotions," *Viator* 20 (1989): 161–182, Hamburger also offers a brief and useful look at the history of late medieval devotional imagery. Walter Blank's "Dominikanische Frauenmystik und die Entstehung des Andachtsbildes um 1300," *Alemannisches Jahrbuch* (1964): 57–87, provides a summary of the development of the convent literature.

51. 51 See Pamela Sheingorn, *The Passion of Saint Ursula* (Toronto: Peregrina, 1991). The brief introduction discusses this image. While no comprehensive study exists examining the construction of Mary in the medieval period, it is plausible that the popular image of the *Schutzmantelmadonna* also has roots in realism, that is, the manner in which women used their cloaks to protect their children.

52. From Adelhausen, 171: "Unser herre erschien ir ouch ze einem male als ein kint an der winacht nacht under metti und was bi ir under irme mantel die metti und davon enpfing si grosse gnade und froyde." This also occurs in the Weiler chronicle, 72, Töss, 87–89.

53. From Weiler, 72: Da kom unser herr Jesus Christus ein allerwunniklichstez kint und . . . daz kindlein ging unter den mantel und sass auf ir schoss und hetten grosse frewde mit einander.

54. Images typically "come alive" in the tactile and auditory experiences. Most often it is Christ on the cross who comes to life comforting the nun in some way. The best example of this is in the Adelhausen chron-

icle, 174. Statues of Mary also frequently come to life and speak. In the Dominican convent literature figures of Mary are far more likely to "come alive" than are figures of any other holy person. David Freedburg, *The Power of Images: Studies in the History and Theory of Response* (Chicago: University of Chicago Press, 1989), provides a useful discussion on miraculous images in chapter eleven, especially 299–303. While Freedburg does not relate it to gender, he does suggest that images of Mary from the eleventh century forward were the most likely to "come alive." Casearius of Heisterbach's *Dialogus miraculorum* narrates the stories of copious miraculous images of this sort. In Karl Drescher, ed., *Johann Hartlieb's Uebersetzung des Dialogus Miraculorum von Caesarius von Heisterbach,* (Berlin: Weidmann, 1929).

55. From Katharinenthal, 160: die gieng fur unser frowen bild da si unsern herren an ir arm het und nam des kindlis fussli in ir hand mit grosser andaht, do ward daz fussli fleisch und blut in ir hant.

56. The image of the playful Christ-child does not lend support to Christine Klapisch-Zuber's argument that these women confused the border between play and piety. They engage in the vision, performing a maternal role which unites them with the Holy (human) Child. Nothing in these passages should lead us to believe that expressing and imitating Mary's joyful engagement with Christ was regarded as profane behavior by the nuns. (See, for example, the passage quoted in note 30 above.)

57. From Katharinenthal, 161: "ain schwester, die was eines tages in dem kot an ir gebett, do erschien ir unser herre als ein kindli und was ir gar herzlich wol mit unserm herren . . . do gieng si dannen nach orden ze tisch und do si uber tisch kam do sah si daz kindli by ir sizen und hat vil spils mir ir. davon kam si in als uberflussig gnad. . . ." For other typical examples of this type of Christ-child vision see 162, 174, 176; in Kirchberg see 114, 115; in Weiler see 70; in the *Büchlein* see 29.

58. From Katharinental, 160: do die eines tages das krut wolt trucken und sie ein ballun gemachet do erschain ir unser herr als ein kindli und nam ir die ballun uss der hand und warff ir si do wider; also ballet si und das Jesusli mit einander und was ir als wol mit dem Kindlin. . . .

59. This comes from Letter 2, written on Christmas between 1332 and 1338: "mit dem send ich dir ein hailiges maienbad, das uns von im geben ist in diesen acht tagen." Strauch's comments (322) posit that what Heinrich had in mind was the bath given to newborn infants eight days after birth. The bath that Heinrich sends to Margaretha is composed of blood and milk, mixing the images of the circumcision and baptism.

60. Rosemarie Rode, "Studien zu den mittelalterlichen Kind-Jesu-Visionen" (Ph.D Diss., Frankfurt, 1957), 84, makes the claim that the "spiritual house" Elsbeth mentions here is a reference to a physical crèche-like scene displayed during Advent in the cloister. Johannes Janota, *Studien*

zu Funktion und Typus des deutschen geistlichen Liedes im Mittelalter (Munich: Beck, 1968), 143, makes the same claim.

61. *Das Leben der Schwestern zu Töss*, 36: Won sy nun als fil gewainet, so befalch man ir ze dem adfent unserm heren das badly ze machen (als wir gewonhait hand ze machen ain hus und alles das des er mangel hat, do er uff ertrich was) und do sy ze ainem mal mit hertzlicher andacht wainet, do erschan ir unser herr gar mineklich, als er ain kindly was, und sass in ainem badly vor ir, und als sy ainen trehen vergoss, der ward bald ze ainem schonen gold knopfly und fiel in das badly und schlug in das zart kindly mit dem hendly unden in das badly, und was das als gar mineklich schon anzesechen das sy grossen trost davon enpfieng.

62. Several *vitae* indicate that although formal oblation was forbidden, noble parents still offered their children to monasteries. One *vita* from Oetenbach verified for 1327 tells of a nobleman offering his infant daughter to the convent. See *Die Stiftung des Klosters Oetenbach* ed. H. Zeller-Werdemüller and J. Bächthold, in *Zürcher Taschenbuch auf das Jahr 1889*, 234: "Als si noch in dem alten closter warent, das do gennent wirt daz alt oetenbach und in grosser armut lebten, do gewann ein edler graf von Werdenberg libe zu inen und opfert got sein kint dar ein, do das kint neurt II jar alt was." Many other *vitae* state that the sister lived in the convent from her infancy to her old age. (From *Vitae Sororum d'Unterlinden*, 431: "sub regulari tramitte ab infancia usque ad senectutemsuam strennue et deuote Domino militauit. . . .") There are a substantial number of *vitae* that specify that the sister entered the cloister before the age of 5. Out of the 219 *vitae* in the convent chronicles there are 58 that indicate that the sister entered before the age of 12.

63. See Michael Baxandall's *Patterns of Intention: On the Historical Explanation of Pictures* (New Haven: Yale University Press, 1985), especially chapter four where he discusses this question.

Bibliography

Ancelet-Hustache, Jean, ed. "Les *Vitae Sororum* d'Unterlinden." *Archives d'Historie Doctrinale et Littéraire du Moyen Age* 5 (1931): 317–517.

Atkinson, Clarissa W. *The Oldest Vocation: Christian Motherhood in the Middle Ages.* Ithaca, NY: Cornell University Press, 1991.

Austin, John L. *How to Do Things with Words.* Cambridge: Harvard University Press, 1962.

Bauman, Richard. *Verbal Art as Performance.* Prospect Park, IL: Waveland Press, 1984.

Baxandall, Michael. *Patterns of Intention: On the Historical Explanation of Pictures.* New Haven: Yale University Press, 1985.

Bell, Catherine. *Ritual Theory, Ritual Practice.* Oxford: Oxford University Press, 1992.

Berthold, Louise. "Die Kindelwiegenspiele," *Beiträge zur Geschicte der deutschen Sprache und Literatur* 56 (1932).

Birlinger, Anton, ed. "Die Nonnen von Kirchberg bei Haigerloch." *Alemannia* 11 (1883): 10–20.

———. "Die Nonnen von St. Katharinenthal bei Diessenhofen."*Alemannia* 15 (1887): 150–183.

Blank, Walter. "Dominikanische Frauenmystik und die Entstehung des Andachtsbildes um 1300," *Alemannisches Jahrbuch.* 1964, 57–87.

Bugge, John. *Virginitas: An Essay in the History of an Ideal.* The Hague: Nijhoff, 1975.

Burke, P. "L'Histoire sociale des rêves," *Annales* 28 (1973): 223–234.

Bynum, Caroline Walker. *Holy Feast and Holy Fast.* Berkeley: University of California Press, 1987.

Clifford, James, and George Marcus. *Writing Culture: The Poetics and Politics of Ethnography.* Berkeley: University of California Press, 1986.

Dinzelbacher, Peter. *Vision und Visionliteratur im Mittelalter.* Stuttgart: Hiersmann, 1981.

Drescher, Karl, ed. *Johann Hartlieb's Ueberstetzung des Dialogus Miraculorum von Caesarius von Heisterbach.* Berlin: Weidmann, 1929.

———. *Mittelalterliche Textilien aus Kloster Adelhausen im Augustinermuseum Freiburg.* Adelhausenstiftung Freiburg im Breisgau: Karl Schillinger, 1985, 50–56.

Fisher, Jennifer. "Aesthetic Contingencies: Relational Enactments in Display Culture." Ph. D. Diss., Concordia University, Montreal, Quebec, 1995.

Franck, Sebastian. *Weltbuch.* Tübingen, unedited, 1534.

Freedburg, David. *The Power of Images: Studies in the History and Theory of Response.* Chicago: University of Chicago Press, 1989.

Gehring, Hester. "The Language of Mysticism in South German Dominican Convent Chronicles of the Fourteenth Century." Ph. D. Diss., University of Michigan, 1957.

Goodich, Michael. *Vita Perfecti: The Ideal of Sainthood in the Thirteenth Century.* Stuttgart: Anton Hiersmann, 1982.

Hahn, Karl August, ed. *Der Jüngere Titurel.* Leipzig, 1842.

Hale, Rosemary. "Imitatio Mariae: Motherhood Motifs in Devotional Memoirs." In *Medieval German Literature: Proceedings from the 23rd International Congress on Medieval Studies,* 129–147. Göppingen: Kümmerle, 1989. Reprinted in *Mystics Quarterly* 16 (Dec. 1990): 193–204.

———. "Two Selections from Margaretha Ebner's *Offenbarungen*," *Vox Benedictina* 4 (1987): 320–337.

Hamburger, Jeffrey. *The Rothschild Canticles: Art and Mysticism in Flanders and the Rhineland circa 1300.* New Haven: Yale University Press, 1990.

———. "The Use of Images in the Pastoral Care of Nuns." *Art Bulletin* 71 (1989): 161–82.

———. "The Visual and the Visionary: The Images in Late Medieval Monastic Devotions." *Viator* 20 (1989): 161–182.

Haupt, Moriz, and Edmund Weisser, eds. *Niedhart's Lieder,* 2nd ed. Leipzig: S. Hirzel, 1923.

Hymes, Dell. "Breakthrough into Performance" in *Folk-lore: Performance and Communication,* ed. Dan Ben-Amos and Kenneth Goldstein, 11–74. The Hague: Mouton, 1975.

Janota, Johannes. *Studien zu Funktion und Typus des deutschen geistlichen Liedes im Mittelalter.* Munich: Beck, 1968.

Jedelhauser, C. *Geschichte des Klosters Maria-Medingen.* Leipzig: Vechta, 1936.

Kieckhefer, Richard. *Unquiet Souls: Fourteenth-Century Saints and their Cultural Milieu.* Chicago: University of Chicago Press, 1984.

Klapisch-Zuber, Christine. *Women, Family, and Ritual in Renaissance Italy.* Chicago: University of Chicago Press, 1985.

König, J., ed. "Die Chronik der Anna von Munzingen." *Freiburger Diözesan Archiv* 12 (1980).

Lewis, Gertrud Jaron. *Bibliographie zur deutschen Frauenmystik des Mittelalters* (Berlin: Schmidt, 1989).

———. *By Women, for Women, about Women: The Sister Books of Fourteenth-Century Germany.* Toronto: Pontifical Institute of Medieval Studies, 1996.

MacAllon, John. *Rite, Drama, Festival, Spectacle: Rehearsals Toward a Theory of Cultural Performance.* Philadelphia: Institute for the Study of Human Issues, 1984.

Margaret Ebner: Major Works. Trans. Leonard Hindsley. New York: Paulist Press, 1993.

Martin, Randy. *Performance as Political Act: The Embodied Self.* New York: Bergin and Garvey, 1990.

Miles, Margaret. *Image as Insight: Visual Understanding in Western Christianity and Secular Culture.* Boston: Beacon Press, 1985.

Pfeiffer, Franz, ed. *Deutsche Mystiker des vierzehnten Jahrhunderts,* vol. 1. Göttingen, 1907.

Raitt, Jill, ed. *Christian Spirituality: High Middle Ages and Reformation.* New York: Crossroad, 1987.

Raynor, Alice. *To Act, To Do, To Perform: Drama and the Phenomenology of Action.* Ann Arbor: University of Michigan Press, 1994.

Reinelt, Janelle G., and Joseph R. Roach, eds. *Critical Theory and Performance.* Ann Arbor: University of Michigan Press, 1992.

Rode, Rosemarie. "Studien zu den mittelalterlichen Kind-Jesu-Visionen." Ph.D. Diss., Frankfurt, 1957.

Romuald, Bauerreiss. *Kirchengeschichte Bayerns* 4. St. Ottlilien, 1954.

Schechner, Richard. "From Ritual to Theatre and Back: The Structure/ Process of the Efficacy-Entertainment Dyad." *Educational Theatre Journal* 26 (1974): 455–481.

———. *Performance Theory.* New York: Routledge, 1977.

———. *By Means of Performance: Intercultural Studies of Theatre and Ritual.* Cambridge: Cambridge University Press, 1989.

————. *The Future of Ritual: Writings on Culture and Performance.* New York: Routledge, 1993.

Sciurie, Helga. "Maria-Ecclesia als Mitherrscherin Christi. Zur Funktion des Sponsus-Sponsa Modells in der Bildkunst des 13. Jahrhunderts," in *Maria Abbild oder Vorbild?* ed. Opitz and Röcklein. Tübingen: Diskord, 1990.

Schröder, Karl, ed. "Der Nonnen von Engelthal Büchlein von der Genaden Überlast." *Bibliothek des Litterarischen Vereins in Stuttgart* 108 (1871): 1–44.

Sheingorn, Pamela. *The Passion of Saint Ursula.* Toronto: Peregrina, 1991.

Shilling, A. "Die religiösen und kirchlichen Zustände der ehemaligen Reichsstadt Biberach unmittelbar vor Einführung der Reformation," *Freiburger Diöcesan Archiv,* 19, 1887.

Smart, Ninian. "Understanding Religious Experience." In *Mysticism and Philosophical Analysis,* ed. Stephen Katz. Oxford University Press: New York, 1978.

Strauch, Phillip, ed. *Die Offenbarungen der Adelheide Langmann: Klosterfrau zu Engelthal* (Strassburg,1878).

————. *Margaretha Ebner und Heinrich von Nördlingen: ein Beitrag zur Geschichte der deutschen Mystik.* Freiburg i. Br: Mohr, 1882.

————, ed. *Offenbarungen der Margaretha Ebner* (Freiburg, 1882).

Sullivan, Lawrence. "Sound and Sense: Toward a Hermeneutics of Performance." *History of Religions* 26 (1986): 1–33.

Szarmach, Paul, ed. *An Introduction to the Medieval Mystics.* New York: New York University Press, 1984.

Tambiah, Stanley. "A Performative Approach to Ritual." *Proceedings of the British Academy* 65 (1979): 113–169.

van Engen, John. *Devotio Moderna: Basic Writings* (New York: Paulist Press, 1988).

van Os, Henk. *The Art of Devotion in the Late Middle Ages in Europe.* Princeton, NJ: Princeton University Press, 1994.

Vavra, Elizabeth. "Bildmotiv und Frauenmystik—Funktion und Rezeption." In *Frauenmystik im Mittelalter,* ed. Peter Dinzelbacher and Dieter Bauer. Stuttgart: Schwaben, 1985.

Vetter, Ferdinand, ed. *Das Leben der Schwestern zu Töss beschrieben von Elsbet Stagel* in *Deutsche Texte des Mittelalters,* vil. 6 (Berlin, 1906).

Weinstein, Donald, and Rudolph Bell. *Saints and Society.* Chicago: University of Chicago Press, 1982.

Ziegler, Joanna E. *Sculpture of Compassion: The Pietà and the Beguines in the Southern Low Countries.* Brussels: Brepols, 1992.

Zoepf, Ludwig. *Die Mystikerin Margaretha Ebner.* Beiträge zur Kulturgeschichte des Mittelalters und der Reniassiance, Bd. 16. Leipzig: Teubner, 1914.

CHAPTER NINE

Ritual and Performance in Richard Rolle's Passion Meditation B

William F. Hodapp

Ye that passen by the weye,
Abideth a litel stounde!
Beholdeth, all my felawes,
If any me lik is founde.
To the tree with nailes three
Wol fast I hange bounde;
With a spere all thoru my side,
To min herte is mad a wounde.

[You who pass by the way,
pause a little while!
Behold, all my people,
if anyone like me can be found.
To the tree with nails three
I hang very firmly bound;
with a spear thrust through my side,
to my heart is made a wound.][1]

This eight-line lyric dating from the third quarter of the fourteenth century illustrates a central aspect of late medieval religious culture: devotion to Jesus' Passion and death. In this poem, as in many others like it, the poet creates a dramatic situation in which Jesus, moments before his death, speaks directly to an addressee—the "Ye" who is passing "by the weye"—and invites the addressee to pause and consider his agony.[2] On another level, the poet also creates this situation to encourage his or her contemporary audience members likewise to pause and consider the Passion.

Through a series of present-tense verbs ("abideth," "beholdeth," "hange," "is mad"), the poet imaginatively recovers the scene on Calvary depicted so frequently in late medieval painting and sculpture and draws readers into the dramatic world of the poem, breaking down, if only for "a litel stounde," the barriers of time and space separating the historical event of Jesus' Passion and death from fourteenth-century England.

The poem's dramatic force is further emphasized when we consider how such poetry was typically consumed in the Middle Ages. Medieval people most commonly "read" poetry through the ear, that is, by reciting it aloud either to themselves or to one or more listeners.[3] In such an oral/aural situation, the reader assumes for a moment the poem's subject position while often drawing his or her auditors into the poem's object position through the act of recitation.[4] This practice of oral recitation invites the reader to perform the poem's persona, much like an actor performs a role on stage, by entering into the pattern of behavior inscribed in the poem. The term "perform," here implies a sense of "carrying out" a prescribed action or pattern of behavior, as in "to perform one's duties" on the job or "to perform well" at the Olympics. The term "performance," then, can cover a range of activities, including theater, dance, music, sport, ritual, and work. As Richard Schechner and Willa Appel suggest, performance often fosters transformation of being or consciousness, whereby the performer and sometimes spectators are "changed by means of performance," either permanently, as in initiation ritual, or temporarily, as in theater.[5]

In the case of "Ye that passen by the weye," the reader and his or her audience are momentarily transformed through performance into the roles of Jesus and his contemporaries. As the present-tense verbs break down time-space barriers, the poem evokes a meditative pause, during which Jesus' Passion becomes immediate and present for those who enter and participate in the poem's dramatic world. The use of present-tense verbs to break down time-space barriers through performance, so evident in this poem, provides a key element for approaching other medieval devotional texts as well.

Like this poet and other medieval artists and writers, the fourteenth-century English mystic Richard Rolle (ca. 1300–1349) attended to Jesus' Passion in his own writings. Critics and scholars have long ascribed two Middle English Passion meditations to Rolle: what editors have come to call Meditation A and Meditation B. Meditation A, surviving in one manuscript with a fragment in another,[6] is a rather straightforward text in which Rolle delineates how one is to meditate. Taking the life of Christ from conception to Ascension as his subject, but focusing primarily on the

Passion, Rolle instructs his audience in the steps one should follow to meditate well on Christ's life. In Meditation B, on the other hand, which survives in five manuscripts and in two versions, often distinguished as the Short Meditation and the Long Meditation,[7] Rolle presents not a series of steps—a didactic "how to meditate" manual, of sorts—but a series of devotional prayers. Through these prayers, which focus solely on the Passion and death of Jesus, Rolle invites users of his text to perform a meditation that potentially could transform their spiritual lives. Much like readers of the lyric "Ye that passen by the weye," readers of Meditation B participate in the scenes presented before what Rolle calls their "eye of the heart" as they proceed through the text. Performing this meditation can lead meditators to satisfy to a degree the desire Julian of Norwich was also to articulate within 25 years of Rolle's death: the desire "to suffer with [Jesus] as others who loved him did"; the desire to "have been one of them" present with Christ on Calvary.[8]

In the past, critics of Rolle's Passion meditations have tended to treat Meditation A and Meditation B as indistinct by focusing on their conventions and possible sources and on their possible function as exercises for novices in the spiritual life.[9] While illuminating and important, especially for understanding Meditation A, this work has generally diffused the importance of Meditation B as a devotional text; as a result, critics have yet to address the performative and transformative aspects so central to Meditation B's devotional force. By examining these aspects of the text in light of notions of ritual, I wish here to build on an earlier discussion in which I argued that Meditation B had a significant purpose in Rolle's scheme of the spiritual life.[10] In particular, the concepts of sacred time, space, and story as they pertain to medieval liturgy provide a theoretical foundation from which to understand ritual in Meditation B. This discussion allows us, then, to explore relations between Meditation B and other ritual-devotional phenomena in late medieval culture, particularly the popular devotional exercise known as the *via crucis* and the Passion sequence in vernacular drama. Finally, this discussion provides a context for revisiting the place of such meditations in Rolle's scheme of the spiritual life and the text's potential transformative effect.

I

Assumptions about rituals in general will underlie and shape any discussion of religious rituals in particular. By way of definition here, then, we can say that rituals in general are structured acts people perform in particular situations to affect a desired result. When used together, two important terms in this definition, "structured acts" and "perform," imply a pattern of activity, in which an individual or group behaves in a more or less prescribed manner. The third term, "desired result," suggests a degree of intentionality underlying this pattern of activity. As Richard Schechner observes, the intention of ritual is primarily to be efficacious.[11] Further, when considering these formal actions and their various functions in human life, we can posit a distinction (for the sake of illustration) between personal and communal rituals. Personal rituals, established and given meaning by individuals, become formalized through repetition, for instance, the customary morning ritual many follow in commencing the day (some individuals would not consider putting on their right shoe before their left). As with the "arming of the hero" ritual depicted in epic and romance, the desired result is often to prepare to face both the physical and mental challenges of the day. Similarly, communal rituals, established and given meaning by a group and/or a decree from an authority figure, also become formalized through repetition, for example, the customary performance in the United States of the national anthem prior to athletic events. The desired result of this ritual, presumably, is both to cultivate a sense of unity among those present and to signal the beginning of the event.[12]

When we turn to the context of religious cultures and communities, we can further define certain rituals, whether personal or communal, in terms of the sacred as it relates to three elements: space, time, and story. According to Mircea Eliade, the sacred is that which pertains to the divine as revealed in the midst of a chaotic world; the profane, in contrast, is that which pertains to nondivine, or what he calls "secular," aspects of life.[13] In Eliade's model of religious culture, the divine manifests itself in time by way of a direct revelation, or what he calls a hierophany and others call a theophany, by which it transforms the quality of a given historical time and place from profane and chaotic to sacred and ordered.[14] Through formal recitation or enactment of sacred stories that recount or repeat the hierophanic act, religious people commemorate, recover, or even participate in the sacred time and space of the hierophanies.[15] As Eliade notes: "Every ritual has the character of happening *now*, at this very moment. The time of the event that the ritual commemorates or re-enacts is made *present*, 're-presented,' so to speak, however far back it may have been in ordinary reckoning."[16] Within the framework of the terms discussed earlier, the desired results of such religious ritual, as Schechner observes, "are achieved by appealing to a transcendent Other (who puts in an appearance either in person or by surrogate)."[17]

Though he approaches religious ritual synchronically rather than diachronically (hence the critique that his approach tends to be static), Eliade's theory of ritual provides conceptual tools useful for understanding space, time, and story as they pertain to hierophanies and rituals in Jewish and Christian cultures.[18] One hierophany in the Jewish tradition, for instance, was the series of plagues God visited upon Egypt prior to the Hebrew exodus. To help the Hebrews avoid the tenth plague, the slaying of the first born (Exodus 11–12:20), God spoke directly to Moses and Aaron, detailing what the Hebrews were to eat and how they were to dress and behave. God also directly established the Feast of the Passover, saying "This day shall be to you one of remembrance: you shall celebrate it as a festival to the LORD throughout the ages; you shall celebrate it as an institution for all time" (Exodus 12:14).[19] Thus, in subsequent Passover celebrations, people have commemorated, even "re-presented," to use Eliade's term, the sacred time and space of the first Passover through ritual repetition of the meal and story.

During the Christian Middle Ages, the three elements of religious ritual—space, time, and story—found their most prominent expression in the liturgical and sacramental life of the Church.[20] Praying the *Horae*, or Liturgy of the Hours, for instance, was in part an effort to sanctify different moments in the day through recitation of psalms, canticles, prayers, and Scripture readings.[21] In the high to late Middle Ages, with the advent of individual recitation and rise in lay devotions, praying some form of the hours became quite popular beyond monastery walls and cathedral choirs. Part I of the thirteenth-century Middle English text *Ancrene Wisse*, for instance, details a liturgical day in the life of an anchoress, complete with hours and rubrics for gestures and movement.[22] Similarly, participating in the liturgical calendar was in part an effort to consecrate the year by celebrating as memorials various seasons and feast days important to salvation history. For instance, Advent, the penitential season preceding Christmas, commemorated the Hebrews' long wait for the Messiah, and the Annunciation, a Marian feast day, commemorated the angel Gabriel's visit to Mary, announcing she was to be the mother of Jesus.[23]

In addition to sanctifying the day and the year, the medieval Church sought to sanctify individual Christians' lives by incorporating them into what St. Paul called the "mystical Body of Christ" (1 Cor. 12:12–31) through the liturgical rites of the sacraments. In these rituals, the Church in part sought to recover the sacred time and space of their foundings, their hierophanies, by reciting set prayers and scriptures and by performing specific actions: the very "actions and words which the Lord has himself laid down," as Dom Odo Casel observes.[24] Thus, in baptism, for instance, the primary rite of initiation, Christians made present the moments of Jesus' own baptism in the Jordan and of his later command to baptize all peoples.[25] As Eliade observes, "when a Christian . . . participates in liturgical time, he recovers the *illud tempus* in which Christ lived, suffered, and rose again . . . the time when Pontius Pilate governed Judaea."[26]

The center of liturgical life for medieval Christians was, of course, the Eucharist, which Jesus instituted through his hierophanic acts at the Last Supper and on Calvary. And, as remains the case in the Roman Catholic Mass today, the central focus of the medieval Eucharistic liturgy was the Canon, which included the ritual words and gestures of consecration, whereby bread and wine were transformed into the Body and Blood of Christ.[27] Concerning the Canon, Joseph Jungmann notes that "The heart of the process is renewed at this very instant [that is, consecration]. The narrative of what once took place passes into the actuality of the present happening. . . . In the person of the priest, Christ Himself stands at the altar, and picks up the bread, and lifts up 'this goodly chalice' . . . it is Christ Himself who is now active."[28] Every time a priest, as *persona Christi,* performed the ritual words and actions of consecration in the Mass, he recovered the sacred space and time of the Last Supper and Calvary. This understanding of the Mass formed the core of high to late medieval Eucharistic theology: St. Bonaventure, for example, observed that Christ, who offered himself in the Passion on earth, now intercedes for the faithful in heaven and is offered anew in the Mass.[29]

While this theory of religious ritual sheds light on the late medieval liturgical and sacramental life of the Church, it also illuminates an impulse underlying many late medieval devotional practices and prayers. As I have discussed elsewhere, meditation on Jesus' life was a core spiritual and devotional exercise in the high to late Middle Ages.[30] Based on *lectio divina* (that is, the practice of reading Scripture and spiritual writings as a preliminary to meditation and prayer), the Liturgy of the Hours, and the Mass itself, such meditation found expression in various forms, from artistic and iconographic renderings of biblical and apocryphal scenes of the Passion upon which one could meditate, to devotional drama, poetry, and prose in both vernacular and Latin intended for personal and communal use. Many of these devotional texts invite what I shall call here a ritual-devotional performance. Like the ritual of the liturgy, devotional texts, such as the lyric "Ye that passen by the weye," seek in part to recover and make present through performance the sacred time and space of events from Jesus' life. Rolle's Meditation B, as both an expression of his own devotion to the Passion and a script, if you will, for others to use in meditation, provides an instance of the kind of ritual-devotional exercise that grew out of the liturgical and sacramental life of the Church and became so popular in the high to late Middle Ages.[31]

II

The manuscripts suggest Rolle composed at least some of his English writings for women he served as spiritual director—a function he clearly approached with care.[32] As Nicholas Watson observes, the level of intimacy these writings evoke indicates Rolle's personal concern for his readers.[33] Yet, as Rosamund Allen notes, his choice of English instead of Anglo-Norman, which he most likely knew as well, suggests he was also hoping to reach as wide an audience as possible.[34] If Allen is correct, Rolle did not succeed in achieving wide readership until after his death. Fundamentally pastoral in nature, the English texts include, in addition to the meditations, a *Psalter and Commentary*, three epistles (*Ego Dormio, The Commandment,* and *The Form of Living*), and various short texts and lyrics. Although his English writings seem to be occasional texts written near the end of his life for a narrowly defined audience, they were widely read by religious and laity, male and female, after his death, and they helped contribute to his broad popularity in England from the second half of the fourteenth through the fifteenth and well into the sixteenth centuries.[35] Indeed, Rolle's post-mortem popularity became so widespread that, in anticipation of his canonization, an *Officium et miracula* of lessons and antiphons was written in the 1380s. Though never canonized, Rolle's cult flourished for nearly 200 years, especially in his native Yorkshire, and his writings, both Latin and English, influenced and shaped the spiritual development of many Englishwomen and Englishmen.[36]

The structure, content, and meditative movement of Meditation B suggests that Rolle intended the text for ritual-devotional performance. Rolle composed Meditation B as a series of 37 devotional prayers, the organization of which falls into four parts: a prologue of 5 petitionary prayers (1–30), a series of 29 meditative prayers (31–490), an *imitatio* exercise (491–530), and 2 concluding meditative prayers (531–60). In the first 4 prayers of the prologue, Rolle expresses gratitude in turn for various gifts from God (intellectual, emotional, physical, and spiritual) and asks for grace to use them wisely in God's service. He concludes the prologue with a fifth prayer in which he emphasizes the Incarnation and Passion, addressing Jesus as the Lord "þat lyghted fro heuyn to erth for loue of mankynd" [who descended from heaven to earth for love of humankind] (24) and requesting mercy and help from Jesus, "for al þy loue þat þou shewedist to mankynd in þyn incarnacioun and in þy passioun" [because of all your love, which you showed to humankind in your incarnation and in your passion] (28–9). In turning his attention to the Incarnation and Passion in this final prayer of the prologue, Rolle establishes two key themes explored in the second part of the text: the series of 29 meditative prayers that constitute the main section of Meditation B. In each prayer of this series, Rolle implicitly explores the mystery of the Incarnation, that God became a man, by explicitly centering on an event or aspect of the Passion, for which he expresses gratitude, followed by a petition for the necessary grace to integrate the event or aspect into his life. This pattern remains unbroken until the end of the twenty-ninth prayer, which does not conclude with a petition. Rather, the meditation moves into the thirtieth prayer, the *imitatio* exercise that constitutes the third part of the text. In the fourth part, then, Rolle offers two meditative prayers on Christ's last words before concluding with a final petition to Mary that he might "hold þis passion in mynd as hertely, as studiously, in al my lif, as þou, lady, and Iohn hadden in mynd when þe peple was gone, and ye abiden stil by þe rode fote" [hold this passion in mind as heartily and as studiously, throughout my life, as you, lady, and John had held it in mind after the people had left and you still stood by the foot of the cross] (557–9).

An additional structural feature of the text further emphasizes the ritual-devotional movement Rolle inscribed in it. Rolle punctuates each of the meditative prayers, except the final one, with a series of prayers in Latin: the Lord's Prayer, the Hail Mary, and excerpts from Matins in the York Hours of the Cross. These excerpts include the Versus, "Adoramus te Christe et benedicimus tibi" [we adore you, O Christ, and we bless you], and its Responsus, "Quia per sanctam crucem tuam redemisti mundum" [because through your holy cross you have redeemed the world], as well as the prayer "Domine Jesu Christe."[37] Rolle's use of these excerpts from the York *Horae crucis*, which was composed early in the fourteenth century, indicates his awareness of this devotional exercise and suggests a close relationship between Meditation B and the Divine Office.[38] Further, because of their antiphonal nature, these prayers indicate Rolle may have intended his text for multiple uses. For instance, whether used communally or personally, the text invites an extraliturgical performance, perhaps as a devotional supplement to the Divine Office, much like St. Francis of Assisi's *Office of the Passion* and parts of pseudo-Bonaventure's *Meditationes vita Christi*,[39]or as a devotional exercise entirely independent from the Divine Office. In any case, as these liturgical prayers punctuate the meditative prayers proper, thereby evoking a pause between each, they underscore the performative impulses of the text: a ritual-devotional performance that could be conducted either communally or personally.

With Meditation B, then, Rolle provides a series of prayers in which he inscribes a petitioner persona. Like others who compose prayers, including Jesus himself with the Lord's Prayer, Rolle articulates an "I/Thou" relationship in the text and invites his readers, at least those who will use the text as intended, to appropriate his language and enter a monologue with Jesus. When the meditator, for instance, devoutly reads the first line or two of the text—"Lord, as þou made me of noght, I beseche þe, yeue me grace to serue þe with al my hert" [Lord, as you created me from nothing, I beseech you, give me grace to serve you with all my heart]— he or she enters the subject position of the discourse, the "I," and addresses the object of the discourse, the "Thou" (that is, Jesus).[40] With this grammatical construction, Rolle invites the meditator to perform the text, that is, to take on the role of petitioner and carry out this petitioner's pattern of behavior as inscribed in the text. In developing this "I/Thou" discourse, Rolle offers an exercise in which the meditator imaginatively witnesses the events of the Passion through a dramatic monologue with Jesus. In a sense, while the poet of "Ye that passen by the weye" gives voice to Jesus on the cross, Rolle gives voice to the observer of the Passion: to the one who passes by the way.

The sacred story Rolle recounts in Meditation B follows the outline of events the Church celebrated liturgically each year during the first two days of the triduum. Like other medieval writers and artists who imaginatively recount the Passion, Rolle harmonizes the gospel accounts and, in the 32 prayers that make up the body and conclusion of Meditation B, recounts nine events of the Passion: Jesus' prayer in Gethsemane, the arrest, the trial, the buffeting, the scourging, the crowning with thorns, the carrying of the cross, the crucifixion, and the death. In an effort to heighten appreciation for Jesus' humanity, Rolle amplifies these scenes, based on the sparse gospel narratives, with specific, imaginative details of Jesus' physical and emotional sufferings.[41]

Rolle's tone and style as he recounts these events underscores the ritual-devotional movement he inscribed in the text. Initially, his tone is

quite reserved. In the third prayer, for instance, he writes: "I thank þe as
I can of al þat ferdnesse and angwishe þat þou suffred for vs when an
angel of heuyn come to comfort þe, and when þou swettest blode for
anguysshe" [I thank you as much as I am able for all the terror and anguish
you suffered for us when an angel of heaven came to comfort you, and
when you sweat blood in agony] (61–3). As the events become more
physical, however, Rolle's tone and style becomes increasingly emotional,
gradually drawing meditators into an affective imaginative involvement
with specific Passion events. In describing the scourging in the fifteenth
prayer, for example, Rolle writes:

> þat was a bittyr peyne. For þe to scourgen weren [chosen men þat
> weren] stronge and stalwarth and willy to slee þe, and hit was longe
> or þey was wery, and þe scourges weren made ful stronge and smert,
> so þat al þy body was bot woundes, and woundes in oon wou[n]de,
> for þe knottes smytten oft in oon place, and at euch strok smot hit þe
> deppyr.

> [That was a bitter pain. For to scourge you men were chosen who
> were strong and stalwart and eager to kill you, and it was a long time
> before they were weary; and the whips were made very strong and
> stinging, so that all your body was nothing but wounds, and many
> wounds on one wound because the knots struck often in one place,
> and at each stroke they smote you deeper.] (189–94)

Rolle's graphic, imaginative description of this scene heightens the meditator's devotional response to Jesus' physical suffering so that, with Rolle,
the meditator can exclaim "And þat was, swet Ihesu, a large yift and a
plenteuous she[w]ynge of þy loue" [And that was, sweet Jesus, a generous
gift and an abundant revelation of your love] (194–5).

As the events increasingly focus on Jesus' physical and emotional
agony, the latter especially when he sees his mother, the devotional movement of the text becomes more urgent, strident, tense, and immediate.
When he focuses on the crucifixion in the twenty-fifth and twenty-sixth
prayers, for instance, Rolle first describes the nailing process in much the
same manner as the scourging, saying:

> þe cros was cast doun on þe ground, and þey leid þe flatte þeron,
> and with cordes drow þy hondes and fete to þe holys, and nayled
> first þat oon hand, and streyned þat oþer to þe oþer hole, and þan

drowen alle þy body, swet Ihesu, doun, to þe holys raght þy fete, and þe naylles, lord, weren blont, for þey shold terre þe skyn and bruys þe fleishe.

[the cross was thrown down on the ground, and they laid you flat upon it and with ropes drew your hands and feet to the holes, and nailed first that one hand, and stretched the second to the other hole, and then drew your body, sweet Jesus, down to the holes near your feet, and the nails, Lord, were blunt so they would tear your skin and bruise your flesh.] (372–7)

Again, the graphic detailed image of the nailing process presented here increases emotions and elicits an imaginative devotional response to Jesus' human suffering. It also sets up the meditator for a more immediate, participatory meditation of the scene, which follows the frenetic activity described above. Rolle writes:

Now, swete Ihesu, me þynketh I se þy body on þe rode al blody, and streyned þat þe ioyntes twynnen; þe woundes now opyn, þy skyn al to-drawen recheth so brode, þy hede corowned with þornes, þy body al woundes, nailles in þy handes and fete so tendyr, and in þe synwes þer as is most peynful felynge. þer is no lennynge for þy hede; þy body is streyned as a parchemyn skyn vpon a rake; þy face is bolned þat first was so fayre; þy ioyntes vndone; þou stondest and hongest on nayllys; stremes of blode ren doun by þe rode; þe syзt of þy modyr encresceth þy peyne.

[Now, sweet Jesus, it seems to me I see your body on the cross, so bloody and strained that your joints burst; your wounds now open, your skin all stretched reaches so widely, your head is crowned with thorns, your body is all wounds, nails are in your hands and feet so tender, and in your sinews there is a most excruciating pain. There is no place to rest your head; your body is strained like a parchment skin on a rack; your face is swollen that once was so fair; your joints are separating; you stand and hang on nails; streams of blood run down the cross; the sight of your mother increases your pain.] (377–81)

In this passage, Rolle's shift into the present tense creates an immediate experience of the event: meditators who perform Rolle's text by entering imaginatively into the petitioner-persona role "see" Jesus' body wracked in excruciating pain and feel the mental and emotional strain between Jesus and his mother. Indeed, the shift to present-tense verbs draws meditators into a participatory experience, much like the audience of "Ye that passen by the weye." In developing this affective exercise, Rolle seems to be following the advice of the anonymous thirteenth-century Franciscan who wrote *Meditationes vita Christi,* one of the most popular meditation handbooks in the later Middle Ages. In this book, written for a Poor Clare, the author encourages imaginative participation in scriptural events, saying in the prologue, "if you wish to profit [from such meditation] you must be present at the same things that it is related that Christ did and said," and later, in the Passion section, "with your whole mind you must imagine yourself present and consider diligently everything done against your Lord."[42] This type of advice, based in what Anne Clark Bartlett describes as a "pedagogy of participation," became prevalent throughout the late Middle Ages.[43]

The movement of the nailing scene in Meditation B draws meditators into a participatory experience of the Passion. From this immediate experience, the text shifts to a devotional response in which the petitioner persona admits a lack of feeling for the Passion and asks grace for a deeper affective response to it. The prayers following the nailing scene, including the body-jarring raising of the cross recounted in the twenty-sixth prayer,[44] continue to build emotional tension until the twenty-ninth prayer, which focuses on Jesus' utterance " 'Dere God, whi hast þou forsak me, þat no þynge þou sparest me?' " [Dear God, why have you forsaken me, that you spare nothing from me?] (478–9). Seeing Jesus wholly abandoned, Rolle writes:

Þer is no bodily peyne lyke þyne. . . . þe fadyr son of heuyn betwix two theues, and amyd al þe world, for al men [shold] hit witte, and on þe hegh holy day when al men comyn to þe cite, and so hit was no priue shame. Þou henge al naked, þy skyn al to-rente, euch lyth from other, with cordes drawen, coroned with þornes, woundes wyde, many and grisly.

[There is no physical pain like yours. . . . the son of the heavenly father hangs between two thieves, and at the midpoint of all the world, so that all men should know of it; and on the high holy day when everyone came to the city; and so it was not a private shame. You hang entirely naked, your skin torn to shreds, each limb drawn

from the others with ropes, crowned with thorns, wounds gaping,
many and gruesome.] (480–6)

In this passage, Rolle meditates on the paradox of the Incarnation, the
theme first introduced in the prologue: Jesus, the God-man, wholly abandoned and in extreme physical agony, is dying. The text's emotional tension, expressed particularly in the present-tense verbs, seems intended to
create a desire for fuller participation in the Passion through a deeper
affective response. The meditative movement culminating in this scene
prepares the meditator to enter into the *imitatio* exercise that immediately
follows it.

As I have discussed elsewhere,[45] this *imitatio* exercise (491–530),
which constitutes the thirtieth prayer, is the climax of the text's devotional
movement. In the exercise, Rolle because of his sinfulness first identifies
with those guilty of crucifying Jesus. Imaginatively prostrating himself at
the foot of the cross, he embraces it and bathes in Christ's blood of mercy
before expressing a desire for a fuller share in the Passion. Feeling unworthy, however, to stand with Mary and John, he identifies with the repentant thief, saying "I hold me worþy for my gret trespas to honge besyde
þe as oon of þe þefes" [I consider myself worthy, because of my great sins,
to hang beside you as one of the thieves] (519–20). Imaginatively posi-
tioning himself on a cross next to Jesus, Rolle imitates the repentant thief,
begging for forgiveness.[46] Meditators who perform the text, who follow
Rolle's lead and enter into the "I/Thou" discourse of the meditative prayers,
also imaginatively imitate the thief whose only recourse is to beg forgiveness. Moreover, like Jesus, who in the meditation empties himself completely in a most horrible and humiliating death, meditators also empty
themselves on a cross. Through this *imitatio* exercise, Rolle leads meditators
to renounce the world by imaginatively embracing the agony of the cross.

In seeking to heighten devotional response to Jesus' Passion and
death through the meditative movement leading to this *imitatio* exercise,
Rolle inscribes a ritual-devotional impulse in the text: an impulse most
clearly evident in the text's implied performance. As the meditator reads
the text, he or she prayerfully considers, and at times imaginatively participates in, the events of the Passion by performing the petitioner-persona
role. Through recounting the sacred story of Christ's Passion, the meditator recovers its sacred time and space—no longer historically or
geographically remote, the events of the Passion become immediate
through the ritual repetition of the story. Again, in Julian of Norwich's

words, the meditator becomes "one of them" present with Christ on Calvary. Thus, as with the performance of liturgical and sacramental rites, the devout ritual performance of Meditation B could potentially transform the spiritual lives of meditators. As a ritual-devotional text that invites performance, Meditation B is closely aligned, at least in spirit, with other ritual-devotional phenomena from the late Middle Ages, in particular, the spiritual pilgrimage exercise known as *via crucis* and the Yorkshire vernacular drama, both of which developed and became quite popular in the fourteenth, fifteenth, and sixteenth centuries.

III

As readers of Meditation B ritually recover to a degree the sacred time and space of Christ's Passion through recitation of the sacred story, they also make a spiritual pilgrimage to Calvary and, in a sense, to other holy places of Jerusalem. One of the three most important pilgrimage sites in the Middle Ages, the other two being Rome and Santiago de Compostella, Jerusalem had long been a destination for pious Christians who venerated various holy sites, including Calvary, the Holy Sepulchre, Gethsemane, and others. Such visits commenced during the patristic period: the fourth-century pilgrim Egeria, for instance, who left a record of her visit to the Holy Land (ca. 380), describes her experiences at numerous holy sites, including some rather interesting and important details of the liturgies conducted at the sites.[47] Most significantly for this discussion, her text reveals that the character of this liturgy was stational, that is, the liturgical action involved movement to several holy places in and around Jerusalem.[48] Visits to the Holy Land such as Egeria's continued intermittently throughout the Middle Ages and, by the fourteenth century, the Franciscans (who had charge of many holy places in Jerusalem) had reinstituted liturgical and devotional processions from site to site, beginning and ending at the Church of the Holy Sepulchre.[49] This Holy Circulus, as it was called, included what became known as the *via dolorosa* or *via crucis*. The desire to pilgrimage to Jerusalem was strong for pious Christians but, unlike Egeria in the fourth century or Margery Kempe in the fifteenth, many were unable to make the journey. This desire, coupled with devotion to Jesus' humanity, contributed in part to the rise of devotion to the Passion. If people could not make an actual pilgrimage to Jerusalem, or if they wished to recapture their pilgrim experiences after returning home, they could imaginatively make a spiritual journey to Jerusalem, and texts like Meditation B provided the means for conducting such a spiritual pilgrimage.

While it is apparent that the *via crucis*, or Stations of the Cross, of modern times came into its present form of 14 stations much later than the early to mid-fourteenth century, the impulse for this devotion, that in part seeks to recover the steps Christ took to his death, reaches back to the earliest pilgrims to the Holy Land. When high to late medieval Christology began to emphasize Jesus' human suffering more than his triumphant resurrection, the impulse to follow in his footsteps was further nurtured. Rolle's contemporary, the Rhineland Dominican and mystic Henry Suso, with whom Rolle is often compared,[50] provides an interesting perspective on the centrality of the Passion to late medieval devotion and a provocative insight into the development of devotional exercises such as the *via crucis*. In chapter 13 of his spiritual autobiography, *Vita servi*, Suso describes in the third person how, following Matins, he frequently accompanied Christ on his "way of the Cross," thereby replicating the holy places of Jerusalem.[51] Designating the chapter room, cloister walk, and chapel as different holy places, Suso would move through his friary reciting psalms, hymns, and Scripture readings from Holy Week liturgies and performing actions to symbolize various events from the Passion. He writes, for instance:

> When he came to the fourth path [of the cloister walk], he knelt down in the middle as though he were kneeling in front of the gate through which Christ would have to go out. Falling down in front of him, he kissed the ground, calling upon him and asking him not to go to his death without him, and that he let him go along because he had a right to go along. He imagined all this to himself as vividly as he could, and he spoke the prayer *"Ave rex noster, fili David,"* etc. and let Christ lead the way. (85)

He then imagines meeting Mary, for whom he offers a *Salve Regina* before, as he states, "he got up quickly and strode after his Lord to catch up to him" (85). Moving into the chapel and up to the choir, then, he concludes his exercise, saying:

> When he came beneath the cross, where he had once experienced the hundred thoughts on the passion, he knelt to watch his Lord being stripped of his clothing and nailed to the cross. Then he took the discipline and with heartfelt agony nailed himself on the cross

> with his Lord, begging him that neither life nor death, joy nor sorrow
> be able to separate his servant from him. (85)

To conform himself to Jesus, Suso performed this meditation with words
and movement and, as he observes, his "imagining was sometimes very
vivid, just as if he were really walking at [Jesus'] side" (85). Through ritual
performance of, and affective engagement with, the sacred story of Christ's
Passion, Suso recovered and "re-presented" in his interior life the sacred
time and space of Jesus' way of the cross. That this exercise played an
important role in Suso's mystical life is evident from his allusion in the
passage above to the "hundred thoughts on the passion." These "hundred
thoughts" formed the core of Suso's most popular work, *Horologium sapientiae,*
and, as he details in his prologue to that text, they came to him as he
stood before the cross after performing this exercise (207).

While the text itself does not indicate definitively that praying Meditation B in the fourteenth century entailed proceeding through a designated space like Suso did, or like the later developed Stations of the Cross
encouraged, the text's structure and its later consumption indicates such
movement was possible. The Latin prayers Rolle uses to punctuate the
meditative prayers, for instance, suggest both meditative pause and ritual
movement. These prayers, especially the *Versus* and *Responsus,* have long
been part of Stations of the Cross exercises and are often recited while
moving from one station to the next. Moreover, even if Rolle may not
have intended movement through a designated space, at least one reader
of Meditation B saw such movement as possible when he or she edited
and adapted Rolle's text earlier this century for use in a modern Stations
of the Cross manual, complete with the Latin prayers and the *imitatio* exercise.[52] Of course, claiming that a fourteenth-century writer intended a
certain use of a text based on later developments in devotional practices,
or even on later uses of the given text, is anachronistic at best, and I do
not wish to make such a claim about Rolle or Meditation B. However, this
later evidence, in conjunction with what we know about medieval stational
liturgy and devotional prayer, suggests movement to or through a designated space while praying Meditation B was possible.[53] Regardless, the
ritual and devotional performance the text calls forth—whether personal,
like Suso's, or communal, like the devotional ritual practiced by pilgrims
in the Holy Land—provided devout meditators an opportunity to make a
spiritual pilgrimage to Jerusalem, as Rolle suggests in the first meditative
prayer.[54] He writes: "I thank þe, lord, with al my hert for þou profered þe
to þat place where þou wist þy deth ordeyned" [I thank you, lord, with

all my heart because you offered yourself to that place where you knew your death was ordained] (31–2). In addition to thanking Jesus, this prayer orients meditators to Jerusalem ("þat place") as a devotional space, and it prepares them for the subsequent meditations on the Passion.

In addition to the spiritual pilgrimage of the *via crucis*, vernacular drama also provides an illuminating touchstone for understanding Rolle's text in relation to late medieval devotional practices.[55] At the same time that we see the spread in England of devotional texts such as Meditation B, we also see the development of the vernacular cycle dramas, which depict various biblical scenes from Creation to Judgment Day. This drama had the potential to transform spiritually its players and audience: a transformative potential most evident in the ritual-devotional impulse underlying its performance. Much like the liturgy itself, and ritual-devotional exercises like Meditation B, this vernacular drama sought to recover, at least to a degree, the sacred time and space of events in salvation history through enacting sacred stories.

When we turn particularly to plays recounting the events of Holy Week, we find an effort to break down time-space barriers between the events of the sacred stories and the lives of late medieval audiences that is similar to the effort we have seen in "Ye that passen by the weye," Suso's *via crucis*, and Meditation B. Indeed, to varying degrees, performance of certain plays invites audience members to enter into the scene presented before them, moving from simple observers to active participants in the play. As we have the text today, the Passion sequence from the York cycle, which was being acted in some form possibly as early as 25 years after Rolle died,[56] encompasses 12 plays, ranging in length from approximately 200 to 548 lines.[57] The sequence begins with a play dramatizing Jesus' entry into Jerusalem, during which Jesus heals a blind man (288–357), heals a lame man (358–91), and encounters Zacchaeus (392–460), all of which seem to be acted at street level among the audience. As Jesus moves through the audience toward the pageant wagon, on which eight burgesses of the city stand ready to greet him, the audience is drawn into the play and becomes the throng welcoming Jesus to Jerusalem: the dramatic time of the play displaces for a moment the ordinary time of the Corpus Christi feast day, and the audience is imaginatively transported through the performance to Jerusalem at the time of Christ. The play ends with the eight burgesses welcoming Jesus with a litany of "Hayll" invocations that echo, and perhaps are modeled on, the "Ave" invocations from the Palm Sunday processional medieval Christians celebrated liturgically each year at the beginning of Holy Week.[58]

Indeed, this movement in the play mirrors the devotional effect of the Palm Sunday processional. During these communal rituals, which were reminiscent of the stational liturgy at Jerusalem, parishioners typically processed through a series of stations, moving through the west entrance of the church building to the Palm Cross, located in the churchyard, then around the east end of the church to the south side of the churchyard, and finally back into the west entrance of the church and up to the rood screen, all the while singing psalms and hymns recounting Jesus' entry into Jerusalem.[59] As Margery Kempe attests, the Palm Sunday processional at times called forth a profound devotional response from the congregation.[60] Similarly, the York *Entry into Jerusalem* calls forth a response that, again, draws the audience into a communal devotional experience, a ritual experience they would find familiar because of the liturgy.[61]

Like Rolle's Meditation B, the York Passion sequence follows fairly closely the chronology of Holy Week events. The *Crucifixion*, in particular, provides an interesting corollary to Rolle's text because the play stages with a darkly comic effect many of the imaginative details Rolle uses in the twenty-fifth and twenty-sixth prayers of his text to amplify the nailing scene and the raising of the cross. While we cannot posit a direct influence of Rolle on the playwright, especially because many of these details became ubiquitous in fifteenth-century English devotional literature, the play evinces a ritual-devotional impulse similar to that inscribed in Meditation B. Together, the nailing scene and the raising of the cross form the central action of the play. In the nailing scene (73–144), for instance, the soldiers are comically inept in spite of their frequent boasts of prowess. Finding that the holes bored for nailing were set incorrectly, they use ropes to stretch Jesus to fit the holes, then they nail him to the cross and pause to marvel their handiwork, saying:

I Miles	Ther cordis haue evill encressed his paynes,
	Or he wer tille þe booryngis brought.
II Miles	3aa, assoundir are bothe synnous and veynis
	On ilke a side, so haue we soughte
[1 Soldier:	The ropes have wickedly increased his pains
	before he was brought to the borings.
2 Soldier:	Yah, both sinews and veins are burst apart on
	each side, just as we sought.] (145–8)

Their commentary echoes Rolle's comments on the nailing scene, only here they are from the perspective of the torturers admiring their work rather than a devout meditator feeling compassion. While the comedy of this scene seems to distance the audience from the soldiers' activities, the commentary still heightens the audience's awareness of Jesus' physical agony. In the raising of the cross (169–252), too, the soldiers deliberately seek to inflict pain by dropping the cross into a hole, much as in Meditation B, saying:

I Miles: Now raise hym nemely for þe nonys
     And sette hym be þis mortas heere,
     And latte hym falle in alle at ones,
     For certis þat payne schall haue no pere.
III Miles: Heue vppe!
IV Miles: Latte doune, so all his bones
     Are asoundre nowe on sides seere.
I Miles: Þis fallyng was more felle
     Þan all the harmes he hadde.
[1 Soldier: Now raise him quickly for the purpose and set
     him by this mortice here, and let him drop in all
     at once, for certainly that pain will have no
     equal.
3 Soldier: Heave up!
4 Soldier: Let it drop so all his bones now
     burst apart everywhere.
1 Soldier: This falling was more cruel than all the
     harms he had.] (219–26)

Again, even though (and perhaps because) the soldiers so obviously delight in their work, a delight the audience would scarcely find admirable, the commentary serves to heighten the audiences' awareness of Jesus' pain, and it sets up the play's meditative center. Not long after the soldiers raise and set the cross, Jesus, who is primarily silent throughout the play (he does deliver a short speech earlier, lines 49–60) directly addresses the audience, much like in the lyric "Ye that passen by the weye," and says:

Al men þat walkis by waye or strete,   [All people who walk by the road or
                                 street,
Takes tente ȝe schalle no trauayle   take heed, you shall no labor lose.
   tyne.
Byholdes myn heede, myn handis,   Behold my head, my hands, and my
   and my feet,   feet,

And fully feele nowe, or ȝe fyne,	and fully perceive now, before you pass by,
Yf any mournyng may be meete,	if any sorrow may be equal,
Or myscheue mesured vnto myne.	or mischief measured to mine.]
	(253–8)

    Through this brief address, the late medieval audience is drawn into
the play again and becomes the people "þat walkis by waye or strete,"
much as they had earlier become the crowd welcoming Jesus to Jerusalem.
Recounting the sacred story recovers, in a sense, the time and space of
the Passion. The gruesome details of the nailing scene and the raising of
the cross remain dramatically present and immediate as the play's audience
is drawn into a communal devotional response to Jesus' human suffering.
As with Rolle's Meditation B, and the spiritual pilgrimage exercises of the
via crucis, this ritual-devotional engagement with the scenes performed in
the plays provide opportunities for both the audiences and the actors of
the drama to be spiritually transformed as they respond affectively to Jesus'
human suffering.

IV

Devotional texts and spiritual exercises such as the cycle drama and the
via crucis invite people to respond to Jesus' life by participating ritually in
the sacred stories. Such responses could be both personal and communal;
in either case, though, they were rooted in what Gail McMurray Gibson
has described as an "incarnational aesthetic," an aesthetic that emphasized
"a suffering human body racked on a cross."[62] In this emphasis on the
Incarnation, meditation on Christ's life, as mentioned earlier, also played
a significant part in the three stages of the via mystica: purgation, illumi-
nation, and perfective union.[63] Performance of such meditations had the
potential to transform devout meditators so as to prepare them for, perhaps
even lead them to, a unitive mystical experience with the divine. Meditation B, through its ritual impulse, similarly evinces the potential for such
transformation; indeed, as I have argued elsewhere, Meditation B serves a
significant purpose in the via mystica that Rolle develops in his English
writings.
    In the epistles, Rolle presents a three-step path to perfection, moving
from an outward to an inward expression of love through three degrees
that correspond to the three stages of the via mystica. Insuperable love, the

first degree, is outwardly active and encompasses the basic tenets of the Christian faith essential for salvation. According to Rolle, once a person faithfully lives the first degree, he or she can proceed to inseparable love, the second degree: an inwardly active love in which the person renounces worldly attachments, follows Jesus in poverty, and is ever mindful of him. Singular love, the third degree, is an inwardly passive state, in which God's grace enkindles the soul with the fire of Christ's love, the soul finds comfort and consolation only in Jesus, and it is drawn into a unitive experience with the divine. Because it calls for completely emptying the self, singular love is difficult to attain: only a few achieve it.

Like other spiritual writers, Rolle places meditation on Christ's life in the illuminative, or second, stage of the *via mystica*, again what he calls inseparable love.[64] As an expression of inseparable love, meditation on the Passion is a key spiritual exercise in Rolle's path to perfection. In *Ego Dormio*, for instance, immediately following a Passion lyric he incorporates into the text, Rolle writes:

> If þou wil þynke þis [the passion] euery day, þou shalt fynd gret swetnesse, þat shal draw þi hert vp, and mak þe fal in wepynge and in grete langynge to Ihesu; and þi þoght shal be reft abouen al erthly þynges, abouen þe sky and þe sterres, so þat þe egh of þi hert may loke in to heuyn. . . . And þan entres þou in to þe þrid degre of loue, in þe whiche þou shalt be in gret delite and confort, if þou may get grace to cum þerto.
>
> [If you will meditate on the Passion every day, you will find great sweetness that will draw your heart upward, and make you fall in weeping and in great longing for Jesus; and your thought will be lifted above all earthly things, above the sky and the stars, so that the eye of your heart may gaze into heaven. And so you enter into the third degree of love, in which you will be in great delight and comfort, if you but get the grace to come there.] (212–17)

Ritual meditation on the Passion, then, has a transformative effect in Rolle's understanding of the *via mystica*. Through performing such a spiritual exercise "euery day," meditators can transcend "al erthly þynges" and move from the second to "þe þrid degre of loue," that is, to a unitive experience with the divine. This "pedagogy of transcendence," as Bartlett terms it,[65] is evident in Meditation B, as well, for, in leading meditators to an *imitatio* exercise in which they imaginatively imitate Jesus and hang destitute on a cross, ritual-devotional performance of the text can prepare them to receive the necessary grace to "loke in to heuyn" and experience ecstatic union with the divine.

The ritual impulse of Meditation B, in conjunction with its participatory effects, suggests that performance was a central aspect of its devotional force. Like various liturgical rites, Meditation B provides a prayer script in which meditators can enter into a devotional monologue with Jesus and ritually recover and repeat the sacred time and space of his Passion. Similarly, it is a ritual-devotional exercise, much like the *via crucis* and the later developed Stations of the Cross, that enabled meditators to make a spiritual pilgrimage to Jerusalem, thereby imaginatively visiting the sacred spaces of the *via dolorosa* and Calvary. Further, as a ritual-devotional script, it functions much like the later developed cycle drama, for which it provides an illuminating corollary. Finally, Meditation B functions as a spiritual exercise through which it is possible for one to progress on the *via mystica* from the illuminative stage to perfective union. Like the addressee of "Ye that passen by the weye" and the audience of the York *Entry into Jerusalem* and the York *Crucifixion*, among several other plays, meditators who take on the petitionary persona of Meditation B "abideth a litel stounde" with Jesus and "beholdeth" his agony. In this ritual-devotional pause, barriers of time and space between A.D. 33 Jerusalem and late medieval England dissolve, and meditators become "one of them," as Julian says, who were present at the Passion. It is through becoming "one of them," that is, through a ritual performance of the text, that it becomes possible for meditators to be spiritually transformed, even drawn into an ecstatic unitive experience with the divine.

Notes

1. From John Grimstone's *Commonplace Book* (Nat. Lib. of Scotland MS Advocates 18.7.21), in *Middle English Lyrics*, ed. Maxwell S. Luria and Richard L. Hoffman, (New York: Norton, 1974), no. 216, 208. Unless noted otherwise, translations of Middle English and Latin texts in this chapter are mine.

2. The poet bases the poem on Lamentations 1:12, "O vos omnes, qui transitis per viam, attendite, et videte si est dolor sicut dolor meus: quoniam vindemiavit me ut locutus est Dominus in die irae furoris sui" [Oh all you who pass by the way, look and see if there is sorrow like my sorrow: for he has made a vintage of me as the Lord said on the day of his raging anger]. Except where noted, I follow the Vulgate in this chapter.

3. Ruth Crosby, "Oral Delivery in the Middle Ages," *Speculum* 11 (1936): 88.

4. This kind of displacement or projection of the reader's self into the subject position of the text is common when reciting lyrics. As Judson Boyce Allen argues, "in most cases the [the lyric] utters the position of a definite but unspecified ego whose position the audience is invited to occupy." "Grammar, Poetic Form, and Lyric Ego: A Medieval *a priori*," in *Vernacular Poetics in the Middle Ages*, ed. Lois Ebin, Studies in Medieval Culture 16 (Kalamazoo: Medieval Institute, 1984), 208.

5. Introduction to *By Means of Performance: Intercultural Studies of Theatre and Ritual* (Cambridge: Cambridge University Press, 1990), 4.

6. Meditation A (MS British Library Cotton Titus C xix, fols. 121r-128r) has the incipit "De Passione secundum Ricardum." The fragment (MS Longleat 29 (Lt), fol. 58v) includes lines 159–69 of the text. See S. J. Ogilvie-Thomson, ed., *Richard Rolle: Prose and Verse*, EETS 293 (Oxford: Oxford University Press, 1988), xlix. Hereafter, in-text parenthetical line references to Rolle's English writings are to this edition of the texts.

7. The short version is in Cambridge University Library MS.L1.i.8; the long version exists in four copies: British Library Cotton Titus C xix (fols. 92v-117v); Bodleian e mus. 232 (fols. 1–18r); Upsala University C 494 (fols. 1–32r); and Cambridge University Library Additional MS.3042 (fols. 36r-78v).

8. *A Revelation of Love*, ed. Marion Glasscoe, rev. ed. (Exeter: University of Exeter Press, 1986), 2.

9. Hope Emily Allen, ed., *English Writings of Richard Rolle* (Oxford: Clarendon, 1931), 18; Rosamond S. Allen, ed. and trans., *Richard Rolle: The English Writings* (New York: Paulist Press, 1988), 45; J. A. W. Bennett, *Poetry of the Passion: Studies in Twelve Centuries of English Verse* (Oxford: Clarendon, 1982), 23; Mary F. Madigan, *The "Passio Domini" Theme in the Works of Richard Rolle: His Personal Contribution in Its Religious, Cultural, and Literary Context* (Salzburg: Institut für Englisch Sprach und Literatur, 1978), passim; Domenico Pezzini, "The Theme of the Passion in Richard Rolle and Julian of Norwich," in *Religion in the Poetry and Drama of the Late Middle Ages in England*, ed. Piero Boitani and Anna Torti (Cambridge: D. S. Brewer, 1990), 49; Nicholas Watson, *Richard Rolle and the Invention of Authority*, Cambridge Studies in Medieval Literature 13 (Cambridge: Cambridge University Press, 1991), 18.

10. "Richard Rolle's Passion Meditations in the Context of His English Epistles: *Imitatio Christi* and the Three Degrees of Love," *Mystics Quarterly* 20 (1994): 96–104.

11. Richard Schechner, "From Ritual to Theatre and Back: The Structure/ Process of the Efficacy-Entertainment Dyad," in *Essays on Performance Theory, 1970–1976* (New York: Drama Book Specialists, 1977), 75.

12. It is impossible to determine if all people who stand and sing the

national anthem find this ritual significant, but many certainly do. For a discussion of the development of communal ritual in an American town, see W. Lloyd Warner, *The Living and the Dead: A Study of the Symbolic Life of Americans*, Yankee City Series 5 (New Haven: Yale University Press, 1959), 103–320.

13. *The Sacred and the Profane: The Nature of Religion*, trans. Willard R. Trask (New York: Harcourt, 1959), 20–1; *Patterns in Comparative Religion*, trans. Rosemary Sheed (New York: New American Library, 1958), 1–4. Though some scholars contest Eliade's notion of the "divine" because he treats it as a self-evident category, this is not the place to examine it. His assumption of the existence of the "divine" in his model of ritual parallels medieval assumptions about divinity. The medieval writers examined here also assumed the divine was self-evident.

14. Eliade, *Patterns*, 2–3, and *Sacred*, 11; Louis Bouyer, *Rite and Man: Natural Sacredness and Christian Liturgy*, trans. M. Joseph Costelloe (Notre Dame, IN: University of Notre Dame Press, 1963), 151–88.

15. Eliade posits a platonic-like division of time into sacred and profane, stating that "insertions of sacred time are linked together so that one might almost see them as constituting another duration with its own continuity.... [thus,] a ritual does not merely repeat the ritual that came before it (itself the repetition of an archetype), but is linked to it and continues it, whether at fixed periods or otherwise" (*Patterns*, 391). See also Eliade, *Sacred*, 68–113, and Bouyer, *Rite*, 186–88.

16. Eliade, *Patterns*, 392.

17. Schechner, *Essays*, 74.

18. Jonathan Z. Smith, for instance, critiques Eliade's phenomenological approach in part because he does not fully account for cultural-historical differences when positing the notion of the *axis mundi* as universal symbol for interpreting ritual. See *To Take Place: Toward Theory in Ritual* (Chicago: University of Chicago Press, 1987), 1–11. On the other hand, Eliade's approach remains helpful in approaching aspects of Jewish and Christian ritual; for example, see C. Clifford Flanigan, "The Roman Rite and the Origins of the Liturgical Drama," *University of Toronto Quarterly* 43 (1973/4): 265–6.

19. *Tanakh: The Holy Scriptures* (Philadelphia: Jewish Publication Society, 1988), 101.

20. By definition, liturgy is "service of God in public worship" (Odo Casel, *The Mystery of Christian Worship and Other Writings*, ed. Burkhard Neunheuser, trans. Charles Davis [Westminster, MD: Newman Press, 1962], 39); see also Louis Bouyer, *Liturgical Piety* (Notre Dame, IN: University of Notre Dame Press, 1955), 1.

21. The *Horae* entail eight times of prayer divided into two offices: the Night Office, or Matins, which was the longest of the hours; and daily office, which, based on Psalm 118:164: ("Septies in die laudem dixi tibi" [Seven times in the day I praise you]), included Lauds, Prime,

Terce, Sext, None, Vespers, and Compline. See Pierre Salmon, *The Breviary through the Centuries*, trans. Sr. David Mary (Collegeville, MN: Liturgical Press, 1962); Bouyer, *Liturgical*, 229–42; Roger Reynolds, "Divine Office," in *The Dictionary of the Middle Ages*, vol. 4 (New York: Scribners, 1984), 221–31; and John F. Baldovin, "Christian Worship to the Reformation," in *The Making of Jewish and Christian Worship*, ed. Paul F. Bradshaw and Lawrence A. Hoffman (Notre Dame, IN: University of Notre Dame Press, 1991), 171–2.

22. Anne Savage and Nicholas Watson, trans. *Anchoritic Spirituality: Ancrene Wisse and Associated Works* (New York: Paulist Press, 1991), 53–65.

23. On the liturgical day, see Casel, *Mystery*, 71–93. On the liturgical year, see Bouyer, *Liturgical*, 185–214; Casel, 63–70; and Eamon Duffy, *The Stripping of the Altars: Traditional Religion in England, 1400–1580* (New Haven: Yale University Press, 1992), 11–52. For a detailed discussion of the origin of the liturgical year, see Thomas J. Talley, *The Origins of the Liturgical Year* (New York: Pueblo, 1986); Smith, *To Take Place*, 88–95; and Baldovin, "Christian Worship," 162–5, 170–1.

24. Casel, *Mystery*, 44.

25. Casel, *Mystery*, 41–7; see also Baldovin, "Christian Worship," 158–9, 166–8.

26. Eliade, *Sacred*, 111.

27. *Sarum Missal*, part 1, trans. Frederick E. Warren (London: De La More Press, 1911), 20–56; Johannes H. Emminghaus, *The Eucharist: Essence, Form, Celebration* (Collegeville, MN: Liturgical Press, 1976).

28. *The Mass of the Roman Rite*, vol. 2 (New York: Benziger Brothers, 1961), 203.

29. *The Triple Way*, in *The Works of Bonaventure*, vol. 1, *Mystical Opuscula*, trans. José de Vinck (Paterson, NJ: St. Anthony Guild, 1960), 74; see also Duffy, *Stripping*, 91–130.

30. "The *Via Mystica* in John Pecham's *Philomena*: Affective Meditation and Songs of Love," *Mystics Quarterly* 21 (1995): 80–90; and "Creating Sacred Time and Space Within: Drama and Ritual in Late Medieval Affective Passion Meditations," *Downside Review* 115 (1997): 235–48.

31. See Thomas H. Bestul, *Texts of the Passion: Latin Devotional Literature and Medieval Society* (Philadelphia: University of Pennsylvania Press, 1996), 26–68.

32. The manuscripts indentify Rolle's primary audience of his epistles as female (H. Allen, *English Writings*, 72, 81; Ogilvie-Thomson, *Richard Rolle*, 1).

33. Watson, *Invention*, 222–6.

34. R. Allen, *Richard Rolle*, 33.

35. John Alford, "Richard Rolle and Related Works," in *Middle English Prose: A Critical Guide to Major Authors and Genres*, ed. A. S. G. Edwards (New Brunswick: Rutgers University Press, 1984), 38. In the 200-year period following his death, his works survived in 500 manuscripts, printed

editions, translations, and anthologies, the sheer volume of which attests to his popularity. See Nicholas Watson, introduction to *Richard Rolle: Emendatio vitae, Orationes ad honorem nominis Jesu*, Toronto Medieval Latin Texts 21 (Toronto: Pontifical Institute of Mediaeval Studies, 1995), 8.

36. R. Allen, *Richard Rolle*, 9–11. While recently scholars of mystical and devotional literature have tended to see the late medieval emphases on Jesus' humanity and on affective piety as being particularly targeted at women (for example, see Caroline Walker Bynum, *Fragmentation and Redemption: Essays on Gender and the Human Body in Medieval Religion* [New York: Zone Books, 1991], 119–50), this does not seem to be the case with Rolle. He may have, indeed, intended his English writings solely for an audience of women; yet, his Latin writings, clearly intended for men, also reflect a concern with Jesus' humanity and a similar affective tenor (for example, see *Emendatio vitae*, ed. Watson, 51–4, and *Orationes ad honorem nominis Ihesu*, passim).

37. "York Hours of the Cross," in *Lay Folks Mass Book*, ed. Thomas F. Simmons, EETS o.s. 71 (London: Oxford University Press, 1879; reprinted R. Clay, 1968), 82–7.

38. R. Allen, *Richard Rolle*, 205, n. 1.

39. *The Office of the Passion*, in *Francis and Clare: The Complete Works*, trans. Regis J. Armstrong and Ignatius C. Brady (New York: Paulist Press, 1982), 80–98; *Meditations on the Life of Christ*, ed. and trans. Isa Ragusa and Rosalie Green (Princeton, NJ: Princeton University Press, 1961).

40. As with medieval lyrics (see note 4 above), displacement of the reader's self into the subject position of the text happens in any prayer text.

41. Many of the details Rolle uses to amplify his text can be found in Latin Passion meditations; for instance, the soldiers' use of ropes for the nailing scene and the effects of raising the cross appear in the thirteenth-century meditation *Dialogus beatae Mariae et Anselmi de Passione domini* (*Patrologia Latina*, 159:283) though here the effect is more reserved than in Rolle, as we shall see (see Bestul, *Texts of the Passion*, 53–4, 66).

42. Ragusa and Green, ed. and trans., *Meditations on the Life of Christ*, 5; see also Bestul, *Texts of the Passion*, 43–50.

43. *Male Authors, Female Readers: Representation and Subjectivity in Middle English Devotional Literature* (Ithaca, NY: Cornell University Press, 1995), 122–3.

44. In the twenty-sixth prayer, Rolle writes: "Swete Ihesu, when þe Iewes heved vp þe cros and made hit falle sore in to þe hole þat was made þerfore, and þan brosten þy woundes and al to-shaked þy body þat honged so sore, lord, swete Iesu, woo was þe pan when þe sore woundes of handes and of fete bare al þe peyns of þy body" [Sweet Jesus, when the Jews heaved up the cross and made it fall painfully into the hole that was prepared for it, which then burst your wounds and completely jarred your body that hung so painfully, Lord, sweet Jesus, woe

were you then when the painful wounds of hands and feet bore all the pains of your body] (402–6).
45. Hodapp, "Passion Meditations," 99.
46. All four gospels mention the two thieves (Matt. 27: 38, 44; Mark 15: 27; Luke 23: 33; John 19:18), but only Luke (23: 39–43) tells the story of the repentant thief. Later writers develop this story further by naming the repentant and unrepentant thieves, Dismas and Gestas respectively, thereby humanizing them to a degree. See, for example, *The Gospel of Nicodemus*, ed. H. C. Kim, Toronto Medieval Latin Texts 2 (Toronto: Pontifical Institute of Mediaeval Studies, 1973), 10.24–5; Jacobus de Voragine, *The Golden Legend*, trans. William Granger Ryan, vol. 1 (Princeton: Princeton University Press, 1993), 53.203–14; and *Cursor Mundi*, ed. Richard Morris, part III, EETS o.s. 62 (London: Oxford University Press, 1876; reprinted R. Clay, 1966), 16738.
47. *Egeria: Diary of a Pilgrimage*, trans. G. E. Gingras, Ancient Christian Writers 38 (New York: Newman Press, 1970), 89–128.
48. Smith, *To Take Place*, 91–92.
49. Herbert Thurston, *The Stations of the Cross: An Account of their History and Devotional Purpose* (New York: Benziger Brothers, 1906), 20–44.
50. Bernard McGinn, preface to *Henry Suso*, trans. Frank Tobin (New York: Paulist Press, 1989), 6.
51. I use the term "autobiography" with hesitation; indeed, the question of authorship remains unsettled. Scholars have attributed parts of the *Vita* to Elsbeth Spagel, a Dominican sister for whom Suso served as spiritual advisor; yet, Suso also contributed to the text, as well as editing and supervising its publication. See Tobin's introduction (38–40) for a full discussion of authorship. In-text page references to Suso's text are to Tobin's translation, *The Life of the Servant* (83–6). On replicating space, see Smith, *To Take Place*, 86–8.
52. *The Stations of the Cross: Taken Freely from the Meditation on the Passion of the Lord by Richard Rolle* (London: Burns and Oates, 1917).
53. Likewise, the opposite is also quite possible, that is, an individual would remain motionless while praying Meditation B. After all, many people today remain seated while praying the Stations of the Cross, even when rubrics indicate standing, kneeling, and processional movement.
54. There is evidence in other texts of processional, stational prayer similar to Suso's. *An Orison of the Passion*, for instance, a mid-fourteenth-century Middle English poem of 154 lines, begins with the rubric: "In seyinge of þis orisone stinteþ and abideþ at euery crose and þinkeþ whate ze haue seide; ffor a more deuout pryer fonde y neuer of þe passione, who-so wolde abidingly sey it" (*Meditations on the Life and Passion of Christ*, ed. Charlotte D'Evelyn, EETS o.s. 158 [London: Oxford University Press, 1921; reprinted New York: Kraus, 1971], 60).
55. Rolle's influence on late medieval devotional practice, especially in

northern England, is particularly evident in how later writers and artists responded to his treatment of the Passion in their writings (Watson, *Invention*, 18).

56. The earliest reference to cycle drama in York dates to 1376, and the list of plays in the *Ordo paginorum* of 1415 suggests that the Passion cycle was well in place by the early fifteenth century if not before; see Richard Beadle, ed., *The York Plays* (London: Edward Arnold, 1982), 19–27. Parenthetical line references to plays from the York cycle are to this edition.

57. Based on the 1463–77 Register copy, the Passion sequence (Beadle, *York Plays*, 205–333) includes the following plays by number, title, and lines: 25, *The Entry into Jerusalem* (544); 26, *The Conspiracy* (294); 27, *The Last Supper* (187/about 53 lines missing); 28, *The Agony in the Garden and the Betrayal* (305/about 40 lines missing); 29, *Christ Before Annas and Caiaphas* (395); 30, *Christ Before Pilate 1: The Dream of Pilate's Wife* (548); 31, *Christ Before Herod* (424); 32, *The Remorse of Judas* (389); 33, *Christ Before Pilate 2: The Judgment* (485/about 54 lines missing); 34, *The Road to Calvary* (349/about 50 lines missing); 35, *The Crucifixion* (300); 36, *The Death of Christ* (416).

58. Duffy, *Stripping*, 27.

59. Duffy, *Stripping*, 23–7.

60. Margery states, "Many ȝerys on Palme Sonday, as þis creatur was at þe processyon wyth oþer good pepyl in þe chirch-ȝerd & beheld how þe preystys dedyn her obseruawnce, how þei knelyd to þe Sacrament & þe pepil also, it semyd to hir gostly sygth as þei sche had ben þat tyme in Ierusalem & seen owr Lord in hys manhod receyuyd of þe pepil as he was whil he went her in erth" [For many years on Palm Sunday, while this creature was at the procession with other good people in the churchyard and saw how the priests performed their observance, how they kneeled before the Sacrament and the people kneeled also, it seemed to her spiritual sight as though she had been at that moment in Jerusalem and saw our Lord in his manhood received by the people as he was when he went about here on earth]. *The Book of Margery Kempe*, ed. S. B. Meech, EETS o.s. 212 (London: Oxford University Press, 1940), 184.

61. Sarah Beckwith, in an illuminating article, examines several specific ways in which acting and ritual was performed in staging the York plays, focusing in part on contested space and the manipulation of the symbol of Christ's body to invoke responses from audiences ("Ritual, Theater, and Social Space in the York Corpus Christi Cycle," in *Bodies and Disciplines: Intersections of Literature and History in Fifteenth-Century England*, ed. Barbara A. Hanawalt and David Wallace, Medieval Cultures 9 [Minneapolis: University of Minnesota Press, 1996], 63–86).

62. *The Theater of Devotion: East Anglian Drama and Society in the Late Middle Ages* (Chicago: University of Chicago Press, 1989), 6.

63. See Bonaventure, 63–94.
64. In *The Commandment*, Rolle writes: "festyn in þi hert þe mynd of his passioun and of his woundes; grete delite and swetnesse shal þou fele if þou hold þi þoght in mynd of þe pyne þat Crist suffred for þe" [fasten in your heart the consciousness of his Passion and of his wounds; you will feel great delight and sweetness if you hold in your mind the thought of the pain that Christ suffered for you] (175–7). In *Ego Dormio*, too, he says, "I wil þat þou neuer be ydel; for be euer other spekynge of God, or wirchynge some notable werke, or thynkynge in hym, and principaly þat þi thoght be euer hauynge hym in mynde. And thynke of[t] þis of his passione" [I desire that you never be idle, but always be either speaking of God, or doing some notable work, or thinking about him principally, so that your thought may be ever remembering him. And think often on his passion] (170–4). He then offers a 36 line lyrical Passion meditation (175–211).
65. Bartlett, 122.

Bibliography

Alford, John. "Richard Rolle and Related Works." In *Middle English Prose: A Critical Guide to Major Authors and Genres*, ed. A. S. G. Edwards. New Brunswick: Rutgers University Press, 1984.

Allen, Hope Emily, ed. *English Writings of Richard Rolle*. Oxford: Clarendon, 1931.

Allen, Judson Boyce. "Grammar, Poetic Form, and Lyric Ego: A Medieval *a priori*." In *Vernacular Poetics in the Middle Ages*, ed. Lois Ebin. Studies in Medieval Culture 16. Kalamazoo: Medieval Institute, 1984.

Allen, Rosemund S., ed. and trans. *Richard Rolle: The English Writings*. New York: Paulist Press, 1988.

Armstrong, Regis J., and Ignatius C. Brady, trans. *Francis and Clare: The Complete Works*. New York: Paulist Press, 1982.

Baldovin, John F. "Christian Worship to the Reformation." In *The Making of Jewish and Christian Worship*, ed. Paul F. Bradshaw and Lawrence A. Hoffman. Notre Dame, IN: University of Notre Dame Press, 1991.

Bartlett, Anne Clark. *Male Authors, Female Readers: Representation and Subjectivity in Middle English Devotional Literature*. Ithaca, NY: Cornell University Press, 1995.

Beadle, Richard, ed. *The York Plays*. London: Edward Arnold, 1982.

Beckwith, Sarah. "Ritual, Theater, and Social Space in the York Corpus Christi Cycle." In *Bodies and Disciplines: Intersections of Literature and History in Fifteenth-Century England*, ed. Barbara A. Hanawalt and David Wallace, 63–86. Medieval Cultures 9. Minneapolis: University of Minnesota Press, 1996.

Bennett, J. A. W. *Poetry of the Passion: Studies in Twelve Centuries of English Verse*. Oxford: Clarendon, 1982.

Bestul, Thomas H. *Texts of the Passion: Latin Devotional Literature and Medieval Society.* Philadelphia: University of Pennsylvania Press, 1996.

Bonaventure. *The Works of Bonaventure.* Vol. 1, *Mystical Opuscula.* Trans. José de Vinck. Paterson, NJ: St. Anthony Guild, 1960.

Bouyer, Louis. *Liturgical Piety.* Notre Dame, IN: University of Notre Dame Press, 1955.

———. *Rite and Man: Natural Sacredness and Christian Liturgy.* Trans. M. Joseph Costelloe. Notre Dame, IN: University of Notre Dame Press, 1963.

Bynum, Caroline Walker. *Fragmentation and Redemption: Essays on Gender and the Human Body in Medieval Religion.* New York: Zone Books, 1991.

Casel, Odo. *The Mystery of Christian Worship and Other Writings.* Ed. Burkhard Neunheuser. Trans. Charles Davis. Westminster, MD: Newman Press, 1962.

Crosby, Ruth. "Oral Delivery in the Middle Ages." *Speculum* 11 (1936): 88.

Dialogus beatae Mariae et Anselmi de Passione domini. Patrologia Latina. 159:283.

D'Evelyn, Charlotte, ed. *Meditations on the Life and Passion of Christ.* EETS o.s. 158. London: Oxford University Press, 1921; reprinted New York: Kraus, 1971.

Duffy, Eamon. *The Stripping of the Altars: Traditional Religion in England 1400–1580.* New Haven: Yale University Press, 1992.

Eliade, Mircea. *Patterns in Comparative Religion.* Trans. Rosemary Sheed. New York: New American Library, 1958.

———. *The Sacred and the Profane: The Nature of Religion.* Trans. Willard R. Trask. New York: Harcourt, 1959.

Emminghaus, Johannes H. *The Eucharist: Essence, Form, Celebration.* Collegeville, MN: Liturgical Press, 1976.

Flanigan, C. Clifford. "The Roman Rite and the Origins of the Liturgical Drama." *University of Toronto Quarterly* 43 (1973/4): 265–6.

Gibson, Gail McMurry. *The Theater of Devotion: East Anglian Drama and Society in the Late Middle Ages.* Chicago: University of Chicago Press, 1989.

Gingras, G. E., trans. *Egeria: Diary of a Pilgrimage.* Ancient Christian Writers 38. New York: Newman Press, 1970.

Hodapp, William F. "Creating Sacred Time and Space Within: Drama and Ritual in Late Medieval Affective Passion Meditations." *Downside Review* 115 (1997): 235–48.

———. "Richard Rolle's Passion Meditations in the Context of His English Epistles: *Imitatio Christi* and the Three Degrees of Love." *Mystics Quarterly* 20 (1994): 96–104.

———. "The *Via Mystica* in John Pecham's *Philomena*: Affective Meditation and Songs of Love." *Mystics Quarterly* 21 (1995): 80–90.

Jacobus de Voragine. *The Golden Legend.* 2 vols. Trans. William Granger Ryan. Princeton, NJ: Princeton University Press, 1993.

Julian of Norwich. *A Revelation of Love.* Ed. Marion Glasscoe, rev. ed. Exeter: University of Exeter Press, 1986.

Jungmann, Joseph. *The Mass of the Roman Rite.* 2 vols. New York: Benziger Brothers, 1961.

Kempe, Margery. *The Book of Margery Kempe.* Ed. S. B. Meech. EETS o.s. 212. London: Oxford University Press, 1940.

Kim, H. C., ed. *The Gospel of Nicodemus.* Toronto Medieval Latin Texts 2. Toronto: Pontifical Institute of Mediaeval Studies, 1973.

Luria, Maxwell S., and Richard L. Hoffman. *Middle English Lyrics.* New York: Norton, 1974.

Madigan, Mary F. *The "Passio Domini" Theme in the Works of Richard Rolle: His Personal Contribution in Its Religious, Cultural, and Literary Context.* Salzburg: Institut für Englisch Sprach und Literatur, 1978.

Morris, Richard, ed. *Cursor Mundi.* EETS o.s. 62. London: Oxford University Press, 1876; reprinted R. Clay, 1966.

Ogilvie-Thomson, S. J., ed. *Richard Rolle: Prose and Verse.* EETS 293. Oxford: Oxford University Press, 1988.

Pezzini, Domenico. "The Theme of the Passion in Richard Rolle and Julian of Norwich." In *Religion in the Poetry and Drama of the Late Middle Ages in England,* eds. Piero Boitani and Anna Torti. Cambridge: D. S. Brewer, 1990.

Ragusa, Isa, and Rosalie Green, ed. and trans. *Meditations on the Life of Christ.* Princeton, NJ: Princeton University Press, 1961.

Reynolds, Roger. "Divine Office." In *The Dictionary of the Middle Ages.* Vol. 4, 221–231. New York: Scribners, 1984.

Salmon, Pierre. *The Breviary through the Centuries.* Trans. Sr. David Mary. Collegeville, MN: Liturgical Press, 1962.

Sarum Missal. Trans. Frederick E. Warren. London: De La More Press, 1911.

Savage, Anne, and Nicholas Watson, trans. *Anchoritic Spirituality: Ancrene Wisse and Associated Works.* New York: Paulist Press, 1991.

Schechner, Richard. "From Ritual to Theatre and Back: The Structure/Process of the Efficacy-Entertainment Dyad." In *Essays on Performance Theory, 1970–1976.* New York: Drama Book Specialists, 1977.

———, and Willa Appel, eds. *By Means of Performance: Intercultural Studies of Theatre and Ritual.* Cambridge: Cambridge University Press, 1990.

Simmons, Thomas F., ed. "York Hours of the Cross." In *Lay Folks Mass Book.* EETS o.s. 71. London: Oxford University Press, 1879; reprinted R. Clay, 1968.

Smith, Jonathan Z. *To Take Place: Toward Theory in Ritual.* Chicago: University of Chicago Press, 1987.

The Stations of the Cross: Taken Freely from the Meditation on the Passion of the Lord by Richard Rolle. London: Burns and Oates, 1917.

Talley, Thomas J. *The Origins of the Liturgical Year.* New York: Pueblo, 1986.

Tanakh: The Holy Scriptures. Philadelphia: Jewish Publication Society, 1988.

Thurston, Herbert. *The Stations of the Cross: An Account of their History and Devotional Purpose.* New York: Benziger Brothers, 1906.

Tobin, Frank, trans. *Henry Suso.* New York: Paulist Press, 1989.

Warner, W. Lloyd. *The Living and the Dead: A Study of the Symbolic Life of Americans.* Yankee City Series 5. New Haven: Yale University Press, 1959.

Watson, Nicholas, ed. *Richard Rolle: Emendatio vitae; Orationes ad honorem nominis Jesu.* Toronto Medieval Latin Texts 21. Toronto: Pontifical Institute of Mediaeval Studies, 1995.

———. *Richard Rolle and the Invention of Authority.* Cambridge Studies in Medieval Literature 13. Cambridge: Cambridge University Press, 1991.

CHAPTER TEN

Spanish Visionary Women and the Paradox of Performance

Mary E. Giles

A tradition of visionary women similar to the one that is widely documented throughout medieval Europe and England does not appear in the religious and historical literature of Spain until the latter part of the fifteenth century and the first decades of the sixteenth. The phenomenon of charismatic women functioning as oracles and teachers of prayer was made possible in large part by the efforts of Cardinal Francisco Ximénez de Cisneros (1435–1517) to open the peninsula to the religious reform that had taken root in lands north of the Pyrenees.[1] Cisneros was deeply affected by the insights of *devotio moderna*, with its summons to an interiorized Christianity in the spirit of the apostolic church. At the same time, he advocated humanist education and employed its methodologies in the educational program of the university he established at Alcalá de Henares.

Cisneros's attraction to interiorized Christianity necessarily put him in contact with the role of visionary women elsewhere. He was especially drawn to St. Catherine of Siena and Angela of Foligno and commissioned translations of their writings into Spanish. Given his interest in *devotio moderna* and the role of charismatic women in advancing religious reform, it was not out of character for him to look favorably upon such visionary women as Madre Juana de la Cruz and Sor María of Santo Domingo, who early in the sixteenth century were spiritual celebrities in Spain. Seen from afar the two women appear to be similar in character and career, but closer inspection in the light of performance theory reveals them to be a study in contrasts that eventually and paradoxically turns in upon itself.

Two Spanish Visionaries

Madre Juana was born in 1480 to a family of farmers in the village of Azaña, near Toledo.[2] Exceptionally devout as a youngster, by the time she was a teenager she was determined to enter the religious life. When her father pressed her to accept an arranged marriage at the age of 15, the future abbess donned men's apparel and fled to the monastery of Cubas, also known as Santa María de la Cruz, a house of the Regular Third Order of Saint Francis. After serving in various offices, she was elected abbess at the age of 28 and held the post until her death on May 3, 1534.

Three years before her election, Madre Juana had begun to experience ecstasies in which she discoursed under inspiration of the Holy Spirit. The provincial of the order initially secluded Juana in her cell, possibly to allay gossip, but eventually people were allowed to witness the ecstasies, notable among them Emperor Charles V, Cardinal Cisneros, and Don Juan of Austria. Lasting 13 years, the ecstatic discourses were transcribed by nuns, principally Sor María Evangelista, and arranged according to the liturgical year of 1508–09 to form what has been called a "sermon-book." Entitled *El libro del conorte* (The Book of Consolation),[3] the sermons are composed of two parts: the first a recasting of an episode from the Gospels, and the second a description of a heavenly liturgy to celebrate the event.[4]

Death in 1534 did not eclipse Madre Juana's fame; she was called "la santa" by popular acclamation during her lifetime and for centuries afterward, even to the present day. In 1981, on the occasion of the fifth centenary of her birth, the cardinal of Toledo led ecclesiastics and local people in Numancia de la Sangra, formerly Azaña, in procession from the plaza of Santa Juana to the site of an ancient hermitage, once dedicated to the Santa Cruz but in popular idiom known as the hermitage of Santa Juana, there to place the cornerstone for a restored hermitage. Accompanied all the while by the music of *dulzaina* and *tamboril*, the crowd moved on to the house identified as Madre Juana's birthplace, and finally to the monastery of Cubas for celebration of the Eucharist by the cardinal archbishop of Madrid.[5]

Sor María of Santo Domingo was born about the same time as Madre Juana in Aldeanueva, not far from Avila, to parents who, like Madre Juana's, were unlettered laborers.[6] Exceptionally devout as a child, María would fast and mortify herself rigorously—not without rewards, however, as conversation with the Blessed Mother, the Lord, and saints in heaven came her way. She, too, chose the religious life, around 1503 entering the monastery of Piedrahita near her home as a third order Dominican.[7]

Despite their general similarities, the two women lived out their visionary vocation in sharply divergent styles. Madre Juana spent her life in the convent with people coming to witness her ecstasies, whereas Sor María was on the move, first to Avila, where she changed residence twice, and then, in the company of men and women, on to Toledo and elsewhere to promote a reform that by then was associated with the monastery of Piedrahita. In 1478 a papal bull officially recognized the efforts to institute reform in the direction of increased austerity that had begun early in the century.[8] The push for reform caused a rupture in the order that even the formal union in 1496 of the province and the reformist faction known as the Congregation of the Observance was unable to heal. At the heart of the reform movement was the monastery at Piedrahita, whose monks saw in their oracular Sor María a Spanish counterpart to Catherine of Siena, Angela of Foligno, and in their own time Sor Lucia of Narni, who was admired by Alexander VI, beatified by Clement XI, and so favored by the duke of Ferrara that he founded a monastery for her in 1501. Sor María's followers were not unaware of the likeness that their oracle bore to the famous Sor Lucia.[9] Like the Italian visionaries, Sor María became a celebrity: the king summoned her to the royal court at Burgos and Cisneros invited her to appear before him; so impressed was Cisneros on observing the ecstatic Sor María that he pronounced her to be "living doctrine." The favor she enjoyed with king and prelate extended to the nobility: the powerful duke of Alba undertook the expense of founding a new monastery for her.

The fame that surrounded Madre Juana and was beneficial to her good name had a dark side for Sor María, as suspicion about her spread on two counts: the genuineness of the raptures, miraculous communion, fasting, and bleeding from the side and her moral behavior with religious and lay men who kept her company. Escalating suspicion finally resulted in a series of informal examinations by church officials: the first in September, 1508; the second scheduled for December of the same year but canceled; the third authorized by Pope Julius II in 1509 but brought to a halt by an explosion of moves and countermoves between her supporters and opponents; and the fourth and last begun later that year in Valladolid, controlled by Sor Maria's powerful friends and concluded with a commendation from the tribunal for her life and holiness as "worthy and deserving of praise."[10] Throughout the inquiries her admirers remained loyal, especially Antonio de la Peña, who served as her defense counsel at the fourth examination and probably was the editor of a small text attributed to her and for which he wrote a preface lauding Sor Maria as continuing the line of prophets dating back to biblical times. Compiled between 1512 and 1518, the *Libro de la oración de Sor María de Santo Domingo* (The Book of Prayer of Sor María of Santo Domingo) contains transcriptions of three ecstatic discourses, called contemplations, and a letter of consolation to a gentleman grieving the death of one García Valdés.[11]

Despite the editor's strong defense and the commendation from the tribunal pursuant to the fourth examination, Sor María did not emerge a winner from her brush with the Inquisition. The Master General of the Dominican order cut short her peripatetic career, remanding her to the safety of the convent, where she was allowed communication by letter or in person only with her confessor, unless otherwise permitted in writing by the provincial, and ordered not to discuss her prophecies and raptures with anyone except the provincial general or procurator of the order.

By the time of Sor María's death, the once favorable climate of tolerance and reform was changing amid threats from abroad and at home to the authority of the Spanish Catholic Church. Of particular concern to ecclesiastical officials were the ideas of Desiderius Erasmus, whose writings had circulated widely in Spain with the blessing of Cisneros;[12] the growth of Protestantism; and the appearance of individuals and groups who regarded personal inspiration by the Holy Spirit as more important for the salvation of their souls than observing the doctrine and rituals of the Church. The *alumbrados*, or enlightened ones, as they were known, included lay and religious men and women from all ranks of society who were united by desire for spiritual rebirth.[13] Especially visible among them were charismatic women, some married, others religious, still others *beatas*, or holy women, living by themselves or in community, all renowned as visionaries, interpreters of Scripture, and teachers of mental prayer.[14] By 1525 the Church was sufficiently apprehensive of the *alumbrados* and their independent ways to have begun investigation of their most visible members and in September of that year to have collected from oral statements of defendants and witnesses a list of 48 alumbrado beliefs that were deemed heretical. These points of heresy constituted a reference book for inquisitors in the trials of *alumbrados*, which lasted well into the 1530s and set ground rules for inquisitorial proceedings against visionary women throughout the sixteenth and seventeenth centuries in Spain and the New World.

Although the different lifestyles of Madre Juana and Sor María, the changing religious climate of Spain, and, for Sor María, the political turmoil within the Dominican order all contributed to the different turns their lives took, the nature of their ecstatic discourse also may have had something to do with Madre Juana's enduring good fortune and Sor Maria's fall from grace. An entry into analysis of ecstatic discourse for the purpose of explaining in part why one woman was revered as a saint in her lifetime while the other was hauled before church tribunals is by way of the relationship of ecstatic discourse and theater. In the case of the two women, that relationship already is established: both the sermons of Madre Juana and Sor María's contemplations are connected either directly to medieval religious theater or indirectly through the popular religious devotions that theater influenced. The insights into ecstatic discourse that comparison with medieval theater has yielded are reason to extend the line of inquiry in the affiliated yet slightly different direction of analyzing the discourse according to modern theories of performance and ritual. The principal theoretician whose work informs the analysis is Victor Turner, who in turn was indebted to Wilhelm Dilthey and Arnold van Gennep.

Ecstatic Discourse as Performance

The theory of performance that Turner presents in *From Ritual to Theatre*[15] is based on William Dilthey's (1833–1911) idea that experience is a process brought to completion only with an act of expression, that is, when the experience is pressed out to other people.[16] The word "performance" is derived from the Old French "parfournir," meaning "to complete" and "to carry out thoroughly"; as such, a performance is what completes the event of expression, this done by drawing forth "what is normally sealed up, inaccessible to everyday observation and reasoning, in the depth of sociocultural life."[17] Both Turner and Dilthey recognize the cultural nature of performance and identify such activities as ritual, ceremony, theater, and poetry as cultural performances that explicate life itself.

In the process of experience, Dilthey identifies five key moments, as the subject (1) experiences a perceptual core, feeling pain or pleasure more acutely than usual; (2) relives past experiences with unusual clarity; (3) has original feelings completely restored; (4) sees interconnections between past and present events; and (5) expresses the process of experience. Turner associates theatrical performance with the fifth moment, when the poet or dramatist, in Dilthey's words, "freely unfolds images beyond the bounds of reality."[18] The entire process implies a projection of time in which the subject moves sequentially through the five moments, with allowance for becoming aware of the intensity of restored events and the feelings they generate; scrutinizing interconnections between past and present events; and creating an expression of the entire performance. In the fifth moment, however, sequential time yields to spontaneity, signifying that which originates without cause or mediator and outside the constraints of time, as in the freely unfolding images that rise up "beyond the bounds of reality."

A prefatory note on the role of spontaneity in postmodern theater may help clarify its importance in ecstatic discourse.[19] For playwrights like Jerzy Grotowski, who displaced the privilege of the written text, spontaneity signifies what is generated immediately in the course of rehearsals and performance. Grotowski stripped the performance of conventions like staging and costumes in order to create an appropriate context for the spontaneity he considered to be essential to the cathartic purpose of performance, which was to effect a psychic and spiritual transformation in the actors, the audience, and himself. The rigor of the performance and rehearsal was such that the actor would undergo a psychic denuding in the presence of spectators, thereby becoming himself a channel through whom the audience also might be stripped and opened to the new vision of reality being created in the moment by the performance.

Ecstatic discourse prefigures—and outstrips—the spontaneity that Grotowski and other modern playwrights value. Addressing the issue of spontaneity in ecstatic discourse, however, is hazardous because the written text is a step away from an original performance that can be recaptured only in part, and then by the grace of acute, imaginative reading. There are hints, however, at the nature of the ecstatic performance in Sor María's statements before her examiners where she suggests a state of consciousness in which time as marking a sequence of events ceases to exist. As an argument in her own defense, she disclaimed responsibility for anything she had said while enraptured on grounds that she neither knew what she was saying at the time of the rapture nor could remember anything of the utterances: she was at the mercy of people who had witnessed the ecstasies and reported on her discourse. Insofar as she did not know and could not remember what she said, Sor María, and by extension Madre Juana, were in the fifth moment of the process when images were unfolding freely, beyond a reality bounded by time and space. They did not consciously strip themselves of those markers of reality or plan a context they believed would be conducive to an experience of spontaneity as did Grotowski with the exhaustive disciplines of mind, body, and emotions that he demanded of his actors and himself. Rather, the visionary women were removed by ecstasy from consciousness of a reality bound by time and space, and in being so removed were made aware of pure spontaneity, the entirety of the discourse transformed for them into a single event, the sequence of moments into but one, the present moment.

Readers probably cannot recover this original performance in its power to affect the spiritual changes reported by witnesses who confessed to being converted to virtue in the presence of the ecstasized holy women.[20] Ecstatic performance was amazing, as men and women from all social ranks were stunned out of their ordinary mode of knowing and were themselves made ecstatic spectators in the sense of existing outside of chronological time in a subject-subject relationship with the enraptured woman and, through her, with God. Although some spectators voiced disbelief and remained unmoved by the performance, for other witnesses distance was collapsed, awareness of the present moment rose within them unsullied by memories of the past or expectations of the future, and there was realized what Turner calls *comunitas*, or consciousness of a deep, mutual understanding with other people.[21]

The ecstasized woman and spectator existing in the purity of the present moment would not have been able to analyze their experience relative to other events and derive meaning from interconnections of past and present experience. That meaning would have to await the hand of the transcriber, a task not incidental, of course, to the texts in question; in the case of Sor María, we are told that several men in attendance would confer after the conclusion of the discourse, sometimes waiting a day or more, in order to agree on what she had said and meant in her enraptured state.[22] Even though Sor María Evangelista was reputed to hold entire sermons in her memory before writing them down, it is likely that she, like Sor Maria's transcribers, consciously worked at remembering Madre Juana's oral text.[23] Given the play of reason in this conscious conferring and remembering by the transcribers, the transcription rather than the original performance would seem to qualify as the five-part process set forth by Dilthey and Turner.

Turner develops his ideas on performance by examining the nature of ritual, with particular attention to rites of passage, according to the tripartite structure of separation, transition, and incorporation presented by Arnold van Gennep.[24] In the first step, separation, the subject goes into a demarcated sacred space and time that removes him from the familiarity of everyday social life. In the second, which van Gennep calls the "margin"

or "limen" (from the Latin, meaning threshold), the subject experiences
ambiguity as new ideas, symbols, and beliefs rise up to challenge old ways.
The third step, incorporation, is marked by symbolic action and phenomena that, depending on what has occurred during the transition, represent
the subject's return to society in a new, relatively stable, and well-defined
position.

Regardless of their experience in steps two and three, visionary
women have in common separation. For the visionary woman, ecstasy is
both the means by which she is separated from her social milieu and the
sacred space in which she experiences herself as being outside of chronological time and in a locus unbounded by cultural conventions that give
her the identity of, say, a third order Dominican or Franciscan. Whether
the visionary woman remains within the convent as Madre Juana did or
travels from place to place like Sor María, she is separated from society
by force of ecstasy. Thus Sor María could undergo the first step in the
initiation ritual when she was enraptured in full view of the royal court at
Burgos; her sacred space was wherever she was, in court, convent, private
home, or on the road. Separation includes symbolic behavior characterized
by symbols of the reversal or inversion of things; ecstasy in itself is symbolic behavior in that the loss of control over the body manifested in
limbs made rigid, speech annihilated, and breathing radically slowed symbolizes the inversion of what might be perceived as the normal disposition
and functioning of the body.[25]

Having been separated by the fact of ecstasy, the visionary woman
then is opened to the transitional stage of the ritual, the limen. This period
is crucial to both the visionary woman and the social constructs that she
represents when the performance is a collective ritual intended for the
benefit of the group. (Analysis of individual rites will reveal the importance
of the second stage as well.) Even though collective rituals are integrated
into the social fabric, the estrangement from the familiar that is realized
through ecstasy makes very real the possibility that normative values will
be rejected rather than reaffirmed at this stage. In the estranged state,
familiar elements that symbolize the history and meaning of the group
may be defamiliarized by a playing that fashions them into novel recombinations. The limen is therefore the context for play, and the phenomena
generated within that context are liminal. How creative the playing becomes depends on the power of the normative social structure to exert its
dominance over the individual or the group and to absorb the play within
the social order. Tribal and agrarian societies generally exhibit through
their religious and governing institutions the power necessary to restrict

the creativity of play to the recombination of familiar elements, which in turn strengthen the cultural order.[26]

Because the arrangement of Madre Juana's sermons corresponds to the liturgical calendar, they seem to be appropriate candidates for examination as collective rites of passage, of which liturgies are traditional examples. The sermon on the Immaculate Conception is typical of the sermon-book in its division into two parts: the first part offers doctrinal innovation as the Lord proclaims through the ecstasized woman the belief in the Immaculate Conception that was popularly accepted at the time but not declared a doctrine of the Church until December 8, 1854. The Lord explains through Madre Juana that even though the evangelists and apostles affirmed the virginity of Mary before, during, and after her birth, they were too busy building the Catholic faith to proclaim the doctrine of her Immaculate Conception. If the Lord has not spoken of his glorious mother's immaculate conception until now, it is because learned men have not known how to proclaim her excellence and virtue. For this momentous work the voice of the ecstatic woman is needed because "even though doctors and preachers and learned men praise and glorify her and speak the truth, they never knew how nor will there ever be completed a knowing how to praise and speak of all the excellence and virtue of his precious mother."[27]

The second part of the sermon is the liturgical celebration in heaven instituted by God, replete with singing, dancing, and instrumental music:

> And the Lord said that on the same day when he spoke and declared the aforementioned things, there were before his Divine Majesty a multitude of angels playing instruments and singing and rejoicing greatly and saying: "Lord, authorize them to remember on earth and celebrate the most chaste and sinless conception of Our Lady the Virgin Mary."[28]

The liturgy is a startling revelation of the Lord's relationship with his mother celebrated throughout with song and dance. As midwife and mother, the Lord draws the baby from the womb of St. Ann and shows her off to the blessed souls in paradise. As lover, he resides within the grown Mary, imaged as "a castle from the waist down and a maiden from the waist up."[29] Extolling her as a warrior castle and a house of prayer, the Lord comes out of the castle-woman and courts her with the music of liturgy:

The Lord said that he was silencing everything that our Lady said, that he would not reply one thing to her, and he put down the guitar and they gave him a pipe and he played it for a while. Likewise, he left it and they gave him another instrument and he played and sang very sweetly, circling the castle adroitly, all the while raising his precious eyes on high and looking at our Lady and saying: Oh, my dove and my beloved! If now you would look at me and fall in love with me and desire to be with me![30]

After she lets down the turrets and windows of her castle, he enters, and "our lady enjoyed him as she wished and desired, very fully and completely." Outside again, he circles the castle until he sees her gazing down on him, whereupon he flies up and enters the windows of the highest towers, there "enjoying himself with his most blessed mother." Then she was turned back into the lady and maiden that she was and "he took her in his powerful arms and took her up to the most high and royal and secret palace of the Most Holy Trinity and there she was exalted and enlightened more than all the cherubim and seraphim."[31]

Although the sermon strikes a familiar note in evoking the sounds and sights of the music, singing, and dancing that was characteristic of popular religious rituals during Madre Juana's time,[32] those liturgical conventions do not drown out the voice of novelty. Consider the role of the woman selected by the Lord to be his channel, revealing through her rather than through learned men of her day the immaculate conception of his glorious mother. These statements on the prophetic role of women and their authority in the Church might have raised eyebrows, but apparently Madre Juana faced no serious recrimination for placing women on at least equal footing with the founders of the Church. Perhaps she was echoing in defamiliarized form a belief that was secured too firmly in popular religiosity to be displaced as heresy. Perhaps the authority granted to the vision by support from important men in church and state also assured her safety. Perhaps, too, the fact that her ecstasies occurred in the seclusion of the monastery and that afterward she resumed her duties as abbess and maintained the monastic routine deflected doubts about her allegiance to the church. Whatever were the determinants, she appears to have reached the safety of the third stage with her sermons incorporated into the normative structure, possibly with modifications by the transcriber to insure their acceptance.[33] Insofar as her novelties did not threaten church authority or deny its doctrines and could be accommodated in existent paradigms of belief, the phenomena of the discourse generated in the transitional stage appear to be liminal.

The situation with Sor María was a different matter. As noted already, she was no stay-at-home visionary. Championed as their oracle by a group of Dominicans intent on instituting the reform agenda that Girolamo Savonarola (1452–98) had exercised with the Italian Dominicans, and likened to the Italian prophetess Sor Lucia, Sor María was paraded around Toledo and its environs, her ecstasies a matter of public viewing. When she appeared before the court, the noted Italian humanist Peter Martyr wrote in a letter of October 6, 1509, that a new kind of devotion was sprouting up, centered on a woman who claimed to be a prophet and the bride of Christ, conversed with God and the Blessed Mother, and subjected herself to severe self-mortification. According to Peter Martyr, the world was not unanimous in its praise of Sor María: even though the king himself was her advocate, some people doubted the authenticity of her visions while others plainly denounced her as a fraud. The ease with which she appeared to go in and out of ecstasy convinced critics that she manipulated her raptures; if true, the criticism would countermand claims by admirers that her ecstasies were divine gifts and, as such, absolutely beyond her control.

Stories of immoral behavior with men fueled the fires of doubt. Apparently Sor María's confessor sometimes would spend the night alone with her, even lying on top of the bed, ostensibly to protect her against the devil and comfort her when she had heart pain. Certainly Sor María did not help her reputation when she indulged her taste for good food, dancing, playing chess, and wearing fine clothes, especially little French hats, bracelets, and scarlet skirts, set off smartly with a red satin purse. The editor of *The Book of Prayer* defends her dress with the ingenious argument that wearing fine clothes proved not her pride but her humility: when people saw her elegantly attired, they thought less of her than if she had not displayed this weakness of hers. Despite protestations of innocence and holiness from herself and others, Sor María was plagued by controversy, in part caused by a naiveté that saw nothing wrong in having her confessor overnight in her room, in part the result of excessive credulity in followers whose good judgment was overruled by emotion, the zest for novelty, and personal ambition.[34]

Because Sor María lived her vocation as a visionary woman in a fashion radically different from Madre Juana's, it is possible that her performance as ritual is individual rather than collective, or liturgical, and that the phenomena of the transitional stage thus are of an innovative order that resisted accommodation. Collective and individual rites contrast in terms of their context and the nature of the phenomena originating in the second stage. The setting of collective rites are tribal and agrarian societies that as such do not distinguish between work and leisure, while individual rites occur in "post-industrial" societies. The label "post-industrial" is not affixed to societies for reasons of chronology but because they are characterized by leisure and the two freedoms that issue from leisure: freedom from institutional obligations and freedom to play creatively.[35] If the playing reinforces and revitalizes social values and can be accommodated by the governing structure, as may be the situation with Madre Juana's sermon on the Immaculate Conception, the phenomenon is liminal, but if the playing deepens creatively to challenge the existent order, then the phenomenon is liminoid. Plural, fragmentary, experimental, and idiosyncratic, liminoid phenomena are characteristic of schools, groups, and movements—the minority group of Dominicans who advocated reform of the order, for example—bent on exposing deficiencies in the existing system. As appealing as these categories of liminal and liminoid are to the advocate of certainty, they may falter before the pressure of paradox in a society that was at once eager for adventures of body and spirit and fearful of their consequences.

The fact that Sor María did not remain cloistered but traveled from place to place in the company of her Dominican brethren suggests that she experienced freedom from institutional obligations in the form of the duties and regulations incumbent upon her as a cloistered third order religious woman. Although it is true that Sor María did not exercise freedom in the matter of her rapture, which by definition and her own admission she could not control, she nevertheless was responsible to some degree for the setting of her ecstasies and for other situations. She had to have agreed to the peripatetic lifestyle that scandalized her critics. She had to have allowed herself to be put on public display at the court and in churches of Toledo and elsewhere so that her raptures could be witnessed. She had to have had a hand in the wearing of fancy clothes, dancing, and playing chess that smudged the image of a penitential holy woman. She had to have said "yes" to having men accompany her at night in her own bedroom. Exactly how much she agreed to and permitted is impossible to ascertain, but even allowing for a large dose of naiveté and the persuasive power of reformers who wanted their very own visionary woman, she could not have been completely oblivious to her behavior outside of rapture. In accepting some responsibility for her actions, Sor María would necessarily have been aware of alternatives, that she could or could not appear, for example, in a certain church where people expected her to be ecstasized for public viewing. If she had regarded the ecstatic performance not as the obligatory work to uphold the system, but rather as a personal event of her choosing, she would have recognized the difference between work and leisure and been free to play creatively, in which case her performance would be the liminoid phenomenon that the normative structure would reject.

A glance at Sor María's ecstatic discourse reveals immediately a startling kind of performance. In a word, her contemplations are one-woman shows. An obvious feature that sets her performance apart from Madre Juana's is that she speaks in the voice of the first person rather than the third person. The opening line of Madre Juana's discourse sets the third-person perspective: "While the Lord was speaking of the conception of our lady the Virgin Mary he said . . ."[36] The perspective is constant throughout the sermon, whether the content is theological ("And the Lord said that if they say and affirm that indeed our lady was born from the lineage of Adam, they tell the truth, but those that say she was born in original sin and bound by it through the sin of our first parents are deceived and in error")[37] or whether it is liturgical ("Then the Lord said that all the blessed souls were circling the castle, playing instruments and singing and rejoicing greatly festive").[38]

Sor María's "Contemplation while Enraptured on Easter Sunday," on the other hand, begins with the ecstatic woman's lament:

> Oh, my God. Oh, my God. Oh, my God. Oh, woe is me. Oh, woe is me who is not resurrected with You. When will I be resurrected in Your love and fear? When is the day of utter love and delight when I will rejoice with You? The day when heaven and earth rejoiced. Oh, my God, how alone and unhappy my soul who comes to You![39]

The first-person voice established with the opening words of the performance, Sor María turns to the Virgin Mary as if to a lifeless form, hidden in darkness on the stage until Sor María illumines her presence with this address: "Oh, most kind and sweet Mother of God and Mother of sinners! Oh devout Mother who wished to be Mother to sinners, Mother of torments and pleasure, Mother of pain, Mother of repose, Mother of repose for those in pain and Mother of pain for Him who was all repose, you who were Mother of pain for Him."[40] She further animates the Blessed

Mother by evoking her actions: "Oh sweet Mother of God, what do you see in these books? Since all the books say that He will rise up, cease weeping now. Ah, how lovingly, softly and meekly she weeps, as if she were not weeping. Yet she weeps so grievously that the tears of her eyes dampen her clothing."[41] She pulls her audience into the performance by saying: "Now see the living mother who saw her son die. See with what love and tears she washes and sweeps the cell while waiting for her Beloved."[42] And she maintains her presence as a character in the performance, speaking now to God, now to the Lord, now to the Blessed Mother, now to Mary Magdalen, Peter, and John, now to her audience.

She effects transitions within her performance from character to character, as when, speaking of God's people's failure to do his will, she asks, "Who does not seek him out of self-interest and amusement?" followed after one line of lament ("Woe is me, for I do not know how to value even this") by the question, "Whom do you seek, sister, with so many tears and moans, and why all this questioning of Him as if you would not recognize Him with the eyes of faith if you had seen Him and as if you would not recognize Him with whom you walked for seven months?"[43] Through conversation Mary Magdalen's identity is disclosed, and when the penitent woman recognizes the Lord in the person with whom she is speaking, Sor María says of the two people: "Behold the cry she utters as she casts herself completely at His feet! Behold Him telling her not to approach and how these words cause her more terror and suffering than what happened in the past!"[44] Then Sor María herself addresses Mary Magdalen:

> Do not fret, sister. Consider that our Beloved does not reject you. But now, draw near so you may awaken more fully by gazing on Him. Since you want all of yourself to be for Him, rejoice with Him in that He wants you to want Him in this way. Consider that when you told Him that you kept yourself for Him and that what you possessed was for Him and His sake, He then showed Himself to you.[45]

Further on the ecstatic woman speaks directly to Jesus: "Oh most benign Jesus, You took the hoe and gave it to us! Take care that the garden we are should be well tilled and cleared with the hoe."[46] Then she recreates the scene at the empty tomb with John, Peter, and the women. Even this little performance within a performance bears the personal, immediate touch of Sor María:

> Behold the women running to them! How they cry out and act joyously, exclaiming that He is risen! Behold the men happy and sad, doubtful and yet not doubting! They rejoice because they wanted to, but then they become sad, saying: "How will we assure the hard-headed ones that He is out of their hands? Since they are so obstinate, how will we be believed when we tell them that we are sure of it (because some women told us) unless we have firm proof?"[47]

Unlike the omniscient narrative voice of Madre Juana that tells the story, interprets events, and comments on meaning, Sor María's first-person narrative is pure stream-of-consciousness. As in a modern novel without the guidance of the observer, the reader of Sor María's transcribed text must grasp responsibility for identifying characters, discerning motivations, sorting out and rearranging events to make of them chronological sense, and bringing the performance alive in the imagination to detect the word or phrase that moves us from scene to scene, character to character, event to event. Sor María is no godlike observer to an action from which she stands apart; physically present within the discourse, she is at once pro-tagonist and playwright.

Embodiedness is the feature that surely separates the performances of the two visionary women. Madre Juana's voice is disembodied, coming from off stage, as it were, narrating, describing, and explaining, while she herself does not participate in the scenes and action she presents. Sor María's voice, on the other hand, is embodied, her physical presence cre-ating rather than merely reporting action. Although Madre Juana must necessarily be present in order to serve as the channel through whom the heavenly liturgy is celebrated, she is not physically engaged in the action as is Sor María, whose body the reader can imagine turning now this way, now that, as over and over she calls her audience to behold the characters in action:

> Behold the two men weeping and our Beloved saying with deep love to St. Peter: "Arise, my friend, arise, prostrate yourself no longer, no longer. May your sin not be placed in my penitence."
>
> He said: "I dare not lift my eyes to look at You for I denied You."
>
> The Lord says: "Rise up, rise up for the love I bear you and look at Me."
>
> Behold him standing and having looked at the Lord, falling

down as if dead and saying: "I gazed upon my Glory and He gazed at me."[48]

In order to understand the transcribed text of Madre Juana's performance, the reader must be aware only of the enraptured woman's voice; the text of Sor María's performance requires awareness of both voice and body, with special sensitivity to inflections of the body as the instrument by which the performance is being created moment by moment. It is the necessary and unavoidable physicality of Sor María's presence in the performance that creates the individual ritual; even when a contemplation resembles liturgy, as does her discourse at Easter, the performance is uniquely hers because her body is both the instrument and the meaning of the ecstatic discourse. Individual and spontaneous, personal and physical, her performance is a liminoid phenomenon because in its embodiedness it is generated in the margins of gender conventions and, as such, challenges those conventions. Perhaps the physicality of Sor María's ecstatic performance nettled men who in turn questioned the authenticity of her visions and gossiped about her personal conduct. For skeptics reared on misogynist traditions that reviled the female body as the source and purveyor of sin, the sexuality of Sor María—the sight, sound, smell, touch of her body—could have sealed their fears that the woman was at best an opportunist, at worst a seducer of men's souls.

The Paradox of Performance

Alike in many respects, Madre Juana and Sor María nonetheless ended their lives on different notes: Madre Juana lived out her days in the peace of a cloister, her fame as a holy woman assured for centuries by the hand of a biographer and dramatist. Only when the process for her beatification opened in Rome in 1621 and the Congregation of Sacred Rites scrutinized *The Book of Consolation* and the *Life* did serious questioning of her orthodoxy take place. The Jesuit Martin de Esparza Artieda censured 17 doctrinal points in *The Book of Consolation,* while Cardinal Gionanni Bona censored 23, among them number 15 that called the negative opinion on the Immaculate Conception a huge error; and number 16, that branded as traitors people who denied the Immaculate Conception.[49] Determined to convince church authorities that Madre Juana's sermons and teachings were orthodox, her supporters argued that the manuscript under review was not hers at all and that a decision should be delayed until the authentic one could be located. The strategy failed. A certain Father Coppens refuted the objections in writing and various papers preserved in archives in Rome reveal that other advocates came forward on behalf of her cause; but official proceedings were abandoned, not to be reopened until 1986. The road to beatification remains blocked by objections; the official catalogue of causes for beatification for the Franciscan order has her name as number 130 on a list of candidates, with the annotation that difficulties in her case must be resolved.[50]

Sor María has survived in name if not in popular devotion. She figures primarily in documents relating to the strife within the Dominican order and in literature on religious reform in the early part of the sixteenth century. With the publication in Spanish of *The Book of Prayer* in 1948, interest in the visionary woman escalated, undoubtedly prompted by increasing scholarly interest in the recovery of visionary women's texts. Until recently most literature about Sor María was the work of men who inherited the biases of Henry Charles Lea and Menéndez Pelayo[51] and the ambiguous image of her conveyed by chroniclers of the Dominican order who disapproved of the reform movement with which she was identified.[52] Sor María was a pivotal figure in a political conflict of such gravity within the Dominican order that Rome and the highest prelate of Spain were called into the fray. The controversy was no trifle; at stake was the very survival of the order. The reformers for whom Sor María spoke prophetically saw grave deficiencies in the system and threatened to secede if their calls for reform were not heeded.

Sor María was no trifle either; she was the dissidents' portable stage and performer. Where she was, there was the stage, and there, too, the performance. Her performance was not the liminal phenomenon of Madre Juana, which could be incorporated by the religious structure at least temporarily, until the process of beatification would require closer scrutiny. Sor María's performance was liminoid, individual, and idiosyncratic in its physicality. It sufficiently jarred institutional sensibilities into calling into serious question the woman's orthodoxy and morality and provoked a summons from the Inquisition, not once but four times, a haunting reminder of how tenuous the line is between glorification and vilification.

The comparison of the two visionaries cannot be left as a tidy arrangement of similarities and differences. Paradox has the final say. In terms of doctrine, it turns out that the saintly Madre Juana was a potential rebel and Sor María orthodox to the bone. Given the serious doubts about Sor María's moral conduct, the genuineness of her visions, and the orthodoxy of their content, a reasonable expectation is to find in her *Book of*

Prayer evidence that she strayed into heretical territory. The facts make for another case: comparison of statements from the 1525 book of *alumbrado* beliefs with the transcribed texts reveals no substantive connection with the *alumbrado* heresy, thus lending credence to the opinion that the real basis for accusations was not the content of her discourse but rather the instrument of it—her body.[53] Whether bodily enacting the performance being created in the moment, traveling around Spain with men and even residing with them, or wearing colorful clothes and dancing, Sor María's sexuality was in the foreground. Had she cloistered herself in discretion, she might not have drawn allegations of heresy and scandal, but neither she nor the men who advised her and whose agendas she served concealed her physicality. Sor María was on display. For this bold defiance of standards of comportment for women, and specifically, for a third order religious woman, she was subject to informal inquisitorial examination, confined to the convent, and unfairly identified with the *alumbrado* heresy.

If Madre Juana were judged only by the reputation for holiness still hers today, no hint of suspicion about orthodoxy and unseemly behavior would come her way. But as Ronald E. Surtz's analysis of her sermons demonstrates, Madre Juana's views on women were anything but conventional: what in this essay have been termed novel recombinations of familiar elements could be interpreted as Madre Juana's strategies for revealing as divinely ordained for women the power and authority denied them by cultural misogyny. If her sermons sound subversive in terms of church doctrine, Surtz would have us remember "that the questionable orthodoxy of some of Juana's visions was the principal reason for the negative outcome of her beatification."[54]

The subversive Madre Juana surfaces in the sermon on the Immaculate Conception, in which she presents the Virgin Mary not only as a castle but also a house of prayer where "prayers and petitions and cries of sacrifice are made with which God is pleased and softened"[55] and a church with many altars where God is consecrated. In joining sacrifice, church, and altar, Madre Juana evokes the image of the priest celebrating the sacrifice of the Mass. The effect is a mixing of the prophetic and priestly roles in the person of the woman who is empowered by God to celebrate a liturgy that by divine authority is being instituted through her word by word. Possibly Madre Juana would have suffered recrimination in her lifetime for her boldness in claiming power and authority for women had her stage been outside of the convent like Sor María's and had she shared the other woman's taste for clothes, diversions, and male companions; but Madre Juana's style was clothed in discretion and a stable environment was hers as well, a situation far different from that of Sor María, who happened to be affiliated with a monastery in open rebellion against its order. Ultimately, the finished look of the contrasting portraits of Madre Juana and Sor Maria as candidates for beatification and trial, respectively, turns out to be illusory. To consider their portraits in the light of paradox is not only to blur the image of two women who appeared to be a study in contrasts, but to realize that in the final analysis the fate of the visionary woman was decided not so much on the content of her performance as on the role of her body in the act of performing, as well as in the actions that shaped the context for her theater. If the visionary woman honored sexual conventions with the decorum of Madre Juana, stardom might be assured, but if like Sor María she was perceived to be flouting those standards in her behavior, it was likely her stage would darken, the curtain fall, and her star be abandoned to the Inquisition.

Notes

1. For the most comprehensive study on this period of religious reform, see Marcel Bataillon, *Erasmo y España: Estudios sobre la historia espiritual del siglo xvi* (Mexico City: Fondo de Cultura Económica, 1966).

2. For information on Madre Juana's life see especially Ronald E. Surtz, *The Guitar of God: Gender, Power, and Authority in the Visionary World of Mother Juana de la Cruz (1481–1534)* (Philadelphia: University of Pennsylvania Press, 1990) and Jesús Gómez López and Inocente García de Andrés, *Sor Juana de la Cruz, mística e iluminista toledana* (Toledo: Diputación Provincial, 1982).

3. Surtz calls the book a "sermon-book" in *The Guitar of God*, 6. *El libro del conorte*, Escorial MS J-II-18, has 454 folios.

4. More information on Madre Juana's life is in the *Vida y fin de la bienabenturada virgen sancta Juana de la Cruz*, Escorial MS K-111–13, 137 folios, attributed to Sor María Evangelista.

5. For an account of the celebration see Gómez López and García de Andrés, *Sor Juana de la Cruz*, 5–9.

6. Scholars are not in agreement on the date of her birth, some placing it as early as 1470, another as late as 1486. See Mary E. Giles, *The Book of Prayer of Sor María of Santo Domingo: A Study and Translation* (Albany, NY: State University of New York Press, 1990), 7.

7. Giles, *The Book of Prayer*, 8.

8. Ibid., 46–61.

9. Antonio de la Peña, who probably edited the contemplations and wrote the "Summary of Her Virtuous and Perfect Life," happened to

have translated Catherine of Siena's life, her letters, and prayers. The first edition of her life was printed by Brocar, 1511, and her letters and prayers were published a year later.

10. The Latin passage is reproduced in Giles, *The Book of Prayer*, 183–82, note 5.

11. The manuscript was discovered in the archives of the University of Zaragoza in 1948 and published in a facsimile edition by José Manuel Blecua (Madrid: Hauser y Menet, 1948).

12. For the influence of Erasmus in Spain see Bataillon, *Erasmo y España*.

13. The bibliography on the *alumbrados* is extensive. Major works include: Melquíades Andrés Martín, *El misterio de los alumbrados de Toledo, desvelado por sus contemporáneos (1523–1560)* (Burgos: El Monte Carmelo, 1976) and *Nueva visión de los "alumbrados" de 1525* (Madrid: Fundación Universitaria Española, 1973); Alvaro Huerga, *Historia de los alumbrados*, 3 vols. (Madrid: Fundación Universitaria Española, 1973); Antonio Márquez, *Los alumbrados: Orígenes y filosofía (1525–1559)*, 2nd. ed. (Madrid: Taurus Ediciones, S.A., 1980).

14. Mental prayer, as distinguished from vocal prayer, requires actively thinking about the words that one is saying aloud or to oneself. Teresa of Avila practiced and taught mental prayer, both in person and in her writings. An influential spiritual treatise on the subject was written by Francisco de Osuna. See the translation by Mary E. Giles, *Third Spiritual Alphabet* (New York: Paulist Press, 1981).

15. Victor Turner, *From Ritual to Theatre: The Human Seriousness of Play* (New York City: Performing Arts Journal Publications, 1982).

16. See Wilhelm Dilthey, *Selected Writings*, ed. and intro. H. P. Rickman (London: Cambridge University Press, 1976).

17. Turner, *From Ritual to Theatre*, 13.

18. Ibid., 15.

19. For a detailed study of the relationship between ecstatic discourse and postmodern theater, see Mary E. Giles, "Holy Theatre/Ecstatic Theatre," in *Vox Mystica: Essays on Medieval Mysticism*, ed. Anne Clark Bartlett et al. (Cambridge: D. S. Brewer, 1995), 117–128.

20. For a summary of the points in her defense see Giles, *The Book of Prayer*, 36–7.

21. Turner, *From Ritual to Theatre*, 48.

22. Vicente Beltrán de Heredia, in *Historia en la reforma de la Provincia de España(1450–1550)* (Roma: Institutum Historicum F. F. Praedicatorum Romae ad. S. Sabinae, 1939), 240–46, includes a statement given by Diego de Vitoria at the examination in 1509 in which he describes the process by which he and other men conferred about the wording and meaning of the transcription, confessing that they did not always agree on the meaning.

23. Gómez López and García de Andrés, *Sor Juana de la Cruz*, 39–42.

24. Turner, *From Ritual to Theatre*, 24.

25. In applying the theories of Turner and van Gennep, I regard their paradigms as fluid and expansive, allowing for interpretations that not only affect analysis of the subjects, but also reveal the capacity of the theories to extend beyond the original application. For a specific critique of Turner's theories as they relate to the study of visionary women, see Caroline Walker Bynum, *Fragmentation and Redemption: Essays on Gender and the Human Body in Medieval Religion* (New York: Zone Books, 1991): 27–51.

26. Ibid., 27.

27. Passages are drawn from the transcription of the sermon by J. Gómez López, "El 'Conorte' de Sor Juana de la Cruz y su sermón sobre la inmaculada concepción de María," *Hispania Sacra* 36 (1984): 601–27. . . . aunque los doctores e predicadores e letrados la loan y encalçan e dizen la verdad, nunca supieron ni sabra acabar de loar e dezir todas las eselencias e virtudes de su preciosa madre (620).

28. E dixo el señor que en este mesmo dia que el fabló e declaró las cosas suso dichas, fueron delante su divina magestad muchedunbre de angeles tañendo e cantando e faziendo muy grandes gozos e diziendo: Acuerdate señor que fazen en la tierra fiesta e memoria de la linpisima e sin macula concepcion de nuestra señora la virgen maria (621).

29. . . . que estar nuestra señora dende la cinta abaxo fecha castillo e dende la cinta arriba doncella (622).

30. Dixo el señor que callava él a todo lo que nuestra señora dezia, no le rrespondía ninguna cosa e dexava la viguela e le davan un añafil e tañia un rato con el. E por semejante le dexava y le davan otro estrumento, e tañia e cantava muy dulcemente andando con tino alrededor del castillo; alçando sienpre sus preciosos ojos fazia en alto mirando a nuestra señora e diziendo: O mi paloma e mi amada!, si agora me mirases e te enamorases de mi e desseases estar conmigo! (625).

31. . . . gozó nuestra señora del como ella queria e deseava, muy llena e cunplidamente . . . estando él gozando con su santisima madre . . . la tomó él de sus poderosos braços e le subio al palacio altissimo e rreal e secreto de la santissima trinidad e alli fue ella ensalçada e inflamada más que todos los cherubines e serafines (626).

32. See William A. Christian, *Apparitions in Late Medieval and Renaissance Spain* (Princeton, NJ: Princeton University Press, 1981) and *Local Religion in Sixteenth-Century Spain* (Princeton, NJ: Princeton University Press, 1981).

33. The question of authorship of the sermons became crucial during negotiations for her beatification in the seventeenth century. Her supporters countered objections to the theology of her sermons by denying that she was their author. See especially Surtz, *The Guitar of God*, 136–38. These actions make plausible the possibility that at the time of transcription modifications might have been made.

34. See especially Giles, *The Book of Prayer*, 21–38.

35. According to Turner in *From Ritual to Theatre*, liminoid phenomena flourish in societies "generated by and following the industrial revolution, though they perhaps begin to appear on the scene in city-states on their way to becoming empires (of the Graeco-Roman type) and in feudal societies (including not only the European sub-types found between the tenth and fourteenth centuries in France, England, Flanders, and Germany, but also in the far less 'pluralistic' Japanese, Chinese, and Russian types of feudalism or quasi-feudalism). But they first begin clearly to develop in Western Europe in nascent capitalist societies, with the beginnings of industrialization and mechanizations, the transformation of labor into a commodity, and the appearance of real social classes. " This type of society "had begun to appear in Western Europe in the second half of the sixteenth century ..." (53)

36. Fablando el señor de la concepcion de nuestra señora la virgen maria dixo ... (615).

37. E dixo el señor que si dizen e afirman que si nuestra señora nascio de linage de adan, que dizen verdad, mas que los que dizen nascio en pecado original e obligada a el por el pecado de nuestros primeros padres, que estan engañados e yerran en ello (617).

38. El luego dixo el señor andavan todos los bienaventurados alrrededor del castillo, tañendo e cantando e faziendo grandes alegrias (623).

39. Pagination is mine, spelling has not been modernized, letters within brackets are indicated by abbreviations in original text. Ay mi dios, Ay mi dios, Ay mi dios. Ay triste yo. Ay de mí triste, q[ue] no se resuscitar co[n]tigo. E qua[n]do resuscitare en tu amor y temor. Qua[n]do en dia q[ue] es todo de amor y de plazer, sabre alegrarme co[n]tigo, el dia q[ue] se alegro el cielo y la t[ie]rra. Ay dios mio y qua[n] sola viene mi al[m]a a ti y qua[n] triste (22).

40. Benignissima y dulce madre de dios y madre de los pecadores. O piadosa madre q[ue] q[ui]so ser madre dellos: madre pa[ra] torme[n]tos y pa[ra] plazer, madre pa[ra] dolor y madre pa[ra] desca[n]so, madre de descaso pa[ra] los q[ue] estaua[n] en dolor y madre de dolor pa[ra] el q[ue] era todo desca[n]so. Fueste madre de dolor pa[ra] el (24).

41. O dulce madre de dios, y q[ue] miras en [e]ssos libros. Y pues todos te dize[n] q[ue] se leua[n]tara: cessa ya de llorar. Y co[n] q[ue] amor y suauidad esta llora[n]do tan ma[n]samete como si no llorasse. Y llora ta[n] rezio q[ue] las lagrimas de sus ojos moja[n] sus tocados (25).

42. Vea ya la madre biuo al hijo q[ue] vido morir. Ved co[n] q[ue] amor y lagrimas riega y barre la celda esp[er]a[nd]do a su desseado (26).

43. ... y quie[n] por su p[ro]pio interesse y recreacio[n] no lo busca? Hay de mi triste q[ue] avn esto yo no se tener. Hermana y a quie[n] buscas co[n] ta[n]tas bozes y gemidos? Y que pregu[n]tar es esse que trahes por el como si le viesses no le conoscerias con ojos de fe? No le conoscerias en siete meses que co[n] el anduuiste (31)?

44. Ved el grito q[ue] da arrojandose toda a sus pies y dizie[n]dole el

q[ue] no allegue. Mas espanto y dolor le da aq[ue]llo que lo passado (32).

45. Hermana no te fatigues. Mira que no te desecha n[uest]ro desseado Mas allegate con esso assi mas porq[ue] despiertes mas en mirarle. Y pues te q[ui]eres toda para el alegrate con el enlo que quiere el por quererlo assi a el. Mira que qua[n]do dixiste que te tenias a ti para el y lo q[ue] tenias pa el y por suyo del, luego el se te mostro (32).

46. O benignissimo Jesu pues tu tomaste y nos das el açada. Mira q[ue] sea bie[n] labrado y apurado co[n] ella el jardin q[ue] somos nosotros (34).

47. Ved como vienen ellas corriendo a ellos y que bozes y que alegria traen, diziendo que es ya levantado. Ved a ellos alegres y tristes, dudosos y no dudan dello. Alegranse porq[ue] lo querrian, y entristecense dizie[n]do: Como certificaremos alos de dura cerviz q[ue] el es ya fuera de sus manos? Como sie[n]do ellos tan duros seremos nosotros creydos dizie[n]doles q[ue] lo sabemos (porq[ue] vnas mujeres nos lo dixero[n]) sino tenemos pa[ra] esto firmeza mayor de certificarseles (36–7).

48. Ved como llora[n] los dos y n[uest]ro desseado dize co[n] mucho amor a sa[n]t Pedro. Leua[n]tate amigo mio leua[n]tate ya no mas ya no mas, y no sea puesto tu pecado en mi p[enite]ncia. Y dizie[n]do el no osare leua[n]tar mis ojos a mirarte pues te negue, dize el señor, leua[n]tate leua[n]tate por el amor mio y mira me. Ved lo leua[n]tado y hauiendo mirado al señor cabe como muerto dizie[n]do Mire a mi gl[or]ia y miro me (38).

49. Gómez López and García de Andrés, Sor Juana de la Cruz, 37. In the sermon on the Immaculate Conception Madre Juana had said forthrightly that people who deny the immaculate conception do not tell the truth and are in grave error (615).

50. Ibid., 14.

51. See especially Henry Charles Lea, History of the Inquisition of Spain, vol. 4 (New York: AMS Press, 1906–1907), 6 and Marcelino Menéndez Pelayo, Historia de los heterodoxos españoles (Mexico City: Editorial Porrúa, S.A., 1982), 312.

52. In his history of the Dominican Order, written around the middle of the century, Juan de la Cruz stated that the monastery of Piedrahita wanted to separate from the province for reasons of increased austerity but also because of growing self-interest. He mentions Sor María as assisting the fathers in the attempt to separate. Cited by Beltrán de Heredia, Historia de la reforma, 135–36.

53. For a detailed analysis see Giles, The Book of Prayer, 63–75

54. Surtz, The Guitar of God, 79.

55. For further analysis of Sor Juana's priestly role see Mary E. Giles, "The Discourse of Ecstasy: Late Medieval Spanish Women and Their Texts," in Gender and Text in the Later Middle Ages, ed. Jane Chance (Gainesville: University Press of Florida, 1996), 320.

Bibliography

Andrés Martín, Melquíades. *El misterio de los alumbrados de Toledo, desvelado por sus contemporáneos (1523–1560)*. Burgos, El Monte Carmelo, 1976.

———. *Nueva visión de los "alumbrados" de 1525*. Madrid: Fundación Universitaria Española, 1973.

Bataillon, Marcel. *Erasmo y España: Estudios sobre la historia espiritual del siglo xvi*. Mexico City: Fondo de Cultura Económica, 1966.

Beltrán de Heredia, Vicente. *Las corrientes de espiritualidad entre los dominicos de Castilla durante la primera mitad del siglo XVI*. Salamanca, 1941.

———. *Historia de la reforma en la Provincia de España*. Roma, Institutum Historicum F. F. Praedicatorum Romae ad. S. Sabinae, 1939.

Bynum, Caroline Walker. *Fragmentation and Redemption: Essays on Gender and the Human Body in Medieval Religion*. New York: Zone Books, 1991.

Christian, William A. *Apparitions in Late Medieval and Renaissance Spain*. Princeton: Princeton University Press, 1981.

———. *Local Religion in Sixteenth-Century Spain*. Princeton: Princeton University Press, 1981.

Dilthey, Wilhelm. *Selected Writings*. Ed. and Intro. H. P. Rickman. London: Cambridge University Press, 1976.

Giles, Mary E. *The Book of Prayer of Sor María of Santo Domingo: A Study and Translation*. Albany: State University of New York Press, 1990.

———. "The Discourse of Ecstasy: Late Medieval Spanish Women and Their Texts." In *Gender and Text in the Later Middle Ages*, ed. Jane Chance. Gainesville: University Press of Florida, 1996, 306–30.

———. "Holy Theatre/Ecstatic Theatre." In *Vox Mystica: Essays on Medieval Mysticism in Honor of Professor Valerie M. Lagorio*, ed. Anne Clark Bartlett et al., 117–128. Cambridge: D. S. Brewer, 1995.

———., trans. *Third Spiritual Alphabet*. New York: Paulist Press, 1981.

Gómez López, Jesús. "El 'Conorte' de Sor Juana de la Cruz y su sermón sobre la inmaculada concepción de María." *Hispania Sacra* 36 (1984): 601–27.

———, and Inocente García de Andrés. *Sor Juana de la Cruz, mística e iluminista toledana*. Toledo: Diputación Provincial, 1982.

Huerga, Alvaro. *Historia de los alumbrados*. 3 vols. Madrid: Fundación Universitaria Española, 1973.

Lea, Henry Charles. *History of the Inquisition of Spain*. 4 vols. New York: AMS Press, 1906–1907.

Márquez, Antonio. *Los alumbrados. Orígenes y filosofía (1525–1559)*, second ed. Madrid: Tayrus Ediciones, S.A., 1980.

Menéndez Pelayo, Marcelino. *Historia de los heterodoxos españoles*. Mexico: Editorial Porrúa, S.A., 1982.

Surtz, Ronald E. *The Guitar of God: Gender, Power, and Authority in the Visionary World of Mother Juana de la Cruz (1481–1534).* Philadelphia: University of Pennsylvania Press, 1990.

Turner, Victor. *From Ritual to Theater: The Human Seriousness of Play.* New York: Performing Arts Journal Publications, 1982.

CHAPTER ELEVEN

Elisabeth of Spalbeek's Trance Dance of Faith: A Performance Theory Interpretation from Anthropological and Art Historical Perspectives

Susan Rodgers and Joanna E. Ziegler

Interdisciplinary work stands to bring much to medieval studies. But this is only so if researchers are well grounded in their respective fields and are not interested in some mere polite sharing of ideas across disciplinary boundaries but rather wish to formulate new, more powerful approaches to difficult cultural materials. In that spirit, this essay is written in order to shed light on one of the most intriguing and unusual examples of medieval women's mysticism. Our subject is Elisabeth of Spalbeek, virgin and visionary, whose thirteenth-century *vita* attests to a holy life of performance. The blending of these two particular disciplines may at times be unsettling to medievalists. The language of anthropology, for instance, may jolt the reader, for it characterizes ecstasy and holiness in ways that may be unfamiliar to medievalists. Yet it is precisely because our approaches, when combined, disrupt customary categories and expectations for interpretive language that we believe such a blending of disciplines may offer fresh and revealing insights. We begin with the situation of Elisabeth and her *vita* as the anthropologist would describe it.

When anthropologists are asked to consider Western medieval mysticism, it seems to have sometimes involved a deep interiority, in which contemplative monks or nuns entered quiet meditative states to touch the divine. Anthropologists would immediately note that ritual techniques employed for attaining such forms of consciousness included intensive chanting and various types of self-denial, ranging from social isolation to food refusal. These are all phenomena quite predictable to cultural anthropologists familiar with the cross–cultural literature on trance. In perhaps the most extreme example of this sort of inward-directed trajectory of faith, medieval holy fasting girls pursued sacredness and union with divinity by asserting that they could subsist solely by consuming the consecrated wafers of the Eucharist. By eating only the Host these young women apparently thought that they were not only consuming the Body of Christ but were in effect uniting their bodies with his. Historian Caroline Walker Bynum has explored with great sensitivity the remarkable worlds of "bodily faith" posited by these twelfth- and thirteenth-century holy women and girls.[1] Perhaps these young women, more than any other medieval devouts, stressed a sense of "closing in" on the self in their pursuit of oneness with God.

When seen in the most general anthropological terms, the religiously motivated food denial of the Middle Ages seems to have focused the ritual celebrant's attention on the body itself, and on its interior states (in this case, on what were probably painful interior states). Many of these holy fasters were involved in other sorts of devotionalism as well (for instance, praying, pilgrimages) but it does not seem too much to claim that for these religious devotees, their bodies became their prime sites for attaining ecstatic union with Christ's flesh. Moreover, if a holy faster was diligent and particularly single-minded in her quest, her body would eventually literally shrink inward, as her food denial, faith, and "hunger for Christ's body" progressed.

Other types of medieval devotion pointed outward beyond the physical body: toward intense ritual interaction with devotional objects such as sculptures (for instance, the Low Country beguines' ritual practices of stroking, handling, dressing, and undressing wooden sculptures of the Christ-child), toward participation in popular drama (the Passion plays), or toward drama-like ceremonial activities such as walking through the

Stations of the Cross. Participation in the Mass itself of course led priestly celebrants and the laity into a series of complex interactions with objects outside the body (with the Eucharist, holy vestments, holy texts) and with ritual architectural spaces (church interiors, shrines, pilgrimage sites).

Medieval mysticism and particularly women's modes of worship within it had another important, if rare, variant, however, one that employed a different vocabulary of bodily symbolism than these other options: that is, active, energetic, outward-thrusting, specifically ecstatic dance. Here, the worshiper would move forcefully and sometimes even exuberantly through such spaces as church interiors, claiming these locales as fields of devotion that they themselves, as performers, could actively shape and define through personal, idiosyncratic choreography. These intensely creative dance performances took place in spaces far outside the boundaries of the human body itself, and, in their ecstatic abandon, these choreographic events went considerably beyond such relatively more church-sanctioned activities as devotion to sacred sculptures, or participation in the Stations of the Cross. In these performances the trance dancer's—that is, the mystic's—body became one cultural site among many extrasomatic, choreographic, and even architectural ones for professing belief and asserting union with the sacred. The individualized creation of such holy dance routines represented something truly innovative within the Christianity of the time: a familiar potential of ecstatic dance, when seen in cross-cultural perspective.

Here in this paper, drawing on anthropological insights like those just discussed but also venturing into art history, we would like to examine the world of faith created in an extraordinary ritual dance life of just this sort: the performance experience of a young Beguine known to us today as Elisabeth of Spalbeek.[2] She lived in a small village near Liège in the mid-thirteenth century and by 1267 her ritual activities had drawn the respectful if amazed attention of Abbot Philip of Clairvaux. A Cistercian and clear admirer of Elisabeth, he wrote a report of her activities, later known as her *vita*.[3] Early on in their association he reported that Elisabeth would engage regularly in such activities as rhythmically beating her chest, caressing and kissing a diptych painted with a scene of the crucifixion, then falling into a distracted, ecstatic state, then moving exultantly around the entire inside of her chapel. In these dances, Elisabeth would perform all the major narrative events of the Stations of the Cross, ending with a kind of tableau representation of Christ's body crucified on the cross. Stigmata appeared on her body and (Abbot Philip reports) she regularly bled from her hands, feet, and side. The main audiences for her performances seem to have consisted of male clergy (the abbot and his monks), while her reputation as a holy girl manifesting signs of divinity seems to have been fairly widespread throughout her parish community. Speaking anthropologically, Elisabeth as a sacred, inspired dancer embodied certain crucial tension-filled power dynamics of her culture and her moment in history. Many of these dimensions had to do with gender and social hierarchy. Through her dance performances, which were indeed also apparently trance events, Elisabeth symbolically became the body of Christ, in intriguing counterpoint to the ways in which the quieter, more physically still mystics of her era claimed to attain union with Christ's flesh via their ritual eating behavior. Beyond temporarily blurring the boundaries between human and divine (as many religious trance activities tend to do), Elisabeth's dances also indexed gender dynamics and matters of domination and resistance within the Christianity of her time and place.

In a social structural sense, at least when viewed anthropologically, Elisabeth was a young girl positioned far from the male clergy-dominated official power centers of the church of her time. Moreover, since her devotionalism took the form of ecstatic trance performances and not the somewhat more socially acceptable types of faith such as the Beguines' sculpture- or liturgy-focused worship, Elisabeth also stood somewhat outside the institutionalized centers of female religious power. But, despite her seeming powerlessness on both these fronts, Elisabeth was remarkably bold: she implicitly tried to create Christianity anew in her nonverbal dance life, in the symbolic arena of her own sensual, moving, young woman's body. This was a decidedly unorthodox renarration of Christian myth and iconography. Dancing from the ecclesiastical periphery, as it were (as anthropologist I. M. Lewis might put the matter)[4] Elisabeth offered her onlookers and the later readers of her *vita* a possibly subversive, alternative vision of the relationship between devout women, women's bodies, and the power and presence of Christ among his believers.

Elisabeth as a holy dancer made stunning theological and gender claims. In ecstatic dance and in "ravishment," as she danced out the Holy Hours (a particular preoccupation), Elisabeth did not simply worship God or Christ but symbolically became the cross, which is to say as well the crucified, male, divine Christ. Elisabeth could theoretically have danced out such assertions in any of a number of public or private spaces, but she chose to do so in a particularly power-laden spot: in church, where the official religion held that Christ should appear most powerfully through the Eucharistic ritual, which only the priest can enact. Elisabeth, as a dancer, asserted that she and not just the official church could narrate the

Passion story, and more, that as a ritual performer she could bring Christ's body into public view, in its bodily entirety. She did this with special emotional poignancy and perhaps even "shock value," for audiences of apparently somewhat awestruck clergy (Abbot Philip himself consistently shows a mixture of amazement and respect when narrating Elisabeth's dance actions).

When seen from our late-twentieth-century, anthropologically informed perspective (where observers tend to be particularly alert to issues of domination and resistance), Elisabeth obviously had a touch of scandal about her, and perhaps also one of illicit beauty. To invoke once again I. M. Lewis's framework for interpreting conventionalized religious worlds and the subversive rituals of resistance that sometimes develop along their peripheries of power:[5] Elisabeth's dances were implicit critiques of the idea that only the official church could mediate divinity and regulate believers' relationships to the body of Christ.

The present-day scholarly literature on the processes at work in many cultures in which social structural power becomes encoded in symbolic representations of the body, as body per se,[6] has clear utility here in interpreting Elisabeth's faith, as does the research literature in history and the social sciences on resistance strategies which take bodily form. However, her form of worship and the particular tone her mysticism took obviously cannot be satisfactorily interpreted without also taking the issue of ritual *performance* into account. This is our focus here in this essay. Elisabeth's body was made divine not just by thought, talk, song, or fasting, but by being put into forceful choreographic motion through a specific type of ritual space. To begin to take some account of that fact, we would like to search for Elisabeth (so to speak) and for her personal symbolism of devotion by approaching her person and her performance epistemology from two disciplinary avenues. We believe that these can be joined together dialogically to good effect and that this methodological approach may have some promise for other students of religion in the Middle Ages.

We draw first on cultural anthropology, the field of one of us (Susan Rodgers, who has done fieldwork in the Angkola Batak region of North Sumatra, Indonesia—an area of the world whose indigenous religions have led anthropologists into productive debates about official faiths and the voices of resistance that develop in tandem with them).[7] We place special emphasis here on the ways in which ceremonial performances (and not just imagined bodies) within religious traditions can act as ways for formulating particularly powerful imageries of the performer's self in relation to divinity, via the manipulation of mythic story lines in relation to bodily states.[8] Also important for us here are anthropological explorations of the internal performance structure and pacing of trance dance events, as these sometimes lead to new conceptions of the dancer's self and body.

The anthropological literature on performance is quite large. Perhaps most familiar to nonanthropologists coming from such areas as theater studies is the ambitiously cross-cultural work of such scholars as Richard Schechner, Victor Turner, and David Napier.[9] We do make use of this type of work, but also valuable to us in examining Elisabeth's trance performances are a range of more closely focused case studies of Asian ritual performances involving issues of gender and social power (for instance, Sally Ann Ness's *Body, Movement, and Culture*, Mary M. Steedly's *Hanging Without a Rope*, Anna L. Tsing's work on Meratus women healers in Kalimantan, and Gananath Obeyeskere's now-classic *Medusa's Hair* and related texts on South Asian holy madness involving women's possession dances).[10] We shall also make one short excursion into the performance literature by ethnographers of Papua New Guinea,[11] a region whose ritual dances are often characterized by rich vocabularies of ritual reversals, of much comparative interest here.

As a general backdrop to this broadly cross-cultural line of inquiry about trance dance and constructions of self, we shall also be sketching in some of the social structural dimensions of Elisabeth's status as a specifically ecstatic sort of religious devotee, with the help of Lewis's influential *Ecstatic Religion*. The latter sort of scene-setting endeavor may seem somewhat unnecessary to anthropologists long familiar with this style of analysis (which along with Mary Douglas's work on witchcraft[12] is by now a staple of the anthropology of religion). However, we include it here for medievalist scholars who may be intrigued to learn how anthropologists might approach a religious devout such as Elisabeth of Spalbeek. In the anthropological sections of the essay we tend to take a broad, comparative, cross-cultural approach in our efforts to place Elisabeth's performances against a backdrop of related ritual events in a wide variety of cultures. Anthropology is used here quite purposely to provide a context for other parts of the paper, which tend to be much more closely focused on the actual text of Abbot Philip's *vita*. We find that a methodology of tacking back and forth between a broad-gauged comparative view and one focused tightly on the medieval text helps us to uncover elements of Elisabeth's dance experience in a stepwise fashion, with one insight building on another.[13]

Beyond anthropology we draw on art history and drama theory, with a particular focus on Elisabeth's dances as theater and her ritual uses of a church interior space. In an art historical perspective, as this can be expanded with the help of certain sectors of performance theory, such spaces as churches can become much more intelligible to us when seen specifically as performance sites. Art history is the field of Joanna Ziegler, a student of Beguine communities and their forms of worship related to sacred sculpture such as Pietà figures. Art historical approaches to medieval women's ritual lives and the objects and architectural spaces they interacted with have tended until recently to draw rather sparsely on performance theory. Here, we find the work of drama theorist Jerzy Grotowski[14] particularly useful in correcting this situation, since he helps us to see Elisabeth's ecstatic dances as a specific form of what might be termed elemental theater.

For both anthropology and art history, we find that a critical use of some of the recent literature on performance stands to push our views of medieval mysticism into new territory. In an admittedly exploratory way in this frankly experimental and methodologically focused essay, we shall set these anthropological and art historical interpretive frameworks to interrogating each other, possibly to expand each other's interpretive scope. All this, to help us "see" Elisabeth and her brilliant choreographic retelling of Christian myth in clearer ways than would be possible if any one disciplinary lens were used alone.

We should make an additional methodological point before going on to look at Elisabeth's *vita* and then proceeding to sketch in some of her social structural setting, as we can reconstruct that with the aid of I. M. Lewis and the standard anthropological literature on trance, shamanism, and possession states. Feminist scholarly approaches to medieval mysticism and to representations of the female body and Christ's body in that period are of quite evident help in interpreting Elisabeth's devotion to Christ and understanding her creative, personalized ritual rendition of herself as Christ and cross.[15] However, here again (although we gratefully draw on feminist analytical frameworks at frequent junctures) we wish to push beyond standard feminist anthropological and art historical approaches to the body (per se), when we look at this small corner of medieval mysticism. When we draw on feminist insights about women, power, and resistance within medieval Christianity, we shall be asking once again how the literature on ritual performance can be productively joined to other scholarship on the body, to once again yield a more complex interpretive framework.

Let us now briefly review Abbot Philip's *vita* in more detail, a plan

that will also allow us to introduce readers to several important contex-
tualizing features of Beguine community life.[16]

Elisabeth Commemorated: Evidence from Philip's Vita

Philip was abbot of Clairvaux, director of the mother house of the Cistercian Order.[17] As such, he was responsible for making visitations to the
houses of the Order. One of these was the Cistercian abbey of Herkenrode
in Liège, nearby Spalbeek. This monastery housed Cistercian nuns, and it
was while visiting there in 1267 that Philip learned of Elisabeth's activities.
He met with her in order to see her stigmata, in his words, "with his own
eyes." Philip interviewed the local devotees and watched her devotional
activities. When he returned to Clairvaux, he drafted a report of his observations, dwelling with meticulous care on the details of her spiritual
enactments. That report is what today we refer to as Elisabeth's *vita*.

In his account of this young Beguine's remarkable activities within
her chapel, Abbot Philip reports (as noted) that she would beat herself
rhythmically with holy pictures, fall into a special state of consciousness,
dance energetically around the church interior, and strike such poses as
balancing on one foot with her body bent double. She would take on all
the roles of the Passion story, and interact fervently with images of Christ
through such activities as kissing a diptych painted with a representation
of the crucified Christ, which she used to induce her trances. She did this,
Abbot Philip reports, with evident pain, emotion, and exultation. Sighs,
moans, and exclamations of joy were regular parts of her Holy Hours
performances. As noted, she regularly bled from stigmata and would end
her major performances in a sort of replica version of Christ on the cross.

To an extent, Elisabeth of Spalbeek and her *vita* fit into some of the
standard categories of interpretation commonly used by medievalist scholars when they consider women mystics of the time.[18] For instance, Abbot
Philip's accent on Elisabeth's body and her physicality throughout a considerable portion of her *vita* conforms to expectations set up for us by such
researchers as Caroline Walker Bynum and André Vauchez. The latter has
asserted that the body was "a primary instrument of communication" in
the later Middle Ages for women proclaiming holiness.[19] Elisabeth emerges
in her *vita* in other fairly expected ways, in light of the scholarship on the
body and women's mysticism: the *vita* documents Elisabeth's feverish embodied spirituality, her Beguine-like status in terms of both her religious

and domestic life, and the prevalence of images in her religiosity of a suffering and crucified Christ.

Yet, when compared with other Beguines' *vitae* or those of other later medieval mystics, Elisabeth's is odd. Especially perplexing is the fact that it never entered the present repertory of mainstream women's mystical texts. Elisabeth of Spalbeek is hardly a familiar name to scholars. This is puzzling, given the fact that Philip's text was later assembled into a fifteenth-century folio with three other examples of women's spirituality, each one of which our current generation has all but canonized, in a scholarly sense (the relatively neglected Elisabeth's companions here were Christine the Miraculous, Mary of Oignies, and Catherine of Siena).[20]

Our record of Elisabeth is unusual in another way. Where so many Beguine *vitae* are concerned with the totality of women's lives, their "words, laughter, tears, sleep, and dreams,"[21] Elisabeth's is exceptionally focused on other things. Abbot Philip is narrating, almost exclusively, *"what she does"* at the Holy Hours of the day: Matins, Prime, Terce, Sext, None, Vespers, and Compline.[22] His report in fact reads like a transcription of movement, a script with an ample provision for the use of the props and established routines to accompany her movements.

He is not a participant in these actions nor does he suggest that he is her confessor, a circumstance otherwise frequently the case with authors of the Beguine *vitae*. Many recording clerics were lifelong friends (*intimier*) with their subjects. Philip, however, spent only a short time with Elisabeth (about six months), after which he returned to his monastery. Nor was Philip Elisabeth's scribe. He was not privy to her visions; indeed, if she had visions of the sort Hadewijch or Lutgard claimed, Philip did not tell us so. She is not recorded as mutilating or lacerating herself, nor is she depressed or melancholy, as scholars have led us to expect from these sorts of texts. Neither does Elisabeth's *vita* underscore those bizarre and incredible actions of the sort that Bynum's writings have made us so mindful: she does not drink the pus of lepers or vomit up the unconsecrated Host. These signs that scholars now identify so strongly with Beguine spirituality may have been present in Elisabeth, but if so, we shall never know, for the abbot chose not to record them.

To our generation, at first glance the iconographic symbolism of these events will seem little out of the ordinary for the period of ca. 1300: a devout Beguine becoming the cross, living Christ's pain, and embodying the Passion physically. Philip's representation of Elisabeth is clearly the product of his contemporary visual and literary world. He drew on an extensive repertory of symbolism and imagery, accessible to him because of his status as cleric and administrator of the abbey. He read and wrote Latin, had access to illuminated manuscripts, visited many churches and chapels in his travels to and from his abbey at Clairvaux, and was familiar with the pious imagery favored by local nuns.[23] Then, too, certain gestures he identifies, such as Elisabeth's prostration, were clearly encoded in the manuals on monastic prayer circulating at the time.[24] It is thus likely that Philip crafted his narrative to have his subject displaying those monastic formulae.[25] Historian Walter Simons has interpreted Elisabeth accordingly, as an example of the prevailing ideology of *imitatio Christi* as seen through a monastic lens.[26]

Yet something else is at work. From his text, Philip was patently interested in leaving a record/script predominantly about Elisabeth's movements as they "solemnized" the Holy Hours. He did this scrupulously. The abbot's goal was to pass down not the whole life and catalogue of miracles of Elisabeth of Spalbeek, as most authors of Beguine *vitae* do,[27] but rather to note with exacting detail the wondrous doings of her body in "the distinction of the hours."

His time frame is conditioned and restricted, indeed mapped out, by the sequence of the Holy Hours. Philip's narration is conditioned by a precise, ritual-bound time, the Holy Hour. Elisabeth's devotions are performed at pre-established intervals throughout the day. Philip writes, in fact, that Elisabeth rises to do the Holy Hours "by an unfallible clock that I know not."[28]

There is one other unusual element at work here. Philip describes a chapel to which Elisabeth's room (her living quarter) was attached but closed off by a partition; she could, however, see the altar from her bed.[29] Quite extraordinarily, a chapel still stands, which local legend holds to be the site described by Philip. Not far from the present-day border of Germany, this little shrine is nestled in humble farmland. Quite small-scale, the Spalbeek chapel was totally centralized in Elisabeth's day. It was highly unusual for a village chapel like this to be built in cylindrical form with a central-type ground plan. Yet scholars are convinced that the original structure, which dates from the late thirteenth century, was circular.[30] Sometime in the late fifteenth or early sixteenth centuries, a nave was attached and a splendid cycle of fresco paintings was done to adorn the eastern hemicycle.[31] These enlargements and embellishments likely came about to serve a growing cult to this local heroine.

Elisabeth is the only Beguine mystic in the Low Countries whose cult gave rise to such an extensive architectural and decorative program.[32]

Just as remarkable is that the site is still present. Together, the *vita* (the literary remains) and the chapel (the material remains) allow us to constitute Elisabeth, who presented herself in a particular architectural space. This points to a single performer unfolding her actions before an audience of the abbot, his monks, and God himself. In the analysis that follows, we seek to understand these elements as bold re-assertions by Elisabeth, and Philip, about the public domain for religious ritual: who gets to perform it and where it is performed, as well as who determines the symbol system governing the content of spiritual matters. Beyond this, Elisabeth's ecstatic dances and *vita* throw into high relief some of the usually hidden dimensions of female worship in relation to ecclesiastical power. To explore these matters we turn first to cultural anthropological frameworks for interpreting religious thought and action.

Elisabeth of Spalbeek as Christ and Cross: An Anthropological Interpretation

As historian Robert Darnton has pointed out,[33] at times anthropology's interpretive frameworks that were originally developed for illuminating non-Western village cultures can be usefully brought to the study of Western European historical scenes. In Darnton's own case, in the essays on eighteenth-century France in his book *The Great Cat Massacre*, he makes good use of anthropologist Clifford Geertz's assertion that cultures and certain politically and aesthetically dense cultural scenes within them can be "read" as texts.[34] In his inquiries into such phenomena as popular folk tales, locally authored antiquarian books, and game-like ritual scenes, Darnton focuses especially on power dynamics, and on breakthrough dramas and tableaux where the usually silenced tensions of a culture suddenly erupt to the surface of public space. This approach seems apt for our efforts to search for Elisabeth and describe her dance life, since her performances were so clearly laden with references to hierarchy.

In the years since Geertz's 1972 essay, anthropologists in general have tended to be even more alert to issues of power and resistance within societies stratified by class, gender, and colonial forms of domination. This turn toward deeper power issues has been in part thanks to the influence of Michel Foucault on the social sciences in general.[35] In this newer line of inquiry, several additional questions have come to the fore in anthropological analysis. Many of them relate specifically to the body: How do social structural hierarchies of domination get inscribed on the body, through such mechanisms as physical punishment of "deviant" groups, through dress or decoration, or via ideal body image? How do ideologies of normal bodies get created and maintained, as loci of power for dominant groups? How do women's bodies, and their "worth" in the culture, tend to get configured within such systems of thought and action? Equally important is a range of related questions about resistance within social systems of this sort: Under what social structural circumstances does rebellion tend to break out within hierarchy? What rhetorical forms do resistance voices tend to take? And what of body imagery and folk ideologies of the body within such frameworks of power, control, and resistance?[36]

This sort of concern about power and the body clearly stands to illuminate Elisabeth's dance life. Beyond this, though, anthropology's work on power and the body can also be usefully expanded toward another area of study: recent investigations of performance. First, though, a few background comments on trance, shamanism, and the social structural position of various sorts of inspired persons, as anthropologists have tended to see these matters. In setting out these initial (and, to anthropologists, commonplace) insights about ecstatic religious states, we can also begin to make some tentative comments about Elisabeth's structural place within her church, as a faith community. I. M. Lewis's *Ecstatic Religion* will be a prime source for us here.

Elisabeth of Spalbeek as Trancer

This young Beguine's devotional practices have clear trance elements, at least when seen in relation to material in the large anthropological literature on shamans in trance[37] and on so-called holy madwomen in places such as India, Bengal, and Sri Lanka.[38] The latter sorts of devout women claim to meld their bodies with divine beings in ecstatic performances of various sorts: a phenomenon with clear resonance with Elisabeth's religious movements and actions.

Elisabeth's ecstatic states also take on additional interpretive meaning when seen in relation to the anthropological literature on religious believers who engage specifically in ritual dances designed to contact a supernatural world, in a wide range of societies.[39] Fourthly and perhaps most importantly, Elisabeth's dance life has liminal elements to it, that is, characteristics that connect it to various in-between states in which a ritual celebrant temporarily breaks out of his or her culture's standard social categories to enter chaotic—and deeply powerful—space and time, *for the duration of the performance.* This allies Elisabeth's dance performances to a stage in classic rites of passage, which of course have also been much discussed in the traditional anthropological literature.[40]

Let us take up all these threads of inquiry together as they relate to this thirteenth-century Beguine, especially as these types of anthropological research help us to speculate about Elisabeth's conceptualization of self, in relation to Christ's divinity and body. It seems to us that the domain of self, as this becomes reconstructed in ritual performances, is a particularly promising area of study at the intersection of cultural anthropological research on non-Western religions and scholarship on the Middle Ages that focuses on mysticism.

In the most general sense trance is a state of transport, so to speak— an altered state of consciousness—in which the trancer leaves everyday reality temporarily, typically through the mechanism of repetitive chanting, repetitive exhaustive dancing, hallucinogenic drugs, bodily mutilation, self-starving, or extreme social isolation in such places as caves. Percussive sound such as drumbeats, foot-stomping in dances (involving a beat that reverberates into the body core), or hitting the body in various ways (or, hitting the body with successive waves of sound) seems to be a universal trance-inducing device. The ritual participant leaves normal everyday consciousness (and his or her normal social persona) via a thump-thump beat of great anticipation: of the sacred breaking in. At the end of a trance, percussive sound is also often used to usher the trancer out of the other world and back into normal consciousness.

In this regard, the structure of trance experiences and that of rites of passage overlap. Both schemas posit three stages: a separation from the initial, normal status; a spiritually dangerous but power-filled, in-between, liminal time; and a third period of reincorporation, one that signals rebirth back into regular human society. In rites of passage (for instance, naming ceremonies for infants, first haircuts, adolescent initiations, weddings, funerals), the separation phase is often marked by violence to the body of the initiates (teeth filing, facial scarification, genital surgery, bloodletting, forced vomiting). Then, while in the liminal phase the initiate exists in social structural and cultural limbo, "between categories" in the most fundamental sense. The initiates have fallen outside the social structure temporarily (existing as neither boy nor man in adolescent rites of passage, for instance, but simply as men-in-becoming). In their liminal phase, initiates often dress in ways that denote their non-personhood: for instance, they are wrapped in formless garments of white or black, or their faces or entire bodies are daubed with a substance like clay.[41]

In his provocative essay "Percussion and Transition,"[42] anthropologist Rodney Needham asserts that drumbeat types of sound are probably universal in trance events but also in major rites of passage, as individuals go from stage to stage. Percussive sound serves three purposes in such rituals, Needham writes. It breaks ritual celebrants out of the standard cognitive categories used in their cultures to structure everyday consciousness (thus introducing a "higher level" of reality, from which trancers or ritual initiates may later claim to speak authoritatively); second, percussive sounds propel celebrants into a liminal state where the boundaries of standard categories blur and chaos rushes in; and third, percussive sound eventually leads the trancer out of liminality back into cultural reality, with some measure of safety.

Elisabeth's "Christ dances" clearly had many of these elements, including her use of her hands and arms to beat her body into a trance state; her reliance on the drumbeat of her own footfalls throughout her transport to keep herself in trance and possibly to draw her audience into her own psychophysiological state to some extent; and, her fall into a state of what we infer would have been chaotic personhood while in trance. In her holy performances, Elisabeth was a woman dancing a male life, a human dancing divinity, a thirteenth-century follower of Christ becoming Christ at the time of his crucifixion. We speculate that Elisabeth left behind her normal apprehension of her regular social identity as she entered her trance using her body as a percussive medium. Then, while in the midst of her dance, her selfhood was probably in transition toward its climactic union with her vision of Christ. An aura of danger and unpredictability may also have characterized Elisabeth in trance for her audience. This would be entirely in line with the "out of bounds" scariness often associated with liminal states.

Elisabeth's dances also had shamanistic elements, although it is probably too much to claim that she played a shamanistic role in any clearcut way.[43] According to much of the anthropological literature, shamans are master trancers, master inspired priests. In this they typically stand in contrast to official priests, who attain that status through formal training in well-institutionalized school settings. Shamans generally "receive" their callings as intermediaries to the spirit world suddenly. This often comes as the result of a promise made during a dangerous illness or in some similar brush with death. However, once they become prominent shamans in their societies these individuals often quite consciously polish their skills and try out new techniques for inducing or maintaining trances, all to enhance their public reputations.

These are often of great concern to shamans, along with adequate pay for their healing services. Indeed, many shamans perform curing ceremonies, for patients who have lost their souls or who have suffered bodily invasions of one sort or another. An example of the latter sort of disease etiology and cure would be a situation wherein an enemy of a victim has supposedly cast an arrowhead or bit of dirt into the body of the patient. The shaman then sucks it out as part of a seance journey to the other world.

Other types of shamanistic healing performances entail mass community cures. The ethnographer Knut Rasmussen recorded a now-classic case of shamanship of this sort among the Copper Eskimo, from the 1930s.[44] In this society, if a famine of marine mammals loomed as a threat, an Inuit community would assume that they were being punished by the Goddess of the Sea for taboo transgressions and social sins. Left to their own devices, members of the public were not knowledgeable enough to discern what these sins were, so they called in their village shaman. Going into a song- and cold-induced trance, sitting behind a fur curtain in a snow hut, on the ice, he journeyed beneath the ice floes (he contended, in his narrative song about his mystical trip). He did this to visit the bottom of a mythologized sea. That is, during trance his normal self was replaced with a traveling-self that left the physical body to penetrate deep into supernatural space. At the bottom of the sea lived Takanakapsaluk, the Sea Goddess. She had been exiled there by her father many years ago after a violent scene in which he tried to kill her by throwing her out of their boat. When she grasped the side of the vessel with her hands to save herself, her father chopped off her finger joints. This caused her to sink to the sea floor and die in a physical sense, although she became immortal as a spirit. Each of her finger joints became a type of sea mammal, which is why the goddess now controls the fate of these animals. When human sins pile up (this society conceptualizes sin in frankly material terms), she angrily prevents her beasts from being caught by humans for food, as divine retribution. Each human sin or taboo transgression manifests itself physically on her body as a clump of dirt that attaches to her long hair, which she of course cannot comb out, since she has no fingers.

In trance, the shaman journeys to her home, fights off her guardian spirits, overcomes many dangerous obstacles, and combs out her hair. This calms the goddess enough so that the shaman can ask her what she wants of human society. Confessions of all sins, she answers. This bit of advice the shaman then conveys to his human audience in the snow hut; a mass confession ensues. Some of the neighbors confess envy or minor thefts, but particularly at issue for Takanakapsaluk are the secret, unacknowledged miscarriages of young wives. They often hide these events since custom demands that a household destroy all of its soft things, such as moccasins and the fur lining to the home, when a miscarriage occurs. Once all the deepest sins are confessed, the Sea Goddess is finally satisfied and she releases her seals and walruses. The shamanistic cure is successful.

As background to asking how Elisabeth's dances might relate to shamanship, one of the features of such seances is worth reinforcing here: shamans typically think that some aspect of their person leaves their physical body for a quest journey. While on the trip, shamans are often accompanied (they aver) by spirit familiars (an animal companion, for instance). Further, they hold that they often encounter, fight with, and overcome great obstacles. For instance, they may make sure that their audiences hear (via the shaman's song) that they have done battle with dangerous spirit animals, who wish (for instance) to eat them.

It is evident that Elisabeth of Spalbeek was not precisely a shaman, since this religious specialty generally posits populous spirit worlds as opposed to a monotheistic order of things, and since shamans are often associated directly with healing rituals (ones in which the soul of the patient is recaptured as part of the shaman's journey or ones in which the shaman performs explicitly curative actions). We have no direct evidence that any elaborate healing cult grew up around Elisabeth, during her lifetime at any rate, although the later iconographic program in her chapel does not preclude the possibility.[45] However, there definitely were several shaman-like elements to Elisabeth in trance: her person was ambiguously defined, quite obviously; she combined a long series of binary opposites into her dance self (male/female, divine/human, past/present); she joined worlds—human and divine—together for the short time her trance progressed. The story of Christ's Passion was made manifest in the here-and-now, in her chapel near Liège. She also seemed to have worked for the benefit of her community, possibly to bring her audience into greater closeness with Christ. She was seen by Abbot Philip, moreover, as an essentially good devout girl, as opposed to a threatening person such as a sorcerer.[46] In this, her moral status somewhat resembles that of shamans like those of the Copper Eskimo.

Another type of religious ecstasy, spirit possession, has also often been studied by anthropologists[47] and is worth looking at here as well, again to bring us closer to understanding Elisabeth's dances. In spirit possession, the configuration of symbols about selfhood and divinity is somewhat different than in classic shamanism. In possession states, a spirit from a supernatural world enters and occupies the body of the entranced, possessed person. The occupying spirit often then speaks through the mouth of the possessed. This is sometimes a fearful event for audience members, who often gather around the possessed person to hear what supernatural beings have to say in their regard. In particularly dangerous forms of spirit possession, the "occupied person" appears mad and fully out of control. Gananath Obeyesekere details vivid cases of this from Sri Lanka.[48] He examines a village and town religious world from the 1970s in which women who find themselves in oppressive family circumstances (enmeshed in unhappy forced marriages, for instance) sometimes become possessed by angry deities. The women fall into various forms of frightening behavior, such as eating filth or flailing around their houseyards in an excited manner. Their hair spontaneously forms matted locks, which evoke both pollution fears and public awe, as signs of the presence of holy madness. Sometimes the possessing deities are male, who speak through the women's mouths to berate the other members of the household (something normally blocked by standard rules of family decorum). These holy madwomen gain renown and sometimes become the focus of pilgrimages. They sometimes refuse sexual relations with their husbands, in their devotion to their "occupying" male deities.

Elisabeth in trance showed some of these elements—the air of danger we posit her dances had, her claims to be a site of divinity—but the symbolic dynamics of her selfhood in relation to Christ's divinity seem to have been fundamentally different from those of these Sri Lankan devouts. Christ did not occupy Elisabeth's body as an invader, but rather her self seems to have been eclipsed in a much more beneficent union with his body and divine status. She temporarily brought Christ back into history through the medium of female dance.

Entranced shamans and possessed persons like these South Asian devouts obviously tend to have a common intriguing feature: their identity as persons is tantalizingly ambiguous. This is particularly true of shamans while in ecstasy. They are men dressed as beasts, or women dressed as men, or women who speak with men's voices (male spirits' voices), or persons who combine clothing motifs of two worlds, such as sky realms and the earth. This ambiguity gives them their special, awe-inspiring status: in a single person and body they combine cultural categories that in normal everyday life are kept safely separate. Entranced shamans, and to some extent the possessed too, are sort of collapsed cultural worlds: walking religious events in which normal binary oppositions fall into each other, tensely, temporarily. This ambiguity and chaos is one source of their great powers. Shamans particularly have tapped (momentarily) into the anti-structure of their local cultural universes, as Mary Douglas might say.[49] They are ritual impresarios of the liminal and of its intrinsic closeness to divinity. Elisabeth in trance was a blender of worlds of just this sort, although she was not precisely a shaman or a possessed girl or a holy madwoman.

More intriguing parallels between non-Western religions' forms of ritualized ecstasies and Elisabeth's status as a female trance dancer operating within a conventionalized, male-dominated, hierarchical, official church emerge when one turns to issues of social location, via the work of I. M. Lewis and Mary Douglas.

Trance and Social Location

In indigenous cultures, shamans often claim to speak for the gods or spirits as their most prominent intercessors with humans. Elisabeth of course could not claim to do this fully, as that role of primary priest was already taken by the clergy. But Elisabeth could claim to have a special sort of highly explosive and powerful access to the divine via her ecstatic performances. Here, Lewis's work on peripheral cults versus central cults in his book *Ecstatic Religion* becomes especially useful.

In his excellent cross-cultural, comparative study of various forms of "inspired" religious activity (trancers' pronouncements of messages from spirit worlds, shamans' healing journeys to the beyond, spirit-possessed women's "voices" conveying threats from displeased supernaturals, individuals inhabited by demons), Lewis attempts a sweeping sociology of religious ecstasy. That is, he seeks to correlate the social structural position of religious celebrants to the type of religious experiences they have and then he goes on to relate these to the overall configuration of legitimate and illegitimate (and dangerous) powers posited by the culture as a whole. The tone and form of religious experiences, Lewis asserts, are linked in predictable ways to their practitioners' locations within local political and gender hierarchies. This makes Elisabeth emerge more clearly still. She was performing her passionate dances from the borders of official power, looking in toward the center and implicitly critiquing conventional religious hierarchy.

In brief, Lewis's argument is this. Each culture will tend to have an official, central religious cult, whose ritual specialist representatives (usually men) will claim to periodically "speak for" such entities as founding ancestors. "In these religions," Lewis writes, "the spirits which men incarnate stand at the centre of the stage in the religious life of society and play a crucial, and direct, role in sanctioning customary morality. In these circumstances . . . possession may initially appear as a form of illness or trauma. Yet ultimately it is regarded as the mark of divine inspiration, the certain proof of a person's fitness for pursuing the religious vocation, and the basis for the assumption of leading ritual roles and positions."[50] These official religious experts lend legitimacy to local political elites by simultaneously linking them to ancestral, mythic foundation times and to sources of creativity in the present day: to human fertility, crop production, and so on.

Lewis goes on to note, however, that religious systems often tend also to have their peripheral cults located at the margins of official religious worlds, much as local political elites have their ranks of the dispossessed. Peripheral persons produce religious discourses of protest: sudden, frightening, sometimes very specifically ecstatic breakthroughs of the divine, in such individuals as women who purportedly become possessed by unpredictable and often terrifying demons. Such religious experiences as spirit possession can give a voice (albeit a temporary one) to otherwise silenced persons, such as women in male-dominated village polities or low-caste individuals in rigid hierarchies. Female spirit possession in particular, Lewis writes, often takes on elements of threat and aggressiveness, as well as a certain aura of wild sexuality. Such characteristics tend to be counterposed to the more controlled, calmer, more polite nature of the more acceptable moral persons in such social systems: the practitioners and leaders of the central cult.

Many ethnographic studies have borne out Lewis's predictions here. For brief examples, we can return to Obesyesekere's research on female ecstatics in Sri Lanka. These holy madwomen, whose bodies in trance take on elements of horror and out-of-control female sexuality, were essentially saying the unsayable in their local communities. These women had no effective avenues of protest within their oppressive family circumstances. In this context, they found their voices via ecstatic trance and by practicing shocking, "mad" actions such as eating filth. As Lewis's model goes on to predict, these holy madwomen with their spectacularly awful and ugly crowns of dreadlocks sometimes went on to gain a measure of celebrity and local renown from their possessed actions and odd appearance. As noted, Elisabeth was far from being a holy madwoman of this precise sort, but by energetically nurturing her spiritual calling as an ecstatic dancer she was effectively short-circuiting the usual taboo on young untutored women rising to positions of extreme prominence within the church. In ecstatic performance she was claiming to do no less than to become God (thereby fully negating church hierarchy).

Lewis also discusses an additional form of religious ecstasy of interest to us here: purported spiritual marriages between humans and supernaturals.[51] India and Sri Lanka again provide ready examples here: some of the holy madwomen studied by Obeyesekere considered themselves to be inhabited by male divinities who are simultaneously these women's supernatural incubus-husbands and their infants (thus, a widespread symbolism of "nursing the baby husband" among such devouts). The power dimensions of this situation are evident. Previously relatively silenced, structurally constrained women of no particular social prominence have gained fame and a way to speak back to power, through ecstatic madness linked to sexually "engulfing" a male divinity. We speculate that Elisabeth probably saw the engulfment to have gone in the other direction (with Christ's body engulfing hers), but the power dynamics remain similar: a claim to speak back to hierarchy through ecstatic performance.

Lewis notes that not only entranced persons in peripheral cults but also shamans often play on imagery of sexual union with gods ("ecstatic visions of an incestuous return to the cosmic womb"[52] for male shamans, for instance). He goes on to write, "The metaphor of spiritual marriage is familiar to us from our own Christian tradition. This is the relationship traditionally postulated between the Church and Christ; and, as we know, nuns are specifically bound in spiritual union to the Sacred Bridegroom. Many Christian mystics have used the same idiom, for example St. Bernard, who wrote of Christ as his soul's Bridegroom. . . ."[53] Some of this range of sexual imagery has been explored in the historical literature on Christianity,[54] and any full accounting of the topic of Elisabeth's personal sexual imagery in relation to Christ is beyond the scope of this essay. What is clear in an initial way, though, is that Elisabeth's extinction of her own selfhood in her trance dance as she "became Christ" may well have had the additional metaphor of "marrying Christ," a metaphor quite present to the Beguines.

Standing back from all this comparative anthropological material on inspired states and social location, Elisabeth of Spalbeek's dances emerge as subtly rebellious. She operated within the church (she was not, that is, a heretic) and apparently she saw her devotions as gifts of God, as signs of holiness emanating from her closeness to Christ. She was not "mad" in the sense the Sri Lankan devouts discussed by Obeyesekere were: her demeanor was not overtly "wild" or heavily sexualized (in any obvious way, at least; Abbot Philip takes pains to assure readers that she maintained at all times proper standards of clothing decorum). Further, she was not seen to be animated by evil demons. Far from it: her purported powers emanated from the center (from God and Christ). And, she celebrated holiness in chapel spaces and she presented her body in analogy to Christ's: she bled from his wounds on the cross.

Within her chapel and larger church community, though, as we have seen, Elisabeth was something of a scandal, since her person in trance and in dance movement embodied so many paradoxes of gender and social hierarchy (a woman dancing the male Christ's Passion, a largely unlettered girl showing the divine to audiences of priests). Elisabeth apparently gloried in this role and developed into something of a celebrity and professional trancer, as well as the focus of pilgrimage. Abbot Philip apparently colluded with her in this, and may have used her public career as a holy girl to solidify his own Cistercians' critique of more centrally positioned ecclesiastical authorities.

Anthropology's Newer Literature on Performance: Closer to Elisabeth in Trance

Anthropology's various excursions into the study of trance, shamanism, spirit possession, and "holy madness" all open small windows through which we can begin to glimpse Elisabeth's devotional life, but none of these research trajectories by any means fully explains her remarkable dances. An additional recent line of anthropological inquiry, though, does take us a few more steps in that direction: explorations of ritual performances, qua performance. These events have been studied by anthropology's newer generations of performance theorists in a wide range of non-Western and Western cultures.[55] Especially important for us here are the ways ritual performances sometimes foster transformative possibilities within their local settings to lead participants to form new conceptualizations of self and sacrality, thanks to insights these ritual celebrants gain in the experience of performance itself.[56]

Many of these writers trace their work to the African ethnography and cross-cultural analysis of Victor Turner, both to his seminal essays on the structure of rites of passage and the "ritual process" involved in such ceremonies of life transition and to his later work on performance and "performing ethnography."[57] In the latter, Turner advocates a methodology in which anthropologists use their own experiences participating in performances to discover foreign cultural worlds. His wife, Edith Turner, frequently collaborated with him. We do not draw heavily on this particular line of inquiry here, but rather look toward more concretely situated studies of performance in local religious and social structural context, by students of Asian and Papua New Guinea religious imaginations.

Anthropological studies of performance as a site of cultural transformation, as a domain where culture is remade and reconfigured for ritual participants, stand to help us uncover the crucial aspect of Elisabeth of Spalbeek's dance devotions we so far have left somewhat underexplored: her apparent claims to have transformed herself via choreographic performance into Christ on the cross. We can be more specific here, thanks to performance theory: We wish to look at Elisabeth's stance toward her culture's symbolism of the body of Christ.

As background, we can note that any personal vision Elisabeth may have had of this core field of Christian symbolism was surely just one small part of a quite large, interactive ideological system that involved multiple ways of conceptualizing the body of Christ, by a range of persons: by male clerics, bishops, religious artists of various sorts, and diverse lay publics. Later medieval female religious women often had elaborate ideologies of Christ's body in relation to theirs, as historians have reported.[58] The thirteenth- and fourteenth-century Beguines themselves were like other religious women of the period, with extensive schema for thinking about Christ's body and relating their own to his, in their art, devotional practices, and other spiritual routines.[59] In addition, as we have seen, the beguine communities of the Low Countries pursued a deeply emotional and specifically tactile cult focused on sculptural bodies of the Christchild.[60] Devotional interaction with religious art works such as sculptures of the infant Christ or with Pietà figures was apparently central to these communities' systems of religious beliefs relating to the sacred body of Christ.

Medieval male clerics were apparently caught up in intriguingly contrasting visions of their place in the bodily world in relation to Christ's flesh. Their views took numerous forms. Let one example suffice here to show how imageries of Christ's body tended to be embedded in ritual contexts involving bodily movement in relation to a variety of sacred objects.

Historian Patrick Geary reports that medieval Cluniac monastic communities sometimes participated in the ritual humiliation of saints, a practice that posited an especially powerful array of Christ body imageries.[61] In this ritual, relics of a cathedral's patron saints would be carefully taken down from their normal reliquaries and "humiliated" by being placed on the floor, facing a priest holding aloft a consecrated Host. The monks themselves would then prostrate themselves alongside the relics, thereby taking a similar humbled spatial position vis-à-vis Christ's higher cere- monial body. The monks claimed a common status as holy sufferers in these ritual tableaux and also asserted in rather defiant public form that it was they, and not their secular, wealthy patrons, who controlled access to the divine. Prayer to Christ via relic worship was central to this. The ritual setting was quite dense and involved lament-like hymns and ritualized complaints about the supposed damage done the monastic community by "wayward" patrons. These hymns and prayers also detailed the mutual suf- fering of the monks and the saints' relics, both of which were symbolically cast as being Christlike. Geary reports that such practices would typically take place when a monastic community felt seriously misused by a nor- mally reliable patron. In these humiliation rituals, which emphasized so strongly the Christlike suffering of the "wronged" monks and canons, these men set themselves up as close to Christ's body, but still definitely outside it, praying to it in an evocation of parallel suffering. The abused relics, fragments of dead saints' bodies, were the monks' companions in this effort.

Elisabeth's danced bodily faith seems to have been something quite different: a young girl's assumption of the bodily presence of Christ, entire. This imagined body of Elisabeth's seems to have been a rare personal invention, when set against this range of much more well-institutionalized imageries.

What can anthropology's newer performance literature tell us about Elisabeth's particular apprehension of her self and her body in relation to Christ's body and implicitly to all the other components of the Church as body, as a worshiping community tied to Christ? Several answers emerge, when we borrow first from the work of performance theorist Richard Schechner and then from case studies of performance in Asia and Papua New Guinea.

Schechner is a bold, ambitious comparativist, more so in fact than many anthropologists would hazard to be. His work can be productively suggestive, however, when used as a lens for considering a medieval devout like Elisabeth who was so heavily invested in performance activities. Draw- ing on a dauntingly wide range of historical and ethnographic materials from Native America, South Asia, Africa, and the Arctic, Schechner first makes the by-now familiar points that trance performers tend to see their normal selves to have been taken over or engulfed by a "more real" entity, the visiting spirit or divinity. In trance, Schechner goes on to report, levels of authoritativeness are set up for audience members as they witness the inspired event. The visiting spirit speaks a higher truth, or supposedly sees local social or spiritual conditions in a more penetrating way than the trancer's normal self could ever hope to do.[62]

Schechner then goes on to make more innovative comments about the actual performance nature of trance. There, performers and audience are "transported and transformed"[63] by various measures. In transportative performances (the strongest example of which would be a fairly traditional Western-style theatrical play), the performers enter a performance space and time, temporarily shuck off their normal selves, "take up a role," play it, and then return to their starting point at the end of the performance. Specifically *transformative* performances, however, are more religiously loaded events than these. Here, the protagonist goes through a process of gradually becoming-the-god. The mythic implications and timescape dimensions of the performance scene are obviously much weightier here.

It is important to point out that the two types of performance are not totally unrelated. For instance, both types of events demand a certain cooling-down process to help the actor or ritualist safely re-enter normal space and time again and take up his or her regular social persona. However, this phase is a more spiritually dangerous undertaking in fully transformative events. In these, divinity and a foundational past time have been temporarily re-presented for protagonist and audience; the god has come out of mythic time into the here-and-now. Schechner specifically relates the spiritual gravity of this sort of performances to rites of passage. Initiates there can also be transformed into fundamentally new sorts of persons, through their participation in what Turner called the ritual process. There, they are thought to essentially touch the sacred while in their liminal, limbo period, suspended as they are between social statuses.

In *Between Theater and Anthropology* Schechner explores these ideas in relation to a Papua New Guinea initiation ritual for boys, to Japan's Noh drama, and to Indian ritual performances based on Sanskrit texts.[64] Luckily for us, he is particularly concerned with the performer's definitions of self. In the Papua New Guinea rite of passage, violence to the body, which terrorizes the initiates, catapults the boys into a period in which their previous selves disintegrate. Then the many stages of the arduous ceremony slowly rebuild new "men's selves" for the celebrants. In Noh, with its ties to Zen meditation and Zen-inspired martial art, a highly "distilled" and professionalized training discipline for actors encourages a certain "automatic" approach to doing the performance. These demanding regimes of control can lead to exquisitely "in-the-present" performances that evoke

Zen's maxims about the very character of existence. In Indian ritual drama, a variety of sense experiences (such as memories of food, bodily beauty, lovely sound) enter or seep into the bodies of spectators and performers; this brings them into harmony with the elements of "balance" in the cosmos.

In an equally important series of observations in a chapter entitled "Restoration of Behavior" in the same book[65] Schechner takes up the question of conventionalized behaviors, in ritual performance, that are separable from the "me" of the performer. "Restored behavior," he writes,[66] "is 'out there,' distant from 'me.' It is separate and therefore can be 'worked on,' changed, even though it has 'already happened.' Restored behavior includes a vast range of actions. It can be 'me' at another time/psychological state as in the psychoanalytic abreaction; or it can exist in a non-ordinary sphere of sociocultural reality as does the Passion of Christ or the reenactment in Bali of the struggle between Rangda and Barong; or it can be marked off by aesthetic convention as in drama and dance; or it can be the special kind of behavior 'expected' of someone participating in a traditional ritual . . . ," whether or not that behavior conforms to social reality.

In restored behavior, the performer has a social arena for constituting an essentially ritual self: one that can readily draw on a culture's vocabulary of divine beings. Elisabeth in trance probably engaged in much this sort of self-reconstitution, every time she held a major performance for her audiences of abbot and monks.

Schechner goes on to write that restored behavior, which he takes to be the essence of human performance, "is 'me behaving as if I am someone else,' or 'as if I *am beside myself,* or *not myself,* as when in trance."[67] Further, "restored behavior is symbolic and reflexive: not empty but loaded behavior multivocally broadcasting significances. These difficult terms express a single principle: The self can act in/as another; the social or transindividual self is a role or set of roles. Symbolic and reflexive behavior is the hardening into theater of social, religious, aesthetic, medical, and educational process. Performance means: never for the first time. It means: for the second to the *n*th time. Performance is 'twice-behaved behavior.' "

We speculate, drawing on this, that Elisabeth's movements probably took on for her the quality of routines, which she could think about beforehand and afterward, and rechoreograph from time to time. Indeed, performances have scores in this regard, which can be discussed, consciously critiqued, and changed. Schechner schematizes various types of restored behaviors.[68] These range from obviously acted, on-stage events such as traditional types of Western dramatic performances, to rituals such as communal mask performances in Papua New Guinea, to shamanistic seances, to overt "manifestations of the divine," where the ritual celebrant purports to be "swept away" by a sacred being or force.

Even in this last sort of performance, however, where matters are purportedly beyond human control, ritual routine and standardized mythic frameworks of expectation shape event: surely the case with Elisabeth, where her choreographic creativity was highly constrained by convention.

Schechner highlights one especially important type of event for us here: that consisting of a case in which a performer slips between categories of human/nonhuman almost seamlessly. Schechner writes that this sort of performance is particularly powerful for performer and audience members alike and is especially likely to be seen as an event where the divine breaks in on everyday life. Other types of performances exist further down the path toward conscious rehearsal and conscious ritual control (as in performances with scripts based in holy texts—the formal Mass, for instance).

When seen in this light, what was the nature of Elisabeth's dances, qua performance? And, what manner of body imagery in relation to Christ might have emerged in Elisabeth's dances, when seen via Schechner's model? Her trance performances, we would speculate, were fully transformative events, at least for her: her body became a site where Christ was made manifest.

Elisabeth seems to have dispensed with the more conventional Christian worshiper's stance toward the body of Christ (worshiper outside that body, looking on, praying to Christ) to insert her body and Christ's into each other for the duration of her activities. Was this also seen by Elisabeth as a sexual union with Christ? Again, we hesitate to speculate too much here. The *vita* provides only cloudy evidence here: as we discuss later, her interaction with the image of Christ on the diptych did seem to have loving, erotic elements to it.

Where was Elisabeth's normal self during her transports? Displaced, pushed somewhat offstage, we would speculate: her body became Christ's, and Elisabeth as worshiper fell into some form of sweet extinction, as her performances took on the quality of routines, which she probably hungered to repeat at regular intervals.

Could there have been other important elements to this reconfiguration of self in relation specifically to the performance activity of Elisabeth's dances? Some additional anthropological research suggest so, starting with a classic study by Claude Lévi-Strauss. In "The Effectiveness of Symbols,"[69] an essay on shamanistic healing, Lévi-Strauss urged researchers to look closely at the exact rhetorical structure of such performance elements as the shaman's song. In this famous article about Cuna Indian cures from Panama, the French structuralist asks how a shaman's musical performance about his supernatural journey to the home of a female fertility goddess (obviously a purely mythical event) could possibly actually bring about a physiological cure of a patient, in this case a woman having a difficult time giving birth to a baby.

Lévi-Strauss asserts that the shaman's song and its mode of performance brought about a cure purely through the manipulation of symbols, all without the healer touching the woman in the least. Lévi-Strauss works at several historical removes from the Cuna shamanistic event (he works from a colonial-era, Spanish-language text of the song, not from direct fieldwork with a contemporary society) so the methodological dimensions of this study are problematic. However, Lévi-Strauss's argument about the structure of performance is suggestive for us here, in looking at Elisabeth's dances and asking how she may have maintained so seemingly unlikely a fiction as her claim to be Christ in his final days.

Lévi-Strauss reports that the husband of the Cuna woman in danger fears that the regular village midwife is not up to the task of handling the challenging birth, so he calls in the shaman. This man enters the couple's home, sits on the floor, lights some incense sticks, and proceeds to carve a phalanx of small wooden statues. These are his tutelary spirits, which will aid him on his forthcoming supernatural journey to the home of the creator spirit. The goddess has unexpectedly overstepped her normal, usually beneficent fertility functions and is peevishly holding the pregnant woman's soul; this is preventing the birth.

In trance, the shaman begins his song, which starts out at a rhythmic, very slow beat. The mother reclines in her hammock, listening to the song's narrative but also of course experiencing waves of severe labor pains. Early on in the song the shaman spends several minutes telling the woman how he is starting his trip to the goddess: how he summoned his spirit companions, how he and his helpers walk along a path step by step, how they begin to notice walls closing in on them, how they meet threatening animals who attack them, how they continue to plod along. After several minutes of this, the shaman switches over to a song description of the woman's own, immediate physiological experiences: her pain, her lower body, her contractions, her bodily reality in all its particulars. He then switches back to his narrative about the goddess and the mythic geography leading to her house. The woman hears how he and his party are journeying closer and closer to the goddess, how the walls are now exuding red fluids and closing in on the travelers at an alarming rate.

Lévi-Strauss notes the obvious: the shaman's mythical terrain here is an evocation of the woman's birth canal, with the baby held inside the womb. The shaman and his assistants overcome many obstacles and eventually succeed in meeting the deity and convincing her to release the soul. At this point, the woman's body relaxes and the birth itself proceeds. What has happened? Lévi-Strauss asserts that the woman's apprehension of bodily experience has been manipulated symbolically, thanks to the storytelling structure of the performed song.

Lévi-Strauss calls readers' attention to the pacing of the song. Early on in the performance the shaman switches back and forth between his two levels (mythic, physiological) at a fairly leisurely pace, but as the story progresses and the narrative proceeds toward the climatic encounter with the goddess, the shifts between the levels become increasingly swift. Finally, at the end of the performance the singer is virtually careening musically between mythic geography and bodily experience every few seconds or so. For the pregnant woman, near delirious from pain in any case, the two levels now collapse into each other and she can no longer easily tell one from the other. At this point, the shaman's victory over the goddess on the mythic level seems to the woman to have also occurred in her body, within her reproductive tract. Boundaries have collapsed and the woman enters a kind of holy "flow" of sensory experience.

Lévi-Strauss suggests that symbolic cures of this sort may frequently involve a rhetorical structure like this, building up to a climax, consisting of the unification of diverse planes of felt and mythically shaded experience. Other anthropologists second this assertion, and have documented similar cases.[70] Several examples from Asia and one from Papua New Guinea will show how this pattern of performance can sometimes work out in the field of ritual dance.[71] Let us set out this comparative material very briefly in order to look at Elisabeth's dances anew in this light.

Joel Kuipers, an ethnographer of the Weyewa people of Sumba, eastern Indonesia, points out in an important study of performance aesthetics and the creation of authority (through the delivery of ritual speeches)[72] that orators claim special trustworthiness for their performances by linking these to ancient times, to an era when the Weyewa first ancestors live and spoke "unadulterated truth." This came in the form of rhymed couplets, the same form of talk that today's great orators use. When orators in the present day deliver speeches of this sort they lead their audiences to believe that the past has broken into the present, to provide a source of wisdom and social guidance. Thus social disorder in the here and now can be contained and controlled, through the strategic appearance of the "voice of the ancestors." On the level of choreographic motion, if not ritual speech, Elisabeth's dances may have worked in a related way, to introduce a sort of sacramental authoritativeness to her theological claims.

Anna Lowenhaupt Tsing, another ethnographer of Indonesian peoples (this time, the Meratus Dayak of Central Kalimantan), documents a complementary case of a female shaman who claims power and authoritativeness, this time from the political periphery.[73] In this shaman's construction of self in relation to divinity, ritual inversion is a key symbolic process at work. Drawing on feminist literary critics and their assertions that women's voices show special types of creativity, Tsing follows the career of a charismatic Meratus female healer named Induan Hiling. This shaman was part of a loose circle of unconventional women in Meratus, including other healers and one extraordinary charismatic leader named Uma Adang, who entertained the anthropologist with elaborate "counter-histories" about the Meratus past in relation to nearby state societies that had long sought to occupy this part of Kalimantan. Induan Hiling was also a rebel, of sorts: her "contributions [in composing and delivering shaman's songs about mystic journeys] proceed in dialogue with dominant conventions of shamanism."[74] That is, Induan Hiling composed her performances by inverting and revising standard canons of male shamanistic performance. Induan Hiling also creates remarkable drawings, as a sort of substitute for and commentary on the types of supernatural journeys she is prevented from taking because she is not a man.

Elisabeth's dances also seem composed in counterpoint to more orthodox models of piety, in this case both male ones (the standard Mass, for instance) and female ones (more conventional forms of Beguine devotion). Like the Meratus healer and mythic traveler, Elisabeth employed numerous inversions and revisions of standard Christian worship. She exchanged well-regulated ritual motion for the extravagance of trance; she substituted her female body for Christ's; she catapulted the normally more contemplative performance of the Holy Hours into exuberant dance.

Sally Ann Ness, an anthropologist of Philippine dance (and a student of the ways in which folk healing dances become transformed politically into emblems of ethnic identity on national and international stages) adds another useful insight here. Ness points out[75] that kinesthetic movement within dance acts as a sort of memory bridge between the individual dancer's own self and larger realms of symbolic meaning out in the culture as a whole. Ness sensitively records her own efforts to learn complex dances and her experience of finally getting to know a dance motion so well, by rote, repetitive movement in practice sessions, that her 'bodily memory" took over and allowed her to feel the aesthetic of the dance in question, for essentially the first time. Elisabeth too may well have reached a state of her dance experience where the sheer physicality of her Holy Hours movements may have begun to drive her overall apprehension of what was happening in her trances.

Beyond Southeast Asia, the Kaluli people of Papua New Guinea, whose ritual dances have been expertly interpreted by Edward Schiefflin,[76] employ much this same pattern of choreographic experience leading to transformation. But, these dances add the elements of pain and violence. The Kaluli performance situation is intriguing here, for it involves scenes of great emotional beauty and poignancy (for the local people; to outsiders the dance might well appear bizarre). A key element of Elisabeth's performances must have been their aesthetic impact, their sheer formal power as dance events. How might this have related to Elisabeth's apprehension of self and divinity?

Writing at times in general terms of the anthropology of aesthetics, Schiefflin asserts that dance movement itself, in moving toward a dramatic climax, can facilitate a "confusion" of levels of experience, a process again blending the mythic with the physiological. Looking then to his specific ethnographic case, he reports that the Kaluli ritual dances are "gift dances" performed by visiting parties of men who pay ceremonial visits to their male counterparts in other villages. In part of a ceremony called Gisaro, which involves complex exchanges of food gifts and the incurring and payment of ritual debts, nighttime ritual dances can literally move grown men to tears. Significantly, they do this in important part by evoking different layers of poignant emotional experience and then "crashing these together" at intense points of the choreography. The dances become overwhelmingly beautiful and men burst into tears at these junctures.

The different levels of meaning involve the painful memories Kaluli men have of past friendships in which one partner has now disappeared through death or estrangement. A favorite song or a favorite place to go or a favorite shared food all index such a relationship and now, its loss. These remembered things are all evoked in Gisaro's song lyrics and the combined effect of a rush of nostalgia from all these different layers of memory make the dancers and spectators pensive and sad. However, it is dance movement itself, as well as florid dance costume and even violence, that catalyze the deep emotions of the event.

The ceremony had a simple form. Throughout the night, one by one the four dancers took turns dancing in place or moving up and down the small space in the middle of the hall, singing songs in company with the choruses seated at each end. The songs concerned familiar places in the surrounding countryside known to most of those who were present. As dancer followed dancer, the songs began to refer to specific places on the host's clan lands and recalled to the listeners former houses and gardens and close relatives, now dead, who lived there . . . [After such a song] the senior man, who was sitting with the crowd at the sidelines, brooding and withdrawn, suddenly became overcome with grief and burst into loud wails of anguish. Enraged, he jumped up, grabbed a torch from a bystander and jammed the burning end forcefully into the dancer's bare shoulder. With a tremendous noise all the youths and young men of the host community jumped into the dancing space, stamping and yelling and brandishing axes. The dancer was momentarily lost in a frightening pandemonium of shadowy figures, torches, and showers of sparks. Showing no sign of pain he moved slowly across the dancing space; the chorus burst into song. The senior man broke away from the crowd and ran out the back door of the house to wail on the verandah. This scene was repeated over and over from dancer to dancer during the course of the night.[77]

Drawing speculatively on this material even while admitting that Elisabeth's dances were nowhere near so violent, let us suggest some dance performance correlates to this Papua New Guinea scene, for the young Beguine's case. Anthropologically speaking, as Elisabeth entered trance by beating her body and beginning her rhythmic movements, her normal self was likely still predominant in her consciousness. That is, Elisabeth was probably still conscious of herself as a young female worshiper of Christ, still separate from him. External to herself were the biblical narratives of Christ's birth, life, death, and resurrection, and the narrative (and beauty) of the Mass itself. As her dance progressed, however, and as the events of the Passion played out upon her chapel-stage one by one as she went from mythic event to event, the intensity and pace of the performance heated up and quickened. Early on in her dance (we speculate), when her trance was still light and her apprehension of an "Elisabeth's self"—and body— was still separate from those of Christ, the pacing of the dance was probably fairly slow, measured, and hypnotic. As the dance speeded up, though, and as the mythic trajectory of her Passion story plunged onward toward the crucifixion, we propose that Elisabeth's comprehension of her own bodily existence and of her self as a young Beguine "fell into" that mythic story. With her pounding feet sending shockwaves through her body, with her gyrations becoming more forceful (more violent, we might say), a confusion of levels similar to that of both the Kaluli dancers and the Cuna woman patient may have occurred, allowing Elisabeth to become not-Elisabeth, not-young beguine, not-human, not just godlike, but to effectively re-present New Testament myth and to become Christ. Additionally, in parallel to the Kaluli men's ritual dances, Elisabeth's multivocal performances (composed as they were of costume, images, hairstyle, and dance movement symbols) probably evoked multiple levels of religious meaning and beauty. By the end of her dance, many of our sources would lead us to predict that these different levels of aesthetic and emotional reference had been collapsed together in a performance event of great emotional impact.

Could it be that Elisabeth came to her great insight about her female body in relation to Christ's male divinity only through performance, as opposed to through cooler modes of formal study or contemplation? We would suggest so, and so we turn now to an additional element of her dance life: its character as theater of a particular type, executed within church architectural spaces. Here we turn from these broadly cross-cultural and comparative sorts of anthropological comments once again to take a closer look at the Elisabeth who emerges from Abbot Philip's *vita*.

The Holy Dancer and the Chapel of Performance

To visualize the text and place Elisabeth and her ritual actions sensitively within her mythic world, in relation to her understanding of human personhood, and finally in relation to her architectural setting, we turn again to performance studies. In this section, we delve further into this area by using the drama theories of Polish director and acting trainer Jerzy Grotowski.[78] They enable us to strip off layers of interpretation traditionally applied to medieval mystical behavior, permitting us to envision the content afresh, in terms this time of its character, not just as ritual but as ritual *drama*. This is not at all to say that we reject traditional historical interpretations, for Elisabeth's actions are of course deeply rooted in the social context of her time. After all, the symbolic language she articulates—her vigorous, if singular, display of *imitatio Christi*, her bodily enactments of the Passion, her exhibition of the stigmata—is completely characteristic of the period. Yet strictly historical interpretation does not account for—nor has it even yet acknowledged—the rare variants on mystical behavior that Elisabeth's *vita* also displays.[79] The unusual character of her devotions begs us, by its very exceptional nature, to explore other avenues of interpretation.

Grotowski's investigations into what Peter Brook calls the ". . . nature and science of the mental-physical-emotional processes" of acting offer just such an innovative instrument for looking at Elisabeth's mystical activities. This is because Grotowski's setting is "the ascetic theatre in which the actors and audience are all that is left."[80] This spareness—or *Poor Theatre*, to cite Grotowski's own name for his teaching laboratory—enables us to discard traditional approaches and visualize the material as well as the spiritual characteristics of Elisabeth's essentially sacral theater.

Grotowski defines what is "distinctively theatre, what separates this activity from other categories of performances and spectacle."[81] This approach interests us, for it promises to elucidate not only how Elisabeth's performances are done ritually but theatrically.

In his theoretical work,[82] Grotowski elucidates an acting technique in which there arises a sense of theater eerily close to Philip's observations. When Grotowski instructs an actor, he introduces a radical definition of the art of performance, one we find germane to Elisabeth. In his type of elemental theater, ". . . what is achieved is a total acceptance of one human being by another."[83] We can see correlates of this if we return to the text of Abbot Philip's *vita*.

As Philip begins his narrative he tells how his disbelief collapsed upon seeing Elisabeth:

> Of these marvelous works of the Lord when I, Dan Philip of Clairvaux, heard when I was visiting houses of my order in that country, I gave no credence to him that told me, until I came myself and saw and proved that I had not heard half. Before I shall describe a few of the many marvels, and after my simple consent though that are more notable and more marvelous, as my conscious gains me, begin at those things that I perceived undoubtedly with my eyes, and afterward setting down what I have heard of many other true men.[84]

His total acceptance came through personal witness and observation. He did not characterize his relationship with Elisabeth in the participatory terms of confessor or intimate or friend. This text highlights the narrator as one who doubts, sees, and is moved to believe. Philip's conversion seems very like the "ancient theoretical truth" of theater on which Grotowski's grounds his principles of acting: "It [the theatre] cannot exist without the actor-spectator relationship of perceptual, direct, 'live' communion."[85]

Grotowski's understanding of performances as a special type of human social interaction is suggestive when looking at Elisabeth's dance life. He first describes the public use of the body in theater's terms, this way: "The actor is a man who works in public with his body, offering it publicly. If this body restricts itself to demonstrating what it is—something that any average person can do—then it is not an obedient instrument capable of performing a spiritual act."[86] Philip conveys just this sense, of the above- or beyond-average body, doing the incredible. Describing Elisabeth beating and striking her breast, he asks: "Which of these I shall call more marvelous, I would not, in such a feable and frail creature . . . ?"[87] Of course this has a late medieval ring to it, as it is "to be committed all to God, to whom nothing is hard or impossible." Yet, it is precisely Philip's emphasis on the marvelous body, made to do things beyond the ordinary, that must be understood in more expansive terms. Philip presents himself as a spectator, not of a full life lived, but of a series of pointed and repeated actions, ones that take place in a condensed, focused frame of time, the Holy Hours of the day. That quality of spectator and spectacle pervades Philip's text and builds the narrative structure; it also provides the primary identity with which he endows Elisabeth. She is the one "observed."

As for the specific devotional practices he enumerates, Philip conveys an intensity of relationship but one that is not encumbered by any previous intimate commitment to Elisabeth. Rather, his intensity of language matches hers of movement. Grotowski characterizes such a relationship this way: "The performance engages a sort of psychic conflict with the spectator. It is a challenge and an excess, but can only have any effect if based on human interest and more than that, on a feeling of sympathy, a feeling of acceptance."[88] A historicist understanding tells us that the monk is motivated by a form of Christianity and spirituality he desires to promote. As noted, Cistercian clerics were generally active defenders of women's faith at the time Philip learned of Elisabeth. This historical situation, though, threatens, by virtue of its commonplace nature (for most medievalists), to extinguish what is vital and forceful about Philip's particular narration—the author's nearly obsessive repetition of sympathy and feeling, as the affect arising from her excesses: ". . . there follows in an unspeakable manner of full devout prayers, which, not as I would but as I might, I have described before; but I would want well that my power nor my cunning might not fulfill my will."[89] In fact, Philip opens his narration by remarking on her magical, almost seductive effect, that "... I gave no credence to him that told me, until I came myself and saw and proved that I had not heard half."[90]

Philip is clear that his subject is observed by an audience, beside God. Philip was there ("I perceived undoubtedly with my eyes"),[91] but apparently he was not alone. He confirms what he heard "of many other true men," that "all the country doubtless knows" about her condition.[92] He says later, upon describing Elisabeth's stigmata, that it was seen by "I and my fellows, both abbots and monks, at midnight, and some other hours also. . . ."[93] And that "we saw blood springing out often at the wounds of her hands and of her feet and out of her side on a Friday at noon."[94] These passages tell us that there was not merely an audience but most probably an awestruck and somewhat frightened one.

Although audience presence may be a fairly obvious theatrical element, we must approach it with some sensitivity in the case of medieval mysticism. Besides Philip's own conversion on seeing, there are certain moments that indicate an intensity something like amazement or wonder. Philip repeatedly uses the phrase, ". . . with a manner that may neither be heard nor told"[95] or describes actions that "might be perceived him that never saw. . . ."[96] When she "knocks her own breast with so hard strokes and the thick of her flat hands," he "deems" this "above men's might, how a person may both smite and suffer so many, so swift and heavy strokes. . . ."[97] After the Holy Hours and "many passions of the virgin tormented, there follows in an unspeakable manner full of devout prayers, which, not as I would but as I might, I have described before."[98] And finally, ". . . this suffices at this time for describing the hours many things left of those that fill beside, what for fault of mind and difficulty of matter that refuses feeble pen."[99]

It is no small matter how Philip pays attention to those details that only become highlighted and important when they embellish the theatricality of the event. Growtowski predicts this, when he writes that "[B]y gradually eliminating whatever proved superfluous, we found that theatre can exist without make-up, without autonomic costume and scenography, without a separate performance area (stage), without lighting and sound effects, etc. . . ."[100] Philip refers to a tablet (a two-part hinged panel, which is probably a diptych), "beautifully painted with the image of our Lord crucified," being "taken to her."[101] He goes on at some length about her movements with this tablet, the sounds she makes, the loving sighs she utters, how her "lips are joined to the feet." No one can part her from the image; if the tablet is moved, her whole body is stirred with it. Philip gives us a calculated image of how Elisabeth transforms a simple prop, with someone attending to it (other than Elisabeth: ". . . she covers and closes the same tablet and takes it to somebody beside her"), into a particularly dense scene. Furthermore, it is a scene with its own content, unlike other scenes in the *vita*: the loving, clearly erotic vision of sighing, kissing, and holding tight the sensory record of the loved one. Here, it seems justified to speculate that Philip and his monks may well have participated to some degree in the intense sexuality of Elisabeth's union with Christ's body represented in the diptych—a dimension of spectatorship here of great cultural complexity and one we leave for a later article to explore.

Philip sets up Elisabeth's performance by how she walks, how she enters on stage, we might say. He writes, ". . . she rises up goes out swiftly from her bed and walks in her chamber with a marvelous and mannerly going, as though with angels leading."[102] He describes her hair (". . . she takes violently her hair, that is about her forehead but short . . .)[103] and her costume (". . . clad as she is always with a woolen coat next to her flesh and with a white linen garment somewhat trailing on the earth . . .").[104] He makes us aware of her body as a theatrical presentation: "Also this is to wit that in moving and bearing of her body . . . there falls nothing unseemly nor nothing that may displease men's sight. She never stumbles nor stampers nor wags, and in going down to the earth or lying or rising, all her body hither and thither she is always covered and clad with her own clothes, nor nothing appears unseemly nor unhonest."[105] Philip attends even to the sound of her voice and how her body and face reproduce the sound in their own terms: "Among these she makes . . . large, deep, jocund and lovesome sighs with a clear stirring of breast and throat and with a sweet sounding whispering of her lips."[106] Grotowksi predicts this range of elocutions in especially powerful forms of theater. He instructs, "If we take into consideration for instance the problem of sound, the plasticity of the actor's respiratory and vocal apparatus must be infinitely more developed than that of the man in the street. Furthermore, this apparatus must be able to produce sound reflexes so quickly that thought—which would remove all spontaneity—has no time to intervene."[107]

That Elisabeth is giving herself in these scenes, Philip leaves us little doubt. Yet, is the gift only to God? Or is Elisabeth's performance not an exteriorization for her audience, an outward directed spirituality, a gift in that sense? Such a possibility is forcefully described by Grotowski in a passage that shows him acutely alert to the erotic elements of theater-as-gift: "One must give oneself totally, in one's deepest intimacy, with confidence, as when one gives oneself in love. Here lies the key. Self-penetration, trance, *excess*, the formal discipline itself—all this can be realized, provided one has given oneself fully, humbly and without defense. This act culminates in a climax. It brings relief."[108] Written by Grotowski, these words might just as well have been penned by the abbot, who reports: "Softly, after seeking marvelous and miserable discipline she stretches upward and soon with a wonderly whiteness with help of her own hands or of any others, and so she goes in her chamber, with her arms and hands joined behind her back; also she stood fully upright all stark. And so she solemnizes the hour of prime . . . after which follows anguish, aching, and sorrows; and then she is ravished; and after the ravishing she takes the tablet and beholds it; and then comes comfort, joy and mirth . . . and so born to her bed."[109]

While many Beguines were recorded as falling into frozen or rigid states, these have generally been interpreted as signifying "ecstasy."[110] This is so (readers may predict by now) in a complicated sense. Elisabeth's *vita* invites us to approach the description of this state syntactically as theater, in addition to sanctity. Grotowski understands the performer's preparation: "The performing of this act we are referring to—self-penetration, exposure—demands a mobilization of all the physical and spiritual forces of the actor who is in a state of idle readiness, a passive availability, which makes possible an active acting score." One must resort to a metaphorical language to say that the decisive factor in this process is humility, a spiritual predisposition: not to do something but to refrain from doing something, otherwise the excess becomes impudence instead of sacrifice. This means that the actor must act in a state of trance.[111]

Philip is clear on this, as well: "Nevertheless it is to wit that through this hour and other hours she is ravished, or she rises from her bed and she has in the same state that she is ravished in a good while, all stark as an image of tree or stone, without feeling or moving and breathing, that nothing on her may be touched or stirred, not as much as her little finger but is all the body be with moved with all."[112] She enters this state, he tells us, many times, signaling each of the hours: "Before as in each of the three hours, soon after the ravishing that customarily goes always before the hours, she goes swiftly out of her bed . . ."[113] As for Elisabeth's mobilization, Philip writes, ". . . at midnight after her ravishing she rises marvelously strong to suffer labor and pain, that before in body weak and unmighty. And when she is up . . . then she walks fully and honestly in her chamber, and without blinking, as goes and comes again, she swaps herself upon the cheeks with both hands. And of her strokes may be heard accordingly sound and clear."[114] This accords with Grotowski's sense that, "At a moment of physic shock, a moment of terror, of mortal danger or tremendous joy, a man does not behave 'naturally.' A man in an elevated spiritual state uses rhythmically articulated signs, begins to dance, to sing."[115]

In taking a theatrical perspective, we can specify Elisabeth's mystical identity with still greater precision, in terms of performance as routine. As a spiritual being, a mystic, a living demonstration of Christian ideology, Elisabeth emerges in Philip's narrative as a disciplined woman, one who most certainly refined and *practiced* her art for the benefit of an audience, not only as a personal act of grace. We learn about a spiritual performer who is far removed from being some spontaneous, immediate vessel of divinity, ignited suddenly by the grace of God (a sort of unpracticed, spontaneous behavior that is the usual hallmark of mystical behavior). When we view Elisabeth's actions as theatrical performance rather than as contemporary Christian symbol alone, we confront a mystic who practiced specific actions in truly public performances.

Too many movements are repeated too often for them not to have been a carefully rehearsed, well-nuanced, and precise routine. The major pattern she follows, that of "solemnizing the Holy Hours," is itself a highly stylized routine. Interpreting Elisabeth's performance in this way does not detract from the intensity of her actions or from the authenticity of her beliefs. In many cultures, particularly in Asia, for example, strict physical discipline is the foundation of transcendence and ecstasy, not to mention creativity. As Grotowski puts it: ". . . the true lesson of sacred theatre . . . : this knowledge that spontaneity and discipline, far from weakening each other, mutually reinforce themselves . . ."[116] Indeed this is one of the most difficult and elusive principles of artistry in any field: habitual discipline and routine do not enslave but rather free artists from the conscious control of the intellect so that they can enter that magical place we call creativity. Here, the creative aim was for Elisabeth to embody what "looks like," to be—to enact—Christ. This was not a private affair, at least not in the way Philip would have us believe. For beholders as well as readers— for her publics, that is to say—Elisabeth's theology is performative. It is that "ascetic theatre" of Grotowski's "in which actors and audience are all that is left," set within a complex Christian theological context in which God too becomes part of the audience.[117]

Elisabeth's chapel itself can be understood theatrically, as well. Grotowski again comes to our aid here, writing, "It is therefore necessary to

Spalbeek, Chapel of Our Lady, exterior, view from north (Photo courtesy of the author).

abolish the distance between actor and audience by eliminating the stage, removing all frontiers. Let the most drastic scenes happen face to face with the spectator so that he is within arm's reach of the actor, can feel his breathing and smell the perspiration. This implies the necessity for a chamber theatre."[118] The Spalbeek chapel has all these hallmarks. The structure is diminutive, intimate. Today, with the addition of the fifteenth-century nave, no more than 40 people can fit comfortably inside. In Elisabeth's day, without the nave, it was smaller still. Then it was but a small circular oratory, with Elisabeth's sickroom attached, a place where her mother and sisters, abbot and fellow monks observed, carried props to the performer, were stunned and transformed. They heard her breathing, walking, moaning, and sighing; they watched her robe trail behind her slightly on the ground; and they were shocked by the athleticism of her spiritual celebrations.

As architecture, the Spalbeek chapel was defined by Elisabeth's performances. She endowed it with a theatrical and cultic significance. As

Spalbeek, Chapel of Our Lady, interior, general view to eastern hemicycle (Photo courtesy of the author).

construction it was wholly insignificant; as a permanent "trace" of Elisabeth's spiritual Christian imagination, however, it is a rare and powerful icon. Elisabeth's performances are forever lost, gone from memory, indeed invisible; Philip's text is itself an attempt to write about the undocumentable, that is, about her "performance." Yet, the chapel endures, as a permanent marker of the sacral theater that was. Abbot Philip's role as witness to miracle is key here, for what is really going on in this situation is that the text attempts to secure, to make visible, a performance: the very thing that eludes "regulation and control."[119] The chapel, then, preserves the same desire that Philip had: to "plunge into visibility" the performances, indeed the very artistic selfhood, of Elisabeth.[120] As Philip said, "—and how marvelous this doing is, *who read this, note it well*" (emphasis my own).[121] Which may also be phrased: how marvelous this mystical performance is, all who enter my chapel doors, feel it well.

Conclusion

Medieval mystic women enraptured of divinity obviously existed at quite a distance from our own late-twentieth-century world, with its emphasis on rationality and its discomfort with flagrantly physical images of the body and sacrality. Elisabeth of Spalbeek is thus necessarily an elusive person for us to ever begin to understand, but we hope that through this paper we have helped readers to "see" this extraordinary young visionary's danced faith, to some extent, and to appreciate the centrality of performance to Elisabeth's accomplishments in reformulating Christian doctrine into a holy choreography of great power. Several essentially methodological points are worth reinforcing here, in conclusion to this essay.

First, we have found that the comparative dimensions of contemporary cultural anthropology have been useful in placing Elisabeth into a context of other brilliant ritual performers in other places and times. Many of these performers have operated from the periphery, and have said the unsayable in their societies through trance, possession states, or ecstatic dance itself. Holy mystics like Elisabeth have numerous compatriots in the history of both Western religions and indigenous religions in places like Southeast Asia: a situation that medievalists can perhaps explore productively in the future. There has been, we feel, a sometimes unfortunate tendency to avoid ambitious comparative, cross-cultural projects of the sort we essay here, but we hope that our small search for Elisabeth's faith life has shown that this type of work can be illuminating.

We have found further that performance theory from both anthropology and theater studies have pushed us beyond even the body-and-
power frameworks of interpretation used by scholars such as Caroline Walker Bynum. This way of looking at Elisabeth has helped us to discern
elements of what we speculate to have been her conceptualization of self,
divinity, and architecture. We suspect that her ideational and emotional
world here would have remained more obscure to us, had we not drawn
so heavily on performance theory. Again, we would guess that medievalists
interested in female spirituality in general might find such an approach
productive, in looking at the lives and faith claims of other mystics and
visionaries.

Finally, we have found that our methodology of tacking back and
forth between a close-grained reading of textual sources (Elisabeth's *vita*)
and an ambitious anthropological effort to place a medieval situation
within a cross-cultural context that stretches far beyond Christianity has
been a thought-provoking one. Would our tentative, admittedly speculative insights about Elisabeth's understanding of her dance self in relation
to Christ's body and in relation to church spaces have been possible without this specific methodology? We doubt it: Elisabeth's incandescent unification of human and divine, female and male, past and present, and myth
and choreographic, physical reality seems to us to have been "glimpsable"
in important part thanks to this double attention to the minute details of
her historically situated, recorded *vita* and to her ties to other devout, bold
persons in other worlds of faith. We would guess, further, that any valuable
points we might have made about Elisabeth's ritual-bound but also ritual-
inspired artistry have come from our contrapuntal attention here to text
and cultural and cross-cultural context. Such a methodology has brought
us a bit closer to Elisabeth's aesthetic presence in her chapel, and has
helped us to understand her evident sense that ritual routine can liberate
an individual to stake out a distinctive, danced, felt faith.

Notes

1. The classic studies on this topic are Rudolph M. Bell, *Holy Anorexia*
    (Chicago: University Chicago Press, 1985) and Caroline Walker
    Bynum, *Holy Feast and Holy Fast: The Religious Significance of Food to Me-
    dieval Women* (Berkeley: University of California Press, 1987).
2. For basic references on Elisabeth in English, with complete citations
    of other bibliography, see Walter Simons and Joanna E. Ziegler, "Phe-
    nomenal Religion in the Thirteenth Century and its Image: Elisabeth

of Spalbeek and the Passion Cult," *Studies in Church History* 27 (1990): 117–26, and Walter Simons, "Reading a saint's body: rapture and bodily movement in the *vitae* of thirteenth-century beguines," in *Framing Medieval Bodies*, ed. Sarah Kay and Miri Rubin (Manchester and New York: Manchester University Press, 1994), 11–23.

3. *Vita Elizabeth sanctimonioalis in Erkenrode, Ordinis Cisterciensis, Leodiensis diocesis*, in *Catalogus codicum hagiographicorum bibliothecae Regiae Bruxellensis*, vol. 1 (Brussels: 1886), 362–79, and K. Horstmann, "Prosalegenden: Die Legenden des Ms. Douce 114," *Anglia* 8 (1885): 102–95, esp. 107–18 (cited hereafter as Horstmann). For study of the textual tradition, see Patricia Deery Kurtz, "Mary of Oignies, Christine the Marvelous, and Medieval Heresy," *Mystics Quarterly* 14 (1988): 186–96, and Amandus Bussels, "Was Elisabeth van Spalbeek Cisterciënserin in Herkenrode?" *Citeaux in de Nederlanden* 2 (1951): 43–54.

4. I. M. Lewis, *Ecstatic Religion: A Study of Shamanism and Spirit Possession*, 2nd ed. (London: Routledge, 1989). This was originally published in 1971. See also his *Religion in Context: Cults and Charisma* (Cambridge: Cambridge University Press, 1986).

5. See especially chapter 1, "Towards a Sociology of Ecstasy," in Lewis, *Ecstatic Religion*, 15–31. For useful comparative work of a similar sort, on voices from the periphery, see James C. Scott, *Domination and the Arts of Resistance: Hidden Transcripts* (New Haven: Yale University Press, 1990).

6. We are thinking here Michel Foucault's foundational study, *Discipline and Punish: The Birth of the Prison* (New York: Vintage Books, 1979) and such related case studies in this same research tradition as Londa Schiebinger, *Nature's Body: Gender in the Making of Modern Science* (Boston: Beacon Press, 1993), Anne Fausto-Sterling, *Myths of Gender: Biological Theories about Women and Men* (New York: Basic Books, 1985), Anne E. Becker, *Body, Self, and Society: The View from Fiji* (Philadelphia: University of Pennsylvania Press, 1995), and Helen Hardacre, *Marketing the Menacing Fetus in Japan* (Berkeley and Los Angeles: University of California Press, 1997). Studies of this sort on body and power issues are of course quite numerous today in anthropology, history, women's studies, and cultural studies.

7. In the anthropological research on Indonesian religions in this regard, see especially Mary M. Steedly, *Hanging Without a Rope: Narrative Experience in Colonial and Postcolonial Karoland* (Princeton, NJ: Princeton University Press, 1993), Anna Lowenhaupt Tsing, *In the Realm of the Diamond Queen: Marginality in an Out-of-the-Way Place* (Princeton, NJ: Princeton University Press, 1993), Jane Monnig Atkinson, "Religions in Dialogue: the Construction of an Indonesian Minority Religion," *American Ethnologist* 10/4 (1983): 684–96, and Margaret Wiener, *Visible and Invisible Realms: Power, Magic, and Colonial Conquest in Bali* (Chicago: University of Chicago Press: 1995). In Susan Rodgers's own work in this same

context, of resistance voices in the conceptualization of "traditions" and "local religions," see especially *Sitti Djaoerah: A Novel of Colonial Indonesia* (Madison, WI: 1997), University of Wisconsin Monographs in Southeast Asian Studies idem, *Telling Lives, Telling History: Autobiography and Historical Imagination in Modern Indonesia* (Berkeley and Los Angeles: University of California Press, 1995), and idem, "A Sumatran Antiquarian Writes His Culture," *Steward Journal of Anthropology* 17 (1–2): 99–120, and "The Ethnic Culture Page in Medan Journalism," *Indonesia* (April 1991).

8. A typical case study of exactly this sort, to be discussed below. Claude Levi-Strauss's "The Effectiveness of Symbols," in *Structural Anthropology* (Garden City, NY: Doubleday Anchor Books, 1967), 181–201. Going one step beyond that, to look at performance in relation to politics in an historicized context are monographs such as Sally Ann Ness's *Body, Movement and Culture: Kinesthetic and Visual Symbolism in a Philippine Community* (Philadelphia: University of Pennsylvania Press, 1992). We place particular emphasis in this paper on the anthropological literature on body and ritual motion in island Southeast Asia and Melanesia, but studies of African cultures in this regard are also extraordinarily rich. See, for instance, Sylvia Ardyn Boone, *Radiance from the Waters: Ideals of Feminine Beauty in Mende Art* (New Haven: Yale University Press, 1986).

9. Basic sources here include Richard Schechner, *Performance Theory* (1971; reprint, New York and London: Routledge, 1988); *Between Theatre and Anthropology* (Philadelphia: University of Pennsylvania Press, 1985); *The Future of Ritual: Writings on Culture and Performance* (London and New York: Routledge, 1993); and Richard Schechner and Willa Appel, eds., *By Means of Performance: Intercultural Studies of Theatre and Ritual* (Cambridge: Cambridge University Press, 1990). Victor Turner's main works on performance and such classic topics as the symbolism of rites of passage include *The Forest of Symbols* (Ithaca, NY: Cornell University Press); *The Ritual Process* (Chicago: Aldine, 1969); *Dramas, Fields, and Metaphors* (Ithaca, NY: Cornell University Press, 1974); *From Ritual to Theatre* (New York: PAJ Publications, 1982); *The Anthropology of Performance* (New York: PAJ Publications, 1986); and "Are There Universals of Performance in Myth, Ritual, and Drama?" in *By Means of Performance*, ed. Schechner and Appel, 8–18. See also Victor Turner and Edith Turner, "Performing Ethnography," in *The Anthropology of Performance*.

    Some of David Napier's work especially useful for our discussion includes *Foreign Bodies: Performance, Art, and Symbolic Anthropology* (Berkeley and Los Angeles: University of California Press, 1992) and *Masks, Transformation, and Paradox* (Berkeley and Los Angeles: University of California Press, 1986).

    Also illuminating is Edward M. Bruner, ed., *Text, Play, and Story: The Construction and Reconstruction of Self and Society* (1984; reprint, Prospect Heights, IL: Waveland, 1988).

10. Ness, *Body, Movement, and Culture*; Steedly, *Hanging Without a Rope*; Tsing, *In the Realm of the Diamond Queen*; and Gananath Obeyesekere, *Medusa's Hair: An Essay on Personal Symbols and Religious Experience* (Chicago: University of Chicago Press, 1981). On South Asian possession states see also Owen M. Lynch, ed., *Divine Passions* (Berkeley and Los Angeles: University of California Press, 1990) and June McDaniel, *The Madness of the Saints: Ecstatic Religion in Bengal* (Chicago: University of Chicago Press, 1989).

11. Edward L. Schiefflin, *The Sorrow of the Lonely and the Burning of the Dancers* (New York: St. Martin's Press, 1976).

12. Mary Douglas, *Purity and Danger* (London: Routledge and Kegan Paul, 1966), *Natural Symbols* (New York: Random House, 1970); and Mary Douglas, ed., *Witchcraft Confessions and Accusations* (London: Tavistock, 1970).

13. For another example of this type of dialectic approach by one of us, in relation to a ritual dance in Sumatra, see Susan Rodgers, "Symbolic Patterning in Angkola Batak Adat Ritual," *Journal of Asian Studies* 44, no. 4 (1985): 765–778.

14. Jerzy Grotowski, *Towards a Poor Theatre* (New York: Simon & Schuster, 1968). See the intriguing perspective on the "spiritual" nature of Grotowski's theater as offered by Ronald Grimes, *Beginnings in Ritual Studies* (Lanham, MD, New York, and London: University Press of America, 1982), esp. 151–192.

15. The feminist literature on medieval women's devotional practices is abundant and is cited throughout this anthology. Until this project, feminist authors have generally overlooked performance theory.

16. The literature on the Beguines written in Dutch is vast and important. Some of the basic references in English are: Ernest W. McDonnell, *The Beguines and Beghards in Medieval Culture, with Special Emphasis on the Belgian Scene* (Princeton, NJ: Rutgers University Press, 1954); Joanna E. Ziegler, "The *curtis* beguinages in the southern Low Countries and art patronage: interpretation and historiography," *Bulletin de l'Institut Historique Belge de Rome/Bulletin van het Belgisch Historisch Instituut te Rome* 57 (1978): 31–70, and idem, "Secular Canonesses as Antecedents of the Beguines in the southern Low Countries: An Introduction to Some Older Views," *Studies in Medieval and Renaissance History* n.s. 13 (1991): 114–35; and Walter Simons, "The Beguine Movement in the Southern Low Countries: A Reassessment," *Bulletin de l'Institut Historique Belge de Rome/Bulletin van het Belgisch Historisch Instituut te Rome* 58 (1989): 63–105.

17. For Elisabeth's relation to the Cistercians in her region, see Amandus Bussels, "Was Elisabeth van Spalbeek Cistercienserin in Herckenrode?" *Citeaux in de Nederlanden* 2 (1951): 43–54.

18. The bibliography attached to each essay in this anthology will testify to the immense number of publications on medieval women's mysticism.

19. As quoted in Christiane Klapisch-Zuber, ed., *A History of Women: Silences of the Middle Ages* (Cambridge and London: The Belknap Press of Harvard University, 1992), n. 1130.

20. See K. Horstmann, where these mystics appear together; and Patricia Deery Kurtz, "Mary of Oignies, Christine the Marvelous, and Medieval Heresy," *Mystics Quarterly* 14 (1988): 186–96. For a translation of the "Life of Mary of Oignies," see Margot H. King, *The Life of Marie d'Oignies by Jacques de Vitry* (Saskatoon, Saskatchewan: Peregrina Press, 1986); and for a discussion of Christina Mirabilis, see Robert Sweetman, "Christine of Saint-Trond's Preaching Apostolate: Thomas of Cantimpré's Hagiographical Method Revisited," *Vox Benedictina* 60 (1992): 67–97.

21. Danielle Régnier-Bohler, "Literary and Mystical Voices," trans. Arthur Goldhammer, in *A History of Women: Silences of the Middle Ages*, ed. Christiane Klapisch-Zuber (Cambridge and London: The Belknap Press of Harvard University, 1992), 427–482, esp. 467.

22. See William Hodapp's essay in this volume for a discussion of the liturgical hours.

23. See Bussels, "Was Elisabeth?"

24. For a full discussion, see Simons, "Reading a saint's body."

25. Ibid.

26. Ibid.

27. Ibid.

28. ". . . of matyns & oʒher oures by an vnufaillabil clock ʒat I know not." Horstmann, 113.

29. Some of this material first appeared in the co-authored essay cited above. See Walter Simons and Joanna E. Ziegler, "Phenomenal Religion."

30. H. Jaminé, "Eglise de Spalbeek," *Bulletin de la Société Scientifique et Littéraire du Limbourg* 16 (1884): lxii-lxvi; and "De Kapel van Spalbeek," *De Nieuwe Hasselaar* 2 (February 1978): 3.

31. Simons and Ziegler.

32. One might consult the beguinage church of Sint-Truiden for an extensive fresco cycle of women saints and martyrs. As far as Ziegler knows, however, Elisabeth is the only individual with a chapel that arose specifically to house her activities and cult and, moreover, with one that remains. The architectural nature of dedicated cult sites is a fertile topic for future research.

33. Robert Darnton, *The Great Cat Massacre* (New York: Basic Books, 1984).

34. Clifford Geertz, "Deep Play: Notes on the Balinese Cockfight," *Daedalus* 101 (1972): 1–37.

35. Timothy Armstrong, ed., *Michel Foucault, Philosopher: Essays Translated from the French and German* (New York: Routledge, 1992); Gary Gutting, ed., *The Cambridge Companion to Foucault* (Cambridge and New York: Cambridge University Press, 1994).

36. An excellent example of this sort of inquiry is Nancy Scheper-Hughes, *Death Without Weeping: The Violence of Everyday Life* (Berkeley and Los Angeles: University of California Press, 1992). See especially chapter 4, "*Delirio de Fame:* The Madness of Hunger," and chapter 6, "Everyday Violence: Bodies, Death, and Silence."

37. See, for instance, Claude Lévi-Strauss, "The Effectiveness of Symbols," and "The Sorcerer and his Magic," in his *Structural Anthropology* (New York: Basic Books, 1963). Also core sources are Rodney Needham, "Percussion and Transition," *Man* 2 (1967): 606–614, and Waldemar Bagoras, "Shamanistic Performance in the Inner Room," in *The Chukchee*, vol. 7, *The Jesup North Pacific Expedition*, ed. Franz Boas (Leiden: E. J. Brill, 1904–1909); reprinted in *Reader in Comparative Religion: An Anthropological Approach*, ed. William Lessa and Evon Vogt, 4th ed. (New York: Harper Collins, 1979), 302–307. See also I. M. Lewis, "Trance and Possession," chapter 2 in *Ecstatic Religion*, 32–59, which also provides excellent sources on the topic. For recent case studies of shamanism in action in contemporary societies see Jane M. Atkinson, *The Art and Politics of Wana Shamanship* (Berkeley and Los Angeles: University of California Press, 1989), and Laurel Kendall, *The Life and Hard Times of a Korean Shaman* (Honolulu: University of Hawaii Press, 1988). See also Laurel Kendall, *Shamans, Housewives, and Other Restless Spirits: Women in Korean Ritual life* (Honolulu: University of Hawaii Press, 1985).

38. See for instance Obeyesekere, *Medusa's Hair,* and McDaniel, *The Madness of the Saints.*

39. The anthropological literature on dance is, somewhat surprisingly, relatively small, at least when compared to the huge amount of work on topics such as trance. On dance, see an early discussion, Franz Boas, "Dance and Music in the Life of the Northwest Coast Indians of North America," in *The Function of Dance in Human Society*, ed. Franziska Boas (New York: Dance Horizons, 1944), 5–19. Judith Hanna's work is also important, if perhaps overly directed toward psychoanalytic concerns for our immediate concerns: *To Dance Is Human: A Theory of Nonverbal Communication* (Austin: University of Texas Press, 1979); idem, *The Performer-Audience Connection: Emotion to Metaphor in Dance and Society* (Austin: University of Texas Press. 1983); and idem, *Dance, Sex, and Gender: Signs of Identity, Dominance, Defiance, and Desire* (Chicago: University of Chicago Press, 1988). See also such relatively more historical, contextualized case studies as Ness, *Body, Movement, and Culture* and Jane K. Cowan, *Dance and the Body Politic in Northern Greece* (Princeton, NJ: Princeton University Press, 1990). These are excellent fieldwork-based studies of dance "traditions" created and continually recreated in relation to state power.

40. The basic sources here include Arnold L. van Gennep, *The Rites of Passage* (London: Routledge and Kegan Paul; Chicago: University of Chicago Press, 1960) and Victor Turner's elaboration on van Gennep's

work, in *The Ritual Process* and *The Forest of Symbols* (see especially "Betwixt and Between: The Liminal Phase in Rites de Passage," reprinted in *Reader in Comparative Religion*, ed. Lessa and Vogt, 234–243.

41. Victor Turner's "Betwixt and Between" includes a classic discussion of this process of "falling outside the social structure" in rites of passage.

42. Needham in *Reader*, Lessa and Vogt, 311–317.

43. See I. M. Lewis's discussion of the type of spirit-filled world typically associated with shamans and their journeys (*Ecstatic Religion*, chapter 2): these are religious terrains contrasting with Elisabeth's apparent monotheism.

44. Knut Rasmussen, "Report of the Fifth Thule Expedition, 1921–1924," *Intellectual Culture of the Iglulik Eskimo*, vol. 14, no. 1 (Copenhagen: Gyldendalske Boghandel, Nordisk Forlag, 1929); reprinted in part as "A Shaman's Journey to the Sea Pirit," in *Reader*, Lessa and Vogt, 308–11.

45. Not much is known about the cults active in Elisabeth's chapel. Most speculation centers on the nature of the fresco cycle, with iconographic references perhaps to saints who help afflictions due to nervous disorders. The cycle dates from approximately the late fifteenth century, indicating that the chapel was still in use at that time. In fact, only in our own century has the chapel ceased to operate as a cult shrine. See Simons and Ziegler for further references.

46. It was not until the fifteenth century that behavior like Elisabeth's was condemned in the guise of sorcery, witchcraft, and the like. Also, mystical extremes, such as were common in Elisabeth's time, were in decline by the fifteenth century. Before then, many of the monastic clergy supported women mystics. It is not unlikely that Philip's report was intended to be read as "what a good woman acts like," for there are details, which compare how witches will later be identified. For example, she exhibits no spittle, her clothes are not unseemly. These are traits of bad women. For the connotations of women attached to sorcery and heresy, see Jean-Claude Schmitt, *Mort d'une hérésie: L'Eglise et les clercs face au béguines et aux béghards du Rhin supérieur du XIVe au XVe siecle*, Civilisation et Sociétés 56 (The Hague and New York: Mouton, 1978); see also Ziegler, "The *curtis* beguinages," 59–64.

47. Valuable, close-grained case studies include Jane Belo, *Trance in Bali* (New York: Columbia University Press, 1960).

48. Obeyesekere, *Medusa's Hair*.

49. Mary Douglas's *Purity and Danger* contains an extensive discussion of the ways in which village societies conceptualize "official" power structures associated with moral goodness and controllable powers, and then counterpose regimes of "wild," uncontrolled, amoral forces and persons to these.

50. Lewis, *Ecstatic Religion*, 119.

51. Ibid., 52–54, 55–56, 170–171. See especially Lewis's discussion of tarantism, which in southern Italy and Sardinia can sometimes involve

imagined spirit marriages between young possessed girls and Catholic male saints, such as St. Paul.

52. Ibid., 52.
53. Ibid.
54. On the sexual imagery of Christ to women, see Bynum's "The Body of Christ in the Later Middle Ages: A Reply to Leo Steinberg," *Renaissance Quarterly* 39/3 (1986): 399–439. This offers an intriguing response to Leo Steinberg, *The Sexuality of Christ in Renaissance Art and in Modern Oblivion* (New York: Pantheon/October Book, 1983), with an excellent postscript by John W. O'Malley, S.J. More recently, see James Clifton, *The Body of Christ In the Art of Europe and New Spain, 1150–1800* (Munich and New York: Prestel, 1997).
55. See note 9, above. Also illuminating when brought to the study of medieval materials are the essays in Smadar Lavie, Kirin Narayan, and Renato Rosaldo, eds., *Creativity/Anthropology* (Ithaca, NY: Cornell University Press, 1993).
56. Here Richard Schechner is a good guide. See especially his *Performance Theory* on concepts of self in various performance formats; see also his *Between Theatre and Anthropology*.
57. See Victor Turner works cited in note 9, above.
58. The relation of Christ's body to female communities is a complex topic. Joanna E. Ziegler's own research analyzes these relations in terms of religious imagery. For a case study and bibliographic references, see Joanna E. Ziegler, *Sculpture of Compassion: The Pietà and the Beguines in the Southern Low Countries, c.1300–c.1600*, Studies over kunstgeschiedenis, het Belgisch Historisch Instituut te Rome 6 (Brussels and Rome: Academia Belgica, 1992).
59. Ibid.
60. See Rosemary Drage Hale's essay in this volume.
61. Patrick J. Geary, *Living with the Dead in the Middle Ages* (Ithaca, NY: Cornell University Press, 1994), especially chapter 5, "Humiliation of Saints," 95–115.
62. Richard Schechner, *Between Theatre and Anthropology*, "Performers and Spectators Transported and Transformed," 117–150.
63. Ibid.
64. These topics are discussed in chapter 3 of Schechner's *Between Theatre and Anthropology*.
65. Schechner, *Between Theatre and Anthropology*, chapter 2, "Restoration of Behavior." This section of the book also includes a thought-provoking discussion of Shaker dancing in the nineteenth-century United States.
66. Ibid., 36.
67. Ibid, 37.
68. Ibid., 38–40.
69. Lévi-Strauss, "The Effectiveness of Symbols," 181–201.
70. Much of the medical anthropology literature on symbolic healing

makes use of a similar argument. For a contemporary exploration of this theme see Thomas J. Csordas, *The Sacred Self: A Cultural Phenomenology of Charismatic Healing* (Berkeley and Los Angeles: University of California Press, 1997).

71. Island Southeast Asian societies and ones from Papua New Guinea are rarely considered together in comparative studies by anthropologists, as cultures in the two areas have marked differences of language family, social organization, gender ideology, and colonial history. However, some of the research on performance in these two different culture areas does seem to be running along parallel theoretical tracks today.

72. Joel Kuipers, *Power in Performance: The Creation of Textual Authority in Weyewa Ritual Speech* (Philadelphia: University of Pennsylvania Press, 1990).

73. Anna Lowenhaupt Tsing, " 'Riding the Horse of Gaps': A Meratus Woman's Spiritual Expression," in *Creativity/Anthropology,* ed. Lavie, Narayan, and Rosaldo, 100–132.

74. Ibid., 108.

75. Ness, *Body, Movement, and Culture.*

76. Schiefflin, *The Sorrow of the Lonely and the Burning of the Dancers.*

77. Ibid., 23.

78. Grotowski, *Towards a Poor Theatre.*

79. Simons, "Reading a saint's body."

80. Grotowski, 33.

81. Grotowski, 15. It will be useful in understanding the nontextual basis of Elisabeth's performance, as well as Grotowski's emphases, by reading Jody Enders splendid study, *Rhetoric and the Origins of Medieval Drama* (Ithaca, NY: Cornell University Press, 1992).

82. Grimes, *Beginnings in Ritual Studies.*

83. Grotowski, 25.

84. Horstmann, 107.

85. Grotowski, 19.

86. Grotowski, 33.

87. "Whiche of þese I schalle calle moor meruilos, I woot not, in suche a febil and freel creature . . . Horstmann, 111.

88. Grotowski, 47.

89. . . . þere folowe vnspekabil maners of ful deuoute prayers, þe whiche, not as I wolde but as I myȝht, I haue discriued byfore; but I woot wel þat my power nor my cunnynge myghte not fulfille my wille. Horstmann, 113.

90. I gaf no credens to hem þat tolde me, til-tyme þat I come my-selfe and sawe and proued þat I hadde not herde þe halfe. Horstmann, 107.

91. Horstmann, 111.

92. Horstmann, 108.

93. . . . leste þe herers of þis happely wil not leue siche meruels for þe whiche wee abbotis and monkes ȝede to see þe same virgyn and taryed wiþ hire so many oures. Horstmann, 114.

94. Ibid.

95. . . . wiþ a maner þat may neiþer be herde ne tolde. Horstmann, 109.

96. Horstmann, 110.

97. And þenne sche pulliþ oute hir handys fro byhynde her backe and knokkith hir owne breste with so harde strokes & þicke of hir plat handys, þat all þat se haue mykel meruayle and deme hit aboue mannes myghte, how o persone may booþ smyte and soffre so many, soo swifte and heuy strokes, þogh hee hadde prosperite of nature, age, heele & complexion. Horstmann, 111.

98. Ferþermore, after many maneres of representacyouns of our lordes crosse and many passyouns of the virgyn turmentyd, þere folowe vnspekabil maners of ful deuoute prayers, þe which, not as I wolde but as I my3ht, I haue discriued byfore; but I woot wel þat my power nor my cunnynge myghte not fulfille my wille. Horstmann, 113.

99. þis sufficiþ atte þis tyme for discriuinge of þe oures, many þinges lafte of þos þat fil be-syde, what for defaute of mynde and difficulte of mater þat refusith a febil penne. Horstmann, 114.

100. Grotowski, 19.

101. The passage in which Elisabeth takes the diptych and performs with it is found in Horstmann, 110–111. Here is a selection: "And þen anon is taken to hir a tabil, ful wele depynte with an ymage of oure lorde crucifyed; and holdyng þat open and vncouerd wiþ booþ handys, ful deuoutly she lokiþ on oure lorde and often and þikke sche seiþ þese woordys: 'zouche here, zouche heere,' þat is to sey in Englysche: swete loord, swete lord, and wiþ hire clene virgyn-lippys she kysseþ often sweetly þe feet of oure lordis ymage. Among þees she makiþ fro hire priue herte rotys large, depe, iocunde & lufsum sighes wiþ a clere stifrynge of breste and þhroot and with a swete sounynge whysperynge of her lippes."

102. . . . and walkith in here chammbyr with a merueylous and a manerly goynge, as hit is trowed, with aungels ledynge. Horstmann, 108.

103. Also oþere-while sche takith vyolently hir heer, þat is aboute her forhede but short . . . Horstmann, 109.

104. And whanne sche is vp, cladde as sche is alle-wey wiþ a wollen coot next her flesch and with a whyte lynnen garnemente sumwhatly trailynge on þe earthe, þan sche walkeþ ful honestly in hir chaumbyr . Horstmann, 108.

105. Also þis is to witte þat in mouynges and berynges of body of þe forseyde virgyn þere fallith no þinge vnsemely nor no þinge þat may displese mannes syghte. . . zit stumbliþ sche neuere ne stamperþe ne waggiþ, and in doynge doune hir-selfe to þe erþe or liggynge or risynge, alle hir body hider or þider she is alwey couerde & bycladde with hir own cloþes, nor no þinge apperith vnsemely nor vnhonest. Horstmann, 114.

106. Horstmann, 110.

107. Grotowski, 35.
108. Grotowski, 38.
109. Horstmann, 110.
110. Simons, "Reading a saint's body," 16–17.
111. Grotowski, 37.
112. Horstmann, 110.
113. Horstmann, 112.
114. . . . and of hir strokes maye be herde acordaunte sowne and cleer. Horstmann, 108.
115. Grotowski, xxx.
116. Grotowski, 121.
117. A. L. Becker's "Text-Building, Epistemology, and Aesthetics in Javanese Shadow Theatre," in *The Imagination of Reality: Essays in Southeast Asian Coherence Systems,* ed. A. L. Becker and Aram Yengoyan (Norwood, NJ: Ablex, 1979), 211–44, provides valuable comparative context here: on a shadow puppet play presented to human audiences and an "unseen audience" of the gods. Becker's use of linguistic analogies in explaining how complexes performances are produced, in terms of ways to establish artistic coherence, is also illuminating for our case.
118. Growtowski, 42.
119. Peggy Phelan, *Unmarked: The Politics of Performance* (London and New York: Routledge, 1993), 148.
120. Ibid.
121. . . . and how merveylous þis doynge is, ho so rediþ þis noot it wele." Horstmann, 112.

Bibliography

Armstrong, Timothy, ed. *Michel Foucault, Philosopher: Essays Translated from the French and German.* New York: Routledge, 1992.
Atkinson, Jane Monnig. "Religions in Dialogue: The Construction of an Indonesian Minority Religion." *American Ethnologist* 10/4 (1983): 684–96.
———. *The Art and Politics of Wana Shamanship.* Berkeley and Los Angeles: University of California Press, 1989.
Bagoras, Waldemar. "Shamanistic Performance in the Inner Room." In *The Chukchee,* vol. 7 of *The Jesup North Pacific Expedition,* ed. Franz Boas. Leiden: E. J. Brill, 1904–1909.
Becker, Anne E. *Body, Self, and Society: The View from Fiji.* Philadelphia: University of Pennsylvania Press, 1995.
Becker, A. L. "Text-Building, Epistemology, and Aesthetics in Javanese Shadow Theatre." In *The Imagination of Reality: Essays in Southeast Asian Coherence Systems,* ed. A. L. Becker and Aram Yengoyan. Norwood, NJ: Ablex, 1979.

Bell, Rudolph M. *Holy Anorexia*. Chicago: University of Chicago Press, 1985.

Belo, Jane. *Trance in Bali*. New York: Columbia University Press, 1960.

Boas, Franz. "Dance and Music in the Life of the Northwest Coast Indians of North America." In *The Function of Dance in Human Society*, ed. Franziska Boas, 5–19. New York: Dance Horizons, 1944.

Boone, Sylvia Ardyn. *Radiance from the Waters: Ideals of Feminine Beauty in Mende Art*. New Haven: Yale University Press, 1986.

Brenneis, Donald, "Performing Passions: Aesthetics and Politics in an Occasionally Egalitarian Community." *American Ethnologist* 14/2 (1987): 236–50.

Bruner, Edward M., ed. *Text, Play, and Story: The Construction and Reconstruction of Self and Society*. 1984; reprint, Prospect Heights, Illinois: Waveland, 1988.

Bussels, Amandus. "Was Elisabeth van Spalbeek Cistersciënserin in Herckenrode?" *Citeaux in de Nederlanden* 2 (1951): 43–54.

Bynum, Caroline Walker. *Holy Feast and Holy Fast: The Religious Significance of Food to Medieval Women*. Berkeley: University of California Press, 1987.

————. "The Body of Christ in the Later Middle Ages: A Reply to Leo Steinberg." *Renaissance Quarterly* 39/3 (1986): 399–439.

Clifton, James. *The Body of Christ In the Art of Europe and New Spain, 1150–1800*. Munich and New York: Prestel, 1997.

Cowan, Jane K. *Dance and the Body Politic in Northern Greece*. Princeton, NJ: Princeton University Press, 1990.

Csordas, Thomas J. *The Sacred Self: A Cultural Phenomenology of Charismatic Healing*. Berkeley and Los Angeles: University of California Press 1997.

Darnton, Robert. *The Great Cat Massacre*. New York: Basic Books, 1984.

"De Kapel van Spalbeek." *De Nieuwe Hasselaar* 2 (February 1978): 3.

Douglas, Mary. *Purity and Danger*. London: Routledge and Kegan Paul, 1966.

————. *Natural Symbols*. New York: Random House, 1970.

————, ed. *Witchcraft Confessions and Accusations*. London: Tavistock, 1970.

Enders, Jody. *Rhetoric and the Origins of Medieval Drama*. Ithaca, NY: Cornell University Press, 1992.

Fausto-Sterling, Anne. *Myths of Gender: Biological Theories about Women and Men*. New York: Basic Books, 1985.

Foucault, Michel. *Discipline and Punish: The Birth of the Prison*. New York: Vintage Books, 1979.

Geary, Patrick J. *Living with the Dead in the Middle Ages*. Ithaca, NY: Cornell University Press, 1994.

Geertz, Clifford. "Deep Play: Notes on the Balinese Cockfight." *Daedalus* 101 (1972): 1–37.

Grimes, Ronald. *Beginnings in Ritual Studies*. Lanham, MD, New York, and London: University Press of America, 1982.

Grotowski, Jerzy. *Towards a Poor Theatre*. New York: Simon & Schuster, 1968.

Gutting, Gary, ed. *The Cambridge Companion to Foucault*. Cambridge and New York: Cambridge University Press, 1994.

Hanna, Judith. *To Dance Is Human: A Theory of Nonverbal Communication.* Austin: University of Texas Press, 1979.

———. *The Performer-Audience Connection: Emotion to Metaphor in Dance and Society.* Austin: University of Texas Press. 1983.

———. *Dance, Sex, and Gender: Signs of Identity, Dominance, Defiance, and Desire.* Chicago: University of Chicago Press, 1988.

Hardacre, Helen. *Marketing the Menacing Fetus in Japan.* Berkeley and Los Angeles: University of California Press, 1997.

Horstmann, K. "Prosalegenden: Die Legenden des Ms. Douce 114." *Anglia* 8 (1885): 102–95.

Jaminé, H. "Eglise de Spalbeek." *Bulletin de la Société Scientifique et Littéraire du Limbourg* 16 (1884): lxii-lxvi.

Kendall, Laurel. *The Life and Hard Times of a Korean Shaman.* Honolulu: University of Hawaii Press, 1988.

———. *Shamans, Housewives, and Other Restless Spirits: Women in Korean Ritual Life.* Honolulu: University of Hawaii Press, 1985.

Klapisch-Zuber, Christiane, ed. *A History of Women: Silences of the Middle Ages.* Cambridge and London: The Belknap Press of Harvard University, 1992.

King, Margot H. *The Life of Marie d'Oignies by Jacques de Vitry.* Saskatoon, Saskatchewan: Peregrina Press, 1986.

Kuipers, Joel. *Power in Performance: The Creation of Textual Authority in Weyewa Ritual Speech.* Philadelphia: University of Pennsylvania Press, 1990.

Kurtz, Patricia Deery. "Mary of Oignies, Christine the Marvelous, and Medieval Heresy." *Mystics Quarterly* 14 (1988): 186–96.

Lavie, Smadar, Kirin Narayan, and Renato Rosaldo, eds. *Creativity/Anthropology.* Ithaca, NY: Cornell University Press, 1993.

Lessa, William and Evon Vogt, eds., *Reader in Comparative Religion: An Anthropological Approach.* 4th ed. New York: Harper Collins, 1979.

Lévi-Strauss, Claude. "The Effectiveness of Symbols." In *Structural Anthropology.* Garden City, NY: Doubleday Anchor Books, 1967.

———. "The Sorcerer and His Magic." In *Structural Anthropology.* Garden City, NY: Doubleday Anchor Books, 1967.

Lewis, I. M. *Ecstatic Religion: A Study of Shamanism and Spirit Possession.* second ed. London: Routledge, 1989.

———. *Religion in Context: Cults and Charisma.* Cambridge: Cambridge University Press, 1986.

Lynch, Owen M., ed. *Divine Passions.* Berkeley and Los Angeles: University of California Press, 1990.

McDaniel, June. *The Madness of the Saints: Ecstatic Religion in Bengal.* Chicago: University of Chicago Press, 1989.

McDonnell, Ernest W. *The Beguines and Beghards in Medieval Culture, with Special Emphasis on the Belgian Scene.* Princeton, NJ: Rutgers University Press, 1954.

Napier, David. *Foreign Bodies: Performance, Art, and Symbolic Anthropology.* Berkeley and Los Angeles: University of California Press, 1992.

———. *Masks, Transformation, and Paradox.* Berkeley and Los Angeles: University of California Press, 1986.

Needham, Rodney. "Percussion and Transition." *Man* 2 (1967): 606–614.

Ness, Sally Ann. *Body, Movement, and Culture: Kinesthetic and Visual Symbolism in a Philippine Community.* Philadelphia: University of Pennsylvania Press, 1992.

Obeyesekere, Gananath. *Medusa's Hair: An Essay on Personal Symbols and Religious Experience.* Chicago: University of Chicago Press, 1981.

Phelan, Peggy. *Unmarked: The Politics of Performance.* London and New York:Routledge, 1993

Rasmussen, Knut. "Report of the Fifth Thule Expedition, 1921–1924." In *Intellectual Culture of the Iglulik Eskimo,* vol. 14, no. 1. Copenhagen: Gyldendalske Boghandel, Nordisk Forlag, 1929. Reprinted in part as "A Shaman's Journey to the Sea Spirit," in *Reader,* Lessa and Vogt.

Régnier-Bohler, Danielle. "Literary and Mystical Voices." Trans. Arthur Goldhammer. In *A History of Women: Silences of the Middle Ages,* ed. Christiane Klapisch-Zuber, 427–482. Cambridge and London: The Belknap Press of Harvard University, 1992.

Rodgers, Susan. *Sitti Djaoerah: A Novel of Colonial Indonesia.* University of Wisconsin Monographs in Southeast Asian Studies. Madison, WI; 1997.

———. *Telling Lives, Telling History: Autobiography and Historical Imagination in Modern Indonesia.* Berkeley and Los Angeles: University of California Press, 1995.

———. "A Sumatran Antiquarian Writes His Culture." *Steward Journal of Anthropology* 17 (1–2): 99–120.

———. "The Ethnic Culture Page in Medan Journalism." *Indonesia* (April 1991).

———. "Symbolic Patterning in Angkola Batak Adat Ritual." *Journal of Asian Studies* 44, no. 4 (1985): 765–778.

Schechner, Richard. *Performance Theory.* 1971; reprint, New York and London: Routledge, 1988.

———. *Between Theatre and Anthropology.* Philadelphia: University of Pennsylvania Press, 1985.

———. *The Future of Ritual: Writings on Culture and Performance.* London and New York: Routledge, 1993.

———, and Willa Appel, eds. *By Means of Performance: Intercultural Studies of Theatre and Ritual.* Cambridge: Cambridge University Press, 1990.

Scheper-Hughes, Nancy. *Death Without Weeping: The Violence of Everyday Life.* Berkeley and Los Angeles: University of California Press, 1992.

Schiebinger, Londa. *Nature's Body: Gender in the Making of Modern Science.* Boston: Beacon Press, 1993.

Schiefflin, Edward L. *The Sorrow of the Lonely and the Burning of the Dancers.* New York: St. Martin's Press, 1976.

Schmitt, Jean-Claude. *Mort d'une hérésie. L'Eglise et les clercs face au béguines et aux béghards du Rhin supérieur du XIVe au XVe siecle.* Civilisation et Sociétés 56. The Hague and New York: Mouton, 1978.

Scott, James C. *Domination and the Arts of Resistance: Hidden Transcripts.* New Haven: Yale University Press, 1990.

Simons, Walter. "The Beguine Movement in the Southern Low Countries: A Reassessment." *Bulletin de l'Institut Historique Belge de Rome/Bulletin van het Belgisch Historisch Instituut te Rome* 58 (1989): 63–105.

————. "Reading a saint's body: rapture and bodily movement in the *vitae* of thirteenth-century beguines." In *Framing Medieval Bodies,* ed. Sarah Kay and Miri Rubin, 11–23. Manchester and New York: Manchester University Press, 1994.

———— and Joanna E. Ziegler. "Phenomenal Religion in the Thirteenth Century and its Image: Elisabeth of Spalbeek and the Passion Cult." *Studies in Church History* 27 (1990): 117–26.

Steedly, Mary M. *Hanging Without a Rope: Narrative Experience in Colonial and Postcolonial Karoland.* Princeton, NJ: Princeton University Press, 1993.

Steinberg, Leo. *The Sexuality of Christ in Renaissance Art and in Modern Oblivion.* New York: Pantheon/October Books, 1983.

Sweetman, Robert. "Christine of Saint-Trond's Preaching Apostolate: Thomas ofCantimpré's Hagiographical Method Revisted." *Vox Benedictina* 60 (1992): 67–97.

Tsing, Anna Lowenhaupt. *In the Realm of the Diamond Queen: Marginality in an Out-of-the-Way Place.* Princeton, NJ: Princeton University Press, 1993.

————. " 'Riding the Horse of Gaps': A Meratus Woman's Spiritual Expression." In *Creativity/Anthropology,* ed. Smardar Lavie, Kirin Narayan, and Renato Rosaldo, 100–132. Ithaca, NY: Cornell University Press, 1993.

Turner, Victor. *The Forest of Symbols.* Ithaca, NY: Cornell University Press.

————. *The Ritual Process.* Chicago: Aldine, 1969.

————. *Dramas, Fields, and Metaphors.* Ithaca, NY: Cornell University Press, 1974.

————. *From Ritual to Theatre.* New York: PAJ Publications, 1982.

————. *The Anthropology of Performance.* New York: PAJ Publications, 1986.

———— and Edith Turner, "Performing Ethnography." In *The Anthropology of Performance,* by Victor Turner. New York: PAJ Publications, 1986.

————. "Betwixt and Between: The Liminal Phase in Rites de Passage." Reprinted in *Reader in Comparative Religion,* ed. Lessa and Vogt, 234–243.

van Gennep, Arnold L. *The Rites of Passage.* London: Routledge and Kegan Paul, Chicago: University of Chicago Press, 1960.

Vita Elizabeth sanctimonioalis in Erkenrode, Ordinis Cisterciensis, Leodiensis diocesis, in *Catalogus codicum hagiographicorum bibliothecae Regiae Bruxellensis,* vol. 1 (Brussels: 1886), 362–79.

Wiener, Margaret. *Visible and Invisible Realms: Power, Magic, and Colonial Conquest in Bali.* Chicago: University of Chicago Press: 1995.

Ziegler, Joanna E. "The *curtis* beguinages in the southern Low Countries and art

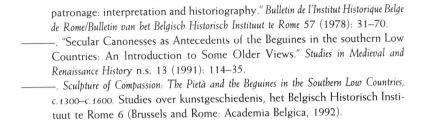

patronage: interpretation and historiography." *Bulletin de l'Institut Historique Belge de Rome/Bulletin van het Belgisch Historisch Instituut te Rome* 57 (1978): 31–70.

———. "Secular Canonesses as Antecedents of the Beguines in the southern Low Countries: An Introduction to Some Older Views." *Studies in Medieval and Renaissance History* n.s. 13 (1991): 114–35.

———. *Sculpture of Compassion: The Pietà and the Beguines in the Southern Low Countries, c.1300–c.1600.* Studies over kunstgeschiedenis, het Belgisch Historisch Instituut te Rome 6 (Brussels and Rome: Academia Belgica, 1992).

Index